Studies in Modern History

General Editor: **J. C. D. Clark**, Joyce and Elizabeth Hall Distinguished Professor of British History, University of Kansas

Titles include:

James B. Bell
A WAR OF RELIGION
Dissenters, Anglicans, and the
American Revolution

James B. Bell
THE IMPERIAL ORIGINS OF THE
KING'S CHURCH IN EARLY AMERICA,
1607–1783

Jonathan Clark and
Howard Erskine-Hill (*editors*)
SAMUEL JOHNSON IN HISTORICAL
CONTEXT

Eveline Cruickshanks and Howard
Erskine-Hill
THE ATTERBURY PLOT

Diana Donald and
Frank O'Gorman (*editors*)
ORDERING THE WORLD IN THE
EIGHTEENTH CENTURY

Richard D. Floyd
RELIGIOUS DISSENT AND POLITICAL
MODERNIZATION
Church, Chapel and Party in
Nineteenth-Century England

Richard R. Follett
EVANGELICALISM, PENAL THEORY
AND THE POLITICS OF CRIMINAL
LAW REFORM IN ENGLAND,
1808–30

Andrew Godley
JEWISH IMMIGRANT
ENTREPRENEURSHIP IN NEW YORK
AND LONDON, 1880–1914

William Anthony Hay
THE WHIG REVIVAL, 1808–1830

Mark Keay
WILLIAM WORDSWORTH'S
GOLDEN AGE THEORIES DURING
THE INDUSTRIAL REVOLUTION
IN ENGLAND, 1750–1850

Kim Lawes
PATERNALISM AND POLITICS
The Revival of Paternalism in Early
Nineteenth-Century Britain

Marisa Linton
THE POLITICS OF VIRTUE IN
ENLIGHTENMENT FRANCE

Karin J. MacHardy
WAR, RELIGION AND COURT
PATRONAGE IN HABSBURG
AUSTRIA
The Social and Cultural
Dimensions of Political Interaction,
1521–1622

James Mackintosh
VINDICIÆ GALLICÆ
Defence of the French Revolution:
A Critical Edition

Robert J. Mayhew
LANDSCAPE, LITERATURE AND
ENGLISH RELIGIOUS CULTURE,
1660–1800
Samuel Johnson and Languages of
Natural Description

Marjorie Morgan
NATIONAL IDENTITIES AND TRAVEL
IN VICTORIAN BRITAIN

James Muldoon
EMPIRE AND ORDER
The Concept of Empire, 800–1800

W. D. Rubinstein
and Hilary Rubinstein
PHILOSEMITISM
Admiration and Support for Jews in
the English-Speaking World,
1840–1939

Julia Rudolph
WHIG POLITICAL THOUGHT AND
THE GLORIOUS REVOLUTION
James Tyrrell and the Theory of
Resistance

Lisa Steffen
TREASON AND NATIONAL IDENTITY
Defining a British State, 1608–1820

Lynne Taylor
BETWEEN RESISTANCE
AND COLLABORATION
Popular Protest in Northern France,
1940–45

Anthony Waterman
POLITICAL ECONOMY
AND CHRISTIAN THEOLOGY
SINCE THE ENLIGHTENMENT
Essays in Intellectual History

Doron Zimmerman
THE JACOBITE MOVEMENT
IN SCOTLAND AND IN EXILE,
1746–1759

Studies in Modern History
Series Standing Order ISBN 978-0-333-79328-2 (Hardback)
978-0-333-80346-2 (Paperback)
(*outside North America only*)

You can receive future titles in this series as they are published by placing a
standing order. Please contact your bookseller or, in case of difficulty, write to us
at the address below with your name and address, the title of the series and the
ISBN quoted above.

Customer Services Department, Macmillan Distribution Ltd, Houndmills,
Basingstoke, Hampshire RG21 6XS, England

A War of Religion

Dissenters, Anglicans, and the American Revolution

James B. Bell

First published 2008 by
PALGRAVE MACMILLAN
Houndmills, Basingstoke, Hampshire RG21 6XS and
175 Fifth Avenue, New York, N.Y. 10010
Companies and representatives throughout the world

PALGRAVE MACMILLAN is the global academic imprint of the Palgrave Macmillan division of St. Martin's Press, LLC and of Palgrave Macmillan Ltd. Macmillan® is a registered trademark in the United States, United Kingdom and other countries. Palgrave is a registered trademark in the European Union and other countries.

ISBN-13: 978-0-230-54297-6   hardback
ISBN-10: 0-230-54297-2   hardback

This book is printed on paper suitable for recycling and made from fully managed and sustained forest sources. Logging, pulping and manufacturing processes are expected to conform to the environmental regulations of the country of origin.

A catalogue record for this book is available from the British Library.

Library of Congress Cataloging-in-Publication Data

Bell, James B., 1932–
    A war of religion : dissenters, Anglicans, and the American Revolution / James B. Bell.
        p. cm. — (Studies in modern history)
    Includes bibliographical references and index.
    ISBN-13: 978-0-230-54297-6 (hbk.)
    ISBN-10: 0-230-54297-2 (hbk.)
    1. United States—History—Revolution, 1775–1783—Religious aspects.
        2. Dissenters—United States—History—18th century. 3. Anglicans—
        United States—History—18th century. 4. Dissenters—United States—
        Biography. 5. Anglicans—United States—Biography. 6. Christianity
        and politics— United States—Church of England—History—18th century.
        7. United States—Politics and government—1775–1783. I. Title.

    E209.B38 2008
    973.3'8—dc22   2008011740

10   9   8   7   6   5   4   3   2   1
17 16 15 14 13 12 11 10 09 08

Transferred to Digital Printing in 2009.

In Gratitude to
William A. Coolidge
and to an
Inspired and Inspiring Band
Of Teachers and Scholars

Raymond W. Albright, Charles E. Batten, John B. Coburn,
Rollin J. Fairbanks, Theodore P. Ferris, Joseph F. Fletcher,
Eugene Van Ness Goetchius, Harvey H. Guthrie, Clifton Lunt,
Lloyd G. Patterson, Henry M. Shires, Charles W. F. Smith,
Owen C. Thomas, Peter Waring, and William J. Wolf.

Contents

List of Illustrations and Tables   ix

Prologue   x

Acknowledgements   xvii

Some Useful Dates   xix

PART I   A Century of Controversies

1   The Seeds of Discord: An English Church Established in Boston   3

2   Discord Enlarged: The Society for the Propagation of the Gospel   17

3   A Handmaiden for Episcopacy: John Checkley of Boston   33

4   The English Origins of a Colonial American Controversy   42

5   Noah Hobart Decries Anglican Expansion: Thomas Sherlock Proposes an American Bishop   58

6   Jonathan Mayhew Fears a Bishop and Challenges the Purpose of the S.P.G.   67

7   Pleas for an American Bishop in the 1760s: Archbishop of Canterbury Thomas Secker and Thomas Bradbury Chandler   81

8   A Radical Response to a Bishop: John Adams, Samuel Adams, and John Wilkes   91

9   The Controversy over a Bishop in the Colonies outside New England   107

PART II   A New Controversy: The Political Sentiments of the Clergymen

10   The Impact of the First Continental Congress and the Local Committees of Safety   123

11   Critics of the Continental Congress and *Common Sense*:
     Jonathan Boucher and Charles Inglis   140

12   A Challenge to Radical Politics: Samuel Seabury, Jr.,
     and Thomas Bradbury Chandler   156

13   Quiet and Militant Patriots   170

14   William Knox Seeks to Establish an Ecclesiastical
     Imperial Policy for the American Church   187

15   The State of the Clergy in 1775 and 1783   195

16   The English Church, a Cause of the
     American Revolution   211

Appendix I
     Political Sentiments of Colonial Clergymen
     of the Church of England during the
     American Revolutionary War, 1775–83   222

Appendix II
     A Summary of the Birthplaces, Birth Years,
     and Colleges Attended by Colonial American
     Church of England Clergymen, 1775   241

Notes   246

Bibliography   294

Index   316

Illustrations

Illustration 8.1 'An Attempt to Land a Bishop in America'
(Courtesy of the Boston Athenaeum)   101
Illustration 8.2 'The Mitred Minuet'
(Courtesy of the Boston Athenaeum)   105

Tables

Table 15.1 Number of clergy in the New England
colonies, 1775–83   199
Table 15.2 Number of Clergy in the Middle Colonies,
1775–83   202
Table 15.3 Number of Clergy in the Chesapeake Colonies,
1775–83   204
Table 15.4 Number of Clergy in the Southern Colonies, 1775–83   208

Prologue

Two principal colonial observers and participating essayists on radical political affairs in the 1760s and 1770s claimed that the question of an American Anglican bishop was a cause of the Revolutionary War. Writing from the vicarage in Epsom, County Surrey, in England in the mid-1790s, the exiled Maryland schoolmaster and parson Jonathan Boucher recalled that during the pre-Revolutionary War years in the colonies, 'Episcopacy was opposed for no reason whatever besides that of thwarting and irritating those who, being known to be friends to the church, were concluded to be also friends to the Crown: how much it was the fashion, at the same period in question, for people of all ranks to speculate, philosophise, and project Utopian schemes of reformation; which, as it was conducted in America, led, as regularly as ever any cause produces its corresponding effect, first, to the demolition of the Church, as that, in its turn, no less certainly led to the overturning the State'.[1] Boucher's assessment of the issue was supported and extended 40 years after the beginning of the War for Independence by John Adams, who recounted to a historian of the conflict that the episcopacy controversy and the authority of parliament to appoint bishops and creates dioceses in the colonies was a cause of the war.[2]

In the train of Professor J. C. D. Clark's study *The Language of Liberty, 1660–1832*, which examines and illuminates the political and intellectual relationship between the British Isles and America, this book considers the experience of the colonial English church between 1686 and 1783.[3] From the founding of James Town in 1607 to the end of the Revolutionary War, the church in America maintained essential transatlantic ties.[4] Connections that were fashioned by the vital need for the recruitment and ordination of clergymen; for the supervision by successive bishops of London; and the assistance of the Society for the Propagation of the Gospel for the financial support of missionaries in the New England, Middle, and Southern Colonies after 1701. Clark persuasively argues that the American Revolution was 'about' law, political authority, taxation, trade, and religion.[5] During the century before the outbreak of the Revolutionary War the English church sustained controversies that underscored the tensions of colonial political and religious conflict. After 1765 and the adoption of the Stamp Act, the debate over the prospect of the appointment of an Anglican prelate was joined with colonial fears and objections to the authority of Parliament. Led by a triumvirate of political leaders, the cousins John and Samuel Adams, in Boston, in league with John Wilkes in London, the question of an American episcopate was inextricably linked with the contentious political issues of taxation, trade, and the quartering of troops.[6] It is my assertion that while the issue marked the annals of the church, it was but one of several disputes that embroiled the church and ministers during the century before the Revolutionary War.

The contribution of this book is twofold. First, it re-examines the several controversies that marked the church's experience between the 1680s and 1770s as elements that forged the religious group's colonial identity and development.[7] Among these topics is the role and purpose of the missionaries funded by the S.P.G. in the colonies and the sustained debate over the historical nature of the ministry initiated in the 1720s by the Boston layman John Checkley. The latter is an argument that I have traced to the question in England over the historic Episcopal office during the sixteenth, seventeenth, and eighteenth centuries and in America between Anglican and Dissenter pamphleteers from the 1720s to the early 1770s. In addition, the persistent efforts by both colonial clergymen and English bishops to seek the appointment of a colonial episcopate is discussed. During a visit to America in 1776, William Knox, a representative of Lord Dartmouth, Secretary of State for Colonial Affairs, presented a final effort to formulate a policy for the colonial English church. His last minute on-the-spot analysis of the situation was too late to be helpful for the American church.

Second, the work examines the significant roles played by the radical political leaders John and Samuel Adams, and John Wilkes, in transforming during the 1760s and 1770s the longstanding disputes from the realm of esoteric ecclesiastical argument to the domain of a fundamental political and civil issue. Fearful of the authority of Parliament to enhance and extend the affairs of the English church, the three critics absorbed the church's experience into the general rhetoric of complaints against imperial policies and causes of the American Revolution. The decisive and pivotal contributions of the men to the episcopacy debate has not received the attention previously from historians of the subject.

For nearly a century before 1776 ecclesiastical leaders in Boston were suspicious of the real purpose of the church's presence in the Massachusetts Bay Colony. Voices of opposition were raised regarding the legitimacy of the church's practices of worship, ordination of clergymen, and the prospect of an appointment of a prelate. After 1702

Congregational ministers issued regular alarms over the increasing number of missionaries in the province sponsored by the S.P.G. Each successive generation of nonconformist church leaders revisited these argumentative subjects. While provincial and London church officials countered that a bishop was necessary in America for the ordination of ministers, to administer confirmation to members, and to consecrate church buildings and churchyards.

In the eyes of many colonial witnesses, the church unlike other religious groups, was not a distinctively American institution. The Anglican ministers were required to maintain close links with London officials, including the bishop of London, archbishop of Canterbury, and the Secretary of the S.P.G. In addition to this array of church officials, the policies of the Council of Trade and Plantations also influenced the course of the institution in the provinces. All of these ties were not only a vital force on behalf of the church's development in America until the Declaration of Independence in 1776, but also imperial associations that aroused and inspired critics.

From the beginning of settlement in America in the early seventeenth century the church was a feature of the English civil apparatus.[8] It was fostered by the royal charters granted to private companies, to proprietors, and in the instructions issued to royal governors. After 1675 the Council of Trade and Plantations with the participation and assistance of successive bishops of London and archbishops of Canterbury shaped and established the church's policies and advancement for the remainder of the colonial period.[9] In the New England, and Middle, and Southern Colonies, the S.P.G. recruited, appointed, and financially supported nearly all of the ministers to these regions. Although the church was established in Virginia, Maryland, North and South Carolina, Georgia, and partially in New York, it was strongest and most prominent in the Chesapeake provinces.[10] Yet at bottom it remained an English institution in an American setting and not an English-American, or American-English church in the colonies.

Despite the fact that the number of congregations and ministers in America were most numerous in Virginia, significantly outnumbering the churches and men in other colonies, the intensity of criticism against the church throughout the colonial era was concentrated in Boston, Massachusetts. Opposition to the presence and practices of the church in the region was led by such Congregational Church luminaries as Increase and Cotton Mather, Jonathan Mayhew, and Charles Chauncy. The origins of the contention against the church are anchored in the dissension within the institution in the homeland during the sixteenth, seventeenth, and eighteenth centuries. It was extended to America at the time of the establishment of a congregation in Boston in 1686. An occasion long proposed by the resident royal customs commissioner, Edward Randolph, that was accomplished after the revocation of the Massachusetts Bay Colony's charter in 1684 and the appointment of a royal governor in 1686.[11] Increase Mather recalled and recited the ecclesiastical and liturgical issues that had been a source of debate between the Puritan and orthodox parties within the Church of England since the mid-sixteenth century. He systematically disputed the manner of worship of the church: the legitimacy of the Book of Common Prayer, the nature of the liturgy, and the surplice worn by ministers. His complaints provided the foundation for the subsequent controversies that the church faced during the remainder of the colonial period: challenges and criticisms that were presented in published sermons, essays, and newspaper articles.

Increase Mather's son Cotton, was the first Congregational minister to pointedly object to the activity of missionaries funded by the S.P.G. in the provinces. He suspected that the men were possibly not serving solely the offices of the church but were also actively undertaking undefined imperial activities on behalf of the English government. It was a plan, he and other critics argued, that aimed to reduce the influence of non-Anglican churches by strengthening the congregations of the national church.

A Boston bookseller, layman, High Churchman, and suspected Jacobite, John Checkley, opened the next controversial era in the early 1720s when he reprinted several English pamphlets. These works addressed the historical legitimacy of the ministerial and Episcopal offices in the church, a debate that cast into question the validity of the Congregational church's ordinations. Checkley's publications not only gave rise to the argument over the prospect of the appointment of a colonial Anglican bishop, but also renewed fears among Congregational church leaders that the civil authority of seventeenth-century English bishops would be reclaimed and transferred to the colonies along with the possibility of persecution of non-Anglicans.

After the Stamp Act crisis of the mid-1760s, the issue of an American bishop was changed by lawyer John Adams and merchant Samuel Adams. No longer was the subject an ambiguous debate between learned Congregational and Anglican ministers. The prospect of a prelate and the role of the church in the colonies were absorbed into the objectionable rhetoric of English imperial policies and administration. These essayists feared the authority of Parliament to appoint colonial bishops, create dioceses, and impose a tithe on the general population to support the English church. From 1768 to the Declaration of Independence in 1776, the two Adams and John Wilkes were the sources of many of the critical accounts to a prelate in America that appeared in the Boston and London newspapers. Their calculating strategy was shrewd, relentless, and effective. No Anglican bishop was ever sent to or visited America during the colonial period; the church's hierarchical structure remained incomplete.

For a brief period after 1772 there was a lull in adverse criticism of the church. Increasing public objections to imperial administrative policies such as the Tea Act of 1773, the Coercive Acts of 1774, and the Quebec Act of 1774 supplanted common outcries over a colonial prelate. A new situation emerged after the meeting of the First Continental Congress in 1774 that reached into the midst of every Church of England congregation. Now a target was a clarification of the political loyalties of the local ministers. During the months immediately after the sessions of the First Continental Congress and before the battles at Lexington and Concord in 1775, in an atmosphere of escalating rebellious opinion, the loyalties of the parsons was openly challenged by their neighbours. The public question was simply, were the ministers allied with the English or the Revolutionary cause? Were the men loyalists or patriots? A handful of the men had identified their sentiments during 1774 and 1775; some of the men immediately embraced the Loyalist cause while others were firmly in the Patriot camp. For many of the clergy, their civil opinions were unknown, while others quietly retired or died without disclosing their sentiments. It was a complicated situation as I have recounted elsewhere, the political dissension and experience meant dire consequences for the church during and after the Revolutionary War, an impact that was felt for nearly a century.[12] Because, on the one hand, as representatives of the English church, the men held a sense of moral obligation to the oath of loyalty to the Crown and Parliament undertaken at their ordination.

The colonial controversy over the appointment of an American prelate has attracted the attention of several historians.[13] David Ramsay, the prominent South Carolina physician, politician, and historian of the Revolution, observed that at the outbreak of the war religion divided the colonists. The Presbyterians and Congregationalists, Ramsay commented, 'were universally attached to the measures of Congress'.[14] Doubtless, mindful of the pamphlet war over the prospect of an American bishop during the 1760s, he remarked that the nonconformists feared the establishment of an English church hierarchy.[15] The Princeton-educated

South Carolinian chronicled the political opinion of the Church of England's parsons in the northern and southern colonies and bluntly noted that the northern ministers 'were pensioners on the bounty of the British government'.[16] He failed to recognise the responsibility and moral obligations of the bishop of London and the S.P.G. for the maintenance of the ministers.[17]

In 1902 Alfred Lyon Cross published *The Anglican Episcopate and the American Colonies*, a study that examined the historical origins of the provision of ecclesiastical authority in the provinces and the supervisory apparatus for administering the church and clergy during the seventeenth and eighteenth centuries. The work has been the primary resource for successive generations of historians referring to the colonial experience of the church. The question of episcopacy was given similar emphasis nearly 40 years after Cross's work was published by John C. Miller's *Origins of the American Revolution*. He suggested that the churchmen viewed themselves as the upholders of the monarchy and British authority in the colonies. Miller observed that not all Anglican preachers fitted into this category and that northern Dissenters and Southern Anglicans after 1774 were allied against British misrule.[18] Bernhard Knollenberg examined in more detail the roots of the American Revolution during the seven years between 1759 and 1766. He concentrated his analysis of the Anglican church's role in these affairs on the efforts of the Archbishop of Canterbury, Thomas Secker, to promote the founding of a mission at Cambridge, Massachusetts, and to set up an episcopate.[19] Knollenberg's conclusions were justifiable, although Secker's two efforts to plant the church in the neighbourhood of Harvard College and to establish colonial bishops were not new. As early as 1727 Timothy Cutler and Samuel Myles, Anglican ministers in Boston, had expressed to the S.P.G. the importance, most likely for conversion purposes, of starting a church in Cambridge. Ever since the first years of the eighteenth century, Anglican parsons in the Middle Colonies and in New England had frequently expressed the need for a resident prelate to supervise ecclesiastical affairs.

Sixty years after Cross had presented his work, Carl Bridenbaugh examined the episcopacy question from a different perspective in *Mitre and Sceptre: Transatlantic Faiths, Ideas, Personalities, and Politics, 1689–1775*. His book differed from Cross's, proposing that religious issues were involved in the Revolution and that some historians had ignored them. It also documented admirably the persistent political effectiveness of the Dissenters' lobby in England in preventing the appointment of colonial bishops, a success that clearly precluded any need for armed rebellion to prevent bishops from being sent to America. Yet *Mitre and Sceptre* followed the same general pattern advanced by the earlier writers, although supplemented with new material from noncon-formist sources. Offering another interpretation of the episcopacy contro-versy, Stephen Taylor has persuasively suggested that Bridenbaugh's study was deeply flawed by his assumption that the fears of colonial Dissenters at the prospect of an English episcopate were an accurate portrayal of reality on both sides of the Atlantic. Phrases like 'ecclesias-tical imperialism' and 'lust for dominion' might be applicable to some American Anglicans, although even then not without qualification, but to apply them to the English bishops reveals not only a predisposition to rely on rhetoric and propaganda for evidence 'but also a fundamental incomprehension of religious thought in eighteenth century England'.[20]

Frederick V. Mills admirable study, *Bishops by Ballot: An Eighteenth Century Ecclesiastical Revolution* (New York, 1978) emphasises primarily the efforts by Anglican church leaders to obtain a colonial episcopate, particularly during the 1760s and 1770s. He follows the account during the period of the reconstitution and reorganisation of the church in the post-Revolutionary War decade.

In my book *The Imperial Origins of the English Church in Early America, 1607–1783* (London, 2004), I briefly noted the controversy over the prospect of an American bishop and the political opinions and loyalties of the ministers in 1775. But the complexity of the issues suggested a more extended analysis of the matter. Although episcopacy was a dominant point in conflict with critics, it was not the only issue in disagreement. Yet the overriding irritant, at least during the decade before the Declaration of Independence, was the fact that the Church of England was the state church under the authority of Parliament, with inseparable ties to civil and ecclesiastical officers in London.

The Revolutionary War transformed the church and required it to forge a new American organisation. Without any political ties, it was allowed to reorganise and reconstitute itself as an institution independent of the authority of Parliament, the bishop of London, the archbishop of Canterbury, and the financial support of the S.P.G.

Acknowledgements

As always when a book is finished, its author looks back on the years of research and writing, and realises with gratitude how many people and institutions have helped in its composition. The nature of the book requires a familiarity with ecclesiastical history, offices, precedents, and practices on both sides of the Atlantic Ocean during the seventeenth and eighteenth centuries. It also demands an examination of the resources, both printed and manuscript that illuminate the unfolding drama of the controversies that gripped the American church from 1686 to 1783. During the course of my research and writing for this book, I have benefited in England from the interest, assistance and criticism of numerous generous persons including Kevin Sharpe, Stephen J. Taylor, and John Walsh.

An anonymous reader generously provided thoughtful and substantive comments on the entire text. Without reservation I am indebted to the Series Editor, J. C. D. Clark, for his wise, persistent, encouraging, and insightful interest in the course of the development of the work, contributions that have strengthened, refined, and enriched the book.

In the United States, several scholars have generously answered my requests for assistance and criticism for which I am most grateful. In particular, I am especially indebted to Dr. James E. Mooney for his kindness, encouragement, and good sense with which he has aided my efforts on the book over several years. He has read each of the versions of the study and offered his thoughtful and keen bibliographical and editorial criticisms. I must unabashedly admit that the book is stronger because of his wise counsel. Professor Otto Lohrenz has on numerous occasions provided to me the benefit of his extraordinarily rich biographical knowledge of Virginia parsons and their political opinions during the era of the American Revolution. Steve Barron of Philadelphia created the program for my 'The Colonial American Clergymen of the Church of England, 1607–1783, Database', a collection of biographical data on the 1280 ministers who were associated with the church between 1607 and 1783. My knowledge of the colonial clergymen is more comprehensive and informed because of his expert counsel. The database is a valuable resource for examining and interpreting the individual's and the church's experience in Early America. Barron's generous and supportive efforts have enhanced the book.

In addition to scholars, I am obligated to the unfailingly helpful staffs of many libraries and archives. In England, my research efforts have been aided at the Bodleian Library, Rhodes House Library, Vere Harmsworth Library, and Rothermere American Institute at Oxford (especially to Dr. Laura Lauer and Mrs. Andrea Beighton, the Assistant Directors), the Lambeth Palace Library, and the Guildhall Library in London. In the United States, the libraries of Princeton University, Yale University, Harvard University, the College of William and Mary, Princeton Theological Seminary, Columbia University, the Episcopal Divinity School, the Library of Congress, and the Family History Library.

My efforts have been considerably eased by the Master and Fellows of Balliol College, in the University of Oxford, who have graciously extended to me the congenial privileges and courtesies of the College for extended periods of research. The publishers have been unfailingly kind, supportive, and constructive at every step in the process of editing and publishing the book.

There are many persons on both sides of the Atlantic who (perhaps without knowing it) have helped me to complete this work through their discussions and publications. I hope in some small way they know my gratitude. Nonetheless, the book remains of my doing and any errors that may remain in the text are my responsibility.

An earlier version of Chapter 3 was presented to the Washington Seminar on American History and Culture led by Dr. James M. Banner, Jr. I am grateful to him and to the participants of the seminar for their beneficial and significant comments.

Whenever reference is made in this book to the Church of England, or Anglican or English church, I mean to the church and its organisation and practices in England. Because the origins, educational and early religious experiences of many colonial ministers occurred in the distant provinces of Scotland, Ireland, and Wales, they were required to submit in all matters to the jurisdiction of the bishop of London and the customs of the English church. Such sister institutions as The Episcopal Church in Scotland, the Church of Ireland, and the Church of England in Wales, differed in varying degrees from practices of the Anglican church.

Dates of the months and years are given here according to the New Style throughout the text; but when reference has been made to manuscript source materials in the footnotes, the Old Style system of dating has been maintained.

Rothermere American Institute
University of Oxford
2006

Some Useful Dates

1603–25	James I, King of England
1604–7	Richard Vaughan, Bishop of London
1607	Settlement of James Town
1607–9	Thomas Ravis, Bishop of London
1610–11	George Abbot, Bishop of London
1611–33	George Abbot, Archbishop of Canterbury
1611–21	John King, Bishop of London
1620	Settlement of Plymouth Colony
1621–8	George Montaigne, Bishop of London
1624	Settlement of New Amsterdam
1625–49	Charles I, King of England
1628–33	William Laud, Bishop of London
1630	Settlement of Massachusetts Bay Colony
1633–45	William Laud, Archbishop of Canterbury
1633–60	William Juxon, Bishop of London
1634	Settlement of Maryland
1636	Settlement of Connecticut
1636	Settlement of Rhode Island
1637	Settlement of New Haven
1638	Settlement of New Sweden
1642–9	Civil War in England
1649–60	Commonwealth in England
1660–85	Charles II, King of England
1660–3	Gilbert Sheldon, Bishop of London
1663–77	Gilbert Sheldon, Archbishop of Canterbury
1663	Establishment of the Carolinas
1663–75	Humphrey Henchman, Bishop of London
1664	Settlement of New Jersey
1675–6	King Philip's War
1675–1713	Henry Compton, Bishop of London
1682	Settlement of Pennsylvania
1684	Massachusetts Bay Charter revoked
1685	Dominion of New England
1685–8	James II, King of England
1686	King's Chapel, Boston, organised
1688	Glorious Revolution

1689	William (1689–1702) and Mary (1689–94), King and Queen of England
	Toleration Act
1689–97	King William's War
	Royal charter issued for Massachusetts Bay Colony, which incorporated Maine and Plymouth Colony within its boundaries
1690	Scottish Episcopal Church outlawed
1698	Society for the Propagation of Christian Knowledge founded
1701	Society for the Propagation of the Gospel in Foreign Parts authorised by Convocation and incorporated by Royal Charter
1702	East and West Jersey united as the royal colony of New Jersey
1702–14	Anne, Queen of England
1702–13	Queen Anne's War
1713	Treaty of Utrecht
1714–27	George I, King of England
1714–23	John Robinson, Bishop of London
1723–48	Edmund Gibson, Bishop of London
1727–60	George II, King of England
1729	North and South Carolina established as royal colonies
1732	Settlement of Georgia
1739–42	War of Jenkins' Ear
1739–45	Great Awakening
1744–8	King George's War
1748–61	Thomas Sherlock, Bishop of London
1754–63	The French and Indian War
1755–69	Parson's Cause
1758–68	Thomas Secker, Archbishop of Canterbury
1760–1820	George III, King of England
1761–2	Thomas Hayter, Bishop of London
1762–4	Richard Osbaldeston, Bishop of London
1763	Treaty of Paris, English control over North America east of the Mississippi confirmed
1764–77	Richard Terrick, Bishop of London
1765–6	Stamp Act
1767	Townshend Acts
1770	Boston Massacre
1773	Tea Act
	Boston Tea Party

1774	Coercive Acts
	Continental Congress
1775	Lexington and Concord
	Battle of Bunker Hill
1776	British forces evacuate Boston
	Declaration of Independence
	Battle of Long Island
	Continental Army evacuates New York City
	and British forces occupy the city
	Thomas Paine, *Common Sense*
	Battle of Trenton
	Anglican church disestablished in North Carolina
1777	State support of clergy ends in Virginia
	Continental Congress flees Philadelphia
	Philadelphia occupied by British forces
	British forces surrender at Saratoga Springs,
	New York
	Articles of Confederation adopted
	General Washington and troops spend winter at Valley
	Forge, Pennsylvania
	Anglican church disestablished in New York
	and Georgia
1778–87	Robert Lowth, Bishop of London
1778	Treaty of Alliance with France
	British forces evacuate Philadelphia
	Continental forces withdraw from Rhode Island
	Savannah, Georgia, occupied by British forces
	Anglican church disestablished in South Carolina
1780	British and Loyalist forces defeated at King's Mountain,
	South Carolina
	First use of the name Protestant Episcopal Church by
	the former Church of England in Maryland
1781	British forces surrender at Yorktown, Virginia
1782	William White, *The Case of the Episcopal Churches*
	in the United States Considered
1783	Treaty of Paris
	Loyalists sail from New York
	British evacuate New York City
	Protestant Episcopal Church organised in
	Maryland
1784	The Episcopal Church is organised in Pennsylvania
	and Massachusetts

	Samuel Seabury of Connecticut is consecrated the first bishop of the Protestant Episcopal Church in the United States of America
1785	The Episcopal Church is organised in Virginia, New Jersey, and South Carolina
	First General Convention of the Protestant Episcopal Church in the United States of America
1786	English Parliament enacts statute to allow for the consecration of American bishops by English prelates
	Anglican church disestablished in Virginia
1789	General Convention of the Episcopal Church adopts for use a revised liturgy from that of the English church and a revised Book of Common Prayer

Part I A Century of Controversies

1
The Seeds of Discord: An English Church Established in Boston

Forty years after the history-making events at Lexington and Concord, John Adams wrote to Jedidiah Morse, a geographer and historian as well as a Congregational minister, remarking strongly that the episcopacy question had been a lively and divisive issue at the time of the Revolution.[1] Adams asked Morse rhetorically, 'Where is the man to be found at this day, when we see Methodistical bishops, bishops of the church of England, and bishops, archbishops, and Jesuits of the church of Rome, with indifference, who will believe that the apprehension of Episcopacy contributed fifty years ago, as much as any other cause, to arouse the attention, not only of the inquiring mind, but of the common people, and urge them to close thinking on the constitutional authority of parliament over the colonies?'[2] The former president of the United States was certain that 'The objection was not merely to the office of bishop, though even that was dreaded, but to the authority of parliament, on which it must be founded'.[3] Continuing, Adams remarked, 'But if parliament can erect dioceses and appoint bishops, they may introduce the whole hierarchy, establish tithes, forbid marriages and funerals, establish religions, forbid Dissenters, make schism heresy, impose penalties extending to life and limb as well as to liberty and property'.[4] He noted that 'It [the scheme for a colonial episcopate] spread a universal alarm against the authority of Parliament. It excited a general and just apprehension, that bishops, and dioceses, and churches, and priests, and tithes, were to be imposed on us by Parliament ... If Parliament could tax us, they could establish the Church of England'.[5] Following in Adams's clear and precise footprints, the nineteenth-century English historian James Grahame, 20 years later, identified the episcopacy controversy as one of the causes of political discontent among the colonists in his popular *History of the United States*, which was published in both London and Philadelphia.[6]

Adams's emphasis on the significance of the episcopacy issue in the political debates leading to the Declaration of Independence is understandable because it loomed large on the Boston public scene for half a century. While it was a major dispute accompanied by a barrage of pamphlets published by opponents and advocates, it was one of a series of controversies that faced the institution, particularly in New England and the Middle Colonies, for nearly a century. In retrospect, the continuing experience of the Church of England in Colonial America was shaped at least in part by the arguments raised by critics of the church's practice and polity. Each of the debatable issues during the late seventeenth and eighteenth centuries essentially challenged the church. Called into question were the content of the Book of Common Prayer, liturgical practices of worship, and the ceremonial dress of the clergymen, all seeds broadcast by Increase Mather in the 1680s that germinated and flowered throughout the colonial era. In every instance the church was vulnerable to objections by critics on these matters.

Ceaseless pleas by individual provincial Anglican church leaders and by numerous conventions of the ministers were made to London church officials during the eighteenth century requesting the appointment of a prelate to complete the hierarchical organisation. Their petitions were unanswered. Without the presence of a supervising bishop, the church leaders were placed in the awkward position of attempting to define and defend the historical nature of the church, priesthood, and episcopacy. It was a debate that generated considerable heat and that contrasted the positions of the Anglican and reformed churches on the subjects. New England Congregational church leaders and critics shaped their argument around the memory of the political influence of seventeenth-century English prelates and were fearful of a repetition of the objectionable consequences should such an officer be introduced in the colonies.

The origin of the several controversies that engulfed the Anglican church in Colonial America is intertwined with the English civil and ecclesiastical policies formulated by the Council of Trade and Plantations in the 1670s, 1680s, and 1690s – policies that led not only to the founding of the first Anglican congregations in Boston, New York, Philadelphia, Newport, and Charles Town during the period, but cumulatively cast the church as a cause of the American Revolution.[7] The occasion of the establishment of the first Anglican congregation in Boston in 1686 initiated strident published objections to the presence of the church in the community by Mather, minister of Boston's Second Church and president of Harvard College.

Mather's personal and professional genealogy was linked to two of the notable Puritan leaders of the colony's first and second generations: he was the son of Richard Mather and the grandson of John Cotton. While his father and grandfather proclaimed and defined for their audiences the differences between the Puritan church in Massachusetts and the Anglican church in England, Increase Mather was obliged to direct his criticisms in the midst of the newly established English congregation in Boston. His published tracts regarding the Anglican church echoed his father's objections to the Book of Common Prayer, liturgical vestments, and bishops.[8] It was also a formula systematically honed and argued by John Cotton more than a generation earlier.[9]

Increase Mather's perspicacity sensed, though he could not substantiate his perception, a conspiracy by the English government to introduce the English church to the community as a means to erode the status and influence of the Congregational church in the colony. I have examined in detail in my book *The Imperial Origins of the English Church in Early America, 1607–1783* (London, 2004) the development and implementation of the policies that encouraged and strengthened the extension of the Church of England to colonial mainland America.[10]

The fortunes of the church were ultimately in the hands of secular authorities, especially the Council of Trade and Plantations. As a chief officer of state, the bishop of London was an influential member of the Council, and his advice and guidance were sought on religious issues that came before it. In fact, the Council took no action on any church-related matter without the consideration of the bishop of London. Besides introducing tighter economic and commercial regulations for the colonies, the Council delegated unprecedented duties and responsibilities for ecclesiastical jurisdiction to royal governors and the bishop of London.[11] As a national institution, the church was much more than a church in the strict religious sense of the word. It was a political and social establishment and its position was little changed after the Toleration Act of 1689.

The influential and accomplished civil official John Evelyn took a keen interest in the extension and administration of the colonial church. Evelyn was appointed by King Charles II to the Council for Foreign Plantations in 1672, and the position provided him with information regarding the difficulty of maintaining an Episcopalian presence in the colonies against rival sects. He concluded in 1688 that the lack of ministers in the American provinces was due, in part, to the lack of a resident bishop in any of the colonies. He suggested that a bishop be consecrated to go and reside 'in our forraine dominions'.[12]

England was a Protestant nation, and its civil and ecclesiastical leaders provided for the advancement of the state church in the stronger imperial policies that were forged in the 1670s, 1680s, and 1690s.[13] The church followed the establishment of royal government and governors in Massachusetts, Maryland, New York, and Pennsylvania. It was an important element of a process of anglicisation in the provinces. After the mid-1670s, the extension of the national church to the colonies and the appointments to provincial posts became a component of imperial policy, a course from which civil and ecclesiastical leaders would not deviate until after the Revolutionary War. During the 1670s, the principal policymakers included Thomas Osborne, the Earl of Danby and Charles II's Lord Treasurer; Archbishop of Canterbury Gilbert Sheldon; and Bishop of London Henry Compton.

Increase Mather's objections to the establishment of the English church in Boston were in part shaped by the unfolding challenge of the Massachusetts colony's independent status.[14] During the Puritan Revolution in England the Massachusetts Bay Colony remained neutral because the government considered itself an independent commonwealth after 1649. The tolerance of Cromwell's government towards the Massachusetts Puritans had come to an end with the restoration of the monarchy in 1660. A royal commission had been dispatched to New England in 1664 to investigate the state of affairs in those colonies. It reported that Massachusetts was resisting England's mercantile law, disobeying the Navigation Acts, minting its own currency, restricting suffrage to church members, denying free worship to Dissenters, and generally vitiating the authority of Parliament. The refusal of the Massachusetts Bay Colony leaders to send representatives to England to answer charges, and the even harsher reports of Edward Randolph, who became collector of customs of New England in 1678, led to the revocation of the Massachusetts Bay Colony's charter in 1684. The close union between church and state that had flourished since the province was established in 1629 was broken by the annulment of the charter.

With a royal charter and appointment commission in hand, the new governor of the Dominion of New England, Sir Edmund Andros, arrived in Boston in 1686. He immediately renewed Randolph's plea for the establishment of the first Anglican congregation in Boston and the appointment of a minister to serve it.[15] The new congregation held its first services that year and the presence of the English church in the community was unmistakably associated with the authority of royal government and officials. Bishop of London Henry Compton appointed the Reverend Robert Radcliff, a graduate and fellow of Exeter College in Oxford University, to serve as its minister.[16] Under Andros's administration, funds were raised for the construction of King's Chapel, which opened for services in June 1689.

New England church and state leaders were stunned by the revocation of the charter, the appointment of Andros as the royal governor, and the commencement of Anglican church services in Boston. The events ushered in a decade of cataclysmic and irreversible change in the structure of Massachusetts society, in its politics, and in the nature of its religious community. In affairs of state the rule of local governors was replaced by the appointment of royal officials who were charged to centralise the government.[17] The once-dominant Puritan oligarchy was now forced to accept the presence of the Church of England in the Boston Town Meeting House, parsons outfitted in the hated surplice reciting the liturgy of the corrupt Common Prayer. These circumstances summoned not only heated criticism from Increase Mather but also prompted an intense battle of ideas on such issues for the next 25 years. The exchange on the surface seems to be a confrontation of religious leaders championing either a Puritan or an Anglican point of view on fundamental issues of worship. Increase Mather and several of his closest collaborators lectured, preached, and wrote pamphlets calling the people of New England to return to the purposes and ways of the founders of the colony.

For Increase and his son Cotton Mather, the holy vision for the establishment of the colony more than half a century earlier had been betrayed. The turn of events in church and state affairs signalled for the Mathers a further example of the colony's declension and waywardness from the purpose of its founders. Immediately, Increase Mather took up the battle cry for the Puritan clergy and challenged the legitimacy and presence of the English church. Born and bred in Boston, he was committed to perpetuating his father's and the founders' vision for the wilderness settlement and he served his church, his college, and his colony with distinction. While the first generation came to America to preserve the true church, the second extended this aim to include the preservation of an entire people, saints and sinners. In the 1670s, however, the church and state faced dangers and controversies, weaknesses, and cracks in its foundation. The unsettling consequences of King Philip's war, and the lively debate regarding qualifications for church membership culminating in Solomon Stoddard's acceptance of the Half-Way Covenant, were troubling to Mather. For 20 years the controversial features of 'Stoddardeanism' would grip Mather's mind and pen. These were not the best of times: the decision of the Synod of 1679 about church membership and the failure of the state to suppress competing faiths were marks of division, dissension, and declension. Mather was the leader of the Reforming Synod summoned by the General Court to answer two questions: 'What are the evils that have provoked the Lord to bring his judgements on New England'? and 'What is to be done so that those evils may be reformed?' The delegates met in September 1679, and Mather was prominent in their councils. He was chosen, with others, at the close of the first session, to present the Synod's results to the General Court. In October this work was ready, and was published as *The Necessity of Reformation* (Boston, 1679).[18]

The same committee had been charged with the preparation of a new Confession of Faith. As Mather and Urian Oakes, the celebrated poet and president of Harvard, had been in England between 1653 and 1671 and were interested observers of the 1658 Savoy Conference, their proposed 'platform' for the local churches was, with few changes, the Savoy Confession. This was presented to the second session of the Synod, held in May 1680, at which Mather served as moderator. For Mather, the church was an institution of the chosen of God: it had always been so. The saints were to govern the state: this assumption guided Mather not only as a pastor but also as president of Harvard, and later as the agent of Massachusetts in London seeking the renewal of the charter.[19]

The loss of piety, the changes in sacramental practices, and the lowering of standards for church membership had shaken Increase Mather and eroded the idea of the true church in New England as a saving remnant. The presence of the Church of England in Boston undermined and placed in jeopardy the political and religious legacy of the Puritan founders of the Bay colony. The two Mathers, Increase and Cotton, uncrowned heads of the New England Congregational church in their days, opposed at once and strenuously the intrusion of the English church.

Increase Mather immediately took up the challenge and with voice and pen led the Puritan attack on the doctrine, polity, and practices of the Church of England. As the minister of the Second Church in Boston, fellow of Harvard College from 1675 to 1685, and president of the institution between 1685 and 1701, he was the first nonconformist to speak boldly and critically against the Anglican presence in Boston in 1686. He was also the significant link in the chain of transmission during the third generation from England to New England of Puritan opinions and ideas regarding episcopacy, Anglican religious ceremonies, and the Book of Common Prayer. As the foremost religious and civil leader of his generation, Mather had established and maintained useful ties with English nonconformist church leaders for more than 30 years. His opinion had been shaped by his experience and intellectual inheritance on both sides of the Atlantic.

Mather's prized possession was his collection of books; it comprised more than 700 titles in nearly a thousand volumes. In the catalogue of the collection which he prepared in 1664, we find examples of his interest in the episcopacy issue in the church. His library included such volumes as William Prynne's *Lord Bishops None of the Lord Bishops* (London, 1640) and *Sixteen Quaeres Proposed to our Lord Prelates*; David Calderwood's *The Pastor and Prelate*, of 1628; and *The Presbyterian Government is Divine*. These texts were side by side with the fundamental doctrines and laws of the Anglican church, *Articles of the Church of England* and *Canons Ecclesiastical of the English Church*. New England's most learned cleric had at his fingertips the basic reference works on the basis of which he could launch his attack on the corrupted nature of the episcopacy, liturgical ceremonies, and the Prayer Book of the Anglican church.[20]

Undoubtedly, Increase Mather had heard at his father's table and from his father's lips accounts of the turbulent times for Puritans in England during the 1620s and 1630s.[21] He may have heard the names of the prominent leaders among Puritans and Anglicans. In response to the establishment of King's Chapel in Boston and the conduct of services of worship in 1686, Mather published in the same year *A Brief Discourse Concerning the Unlawfulness of the Common Prayer Worship. And of Laying the Hand on, and Kissing the Booke in Swearing* (Cambridge, 1686; London, 1689). It is the first printed work in the battle of pamphlets that was waged between advocates of the Puritan theocracy in Massachusetts and the agents of the Anglican church.[22] Mather was addressing the unlawfulness, first, of the use of the Book of Common Prayer in church service, and, second, of the custom of kissing the Bible in taking oaths, both contemptible to Puritans on both sides of the Atlantic. But the real question in the minds of the opposing parties – king and colonists – was which of them should rule the colony.

Cotton Mather recorded in his diary under 11 day, 9 month [November], 1686, that after meditating on his usual question, 'What shall I now do for God', he answered that as 'The Common-Prayer Worship now being sett up in this Country, I would procure and assist the Publication of a Discourse written by my Father, that shall enlighten the rising Generation, in the Unlawfulness of that Worship, and antidote them against Apostasy from the Principles of our

First Settlement'.[23] The pamphlet was a direct attack on Common Prayer worship and was certainly attended with potential danger, for Joseph Dudley was president of the New England Confederation and his cunning secretary, Edward Randolph, both with commissions under James II, were actively engaged in promoting the service. *New-England's Faction Discovered* (London, 1690), an anti-Puritan tract attributed to either Dudley or Randolph, reports that copies of the 'scandalous Pamphlet ... intituled "the unlawfulness of the Common-prayer Worship" ... were spread and scattered up and down the Country'.[24]

Increase Mather's *Unlawfulness of the Common Prayer Worship* challenged the position of the proponents of Common Prayer worship. He concluded, 'If you would have a distinct account of the Original of the Common prayer Book, you must know, it was Collected out of three Superstitious Books. The first part of Publick prayer is borrowed from the Papists Breviary. That about Sacraments, Matrimony, Burials, &c. is taken out of the Ritual. The Order of Consecration, Epistles, Collects, &c. is gathered out of the Roman Missal'.[25]

For Mather, the New England Puritan who had walked and talked with leading English Independents during his sojourn in England, 'the English Liturgy is Originally Heathenish as well as Popish is manifest, in that the Popes Liturgy from whence ours has bin derived, is so. The Principal Parts of the Mass Book were borrowed from Idolatrous Pagans. They came from *Numa Pompilius*. The Vestments, Holy water, Incense, &c. in the Roman Liturgy, were taken up from the Heathen; the Bishops of Rome thinking thereby to gain Pagans to the Christian Religion, Just as the Bishops of England thought to gain Papists to the Protestant Religion, by the use of their Ceremony's'. Mather, the future rector of Harvard College and the titular head of the New England church, rhetorically inquired, 'What Vain Repetitions dos the Common prayer Book abound with?', noting that 'In One Service the worshippers must repeat these words, Good Lord deliver us Eight Times over. And wee beseech Thee to hear us, Twenty Times over. The Gloria Patri is to bee repeated Ten Times in the same Morning or Evening Service'. Mather pointedly observed that the heathens were wont to worship their idols in the same manner, and that the Gospel according to Matthew admonishes the reader that 'When ye pray use not vain Repetitions as the Heathens do, for they think that they shall bee heard for their much Speaking'.[26]

Increase Mather's *Brief Discourse* was not a narrow, sectarian, peevish, unprovoked attack on Common Prayer worship. The work is a temperate defence of the Puritan position against the encroachments of the agents of the crown, those advocates of episcopacy, and the unprincipled, growing absolutism of the monarchy. The extraordinary turn of events in Boston prompted Mather to remember that the founders of the Massachusetts Bay Colony and 'those Eminent and Faithful Ministers of Christ who were driven into an American desert, the principal cause of whose Exile, and Sufferings, was because they durst not touch with the Common Prayer Book. And since their being in New England, some of them have by their writings testified against it'.[27]

Mather reminded his reader that his religious education was at the hand of one of the principal founders of the province, his father, the legendary Richard Mather, who 'was an Holy and a Larned man, and one that Suffered much for his Non conformity'.[28] Mather declared that 'should I once go to hear Common Prayer, I Seriously profess I Know not how I should bee able to look my Father in the Face in the other world; much less how I should answer Christ at the great day for my Apostasy from those Principles of Truth, which my Father has instructed me in both by word and Example'.[29] He strongly disputed the motives of the advocates of royal government and the English church in Boston, forcefully suggesting that 'It may be time will discover that some who pretend Zeal for the Common Prayer Book are carrying on a design for Rome. The Liturgy came from thence, and will Perhaps lead thither again'.[30] The Church of Rome was recognised by Puritan leaders on both sides of the Atlantic as the Antichrist. For them the real danger of current circumstances was that an unreformed Church of England might return to the Catholic camp.

Reading the pamphlet today the reader is bound to be struck by the cogency and precision of Mather's argument. The pamphlet had far greater significance, beyond the question of the order and origin of church worship services and the method of taking oaths. It is a political document that defends the Puritan traditions of the Massachusetts colony against the intrusion of an Anglicanism that he perceived sought to erode, if not supplant, the established order. Certainly, events of the period promoted such cautious and protective concern. In France the Edict of Nantes, which for nearly 90 years had sealed a truce between Catholic and Huguenot, was revoked on 18 October 1685. Persecution of Protestants drove thousands of emigrants from France. Some refugees in destitute condition arrived at Boston in August 1686. Mather must have talked with some of these persons. In England, the Catholic policies of James II had given to Archibald Campbell, Ninth Earl of Argyll, and to James Scott, First Duke of Monmouth, an excuse to stir up a Protestant rebellion against him, but the efforts of Argyll in Scotland and of Monmouth in southwestern England had failed hopelessly and tragically.[31]

In quick succession Mather published, in 1688, *A Testimony against Sacred Prophane and Superstitious Customs, Now Practised by Some in New England* and *A Vindication of New England, from the Vile Aspersions Cast Upon that Country by a Late Address of a Faction There who Denominate Themselves of the Church of England in Boston.* Mather's *Testimony* was an attack upon May games, stage plays, dancing, organs, pictures in church, and the like, and owed much to William Prynne's influential work *Histrio-Mastix*, a copy of which Mather had in his library.[32]

The first printed response to Mather's tract seems to have been a London pamphlet, *New-England's Faction Discovered* (London, 1690). The author, identified only as 'C. D.' and who may have been either a colonist or Englishman, presented a vigorous defence of English political and religious policies in New England since 1685. The reader is reminded that on religious grounds the Puritans 'now had the opportunity to make themselves Persecutors of the Church of England as they had before been of all others that did not comply with their Independency; whom they punished with Fines, Imprisonment, Stripes, Banishment, and Death; and all for matters of meer Conscience and Religion only'.[33]

In London, Bishop of Chichester John Williams, a well-known and prolific controversialist, whose reputation included writing with equal vehemence against Roman Catholics and Dissenters, responded to Mather's *Brief Discourse* with *A Brief Discourse Concerning the Lawfulness of Worshipping God by the Common Prayer*.[34] A prominent figure in church and state affairs, he served as a chaplain to King William III and Queen Mary, and as a canon of Canterbury Cathedral. Mather responded to Williams's tract perhaps as early as 1701–2, with *Some Remarks, on a Pretended Answer, to a Discourse Concerning the Common-Prayer Worship.* Declaring that 'The Author of a Discourse written many years ago has had by him above seven Years' to reply with this 'Pretended Answer' to his former *Discourse on the Unlawfulness of the Common-Prayer Worship*, Mather had 'resolved to make no Reply unto it; only to Answer it with Silence, and deserved Contempt. But some worthy Persons in England having desired that he would send them some Remarks upon it, he has at last complied with their importunity'.[35] The principal point at issue between the two pamphleteers was whether the English liturgy was in substance borrowed from the Roman Catholics. Williams claimed that there were certain details in common, but that, in substance, Mather's criticism was a falsehood. Mather took strong exception to that judgement.

At the time Mather was writing *A Brief Discourse*, in the autumn of 1686, he was also composing *A Testimony Against Several Prophane and Superstitious Customs Now Practised by some in New-England*.[36]

Mather's two pamphlets were part of his arsenal of defence on behalf of Massachusetts Puritanism: protecting the community against the invasion of Anglican social practices under the guise of political innovations. The Massachusetts charter had been revoked, local power and independence shattered, and now Massachusetts had become a royal colony, governed by a president, Joseph Dudley, and a council, with commissions from King James.

For Increase Mather this 'declension', associated with the coming of a church which observed saints' days and holy days and tolerated old customs connected with them, called for criticism and protest. On the following 25 January 1686/87, St. Paul's day was kept, the bell rung for service, and the new governor, Andros, attended church. Three weeks later, Shrove Tuesday was celebrated with dancing in the streets. On 23 April 1687, Increase Mather wrote in his diary: 'This Sabbath night was greatly profaned by bonfires, fireworks &c under pretence of honor to ye King's Coronation'.[37]

In his *Testimony Against ... Prophane and Superstitious Customs*, Mather assails health drinking, dicing and cards and lotteries, Candlemas, Christmas-keeping, New Year's gifts, Shrove Tuesday, cockfighting, and dedicating days to saints. He traces the history of these customs and gives the opinions of the ancient and more recent Christian writers upon them. Finally he commits to the Assembly of Representatives the responsibility of seeking from the king a happy settlement and establishment of the college. Harvard had been left without a charter since the revocation of the colony's charter in 1684. As rector of the college, Mather attempted in 1692, 1696, 1697, 1699, and 1700 to sustain the conservative party's interests and obtain a charter, but without success. The English government claimed that nothing should be done 'unfavourable to Episcopacy'.

Cotton Mather, no less forceful than his father against the presence of the Anglican church in Boston, maintained that New England had pledged itself to the Lord's service. A covenant with the Lord embraced all people, yet only the elect would survive the final cataclysm. The fates of the church and state were inseparable. The revolutionary political circumstances of the colony during the 1680s prompted Mather to trumpet a final call to New England. Merely 27 years old, flourishing in his career, and following in the footsteps of his father and the colony's founders, Cotton Mather delivered, on 28 May 1690, the annual election sermon before the General Court. A little more than a year earlier, on 18 April 1689, the colony had deposed the Andros government, and on 6 June 1689, it had resumed its old charter government with the old officials taking their former titles of office. The provisional government was now conducting its election pending the arrival of the hoped-for charter, which Increase Mather and other agents then in England were attempting to obtain.

The preacher compared New England and its restored government to the restoration of the Jews at Jerusalem under Nehemiah after the Chaldean invasion and the Captivity. It was an inspiring and dramatic occasion. Yet conditions in New England were far from calm: there were the heavy costs of the war with the French and the Indians; trade was poor, and money was scarce. Cotton Mather did not fail to call New England to the vision of its founders. He preached a dire message of warning to his auditors regarding the presence in the Puritan community of the recently established Anglican congregation. He proclaimed that the founders of the colony 'came into the Wilderness, because we could finally worship God without that Episcopacy, That Common Prayer, and those unwarrantable Ceremonies, which the Land of our Father's Sepulchers, has been defiled with'. Cotton Mather declared that the vision of the province's founders was to live 'under the pure and full Dispensation of the Gospel', and under their own, not royal, government.[38] He pronounced a call to battle. Mather was a general in the Puritan church challenging his audience to preserve in the purest form the old New England church ways from Anglican defilement. It was at best a difficult fight in an era of increased secularisation, increased materialism, increased demographic growth, and, through the eyes of Mather and many of his clerical contemporaries, an age of spiritual declension and waywardness. The enemy was the familiar foe of old, the Church of England: its customs, its ceremonies, its hierarchies, and its parsons. While the events of the Salem witch trials soon dominated the attention of religious leaders, the shadow of the Antichrist seemed to be everywhere, in the nearby countryside and in an Anglican chapel hard by Boston Common.

The new charter of 1691 and the Toleration Act transformed the church and the state. The magistrate was a secular creature and religious uniformity was dead. The new English church in Boston was a threat to the New England way of Richard, Increase, and Cotton Mather. Like the original non-separating Congregationalists, Cotton Mather had always maintained that the New England churches were a part of the Church of England. He was opposed to the movement led by Solomon Stoddard to form an alliance with the Presbyterians in England. Mather believed that there had been two groups struggling for control of the Church of England since the Reformation. One faction had never accepted the reforms of the sixteenth century and despised the Puritans who carried them further in the seventeenth. This group accepted divine right episcopacy and Episcopal ordination, and used the canons for unscriptural rule. The other group, the 'true Church of England', consisted of nonconformists, the 'legal parts' of the Church of England.

Samuel Myles, the son of a Massachusetts Baptist minister and a graduate of Harvard College, succeeded Radcliff as minister of King's Chapel and presided over the church for nearly 40 years. In the first months after his appointment, Myles demonstrated that he was politically astute and a fervent royalist. Joined by the churchwardens of his congregation, the Bostonians reported to King William III the details surrounding the overthrow of the Andros regime.[39] Their intention may have been to undermine Increase Mather's political efforts in London to obtain the reinstatement of the 1629 Massachusetts charter.[40] Without mincing their words Myles and his associates emphasised that the continuation of royal government in the province was essential for Anglican worship to survive in Boston.[41]

Until the first decade of the eighteenth century the congregation in Boston was the only active Anglican church in Massachusetts and New England. The situation changed in 1702, soon after the founding in London of the Society for the Propagation of the Gospel in Foreign Parts (S.P.G.) and the arrival in Boston of the society's first representatives. It was an event that prompted both Increase and Cotton Mather to renew a defence of New England Congregational church practices and attack Anglican procedures. Questioning the purpose of the English church's activity in New England, Cotton Mather pointedly challenged the role of the S.P.G. in the region. He confided to a colleague in 1716 that the presence of the church in New England was a conspiracy by English civil and ecclesiastical officials to undermine and erode the nearly century-old Puritan religious community. Writing to Anthony W. Boehme, the German chaplain to the court of George I, Mather remarked that 'New England is the only country in America which has much of real and vital religion flourishing in it'. He reported that the S.P.G. missionaries, 'who are of little use but to propagate impiety, come to disturb well-ordered churches of God'. The Anglicans were not concerned with sending clergymen to the 'ungospellized plantations' of Virginia and Maryland but rather to send them to 'a country filled with holy churches and pastors' ... to serve their political and vexatious purposes'.[42]

Mather's notion that the extension of the Anglican church to Massachusetts and New England was a plot launched by English government officials to undermine the Puritan church was an interpretation of the church's presence that was recited by successive generations of critics. Indeed, the church's experience follows the observations of Bernard Bailyn, Gordon S. Wood, and G. B. Warden that the colonists were quick to explain a linkage of political events, particularly after the Stamp Act of 1765, as caused by a conspiracy.[43] Mather, like Samuel Adams in the 1760s and 1770s, maintained the opinion that England's leaders were seeking to violate English and American rights and liberties. Such a conspiratorial sentiment about the church was not limited to the years after 1750 but reached back to its 1686 beginnings in Boston and engulfed its affairs for the remainder of the colonial period.

2

Discord Enlarged: The Society for the Propagation of the Gospel

During the late seventeenth and early eighteenth centuries, the long shadows of controversy stalked the English church when it was introduced in several colonies. In Maryland, New York, South and North Carolina, and Connecticut, the church's initial experience was fraught with tension and intense disagreements with leaders of other religious groups. The disputes stemmed in part from the distinctive privileges that the church received from the policies of the imperial government and partly from objections by Quakers, Presbyterians, and other Protestant religious groups. Only in Virginia, where the church was established by law, did the controversies turn not on the issues of the historic nature of episcopacy or liturgical practices of worship, but on the personal differences and rivalries between the bishop of London's official deputy in the province, Commissary James Blair, and several men who served in succession as royal governors including Edmund Andros, Francis Nicholson, and Alexander Spotswood.[1]

Soon after Increase and Cotton Mather expressed strong disapproval over the English church's presence in Boston, disagreement erupted in Maryland on different grounds. After the proprietary rule of Lord Baltimore was suspended in Maryland in 1691 and the province came under royal control, the legislature in May 1692 adopted among its first acts the establishment of 'the Church of England as by law established' in the Mother Country.[2] The legislation included a tax to be collected beginning on 10 March 1693, a provision that provoked strong objections from the Quakers and Roman Catholics protesting the requirement of their members to pay tithes to support the Anglican church and its ministers. The Quakers forcefully broadcast their dispute in Annapolis and London, and effectively accomplished a disallowance of the 1692 Church Act and an additional act by Order in the King's Council on

4 January 1695/96. The Assembly renewed its effort to establish the Church in 1696 with a similar statute, legislation that brought again strong opposition from the Quakers. In 1700 the Church Act was disallowed and on 7 May the Assembly enacted a new bill with the same purpose as the earlier acts before the Quakers could muster opposition; it was approved by Parliament in 1701.[3] King William III signed the bill, inquiring: 'Have the Quakers the benefit of Toleration? Let the Established Church have an Established Maintenance'. After nearly a decade of debate and legal manoeuvring, the Church of England was established in Maryland. The new act gave toleration to the Quakers and Dissenters and provided a stipend for every minister of the English church in Maryland. The colony included among its residents many confessions including Presbyterians, Independents, Anabaptists, Quakers, and Catholics. Commissary Thomas Bray, in Maryland in 1700 for a visitation of the clergy and churches, conducted a survey of provincial church affairs. The results showed that a large portion of the people were Anglicans and that the Quakers, instead of constituting the majority they claimed before the Board of Trade, actually made up only about 10 per cent of the population, with an estimated 8 per cent of the remainder Roman Catholic.[4]

In New York, Governor Benjamin Fletcher implemented his royal instructions relating to ecclesiastical affairs and led the effort for the legislature to adopt the Ministry Act of 1693 that established the Anglican church in the four lower counties of the colony.[5] Presumably the act was an intentionally vague piece of legislation that allowed for a 'good sufficient Protestant minister' to serve in each county. Governor Fletcher realised that to specify the Church of England as the religious institution to be settled in the colony would have raised the wrath of the Dutchmen who were a majority in the colonial assembly. Members of the Dutch Reformed Church, for some unknown reason, did not raise objections before the statute was passed, as the provision for church-wardens and vestrymen suggested an unfamiliar type of ecclesiastical organisation. Perhaps they intended from the beginning to try to profit from its vagueness. Later members of the Dutch church claimed that since the act was broadly defined they and their ministers had a share in the benefits of the law too. Governor Fletcher, however, declared that the law established only the Church of England and its clergymen. Furious over the governor's high-handed tactics, members of the Dutch Church directed sharp criticism towards him and his successors until their denomination was given similar privileges in 1770.[6]

Between 1692 and 1695, John Miller, a graduate of Trinity College, of Cambridge University, serving as the chaplain at the fort on Lower

Manhattan island, was the only Anglican cleric in New York. A keen observer, Miller gathered a collection of notes and drawings on the province. On learning of his father's death in 1695, Governor Benjamin Fletcher gave him permission to return to England after the minister had arranged for religious services to be held at the fort during his absence. He sailed for England on 11 July and en route his vessel and its passengers were taken prisoners by French privateers. Miller threw his papers on civil and ecclesiastical affairs in New York overboard so as not to give the French any intelligence of the colony. For a short period of time he was imprisoned in France before being released and travelling to London sometime in 1696. He immediately set to work writing an account of his New York experience and dedicated the manuscript to Bishop of London Henry Compton but it was not published until 1843.[7]

Miller's manuscript reviewed the state and history of New York and provided plans and ideas of his own for the governance of the colony. In particular, he proposed a formula for establishing an episcopate in America to serve the provinces of New York, New Jersey, Connecticut, and Rhode Island, with the bishop headquartered in New York. The official was to serve as a suffragan bishop under the jurisdiction of the bishop of London with a salary of £1,500 per year, together with all licenses of marriage and probate of wills, and the things usually belonging to bishops in England.' He added that the King's Farm could serve as the seat for himself and his successors.[8]

Compton embraced the plan and as an influential member of the Council of Trade and Plantations arranged for Miller to present his report at two meetings of the Council on 28 August and 4 September, 1696.[9] His comments on Indian affairs in the Mohawk River valley were given serious consideration by the Council members and subsequently a vigorous imperial policy on the matter was implemented during the early years of the eighteenth century.[10] At the time his proposal for an American bishop was not given favourable attention by London civil and ecclesiastical leaders but Compton returned to the issue in 1707 when he urged the appointment of an American prelate. The lack of official support for his plan prompted Miller to abandon returning to New York and he remained in England, becoming vicar of the parish at Effingham in County Surrey, a post that he served until his death in 1724.

A decade after the adoption of the Ministry Act of 1693, controversy exploded on Long Island. The statute provided for the settlement of two 'sufficient Protestant ministers' in Queen's County. The dispute centred in the village of Jamaica, where one of the ministers appointed under the act was to be located. In that town the Dissenters, who constituted most of the population, had called a minister of their own and started to build a church. When the statute for settling the ministry was passed, they stopped building, and the church was completed and a parsonage built by the local vestry elected under the act. This body was composed of Dissenters, and in 1702 it called a dissenting minister to the parish. In the same year, the Society for the Propagation of the Gospel sent a missionary to Jamaica, Patrick Gordon, but he died before he could be inducted.[11] A successive appointee, William Urquhart, was formally inducted by Governor Lord Cornbury in 1704. The governor ordered the dissenting minister to yield the church and parsonage to Urquhart. As William W. Manross has noted, this was an arbitrary proceeding, because the right to their possession had never been legally determined but was complied with for the time being and given an ex post facto legality by an act of the Assembly in 1706.[12]

Urquhart remained in possession of the property until his death in 1709, but during the vacancy that followed the Dissenters seized both the church and parsonage, and some justices of the peace who fined them for taking the former were dismissed. In 1710 the local vestry called another dissenting minister, and the same year an S.P.G. missionary designated for the post, the Reverend Thomas Poyer, arrived in the colony. Robert Hunter, who was then governor, was probably as much concerned for the interests of the church as his predecessor Lord Cornbury had been, but he was more scrupulous as to the means he used to promote them. He told Poyer that the only legal method to obtain either the property or his salary was to bring suit for them in the colonial courts, and offered to bear the costs of the action himself. Poyer, who without parsonage or salary from the colony was maintained solely by his stipend from the Society, was authorised by London officials to initiate a suit for his salary. His case was lost in the lower court but finally was decided in favour of the English church by Chief Justice Lewis Morris, a member of the Society for the Propagation of the Gospel, in 1723 (although Poyer experienced some difficulty in collecting the arrears). The right to the church building was a separate issue, perhaps because the structure had been begun by the Dissenters before the passage of the Ministry Act of 1693 and a jury under Morris subsequently decided that it belonged to the Presbyterians. The Anglicans were forced to meet in the town house and soon afterwards built another church.

In the three colonies south of Virginia, – South Carolina, North Carolina, Georgia, – the English church was established after extensive political manoeuvring and dissension. The earliest wave of English settlers in South Carolina came by way of Barbados, arriving in the spring of 1670 and naming the settlement Charles Town. Yet as M. Eugene Sirmans has convincingly described, the young colony was torn into bitter and protracted factionalism between proprietary and anti-proprietary groups.[13] The community was divided between the old and new immigrants. A majority of the old colonists were Barbadian Anglicans, while many of the recent immigrants were English and Scottish Dissenters.

As he had done in Boston and Philadelphia a decade earlier, Customs Commissioner Edward Randolph set the course for the English church in South Carolina.[14] He doubtless reported the situation to Bishop of London Henry Compton and his secretary Thomas Bray during his 1697 visit to the city. Within a few months the Dissenters and Anglicans in the Common House of Assembly dropped their political sparring and speedily enacted legislation providing for an annual salary drawn on the public revenue of £150 colonial currency per year for a minister of the English church in Charles Town.[15] To satisfy objections to the statute, the tax to support the minister was to be paid only by members of the Church of England. All other religious groups, except Roman Catholics, were allowed to impose a levy on their membership for the maintenance of their house of worship.

During the next stage of the development of the Carolina church, partisans of the Proprietors in the Assembly contrived to establish the English church by law in 1704 with financial support by taxation.[16] As in Maryland in the 1690s, opposition to the proposed statute was centred in the Quaker community. They objected to the establishment of the church protesting that a portion of their tax payments would support the maintenance of Anglican parsons and churches; and also on principle they were opposed to the necessary oaths of officeholders of allegiance to the King as the head of the Church and State. For the Quakers the taking of oaths was anathema. Nonconformists, disfranchised, raised such a strong protest that the Church Act was modified in 1706.[17] In South Carolina the Assembly, still under proprietary control, adopted on 30 November 1706 the church act that was in force until the church's disestablishment in 1778.[18] Under the provisions of this statute, parishes and glebes were to be laid out and parsonages built and the clergy were to be paid set salaries from the public treasury. Six parishes were set up: one at Charles Town, the provincial capital, and five others in the rural communities along the seaboard.[19] To settle the matter promptly, the political franchise was restored to non-Anglicans and the Anglican church remained established until after the Revolutionary War.

The charters granted by King Charles II to the Proprietors of the Carolina Province in 1663 and 1665, present-day North Carolina, anticipated that the Church of England would become the established, tax-supported church of the territory.[20] A provision for the establishment of the church included in the Concessions and Agreement, the Fundamental Constitutions in several versions, and the instructions sent to the governors.[21] Presumably as a gesture to encourage settlement, the religious stipulations in the charters of 1663 and 1665 also provided for toleration for Dissenters. The Proprietors did nothing about installing the Anglican church; instead they permitted any Protestant group to worship as it pleased. The province was a refuge for Quakers, Baptists, the unchurched, and Anglicans. The Quakers during the last decade of the seventeenth century were in complete control of the government, a matter of concern to Anglicans and not remedied until Henderson Walker, an active churchman, became governor in 1699.

The North Carolina legislature adopted the Vestry Act of 1701 that favoured the Anglican church.[22] The statute provided for the creation of five parishes, one for each of the precincts of old Albemarle County (Chowan, Perquimans, Pasquotank, and Currituck), and one for Pamlico Precinct in Bath County. Vestries of 12 members for each parish were authorised to levy a tax of not more than five shillings a poll for the building of churches, buying of glebes, and hiring of ministers. The salary of each minister was fixed at £30 annually.

Right away Quakers, Presbyterians, and some Anglicans objected to the Vestry Act, perhaps partly on principle and partly because it increased taxes. The adversaries were mindful that they would be taxed to support an established church. After waging a strong campaign, the opponents of the 'Church Party' returned a majority to the Assembly of 1703, determined to repeal the law. The Proprietors, however, politically shrewd, spared them the trouble by returning the law disallowed, with the face-saving qualification that the salary was not considered 'a competency for a minister to live on'. Before the news of the disallowance of the Vestry Act of 1701 reached the colony, however, the churchmen proceeded to implement the law. The 1701 statute was disallowed by the Privy Council and replaced by a similar act in 1704.[23]

The London-based Society assigned the first missionary to North Carolina in 1704, John Blair, a graduate of Glasgow College. On his arrival in the province he observed that the population was 'exceedingly scattered' and the people 'backward in religious matters and little disposed to assist in the support of a minister of the Church of England'. After a brief period he returned to England 'enfeebled with poverty and sickness', having found North Carolina 'the most barbarous place in the Continent'.[24]

Blair remarked that the residents of Carolina were a mixed religious community and were divided into four groups: 'first the Quakers, who are the most powerful enemies to Church government, but a people very ignorant of what they profess; ... a second sort being of no religion, but would be Quakers, if by that they were not obliged to lead a more moral life than they are willing to comply to'. A third group were identified as something like Presbyterians, comprised 'idle fellows who have left their lawful employment and preach and baptise through the country, without any manner of order from any sect or pretended Church'. Blair noted a fourth segment of the provincial community, who firmly and zealously supported the interest of the Anglican church, fewest in number though 'the better sort of people, and would do very much for the settlement of the Church government ... if not opposed by these three precedent sects'. The parson observed that the three sects were united in opposition to the establishment by law of the Church of England in the colony.[25]

In spite of Quaker strength in the Assembly, Governor Henderson Walker got another bill through in 1703.[26] It provided that all members of the Assembly must be communicants of the Church of England and also must take an oath of allegiance to Queen Anne. The latter requirement denied the right of affirmation, which Quakers had made previously because an oath was unacceptable to them. Governor Robert Daniel, who succeeded Walker in 1704, and some Anglican leaders in the legislature contended that the oath had nothing to do with the question of the established church, but the Quakers maintained that it was aimed directly at them and denied their rights. Daniel's position was so unpopular with Presbyterians that they joined the Quakers in securing his removal from office in 1705.[27]

Thomas Cary, a Charles Town merchant, succeeded Daniel as provincial chief executive. He had been considered friendly to Dissenters in South Carolina, but his conduct in North Carolina was more offensive to the Quakers than that of his two predecessors. Not only did Cary enforce the oath of allegiance and deprive Quakers of their seats in the Assembly, but he imposed a fine of five pounds on anyone assuming any office without taking such an oath. According to the Anglican missionary, William Gordon, 'this so nettled the Quakers' that in 1707 they sent John Porter to London to protest to the Proprietors.[28]

The legislature passed a law relating to the church establishment in 1711 that declared that all laws in force in England for the establishment of the Church and for granting indulgence to Protestant Dissenters were to be in effect in North Carolina.[29] Dissenters, under English law, could hold office if they took the qualifying oath. 'This oath affirmed the belief in the Trinity and subscribed to the thirty-nine Articles, with reservations permitted on ecclesiastical government and infant baptism'.

In 1715, a new vestry act was passed by the provincial legislature that created nine parishes instead of the original five; it named 12 vestrymen in each parish and prescribed their duties, the levy of 'a poll tax not exceeding five shillings per Poll on all the Taxable persons in the parish' to pay the minister's salary.[30] The first paragraph of this new law listed two reasons for its enactment: first, 'This province of North Carolina being a member of the Kingdom of Great Britain; & the Church of England being appointed by the Charter from the Crown to be the only Established church to give Publick encouragement in it'; and second, 'to express our gratitude' to the S.P.G. 'for the promoting our Holy Religion by making such provisions for the building of Churches & Chappels & maintenance of the clergy as the Circumstances of the Government will admit'.[31] This was the last vestry act passed under the Proprietary government because the colony came under royal control in 1729; it remained in force until 1741. The law of 1715 was accompanied by an 'Act for Liberty of Conscience', which placated the Quakers by allowing them the right of affirmation and gave all Dissenters what they had demanded in legal protection.

The Proprietary government in the province ended in 1729 and it became a royal colony. At that time there was no parson in the province. Under royal administration, the colony experienced phenomenal growth of population, largely of non-English extraction. Scotch-Irish and German colonists, most of whom reached North Carolina by travelling over the great wagon road that led from Pennsylvania through the Valley of Virginia, located in the Piedmont and the far western counties. The United Brethren, or Moravians, settled principally in Forsyth County, where they became singularly prosperous.

In 1741, the Assembly passed a vestry act that was a sharp departure from earlier laws.[32] It provided that the vestry, instead of being named by the Assembly, should be elected by the freeholders of each parish every two years. Another vestry act was passed in 1754, due largely to the urging of Governor Arthur Dobbs but was disallowed.[33] The Bishop of London had steadily objected to the vestries' claim of the right to choose rectors rather than to accept the London prelate's licensed minister for a particular post and he had repeatedly advised the Board of Trade to recommend to the King and Privy Council the disallowance of all such laws. The 1754 act met the same fate. During the next decade the colony experienced a triangular fight between Dissenters, democratic English churchmen, and supporters of the rights of the Crown. The Dissenters stubbornly resisted a church establishment, the Anglican churchmen sought the right of presentation, and the Crown opposed both parties. Within the next ten years five other church laws were passed, two in 1758, two in 1760, and one in 1762.[34] But all were disallowed on the ground that the right of presentation by vestries was 'incompatible with the right of the Crown and the ecclesiastical jurisdiction' of the bishop of London.

Finally in 1765, Governor Arthur Dobbs got a vestry act passed that was approved by the King, the Privy Council, and the Bishop of London.[35] This law excluded any reference to the method of 'presentation'. At the time there were only six parsons and 32 parishes in the colony. The 1764 act that was passed for five years was renewed in 1768 for another five in 1774.[36] But the vestry act, and with it the Established Church, was not to receive its 'quietus' from the dissenting interests in the Assembly. 'Both went down along with other monarchical institutions, before the revolutionary movement of 1776', for when the convention of that year came to adopt a constitution for the newly independent state, churchmen joined with Dissenters in inserting a section prohibiting the 'establishment of any one religious Church or Denomination in this State in Preference to any other'.[37]

During the first two decades of the eighteenth century the English church made modest progress establishing congregations in Massachusetts and Rhode Island, three and two churches respectively. Each church was served by ministers recruited and paid by the S.P.G. Without exception, the churches' membership was small. In Newbury, Massachusetts, many of the founding Anglican church members were disaffected members of the local Congregational Church who objected to paying taxes to support its minister. If the members were reluctant to support the Congregational establishment they were no more enthusiastic about financially aiding the new English church. In fact few Church of England congregations in New England or throughout the colonies became self-supporting during the colonial period.[38]

A dramatic conversion in September 1722 of several Connecticut Congregational ministers to the Church of England sent shock waves throughout the New England Congregational Church network.

For 15 years an occasional New York minister maintained irregular Anglican services in the colony without a church being built or a permanent congregation established. The Yale College commencement on 12 September began a new era for the English church began in the province when the rector of the college, Timothy Cutler, a former Congregational minister in Stratford, Connecticut, renounced his ordination and led the defection of several men to the Anglican church.[39] Among the 'Yale Apostates' were Daniel Browne, the college's tutor; Samuel Johnson, a former tutor now a minister in West Haven; James Wetmore minister in North Haven; and three somewhat less ardent ministers in nearby towns. During a period of several years these men had been reading and discussing many works of Anglican divinity and recent philosophy that had been given to the Yale library by various English donors. They were attracted by these broader, more urbane attitudes, and became less committed to the stricter doctrines of New England theology. They also began to have serious doubts as to the validity of 'presbyterial' or non-Episcopal ordination. Finally, after stating their doubts to the college trustees, they were asked by the Reverend Gurdon Saltonstall, a trustee who was then also governor of Connecticut, to discuss their problems with a group of Congregational ministers. On the day after commencement, 13 September 1722, this historic conference was held in the college library, but to no effect other than to strengthen the resolve of the emerging Anglicans, who very soon thereafter proceeded to England for ordination.[40] After returning to America in 1723, Cutler began his long ministry at Christ Church (the Old North Church) in Boston and Johnson went to Stratford, Connecticut, where he completed the first Anglican church building in the colony.

The experience of the church in Virginia varied from the other colonies. Although established by law in 1619, Quaker and Presbyterian groups were present in the province during the seventeenth century.[41] Professor John K. Nelson has cogently summarised the presence and influence of dissenting groups in Virginia during the seventeenth and eighteenth centuries noting in particular that the numbers of Dissenter members of Anglican parishes were modest until the 1740s and 1750s.[42]

During the early years of the eighteenth century, Virginia officials, seeking settlers, sponsored the importation of French and German Protestants and as an inducement offered temporary relief from parish levies. Released from the tax, they were able to form their own congregations, build churches, and recruit ministers.[43] With the migration of the Scots Irish and Germans in the 1730s, largely from Pennsylvania, new settlements took place in the Shenandoah Valley and pushed eastward into the Piedmont and westward into the Appalachian mountain valleys. The settlers brought into the Virginia backcountry a variety of religious groups, including Presbyterian, Baptist, Lutheran, and Reformed.[44] Each of the new settlements was provided by provincial legislation with parish and county organisation. For the first time in the colony's history the majority of the new residents were not of English descent or Anglican in religion. Yet under the law all Protestant Dissenters were parishioners in eighteenth-century Virginia and were required to pay the annual parish levies on the same tithable basis as all other parishioners. To maintain their own ministers and erect meeting-houses, Dissenters relied on voluntary contributions. Occasionally Dissenters dominated Anglican parish vestries.[45]

The S.P.G. was founded in 1701 for the purpose of recruiting and financially supporting ministers for colonial congregations, an effort that pragmatically aided the implementation of the imperial ecclesiastical policies of the Board of Trade. Although it was not a chartered agency of the state church funded by the government, it was a philanthropic institution of the church, governed by Anglican leaders for the purpose of recruiting, appointing, and supporting missionaries overseas. More than half of the original 94 English members of the Society were clergymen, led by the archbishops of Canterbury and York, and the bishop of London. Between 1702 and 1783 more than 300 missionaries were sent by the Society to serve American provincial posts.

An immediate task of the Society's leaders was to recruit colonial governors for membership as a means for gaining access to information on the state of the church in their provinces. Elected to membership were such civil leaders as Francis Nicholson of Virginia, Lewis Morris of New Jersey, and Joseph Dudley of Massachusetts. The founding of the Society and the dispatch of its initial missionaries into New England ignited suspicions of the purpose of the organisation among Congregational church leaders. They perceived the Society in the provinces as an agent of the imperial religious Anglicisation policies developed and implemented by London-based civil and ecclesiastical officials.

An offspring of the Reverend Thomas Bray, the organisation was a legacy of his more than five years of efforts during the 1690s as secretary to Bishop Compton to enlist ministers for the American church. His knowledge of the colonial church had been further honed by a visit to Maryland in 1700 as Compton's commissary for the church and clergymen.[46] The establishment of the S.P.G. was the formalisation of Bray's efforts to place the enlistment of ministers to serve overseas posts on a permanent and professional basis within the Church of England.

From its founding, the Society cast eye and influence on American church affairs. In London the S.P.G.'s leaders agreed to appoint a deputy to travel to America and survey the state of the religious scene. Rather than examine the circumstances of the church in Virginia and Maryland where the church was established by law, Society officials decided to send its first emissary to New England and the Middle Colonies. The strategy was complicated by the S.P.G.'s curious decision to appoint the recently converted Quaker George Keith to undertake the study.[47] For two decades Keith had been a familiar antagonist of the Pennsylvania Quakers and the New England Puritans during earlier visits to America. Sailing for America on 24 April 1702 aboard the ship *Centurion*, Keith was in the company of the Reverend John Talbot, the chaplain aboard the vessel; and Joseph Dudley, governor of Massachusetts; and Lewis Morris, governor of New Jersey.[48] On his arrival in Boston during the summer, he was welcomed at the home of Samuel Myles, rector of King's Chapel.

Keith's appearance in the colonial capital attracted critical attention, not only as a sometime-Quaker nemesis to the Puritan establishment but also as a representative of the recently formed Society. Not flinching to declaim the historical authority of his new ministry, he mounted the pulpit at King's Chapel in Boston on 14 June, the first Sunday after his arrival in the town, and preached a sermon on the theme of the apostolic tradition in the Early Church.[49] On the one hand, he attacked the Quaker emphasis upon the Light within, while, on the other hand, Keith warned his listeners against 'false Teachers and wild Enthusiasts', declaring that his aim in coming to the New World was 'to heal up the breach [among Protestants] if possible, and be a Peace Maker to all such as with a peaceable and calm Spirit are willing to hear'. He also offered in his sermon 'Six plain brief Rules', that 'being well observed, and put in Practise, would bring all to the Church of England, who dissented from her', an opinion that did not escape the attention of Boston Congregational ministers.[50]

Increase Mather promptly mounted a challenge to Keith's ideas for godly living.[51] He claimed that Keith's first rule, enjoining obedience to superiors, 'would do very well among Papists. The Divine Law binds men to do nothing which is not for edification ... which whether the thing required be so, every man has liberty to examine by the judgement of discretion'. He disputed Keith's fourth rule, 'that the Dissenters ought to joyn, in Acts of Publick Worship with the Church [of England]', despite 'the great mixture of unsound Members in that Church'. Mather declared that 'the Ceremonies enjoyned by the Common Prayer Book ... the Nonconformists believe ... are forbidden in the Second Commandment'.[52]

Keith replied to Mather's stirring criticism in a sermon delivered in June 1702 and that was later published.[53] He noted in his *Journal*, that in his sermon and publication he attempted to answer Mather and refute the validity of his objections. Noting that the tract was printed in New York because 'the Printer at Boston not daring to Print it, lest he should give offence to the Independent Preachers there'.[54]

Keith's self-serving proclamation that his mission to New England and the other colonies was with the intention of bringing unity to the various religious groups met with failure. Under the best of circumstances he was not the person to undertake such a project. The long-standing hostility between Keith and the Congregational ministers in Boston, the legacy of their controversies in 1688 and 1690, exacerbated and sustained differences with the English church and reinforced suspicions regarding the Society's purpose.

Within its first five years, the S.P.G.'s presence was evident in every colony outside Virginia and Maryland, an influence that escalated in every decade until the 1760s and was sustained until the outbreak of the Revolutionary War. Following in the wake of the new interest by London officials in American church affairs the provincial clergymen responded vigorously on two fronts. First, there was an increasing trend for conventions of the men to be held at least once or twice a year to discuss matters of mutual interest.[55] Second, under the leadership of John Talbot of Burlington, New Jersey, the drive for an American prelate gained momentum. Arriving in Boston with George Keith in 1702 he travelled throughout the colonies examining the state of religious affairs. An accomplished, experienced, and strong-willed man, Talbot was appointed to his New Jersey post at the mature age of 52, and assigned to Burlington, the capital of West Jersey. Educated at Christ's College, Cambridge University, he had briefly served as a fellow of Peterhouse, at Cambridge, and had had a large parish at Icklingham St. James in Suffolk and later at Fretherne in Gloucestershire.[56]

Inevitably, the recently appointed missionaries of the S.P.G. recognised that the English church was impeded by the lack of a bishop. Talbot reported to London officials in 1703 a plea that would be heard frequently until 1776, that there was no prelate to confirm church members or to ordain candidates for the ministry. As it was necessary for men to travel to England for ordination he observed and feared that several candidates would lapse 'back again into the herd of Dissenters'. He noted the scarcity of clergymen and that 'several Counties, Islands, and Provinces, which have hardly an orthodox minister am'st them', might have been supplied if there was a bishop in America.[57]

Talbot recommended to the bishop of London and officials of the Society that a new kind of prelate be appointed for the colonies; an official charged to perform solely spiritual duties and not exercise civil responsibilities. It was not a novel proposal, a similar plan had been mooted in the early 1670s, in 1696, and in 1700 the noted scholar and theologian Henry Dodwell had urged Archbishop of Canterbury Thomas Tenison to press for such an appointment.[58] Talbot did not suggest how the bishop was to be supported, whether by funds from the Society, the English government as in the homeland, or from an assessment of colonial Anglican parishes. Not a shy man, it remains unclear if his persistent effort to secure a colonial prelate was a self-serving gesture to obtain for himself an Episcopal mitre. In 1706 he sailed to England to advance his plan before the London Society and with government officials. His proposal won the encouragement and endorsement of the Society, Queen Anne, and the Bishop of London Henry Compton.[59] Ageing and in declining health, Compton recognised after supervising affairs of the overseas church for 30 years that there was a need for a colonial bishop to superintend the clergy and church.

The politics of the appointment of a provincial prelate was not easily accomplished because it required the approval of the Crown and Parliament. Bishop Compton had to wrestle with two complex questions as he advanced his proposal. His first concern was simply: What sort of bishop should be appointed for America? Secondly, considering the different political circumstances between the provinces and England, should an American prelate replicate the English officer in the traditional English mould of the bishops who presided over a diocese such as Exeter, Salisbury, or Norwich? Compton concluded that should an English bishop be appointed, he would not be acceptable to colonists on the grounds that they would reject an official who exercised both civil and ecclesiastical authority. Religious and political circumstances in the colonies suggested that a bishop exercising a modified role would probably be acceptable.[60] The bishop of London recommended that an American prelate would exercise supervision over the lives and morals of both the clergy and laity. Taking an innovative tack, Compton urged that a suffragan bishop be appointed to the colonies, an officer of the church who would perform duties similar to those exercised by a commissary with the additional Episcopal authority to confirm men and women, and ordain candidates for the ministry. The prospective solution for an American episcopate was creative as a suffragan bishop served as an assistant to a diocesan prelate.[61] Such an officer would not be independent but serve under the authority of the bishop of London as his deputy.

The 'Suffragan Bishops Act' initiated by Henry VIII in 1535 (26 Hen. 8. C. 14, 5.1), provided that 26 prelates could be appointed to office.[62] Between 1534 and 1592, 17 suffragan bishops were appointed to serve the church. After that date these officials were not used until 1870, though the canon law of the Church of England continued to provide for the officer. Such an official had all of the necessary requisites for assignment as a spiritual prelate in the colonies and none of the disadvantages. Presumably, if the appointment was tried and failed, the official could be withdrawn from the provinces.

To accomplish an appointment of an American prelate, Compton needed to enlist the support of the Crown, the Lord Chancellor, and other key government ministers. His proposed solution was at once strategic, and bold yet fraught with risk. It was legally possible for the bishop of London to appoint a suffragan bishop without the consideration or approval of the Crown or Parliament. Such a course of action, although personally risky, could neatly avoid acrimonious disagreements with government and Parliamentary officials. For reasons that remain unclear, nothing came of Compton's plan. Possibly the Bishop of London consulted with leading officers of the government and found little support for the proposal.

Based on the encouragement of Bishop Compton and Queen Anne, Talbot, after returning to Burlington, New Jersey, set out to locate an appropriate house as an Episcopal residence in 1707. For more than five years the S.P.G. actively supported the plan and frequently directed Governor Robert Hunter of New York to conclude the purchase of the house and prepare it for occupancy. The deaths of Bishop Compton and Queen Anne the next year put an end to the project. Fifteen years later, in 1728, William Becket, the Society's missionary at Lewes, Delaware, recommended to the S.P.G. to purchase a tract of land along the disputed border between Pennsylvania and Maryland for the use of a suffragan bishop. Nothing came of this renewed overture for a bishop's house.[63]

The death of Compton in 1713 did not quench the fear of the advancement of episcopacy in the colonies. In South Carolina the clergy of the English church held a series of meetings in early 1711–12 under the guidance of Commissary Gideon Johnston and issued a memorandum on the 'state of the church' in the province for the London-based Society. Recounting the criticisms of Compton's authority over ecclesiastical affairs in the province, the Anglican parsons recognised the fragility of the situation. They noted that 'The many hard words that have been frequently bestowed on the late most worthy Bishop of London when His Right was occasionally Asserted and Defended by any of his Clergy are a further Proof of some Mens Aversion to Episcopacy whatever they may pretend to the Contrary, for at Every turn they accused him for being a Pope, nay worse than the Pope because (as they said) he would feign Extend his Diocese and Authority, farther than the Pope ever did'.[64] The assembled clergy continued that the Episcopal critics 'added what have we to do with the Bishop of London or he with us? Must we go to London and the Lord knows where to complain against ill Clergymen, and to prosecute them in the tedious forms of the Ecclesiastical Courts'? The parsons pleaded that in the early church wherever Christianity was established a bishop was settled and observed that the church in America is 'Neglected in this respect, It is but reason that we should do Justice to our Selves'.[65]

The first two decades of the eighteenth century found the English church in America entangled in numerous controversies. Efforts to extend and establish the institution in the colonies of South and North Carolina were met with sustained objections from leaders of the Quaker and Presbyterian religious groups. In part, these disputes were similar to the Quaker legal objections to the several legislative Acts establishing the Church of England in Maryland during the 1690s and early 1700s. But the issues were also linked to efforts by London civil officials to establish the church in both colonies as a segment for strengthening royal government in each of the provinces. In addition, the appearance of the S.P.G. missionaries in the New England, and Middle, and Southern colonies during this period raised questions among critics regarding the purpose of the organisation in diverse religious communities. Many observers suspected that the introduction of the English church and ministers indicated the possible initiation of imperial policies intended to undermine the strength and membership of independent congregations.

3

A Handmaiden for Episcopacy: John Checkley of Boston

Between the establishment of the first Anglican congregation in Boston in 1686 and the year 1720, the community experienced many changes. In 1690 Boston was the largest town in America with a population of about 7000 residents that increased to an estimated 12,000 persons in 1720.[1] The economic and political influence of merchants, built on a flourishing and expanding maritime commerce, affected town and provincial affairs. Following the revocation of the Massachusetts Bay Colony's charter in 1684 and the establishment of royal government in 1686, imperial government encountered unsettled political circumstances in the 1690s and an uneasy acceptance under governors Joseph Dudley and Samuel Shute between 1702 and 1719. Both men were Anglicans and members of the S.P.G. Yet as G. B. Warden has persuasively recounted, from 1692 to 1775 'the Bostonians steadfastly refused to elect any Anglican as a Representative to the General Court (legislature) and elected only one Anglican Selectman'.[2]

Carl Bridenbaugh has noted that several factors in the period between 1690 and 1720 contributed to a definite cultural advancement in Boston, Newport, New York, Philadelphia, and Charles Town. He declared that 'None of the colonial towns, and no English provincial city, compared with Boston in cultural attainments in this period. Direct contact by sea with Europe kept Bostonians alive to the intellectual currents of the age'.[3]

But Boston was not a mere imitation of an English community despite the presence of royal government and officials because the town meeting system symbolised the life of the municipality and the spirit of its citizens.[4] The first American newspaper was established in the town in 1704, the *Boston Newsletter*, to be followed more than a decade later by the *Boston Gazette* and the *New-England Courant*.[5] In the aftermath of the establishment of royal government, the political power of Increase and Cotton Mather was broken in the 1690s, although they both remained influential leaders in the Congregational Church. Nonetheless, at the same time a new generation of influential ministers was emerging in Boston: Benjamin Colman at the Brattle Street Church and Charles Chauncy at the First Church.[6] By 1722, Boston was a religiously diverse community that included seven Congregational churches and one congregation each of the Baptist, Quaker, French Protestant, and Anglican religious groups.[7] The liberal-minded Colman had spent several years in England during the 1690s and maintained correspondence after he returned to Boston with such Anglican luminaries as bishops White Kennet of Peterborough, Henry Compton of London, and Benjamin Hoadly of Salisbury. A leader of the low-church faction and a Whig, Hoadly advocated at the beginning of his career conformity of the religious rites from the Scottish and English churches for the sake of union. Yet he maintained another turn of mind when in 1732 he wrote to the rector of Yale College at the time, the Reverend Elisha Williams, of Dean George Berkeley's donation of books to the library, urging them to 'decline the gift if it were accompanied by conditions tending toward the introduction of Episcopacy'.[8]

The next round of the controversy between Anglicans and non-Anglicans was launched by a Boston layman John Checkley in the 1720s. His efforts shaped the controversy over the establishment of an American episcopate for nearly half a century. A Boston bookseller and fervent Anglican, Checkley was reputed to be an avowed Jacobite. A confirmed High Churchman, he was not one to equivocate, and bluntly attacked and disputed in print the validity of the Congregational ministry and ordination. He declared that it was not a ministry connected with the historic church of the first century, the apostolic church, an institution whose offices and ceremonies were revered and maintained uninterrupted by the Church of England. An urbane, opinionated, and flamboyant layman, Checkley was a thorn in the side not only of the Congregational hierarchy of the city, but also of his fellow churchmen, both clerical and lay, at King's Chapel in Boston. He marshalled in his pamphlets the theological and doctrinal content regarding the nature of the ministry and of the episcopacy through the centuries and set the stage for the lively ideological discussion over the nature of the office and its possible establishment in the colonies.[9]

In 1719 Checkley issued an edition of the Reverend Charles Leslie's essay, *The Religion of Jesus Christ the only True Religion, or a Short and Easie Method with the Deists* (Boston, 1719).[10] A non-juror, fiercely loyal to

James II, Leslie was a zealous and controversial partisan. He attacked in his writings the publications of such Whig divines as Gilbert Burnet, bishop of Salisbury, and John Tillotson, archbishop of Canterbury. Nobody who advocated a contrary position escaped his wrath. Besides the violent criticisms of the nonconformists he also levelled charges against the Quakers and wrote at length of the wickedness of mixed marriages. Leslie had complained that many clergymen were forced to rely on modern German and Dutch systems of theology, thus bypassing the primitive church fathers. He hoped to see the study of the ancients renewed in the churches and universities of eighteenth-century England as Laud had championed 80 years earlier.[11] The importance of the patristic period for high churchmen was demonstrated in variety of ways, including their prodigious efforts in scholarship, their sacramental and liturgical practises, and the defence of episcopacy.[12]

The purpose of Checkley's publication was two-fold: to present a strong Christian apologia in reply to the rationalistic challenges of the deists and to argue for the edification of his Congregational audience that the three orders of the ministry were an early church creation and had been in existence since the days of the apostles. His pen was driven by a sharp wit and a heavy dose of sarcasm, and Checkley was not content to limit his attack on Congregational church polity to the nature of the ministry. He published another work concerning Election and Predestination which brashly attacked the two cardinal doctrines of the Congregational creed.[13]

Accompanying Checkley's challenge to the legitimacy of Congregational ministerial authority was the shattering announcement at the Yale College commencement in September 1722 of the conversion of Rector Timothy Cutler and several Yale tutors and graduates from the Congregational to the Anglican ministry. A graduate of Harvard College in 1701, Cutler became minister of the Congregational church in Stratford, Connecticut, in 1710, and head of Yale College in 1719. Perhaps influenced by Samuel Johnson, a Yale tutor who was increasingly troubled about the theological integrity of Congregational ordinations, the men declared to the Yale Trustees on 13 September 1722 their doubts about the validity of Congregational ordination. Cutler was dismissed from his post on 17 October and he and Johnson and Daniel Browne sailed from Boston for England on 5 November. Cutler's passage was paid by the members of the congregation of the new English church established in Boston's North End, Christ Church, better known today as the Old North Church. On his return from ordination in England, Cutler became rector of the congregation.

In late 1722 or early 1723, Checkley boarded a ship for England in quest of orders. After eight months in London pleading with the bishop of London to make him a priest but to no avail, he returned to Boston with Samuel Johnson of Stratford, Connecticut. His effort to defend and establish Anglican practices and ideas in Puritan Boston was undeterred despite his disappointment in his trip for ordination. After his return to Massachusetts, Checkley published a pamphlet entitled, *A Modest Proof of the Order and Government Settled by Christ and his Apostles in the Church* (Boston, 1723).[14] He forcefully stated the legitimacy of Anglican orders, declaring: 'That the Ministers of the Church of England, who freely own that the power of ordination was first vested in the Apostles, and from them, through all ages since, in a succession of Bishops, from whence they derive their own ordinations, and to be acknowledged true Ministers of the Gospel'.[15] Checkley had said in print what no Anglican parson had expressed either before or after 1723 in New England or elsewhere in the colonies, dramatically voicing an orthodox Anglican view of the ministry. For Checkley, the laymen 'ought to endeavour after all the assurance they can attain to, that they have the means of Grace in the Word and Sacraments, duly administered and dispensed unto them, by persons fully authorised for those holy Offices'.[16] He pointedly remarked 'that it is a very criminal presumption and an unsufferable insolence in some, to value their gifts so high a rate, as to think themselves by the virtue of them, entituled to the Ministerial Office, without being admitted by the Imposition of the Hands of those, who Christ has ordered to preside over the affairs of the Church'.[17] His final attack on the validity of the nonconformists' ministry discarded in essence their credibility as pastors, 'That since there is no approaching before God's Altar, without the appointed Rites of Consecration, nor any medling with his Institutions without his Order and Command. Those invaders of the Sacred Services, cannot be said to be the Ambassadors of God, or accounted the Stewards of the Mysteries of Christ, who presume to touch those holy Things, with their unhallowed Hands'.[18] Checkley was firmly convinced of the apostolic ministry: 'This is the nature and true notion of a Gospel ministry, as we find it founded by our Saviour and his Apostles'.[19]

Checkley's efforts caused an immediate stir in the ranks of Congregational church leaders and prompted a reply from the Hollis Professor of Divinity at Harvard College, Edward Wigglesworth. *In a Letter to a Friend* (Boston, 1724), Wigglesworth cogently argued about the historical validity of Presbyterian ordination, based on biblical texts and theological writings.[20] He observed 'that Bishops and Presbyters are one and the same order by Divine Institution; and that they succeed the Apostles in all their ordinary Powers, of which that of Ordination is one; which is warrant enough for Ordination by Presbyters, and the very same warrant which those have for it, who are now by Custom, and humane Constitution, dignified and distinguished with the Title of Bishops'.[21] Embracing the writings of the English nonconformist minister Isaac Barrow, Wigglesworth concluded that Apostleship was a personal and temporary office and in all respects extraordinary, not the foundation for prelacy.

> 'To deny Presbyters the power of Ordination, is in effect, to deny the validity of all the Administrations of those who are not under the Episcopal Form of Government, or who, if under it now, yet derive the succession of their Bishops from such as were ordained by presbyters, which is to number for the biggest part of the Protestant Churches, and in all probability the Church of England itself, among aliens from the Commonwealth of Israel, and strangers from the Covenants of Promise, who have no hope, and are without Christ, and without God in the World'.[22]

In New Jersey, Jonathan Dickinson, a Presbyterian minister at Elizabeth Town and a founder and first President of the College of New Jersey (now Princeton University), joined the debate by publishing *A Defence of Presbyterian Ordination* (Boston, 1724).[23] A graduate of Yale in 1706, he was a leader in the New Jersey Presbyterian synod and his pen was active in all the religious controversies of his day. Refuting Checkley's argument line by line, Dickinson proclaimed persuasively that divine right of episcopacy was not known in the primitive church, or professed by the reformers, and not in the Church of England at the beginning of the Reformation.[24]

An unknown New England pamphleteer who applauded Dickinson's tract sharply criticised Checkley's *Defence of the Modest Proof*, noting that it was 'full of wild conceits, foolish bigotry, and impudence, and appearing with equal symptoms of weakness, vanity, rage, and despair; surely the puny scribler deserves little thanks from his party, nor have they the least reason to glory in any service he has done their cause'.[25] Bluntly proclaiming that some persons in the towns who 'dislike our grave worship, our searching and faithful sermons, our pure administration and discipline', and who are 'led by worldly principle, lovers of their ownselves, covetous', are seeking nothing more than 'to save a few charges [taxes]'.[26] The anonymous writer challenged the cost of maintaining the hierarchy of the Church of England, bishops, chancellors, registrars, proctors, archdeacons, commissaries, surrogates, and deans.[27] Fearing that if the English church would be reproduced in New England as it was maintained in Old England, the author proclaimed the burden on the colonial taxpayer would be substantial: 'If once the Diocesan Episcopacy Hierarchy be planted in New England how will the land soon be burdened with a swarm of ecclesiastics now unknown to us! Unto whose maintenance in Ease and Grandeur Vast sums will be requisite, perhaps exceeding our whole ordinary expence hitherto Ecclesiastical, Civil, and Military put together'.[28]

While in London seeking ordination in 1722 and 1723, Checkley purchased the rights to publish Leslie's immensely popular *A Short and Easie Method with the Deists Wherein the Certainty of the Christian Religion is demonstrated* in Boston. It was a reprint of Leslie's 1721 publication and included *A Discourse Concerning Episcopacy*, first printed by Leslie in 1698. The tract was perfectly tailored to outrage Boston readers: Massachusetts authorities brought Checkley to trial for the publication of these essays, found him guilty, and fined him £50.[29]

The publication of the condemned book on *Episcopacy* and the prosecution of the trial caused much discussion among both Anglican and nonconformist parsons in Boston. Checkley had the support of all but two of the Church of England ministers for his position. Interested parties made many representations on both sides of the controversy to Lieutenant Governor William Dummer and Bishop of London Edmund Gibson, but both officials sidestepped the debate carefully and diplomatically. Cotton Mather saw an impending danger ahead as a consequence of Checkley's attack on the nature of the Congregational ministry and thought something must be done. He shrewdly felt that a General Convention of the Ministers should be held in 1725 to consider the matter.[30] The two prominent divines of the English church in Boston, Samuel Myles and Timothy Cutler, thought otherwise and prevailed upon Bishop Gibson to intercede with government officials in London and force the cancellation of the proposed meeting.

The debate launched by Checkley regarding the nature and antiquity of the Episcopal office and validity of Presbyterian ordination was occasionally in the spotlight for the next 30 years. For the Congregationalists and Presbyterians, Jonathan Dickinson circumscribed the controversy with his clever and cogent tract *The Scripture-Bishop, or the Divine Right of Presbyterian Ordination & Government* (Boston, 1732).[31] The work was the model for James Wetmore's rejoinder which argued the Anglican position, *Eleutherius Enervatus or An*

Answer to a Pamphlet, Intituled, the Divine Right of Presbyterian Ordination &c. Argued (New York, 1733).[32] Wetmore chastised his adversaries and urged 'whoever will take the pains to read Mr. Hooker's Ecclesiastical Polity (which was never yet answered, though wrote above one hundred years ago) will find all those objections answered, with such strength of reason and clear evidence from Scripture and Antiquity, that nothing but obstinacy can withstand'.[33] Several other parsons of the English church rushed to print and supported Wetmore's position, including Arthur Browne of Providence, Rhode Island, and John Beach, a former Congregational minister, of New London, Connecticut.[34] Dickinson immediately rebutted his Anglican adversaries with a further defence of Presbyterian ordination and government.[35]

Samuel Johnson, one of the Yale Apostates of 1722, the celebrated minister of the church at Stratford and the doyen of the Anglican parsons in New England, contributed *A Letter from A Minister of the Church of England to his Dissenting Parishioners* (New York, 1733).[36] He claimed his pamphlet was necessary because 'all imaginable pains have been taken to frighten you from coming within the Doors of the Church'.[37] Johnson concluded that as Connecticut was an English colony governed by English laws, his manner of address to his 'Dissenting Parishioners' was customary and appropriate.[38] The tract triggered a heated exchange with John Graham, a scion of the Marquis of Montrose, who had emigrated to America in 1718 and begun a 40-year ministry in 1733 at the Congregational church at Southbury in Connecticut. Educated at the Glasgow College, Graham made a career of entering into vigorous debates with Quakers, politicians, and Anglicans. His attacks against Samuel Johnson's letters to his 'Dissenting Parishioners' at least brought him an honorary M.A. degree in 1737 from Yale. His sharp, focused, and penetrating refutation of Johnson's remarks retraced now-familiar ground regarding the Puritans' understanding of the office of priest and presbyter, of the use of 'sureties: and the sign of the cross at baptism, and the practise of observing Holy Days during the year'.[39]

Interest in the issue diminished for several years after 1733. Quite possibly the participants on both sides of the issue had exhausted their arsenals of ideas on the subject. On the Anglican side there was no parson or layman who could pick up Checkley's pen and carry forward the discussion with his sharp, sarcastic, and clever style. He did not take up the quill again to champion the cause, or any other issue, during the last 30 years of his life. After Checkley's long-sought ordination in 1738, he settled into the quiet regular routine of a small-town parson and schoolmaster in Providence, Rhode Island.

Samuel Johnson, however, pursued the issue from another vantage point, he relentlessly pleaded throughout his career with London officials for the appointment of an American prelate. Writing to a fellow Yale graduate and Connecticut native in London in December 1735 for ordination, Jonathan Arnold, Johnson suggested that he should inform Bishop of London Edmund Gibson of the political circumstances in the colonies. As Gibson had mentioned that 'this Country's affecting an Independency on Great Britain as argument with the Court against sending bishops hither, pray let it be everywhere known that that troublesome obstreperous temper that so sturdily opposes the Court, and occasions so many complaints home and among the Dissenters and that would be independent of England if it could, is what prevails among Dissenters and flows from their Republican antimonarchical principles and that the contrary is that of the church which ever pleads and glorys in our dependence on the Crown, and Submission to it, and that therefore nothing could so effectively tend to secure our dependence as sending a bishop'.[40] For Johnson, the Episcopal office was not only an essential characteristic of the hierarchical national church, but also a pragmatic element of imperial authority linking the colonial church and its members to the motherland.

In 1741, the question of an American bishop was brought into public discussion again by Bishop of Oxford Thomas Secker, who became archbishop of Canterbury in 1758. A staunch ally of Bishop of London Gibson, he was held in high esteem among powerful church leaders.[41] Secker delivered the anniversary sermon before the members of the S.P.G. on 20 February 1740/41, at St. Mary-le-Bow Church in London and dramatically polarised the discussion regarding the appointment of an American bishop. Acknowledging the efforts of the Society to expand and support the church in America, he applauded the Society's generosity to underwrite such programmes as charity schools, and the work of missionaries among the Native Americans.[42] Secker elaborated that the appointment of colonial bishops would enable native colonists to ' be ordained without the inconvenience of a long voyage'; that 'vacancies might be supplied in much less time'; that 'the primitive and most useful appointment of confirmation might be restored; and an orderly discipline exercised [established] in the churches'. Attempting to defuse potential criticism from nonconformists, he reminded his audience that such an establishment would not 'encroach at all, either on liberty of conscience, which ought ever to be sacredly preserved; or on the present civil rights, either of the governors or people in our colonies'. The bishop of Oxford concluded that a colonial episcopate would not bring the colonies 'dependence on Great Britain into any degree of that danger, which some persons profess to apprehend so strongly on this occasion, who would make no manner of scruple about doing other things much more likely to destroy it; who are not terrified in the least, that such numbers there reject the Episcopal order entirely: nor perhaps would be greatly alarmed, were ever so many to reject religion itself; though evidently in proportion as either is thrown off, all dependence produced by it ceases of course'.[43]

For five years after Bishop Thomas Secker delivered his 1741 Anniversary Sermon before the members of the S.P.G. in London the controversy over episcopacy simmered.[44] It is difficult to recapture the intensity and momentum of the eighteenth-century dispute over the legitimacy of the historic office of bishop. Yet, as we have seen, the debate was not new in 1741 either in England or the colonies. In fact the contrasting points of view had gripped contesting parties in the English church for at least two centuries. At bottom the fiery and contentious polemics were not limited to the nature of the office of a prelate and its feared introduction into the colonies but were more broadly a conflicting examination of the doctrine of the ministry.

4

The English Origins of a Colonial American Controversy

The debate unleashed by John Checkley over the historical nature of the Episcopal office was a lineal descendant of a similar dispute within the Church of England in the sixteenth century and the publications of John Cotton and Richard and Increase Mather in Massachusetts during the seventeenth century. It was a dispute marked by the division and dissension of the church's reformed and traditional parties over the historic nature of the ministry and the office of bishop since at least the 1560s. The issue had been irregularly but vigorously revisited by Congregational and Anglican pamphleteers in the New England and Middle Colonies during the century before the outbreak of the American Revolution.[1] Since the age of King Henry VIII's reformation of the church in the sixteenth century, the institution had been embroiled in ecclesiastical and secular political conflicts. At stake were several fundamental matters: the nature of the Episcopal office; the structure and content of the Book of Common Prayer; whether a Catholic or Protestant monarch was to reign; and the power of the Crown and the constitutional role of Parliament. Not least important was the question as to who controlled the church's purse, Parliament or the bishops through their Convocations. The question of the nature of episcopacy was shaped by the sixteenth-century debate, renewed in England during the 1630s and 1640s and recalled irregularly and vigorously by Anglican and non-Anglican colonial pamphleteers between 1720 and the early 1770s.

Particularly in New England, the controversy was anchored in a complex matrix of opinions regarding the nature of the region's settlements and churches. The colonial Congregational pamphleteers of the 1750s and 1760s vigorously revisited the memory of Archbishop William Laud's strictures against the Puritans in the late 1620s and 1630s, the exodus of English peoples to Massachusetts in the 1630s, and the contemporary criticism of provincial civil leaders of imperial administration. Since the era of Increase and Cotton Mather during the late seventeenth century, New England church leaders had occasionally proclaimed that the presence of the English church in the neighbourhood represented a conspiracy by English civil and ecclesiastical officials to undermine and erode the more-than-one-century-old religious community. The controversial Boston Congregational minister Jonathan Mayhew declared in 1763 that the activity of the London-based S.P.G. in New England was a plot to establish bishops and root out Presbyterianism.[2] He articulated a manner of conspiratorial reasoning that Bernard Bailyn has contended became a commonplace way of thinking in mid-eighteenth-century Colonial America.[3]

English ecclesiastical leaders since the medieval period had pondered the issue restrained by the little evidence provided by the New Testament writings regarding the practice of the ordination of ministers in the primitive church. Undoubtedly, there were a variety of offices and duties of ministry in the first century, varying from one locale to another.[4] At least some of these offices were conferred by prayer and the imposition of hands, and it would appear that in some cases the people selected the candidates. Beyond this, however, it is impossible to go. The oldest extant ordination rites date from the beginning of the third century and are contained in a document known as the *Apostolic Tradition*, believed to have been written by St. Hippolytus at Rome. By this time the three orders of bishops, priests, and deacons had emerged as the universal ministry of the church.

The medieval theologians did not have the advantage of knowing the history of the Christian ministry or of the rites of ordination that they found in Pontificals. They were compelled to make their theological statements simply on abstract principles and on current usage. This inevitably produced considerable difference of opinion. There were various points of view as to how many different orders there were: seven was the most commonly accepted number, but some thought that there were eight, or even nine. These differing interpretations were occasioned partly by some uncertainty as to whether the episcopate formed a separate order, distinct from the priesthood, or were simply a different degree in the same order.

In the sixteenth century, the continental reformers believed that the scriptures did not warrant the hierarchical structure of the ministry of the medieval church and must therefore be replaced by the ministry that, they believed, was clearly prescribed in the New Testament.

They substituted a ministry of the word for the sacrificial priesthood, and attempted to restore to the diaconate what they regarded as its scriptural function, the care of the needy. Calvin completely eliminated the office of bishop from his church order and in the Lutheran Reformation a Lutheran episcopacy existed in some countries. Bishops were not, however, necessary for implementation of Luther's Reformation.

Paul F. Bradshaw has succinctly described that 'The first signs of the influence of the ideas of the continental reformers at an official level in England appear in *The Institution of a Christian Man, or the Bishops' Book* as it was more popularly called, published in 1537. It rejected the idea that there were of necessity seven or more orders. The institution of the minor orders by the early Church had no foundation in the New Testament where there is no mention made of any degrees or distinctions in orders but only of deacons or ministers, and of priests or bishops'.[5]

A few years later a more radical questioning of the traditional beliefs by some of the English bishops and divines, and in particular by the archbishop of Canterbury, Thomas Cranmer, can be seen. He noted that, 'In the New Testament he that is appointed to be a bishop or a priest, needeth no consecration by the Scripture, for election and appointing thereto is sufficient'.[6] Cranmer believed that 'the bishops and priests were at one time, and were not two things, but both one office in the beginning of Christ's religion'.[7] Others allowed that the apostles were ordained as priests and bishops at the same time, but maintained that the two orders were still distinct from the first. The majority were inclined to the view that according to the Scriptures only bishops could ordain. Cranmer was much more radical stating that 'A bishop may make a priest by the Scripture, and so may princes and governors also, and that by the authority of God committed to them, and the people also by their election; for as we read that bishops have done it, so Christian emperors and princes usually have done it, and the people before Christian princes were, commonly did elect their bishops and priests'.[8] A revised version of the *Bishops' Book* in 1543 maintained the view that in the New Testament there were only two orders, bishops or priests, and deacons, and that these were conferred by prayer and the imposition of hands.

Cranmer also held the view that ecclesiastical power is not superior to civil power, but that both are derived equally from God. This is not so much a low doctrine of ordination but a high doctrine of civil power. The Archbishop wrote that 'All christian princes have committed unto them immediately of God the whole cure of all their subjects ... the civil ministers under the king's majesty in this realm of England be those whom it shall please his highness for the time to put in authority under him ... the ministers of God's word under his majesty be the bishops, parsons, vicars and such other priests as be appointed by his highness to that ministration'.[9] The archbishop's view that bishops and priests were one order was in line with the teaching of the other writings of the period, and with the opinion of many medieval theologians. The statements about the power of the king made by Cranmer were more likely the result of timely political desire, to set the authority of the king against that of the Pope, than the products of deep theological reflection. It certainly has no precedent in patristic or medieval theology.

The first Anglican Ordinal was published in 1550 under the title *The Forme and Manner of Makying and Consecratying of Archebishoppes, Bishoppes, Priestes and Deacons*. Although the Act of Parliament had provided for rites of ordination for the minor orders as well, it is hardly surprising, in view of Cranmer's belief that the minor orders had no scriptural foundation, that he made no use of this provision in drawing up the Ordinal, particularly as the minor orders had fallen into disuse in England. He provided rites for the diaconate, priesthood, and episcopate, the last to be used also for consecrating archbishops. The rite itself confirms that Cranmer did not think of the episcopate as a separate order. From the wording of the prayers, formulas, and questions in the examination, as well as from the choice of Gospels, that the function for which bishops were commissioned was thought of as the pastoral oversight of the church, as it had been in the medieval rites. The Ordinal also shows that Cranmer did not think of the diaconate and the priesthood in the traditional way as two consecutive orders, but as two completely different sorts of ministry.[10]

As soon as the Ordinal was published, it met with criticism from those who desired a more Protestant type of service. With the accession in 1553 of Catholic Queen Mary the medieval ordination rites were restored. During her reign many Englishmen were forced to flee to the Continent to avoid persecution, and there they came into close contact with the ordination rites used in the reformed churches. It would appear that from the first the exiles at Frankfort adopted the reformed structure of ministry. When Elizabeth came to the throne in 1558, the exiles returned to England and many desired to continue the ministry to which they had become accustomed. To their dismay the Ordinal of 1552 was restored with only small alterations. The Puritan party within the church of England found the Ordinal objectionable and throughout Elizabeth's reign they maintained a constant pressure for its reform. They regarded it as identical with the mediaeval rites and thought that

those ordained by it were not duly ordained according to the require-
ments of the New Testament. Their ideal was the structure of ministry
and ordination found in the continental reformed churches, and many
refused to subscribe to the Thirty-nine Articles of Religion until that
should be established in England.[11]

During the 1560s, the tracts of Archbishop of Canterbury John
Whitgift representing the conformist position fuelled the debate in
England and with the counter argument for the Presbyterian position
opinion eloquently presented by the Lady Margaret Professor of
Divinity at Cambridge University Thomas Cartwright.[12] The debate was
rekindled and blazed two decades later with the publication of the
Marprelate Tracts.[13] The Puritans voiced several complaints. They
wanted the congregation to have not only the opportunity to examine
the candidates and to object to them, but also the right of electing
them, as they believed was the practice of the primitive church.
Complaining about the absence of lay elders, who they believed were
demanded by the New Testament, the Puritans strongly criticised the
distinction between bishops and priests, believing that the New
Testament required the equality of ministers. Therefore they resented
some powers of the ministry being given to one man, the bishop, and
not being shared by all ministers and elders. In particular they thought
it wrong for the bishop to ordain alone, but they agreed that imposition
of hands should be used. Archbishop Whitgift did not attempt to argue
that only bishops could ordain. Indeed he was ready to admit, 'in the
apostles' time there was divers manners of ordaining and electing ministers. For sometime one alone did choose and ordain, sometimes,
many, sometimes ministers only, and sometimes the people also'. He
was concerned only to defend the right of bishops to ordain without the
assistance of others, and to insist that the New Testament did not
require other ministers always to be involved in ordination.[14]

Although the evidence is not conclusive, it would seem that the
Elizabethan bishops did not argue that the New Testament demanded
that only bishops should ordain, in the same way that the Puritans
argued that it demanded that ordination must be by elders and ministers together, but they simply defended the position that ordination
must be by men with lawful authority, and that in England this
authority lay with the bishops alone. The Puritans not only criticised
the Ordinal but made positive efforts to secure reforms during the 1580s
including an effort to replace the Prayer Book with a version of the
service book which had been used by the exiles at Geneva. Their efforts
were defeated.[15]

The situation in Scotland was different from that in England. There the Anglican Ordinal had never been introduced and the structure of ministry found in the continental reformed churches had been adopted. The method of ordination was that prescribed in the Genevan service book, that had been brought back to Scotland by the reformer John Knox in 1559 and which became the foundation of the Book of Common Order of the Church of Scotland. Episcopacy was not introduced until 1610, under the pressure of King James I (formerly, before 1603, King James VI of Scotland). Three ministers were sent to England to be consecrated as bishops, and from this time onwards Episcopal ordination became the rule in Scotland, although no attempt was made to reordain all those who had previously received ordination from ministers and superintendents only. It was not until 1620 that an Ordinal appeared. It is particularly interesting as an example of a compromise between the Anglican Ordinal and the ordination practice of the reformed churches. Had the climate of opinion been more congenial, such rites might well have been adopted in England as a concession to the demands of the Puritans, since they meet almost all their objections to the Anglican rites.[16]

It was with Charles I's archbishop of Canterbury, William Laud, that the issue followed a different path. He was determined to exercise his authority and employ whatever methods to maintain religious uniformity at home, in Scotland, and in Ireland, and over the English subjects resident as merchants or colonists overseas. He was a bitter opponent of Calvinism and Puritanism and his goal was to see the Church of England 'catholic and reformed' in the spirit of John Jewel and Richard Hooker but with greater emphasis on ceremony and ritual. He was consequently disliked by the Puritans, who branded him as an 'Arminian', which he was, and accused him of wishing to destroy the work of the reformers and effect reconciliation with Rome, which he did not. Furthermore, the fact that Laud was a favourite with Charles I made him suspect in the eyes of the Protestant party.[17]

During the years between 1629 and 1640 Laud worked in close contact with the King. The policy of 'Thorough' so rigidly enforced by Thomas Wentworth, Earl of Strafford, in secular affairs in Ireland was equally strictly imposed by Laud on the church. Faced with the danger of separatism and division, Laud hoped to preserve the unity of the Church by the measure of uniformity and by enforcement of the law. He found much slackness and disorder in the churches. Many were falling into decay; dirt and desecration were common; clergy neglected their duties or indulged their capriciousness in the conduct of worship.

Laud was determined to stop all of this. He demanded obedience to the bishops and to the Prayer Book, and he used his powers in the courts of law to see that such obedience was enforced.[18] It was here that pamphleteers such as William Prynne, Henry Burton, and John Bastwick were tried for writing scurrilous attacks upon the bishops and were sentenced to have their ears cut off.[19]

Paul Bradshaw has succinctly described the change in opinion towards episcopacy among many Anglicans at this time creating a wider division with the Puritans. The sixteenth-century churchmen regarded episcopacy as one possible type of church government, but in the seventeenth century the belief became common that episcopacy was of divine institution and therefore only bishops could validly ordain.[20] For those men in England who refused ordination by bishops and were ordained by presbyteries or by congregations, their Puritan ordinations were regarded as invalid. Some Puritans had changed their attitude towards episcopacy and would have accepted a more moderate episcopacy, where the functions of the office shared with the ministers, as they believed was the practice in the early church but the uncompromising attitude of the English bishops towards them, however, made them determined to abolish episcopacy 'root and branch' and establish the Presbyterian system.[21]

The Episcopal party renewed their efforts to seek a compromise and began to put forward various schemes to reduce episcopacy somewhat in the hope of reaching a compromise with the Puritans. The archbishop of Armagh, James Ussher, a former student and fellow of Trinity College in Dublin in 1641, proposed a scheme for the government of the church by the bishop together with his synod of clergy, which he believed was the practice of the early Church.[22] Under this plan the bishop would still remain the minister of ordination, but would act with the advice and consent of the other ministers.[23] All this came too late, however. The Puritans refused to compromise with the objectionable episcopate; the bishops were ejected from Parliament and imprisoned or forced to flee.

In 1641, when the English Parliament began to dismantle the regime of Charles I, the most systematic and untamed attack was not upon the political and legal agents of Stuart tyranny, but upon the Church of England. Having overturned Archbishop Laud's innovations in doctrine, discipline, and ritual, and having excluded the bishops from the House of Lords, Parliament began to consider more fundamental remodelling of the national church.[24] The diocesan episcopacy was to be abolished, her courts to be demolished, her parish clergy to be purged of all deleterious and scandalous priests, and her wealth to be applied to more godly purposes. But then civil war overtook the nation and more urgent problems claimed Parliament's attention. Under the pressure of financing and fighting a war against the king, the parliamentarians' early enthusiasm for reform of the church gave way to irregular purges of the clergy and to a piecemeal demolition of what now appeared as a largely irrelevant institution. The Book of Common Prayer was banned and Parliament imposed the Westminster Assembly's Directory of Public Worship upon the nation.[25] In general, the episcopate had abdicated the spiritual and intellectual leadership of the church.

Episcopacy was abolished and in 1643 the Westminster Assembly, a body of Puritan divines appointed by Parliament, was directed to frame an alternative system of church government and ordination. Presbyterianism was hardly established, however, before the Independents gained the upper hand, and the ordination procedure was thrown into chaos; men were ordained either by presbyteries or by congregations, with imposition of hands or without, by the call of the Church or by their own sense of vocation.

Most Puritans in England during the 1640s and 1650s favoured a Presbyterian church polity, one with a national church, centralised authority, and admission to the sacraments almost as broad as the Anglican communion. Another faction, the Independents, who were closely allied to New England Congregationalists in ideas about church government, wanted particular independent churches, no central authority, and sacraments only for visible saints. They were a minority revolutionary party, kept in power for the time being in England by Cromwell and his army.

The Civil War began in August 1642 when Charles raised his standard at Nottingham. How far it was a religious and how far a political or class struggle continues to engage historians. Roughly speaking, on one side were ranged the king and Anglicanism, represented by episcopacy and the Prayer Book, and on the other side stood Parliament and Puritanism, whether Presbyterian or Independent. To those on the king's side the parliamentary party represented anarchy, antinomianism, and Protestant insurrection against the declared will of God. The Puritans, on the other hand, were no less inspired by religious convictions and equally convinced that they had the Bible on their side. They feared Rome and held the belief that the bishops were trying to undo the work of the reformers. They stood for the Protestant faith, for the individual conscience, for private judgement against royal authority, sacerdotalism, and prelacy. The fact that, on each side, religion and politics were in alliance meant fierce passions were aroused and bitter divisions created.

As soon as the war began, Parliament made plans for enlisting the support of the Scots. Having first abolished episcopacy, a meeting of Puritan leaders was held in London, the Westminster Assembly, which proceeded to draw up a religious agreement which might serve as a basis for an alliance with Presbyterian Scotland. Scotland had declared its faith in the Covenant of 1638, and it was an amended form of this document that was discussed by the Westminster Assembly in 1643. The result was the publication of the Solemn League and Covenant that was imposed upon all Britons over the age of 18. It declared that they had entered into 'a mutual and solemn league and covenant' for 'the extirpation of popery and prelacy', that is, Church government by archbishops, bishops, their chancellors and commissaries, and all other ecclesiastical officers depending on that hierarchy.[26]

When this became law in February 1644 it meant the end of the Church of England whenever Parliament could make its will obeyed. Many of the clergy were Puritan at heart, and these signed the Covenant gladly and continued in their benefices as Presbyterian ministers rather than as priests of the Church. All those, however, who could not conscientiously subscribe to the Covenant, were ejected from their livings, local committees being formed to examine any waverers on matters of politics, religion, and morals.[27]

The fall of episcopacy led also to the fall of the Book of Common Prayer, which in 1644 was declared illegal and was replaced by the Directory of Public Worship. The Directory was soon followed by the setting up a Presbyterian form of government for the Church of England with 'classes' and provincial and national assemblies. Presbyterianism, however, whether as a theology or as a method of government, was proving no more popular in England than episcopacy.[28]

The end of the Civil War at Naseby in 1645 was followed by a period of endless intrigues between the king, Parliament, the army, and the Scots. After two years of negotiations, during which little progress was made, Charles made a last bid in 1647 for Scottish support by agreeing to establish Presbyterianism in England for three years, and then he fled to the Isle of Wight. This so aggravated the Independents that war broke out again immediately. Cromwell's army was victorious; the House of Commons was 'purged' of any likely opponents, Charles I was brought to London, tried before a special court of commissioners, and sentenced to death. On 30 January 1649, he was beheaded.

The Anglican Church was by no means united in its opposition to the Puritan state. The Church was deeply divided between the 60 per cent or so of those who conformed to the new regime, and the much smaller group of uncompromising Laudians who had retired into hiding or exile, with an intermediary group of disaffected conformists who accepted the new way under protest, said some of their Prayer Book offices in private, and continued to hold their benefices. It fell to a small group of Laudian clergy to see that the ministry was maintained, that the right influences were brought to bear on Charles II, and that the clergy and laity in England were prepared to play their part when the moment arrived. There is evidence that a certain number of priests and deacons were ordained by bishops in England in order that the supply might be kept up.[29] The consecration of bishops presented a more complex problem since the initiative lay with the future king who, being in exile was scarcely in a position to make any nominations. Various suggestions for overcoming this difficulty were made, particularly by Edward Hyde in 1655 and 1659, but none was found to be workable, and the Restoration taking place before the situation had become desperate to solve the problem.

As John Spurr has argued cogently, the triumphant Presbyterians of the 1640s kept up a barrage of anti-Episcopal polemic throughout the 1650s. Nonetheless, the authorities of the Interregnum turned a blind eye to the continued use of Common Prayer as long as it posed no political threat. But on 24 November 1655, in the aftermath of a royalist rising, Cromwell issued an order against the employment of Anglican ministers and the use of the Prayer Book. Anthony Sparrow, a future bishop, published *A Rationale upon the Book of Common Prayer* that described and justified the liturgy in every detail. Interregnum Anglicanism cannot be defined in a paragraph. It obviously owed much to the continuing use of the Book of Common Prayer.[30]

Parliament, called for the autumn of 1656, held out the prospect of clerical reconciliation and concerted action against religious extremism. A plan for 'primitive' or 'reduced' episcopacy, which had first been proposed in 1641 by Archbishop James Ussher in his tract *Reduction of Episcopacy unto the Form of Synodical Government*, was reconsidered in the hope of staving off the parliamentary attack on Laudian 'prelacy'. Although one royalist thought it was 'dispersed by the Presbyterians among their friends' and Richard Baxter took an interest; it was actually promoted by Nicholas Bernard, Ussher's chaplain, and John Gauden, later bishop of Exeter. For several years Gauden had been recommending this dilute form of Episcopal government in which the bishop was *primus inter pares*, 'ruling with joint counsel, not levelled with younger preachers and novices, not too much exalted above the graver and elder presbyters; neither despised of the one nor despising of the other'.[31] Now, presumably in the hope of erecting some sort of national church organisation, Gauden began to sound out clerical sympathy for primitive episcopacy and was heartened at the response in Essex and London, where 'not only Presbyterians and Independents ... but even Episcopal men are upon a very calm temper'.[32]

The conciliatory Gauden and his allies could plausibly claim to speak for a larger number of Anglican clergymen. Moreover Gauden continued to build bridges with moderate Presbyterian leaders. And some of the leading English Presbyterians were, as they told the king, 'no enemies to moderate episcopacy'. Negotiations between Episcopalians and these moderate Presbyterians seem to have begun in early March 1660. Towards the end of that month, Dr. George Morley, Edward Hyde's agent, arrived to steer them towards acceptance of the Church of England, and on 30 March John Barwick, another of Hyde's men and loyal to Charles II, reported much support in London for episcopacy and the Prayer Book. The Presbyterians saw three matters of difference: church government, the liturgy, and the ceremonies. In church government they accepted and agreed to Ussher's model of reduced episcopacy 'without a word of alteration'; they were convinced of the need for a liturgy, but only asked that since the Prayer Book 'hath in it many things that are justly offensive and need amendment', it should be revised by 'some learned, moderate, and godly divines of both persuasions'; finally, they begged that 'indifferent' ceremonies such as kneeling at the sacrament, bowing at the name of Jesus, making the sign of the cross in baptism, and the use of the surplice, should be left to the conscience of each minister. When it finally came, the reply of 'the bishops' was, in Baxter's words, nothing but 'a paper of bitter oppositions by way of confutation of our former proposals' – it certainly refused any concession, though tempering this intransigence with pleas for unity. This reply flew in the face of royal policy, parliamentary opinion, and much Anglican enthusiasm for reduced episcopacy. It is not clear who composed it, but it does show that the church party, just like the Presbyterians, included hard liners who would press for the restoration of the old regime at every occasion.[33]

Oliver Cromwell died in 1658 and his son Richard, who succeeded him as Protector, was a failure and resigned in 1660. When Charles II returned to England in May 1660, the religious situation was exceedingly delicate. The Presbyterians were in power in the Convention

Parliament, but the question of the restoration of the episcopacy and the Prayer Book was bound to arise before long. Some of the Puritans were in favour of a compromise, a form of 'moderate episcopacy'.[34] Royal and parliamentary policy, however, still seemed directed towards a broad-based church and a moderate religious settlement. The Convention Parliament which had assembled on 25 April included one group, led by William Prynne, that sought the kind of Presbyterian church envisaged by Parliament in the 1640s, and a larger, but more amorphous, party of Episcopalians. After long and disorderly debates on 9 and 16 July, the whole matter was referred to the king and such divines as he should be pleased to nominate.[35]

Within a few months, the moderate settlement for the church and episcopacy collapsed, in part because of the spontaneous recovery of the Church of England in the counties, cathedral cities, and parishes of England. Episcopacy returned with the bishops: those who had survived since the 1640s reclaimed their sees, and the new appointees of September and October 1660 took possession of their palaces and cathedrals.[36] But the advocates of prelacy underestimated the zeal and determination of their critics. The Episcopal party had spent the last 15 years preparing for this moment, and they were not in the mood for compromise. With the assistance of Edward Hyde, now Lord Clarendon, they intended to see to the restoration of the Church of England, as they had known it in the days of Laud, as the one and only legal and established church of the land.

Thanks to the careful work that had been done, the king was on their side. The court, acting on the principle of 'No bishop, no king', assumed that the restoration of the monarchy inevitably involved the reestablishment of the Church of England. In 1641 the bishops had been excluded from the House of Lords. The court now orchestrated the moves which resulted in the decision of June to repeal that act so that the bishops could assume their seats at the opening of the second session in November. When the new Cavalier Parliament met, the majority were Anglican churchmen; new bishops were appointed and began their assignments. Episcopacy had been restored without a struggle, although its power was modified. There was no High Commission and no other prerogative courts to enforce the will of both the government and the bishops when they conflicted with the views of Parliament and common law courts. Nor were bishops associated with the government in the same close way that they had been before 1640.

The Act of Uniformity received the royal assent on 19 May 1662, and came into force on 24 August. The Act of Uniformity was the work of many hands, the product of parliamentary horse-trading rather than theological self-definition; it did not create a breach with English Protestantism, for that had been growing over the preceding two decades, but it did prevent the union of moderate Presbyterians with the established church and set the legal boundaries within which a Restoration Anglicanism would be elaborated. The settlement of 1662 was a political, indeed an Erastian, solution to the religious divisions of the English; moreover, it was based on a conspicuously narrower interest than was the political settlement. None of this augured well for its stability or survival.

Following Charles II's restoration to the throne in 1660, the bishops and clergy in exile returned to England. Even prior to this some had advocated the adoption of one of the schemes for a reduced episcopacy to secure agreement with the Puritans.[37] But the majority of bishops were in no mood to make concessions to the Puritans. Their exile on the continent might have made them feel more charitable towards the reformed churches there, but it had the reverse effect on their feelings towards those who had driven them out of England. They ignored these suggestions and immediately embarked upon a policy of re-ordaining those who had not received Episcopal ordination, sometimes going so far as to demand a full renunciation of their former orders from them. Nevertheless, many Puritans, encouraged by the king's attitude towards them on his return to England, were still hopeful that a compromise might be reached and were now ready to accept Ussher's scheme for a modified episcopacy. Now it was the turn of the bishops to reject Ussher's plan, as the Puritans had done almost 20 years earlier. The bishops were determined to pursue their policy of re-ordaining all who had not received Episcopal ordination, and would not be swayed by anyone. The prelates had made Episcopal ordination necessary *de facto*; it only remained for them to revise the Ordinal and make it necessary *de jure*, and victory over the Puritans would be complete.[38]

The most notable feature of the 1662 revision of the Ordinal by Convocation is the requirement of Episcopal ordination as an absolute necessity for admission to the ministry of the Church of England. Perhaps unintentionally, although that seems most unlikely, it declared that non-Episcopal ordination was invalid in the opinion of the Anglican church, for all, both those in England who had refused to be ordained by bishops and those from foreign reformed churches.[39]

In 1662, a large number of ministers who were unable in conscience to accept that their non-Episcopal ordination was invalid were compelled to leave the ministry of the Church of England. Among these and among Anglicans too, there were many who did not regard this schism as a final break and who entertained high hopes that a compromise might be reached which would secure the comprehension of the Dissenters within the Church of England. Thus throughout the rest of the seventeenth century various schemes were proposed for uniting the Presbyterian and Episcopal ministries.[40]

Later plans offered no new methods but merely reiterated earlier proposals; a Comprehension Bill of 1680 proposed that those ordained by presbyters between 1644 and 1660 should be accepted with re-ordination, but this and other bills were unsuccessful. In 1689 a commission was appointed to revise the Prayer Book to facilitate comprehension; John Tillotson, then dean of Canterbury and a member of the commission, prepared a list of concessions that might be made. Among them he suggested that all future ordinations should be Episcopal but that those who had been ordained in reformed churches abroad should be accepted into the ministry of the Church of England without re-ordination, and that those who had received only Presbyterian orders in England should undergo a conditional ordination. Nothing came of this plan, and, although attempts at comprehension continued to be made, there do not seem to have been any more serious attempts in this century to find ways of reuniting the ministries or of revising the Ordinal to make it acceptable to both parties.[41]

New England critics of an American bishop in the 1750s and 1760s drew on Richard Baxter's pamphlets on episcopacy.[42] His *Five Disputations of Church-Government and Worship* (London, 1659), *Church-History of the Government of Bishops and Their Councils Abbreviated* (London, 1680), and *A Treatise of Episcopacy* (London, 1682) were designed to discredit the early-seventeenth-century Laudian idea that diocesan prelacy is essential to the organisation of a true church.[43] Baxter's works recount the development of episcopacy and the papacy and are shaped as damning reproof to English Episcopalians of what he called 'the new Prelatical Way'. He discerned correctly two traditions in the English church since the Henrician Reformation: the one consisted of 'Protestants', the old moderate sort of bishops who from the 'first Reformation' were 'sound in Doctrine', and 'differed not in any considerable points from those whom they called Puritans', taking 'Episcopacy to be necessary *ad bene esse Ministerii & Ecclesiae*, but not *ad esse*'. There was also 'a second sort of Episcopal Divines of the last edition ... who differed from us in greater matters than Episcopacy'. They were innovators in three ways: they forsook the doctrine of the 39 Articles, the *Homilies*, and the Synod of Dort for the teaching of the Jesuits and

Arminians; they no longer took the pope to be the Antichrist, but inclined to accept him as patriarch of the Western church; and, insisting that episcopacy (English diocesan prelacy) was laid down *jure divino*, they disowned continental reformed churches and refused to acknowledge the validity of non-Episcopal orders. A state of affairs that began 'in Laud, Neale, Howson, Corbet, and Buckeridge with Montagu' and whose concept of the church became official orthodoxy in the Act of Uniformity of 1662, Baxter despaired of reconciliation: 'Do you think that all men that have eyes do not see that between the old Episcopal Divines and the new ... there is much more difference then between the Presbyterians and them'?[44]

Baxter allowed that there was little dispute as to the exact nature of the early polity, nor as to the fact that it changed, nor as to the form of that change, but the change itself, 'whether it was well or ill done, is all the controversie, of the chief'. The first chapter of his *Church-history* showed 'How Prelacy became the diseasing tumour of the Church'. It was his declared intention to trace the stages by which the clergy forsook 'Christian Purity, Simplicity and Love' and ascended 'to the Papal height'. Baxter declared that those who had been guides and preachers 'degenerated to a similitude of Civil Magistracy'. He concluded that this 'was not well done ... [and] hath confounded the Christian world'. *Church-history* reveals the inadequacy of diocesan prelacy, and he develops the idea with extraordinary skill.[45] Baxter's account of the history and weaknesses of episcopacy would be forcefully recited again nearly one hundred years later in the monumental work *A View of Episcopacy*, published by the venerable Boston Congregational minister Charles Chauncy.

In Scotland the Restoration religious settlement re-imposed an Episcopalian system of church government on a predominately Presbyterian population.[46] Some observers of the two ecclesiastical systems in the country noted that there was a high degree of similarity of church government.[47] Yet there flourished in Scotland as in England for a century past a lively debate between church leaders regarding the historic nature of episcopacy.[48] Gilbert Burnet, an artful observer of public affairs and who later became bishop of Salisbury, published several pamphlets on the issue. He also attacked the Scottish bishops for relinquishing their primary pastoral duties in favour of obtaining political influences.[49] The political divisions continued to stir both church groups during the 1670s.

The fluctuating course of Scottish ecclesiastical policy also stirred up divisions between those who were prepared to retain their allegiance to the monarch and those who were unable to compromise with civil authority.[50] An atmosphere of disputatious belligerence surrounded the Scottish Episcopal Church until it was disestablished and outlawed in 1690. It was against this background that several Scottish-born and educated clergymen, such as James Blair of Virginia, migrated to the colonies in the 1680s and 1690s. As Clare Jackson has persuasively argued, between 1660 and 1690 lively debates occurred on civil and ecclesiastical issues in the country on such matters as the divine right of kingship, a hereditary and absolute monarchy, an absentee monarch, the role of parliament, and the efficiency of the two ecclesiastical systems, Episcopal and Presbyterian.[51] The Revolution of 1688–9 brought the religious question in Scotland to a head again. After James II's flight to France in December 1688 and the accession to the throne of his son-in-law William of Orange on 11 April 1689, the way was clear for the Scottish Parliament to resolve the issues. In 1690 the Episcopal Church was disestablished and replaced by the Erastian Presbyterian Church. The Scottish Episcopal Church was banned by statute from holding services attended by more than five persons until the repeal of the Penal Laws in 1792.

The English and Scottish debates over the nature of episcopacy, the ministry, and the church during the sixteenth, seventeenth, and eighteenth centuries were retold in detail by colonial Anglican church advocates and critics. In many instances the pamphlets representing both points of view were nearly verbatim transcriptions of earlier English publications. The old controversy over the historical Episcopal office was vigorously renewed with familiar language in New England colonies.

5

Noah Hobart Decries Anglican Expansion: Thomas Sherlock Proposes an American Bishop

From the late 1720s to the 1760s a wave of religious enthusiasm swept irregularly over large regions of the colonies. It was part of a much broader movement, an evangelical upsurge, taking place simultaneously in England, Scotland, and Germany. Known as the -Great Awakening, the movement began as early as the 1720s among New Jersey congregants of the Dutch Reformed church led by Theodore Frelinghuysen. About the same time, William and Gilbert Tennent spurred a similar revival among New Jersey Presbyterians. In 1734, Jonathan Edwards began preaching a powerful message of revival to Congregationalists in the Connecticut River valley of Massachusetts.

These isolated outbursts of religious enthusiasm were reignited when George Whitefield arrived in Georgia in 1738. During his 15-month tour of the colonies, Whitefield preached a revival message in Charles Town, Philadelphia, New York, and Boston. His emotional speaking style made audiences shed tears of despair and joy, and thousands of persons flocked to his sermons.

In New England the movement flourished briefly, leaving in its wake bitter doctrinal disputes between the 'Old Lights' and the 'New Lights' within the Congregational Church and 'Old Sides' and 'New Sides' within the Presbyterian Church of the Middle Colonies. Among Congregationalists, the 'Old Lights' were led by Charles Chauncy, a Boston clergyman, who opposed the revivalist movement as extravagant and impermanent. The theology of the 'New Lights', a slightly modified Calvinism, crystallised into the Edwardian, or New England, theology that became dominant in western New England, whereas the doctrines of the 'Old Lights', strong in Boston and the eastern vicinity, were destined to develop into the Universalist and Unitarian positions.

The division between 'Old Sides' and 'New Sides' caused a schism in the Presbyterian Church (1741–58).

Preaching the sermon at the ordination of Noah Welles in 1746, Noah Hobart's address was animated, on the one hand, by a discussion of the historical validity of the ministerial office and, on the other hand, was critical of the growing influence of the English church in the colony.[1] Hobart, the Congregational minister in Fairfield, Connecticut, revitalised the subjects of the legitimacy of ordination. A graduate of Harvard College in 1724, he was the great protagonist of eighteenth-century Connecticut Congregationalism. After a brief teaching stint in Philadelphia, Hobart was settled and ordained as the minister of the First Church in Fairfield by 1733, he held that post until his death 40 years later. His friend Ezra Stiles, rector of Yale College, described his preaching style as of a scholarly character 'not of the passionate and animating kind', but 'calculated to enlighten the understanding, inform the judgement and mend the Heart, rather than move the Passions and fire the Imagination'. Stiles offered that Hobart was 'but a poor Speaker, and made very indifferent Figure in the Pulpit'.[2] The previous decade had witnessed an increasing number of congregations organised by the church and a gradual growth in the number of Congregational converts who became ministers in the English church.[3] Ever ready to preach and practise moral policing of his flock, Hobart listed among the evils of the day 'the Lordliness and Arrogance' of the itinerant 'New Lights', and the 'fixed Prelacy' of the Church of England.[4] He challenged the historical nature of episcopacy, apostolic succession, and the process and validity of Anglican ordination. Commenting that the Church of England 'have put their ministers authority for preaching the Gospel, not upon the foot of Christ's Commission, which he has vested with in Ordination, but upon that of his having the Bishop's License', Hobart reminded his audience of the Puritans' objections in England to oaths in the 1630s and now was critical of the ordination oath of canonical obedience to the bishop and to the civil authority of the head of state required of ministers of the English church.[5]

Echoing the pleas of Increase and Cotton Mather in Boston on the occasion of the establishment of a congregation more than half a century earlier, Hobart was critical of the divisive presence of the English church in Connecticut. Since the declaration and conversion of the six 'Yale Apostates' at the College's 1722 Commencement, the religious group had made steady progress in the colony. Congregations had been established during the intervening years in Fairfield, New London, and Newtown, missions at Derby and Norwalk, and an itinerant parson travelled the western section of the province.[6] In Fairfield there were three or four churches, each an alternative to Hobart's, and an English church led by Henry Caner, that included former members of Hobart's congregation.

Hobart noted in his sermon that the attraction of the English church 'is not much wondered at, if persons, who by their immoral lives, expose themselves to ecclesiastical answers, choose the Communion of that Church, which (at least in its present State in this Country) can exercise no Discipline upon them. But that persons of sobriety and religion, men who are desirous that the Church of Christ should be kept pure, in the present age, are transmitted so to their posterity should forsake us and go over to such a Communion, is to me really unaccountable'.[7] Neither unreasonable nor ill-mannered, the Fairfield minister held that because an Anglican priest could not exercise discipline over the most erring of his flock, he concluded that 'open Irreligion and undisguised Prophaneness [are] dreadfully visible where the Church of England has the Ascendant'.[8]

Challenging Hobart's criticisms of the nature of the Anglican ministry was James Wetmore, who served as the minister at Rye, New York. Educated at Yale with the class of 1714, Wetmore had served as the Congregational minister at Northfield, Massachusetts, before his conversion to the English church. He was one of the 'Yale Apostates' who declared for episcopacy in 1722 and sailed for England for ordination.[9] Wetmore's pamphlet, *A Vindication of the Professors of the Church of England in Connecticut* (Boston, 1747), described the Congregational churches as 'excrescences or tumours', and their members as characterised by bigotry, 'Hypocrisy, and detestable Vices'.[10] He argued stridently but vainly that the Anglican church had come to America with the common law and statutes in Winthrop's fleet and that the English law had been conveniently modified by Puritan practice in church and state.[11]

Responding to Wetmore with his *Serious Address* (Boston, 1748), Hobart rejected the position that the common law and parliamentary statutes ran in America and characterised the Church of England as the 'Prelatic Establishment in the South part of Britain'.[12] To admit that it was part of 'the Constitution of the Nation' would have been to deny the validity of the whole Congregational structure, his own ordination, and even the validity of the vast majority of New England marriages. He argued that a church is, by its nature, a purely local thing.

First addressing the question whether the Anglican Church's establishment in England extended to America, Hobart concluded that it did not. Referring to the expenses required for the Anglican system, he stated that the great number of 'unnecessary ecclesiastical Officers' and the great expense involved in supporting them, made it imprudent for members of that denomination to submit to that order.[13] Another objection that Hobart advanced against persons conforming to the English church was that such a step would tend to bring the colonies into an 'unnecessary and hurtful State of Dependence'.[14] By dependence he meant ecclesiastical dependence; for he stated that the provinces were, and of right ought to be, dependent upon the mother country in all civil affairs. The Fairfield parson argued that such a political relation was advantageous; but a state of ecclesiastical dependence, carrying with it no attendant advantages in the way of trade or civil privileges, would certainly not be beneficial to the colonies, and might be just the reverse.[15] He regarded conformity to the English church to be imprudent for many reasons: first, on the ground of expense; second, because of the tyrannical discipline exercised by that church; third, because of its arbitrary power in appointing and removing ministers; and, finally, because such conformity would lead to the destruction of practical religion.[16]

As early as in 1723, intermittent efforts and pleas were initiated by clergymen in America and London to establish a colonial episcopate. Bishop of London Edmund Gibson explored the matter in 1723, soon after his elevation to the post. New England clergymen, in convention in 1725, urged the appointment of a prelate for political purposes, to secure the loyalty of the people to the king.[17] Archbishop of Canterbury John Potter pursued the matter in 1745 and 1746, followed by Bishop of London Thomas Sherlock's sustained effort from 1748 to 1750. Archbishop of York Robert Hay Drummond, at the request of Archbishop of Canterbury Thomas Secker, prepared a report in 1764, 'Thoughts upon the Present State of the Church of England in America', that noted the ineffectiveness of provincial administration of the church and clergy and made the case for a colonial episcopacy. Drummond proposed the establishment of four suffragan bishops with endowed incomes: at Burlington, New Jersey; the College of William and Mary in Williamsburg; Charles Town, South Carolina; and Codrington College in Bermuda. The report was received cordially but ineffectually by the Marquess of Rockingham, prime minister from 1765 to 1766, and by William Petty, second earl of Shelburne, secretary of state for the South in the succeeding Chatham administration in 1767. The latter official met with Secker and Drummond in 1767 to discuss the proposal, but the deteriorating political situation in the colonies ensured that practical progress was impossible. Archbishop

Secker independently pursued the appointment of a colonial bishop with civil officials between 1764 and 1768 but without success.

Interest in American church affairs was renewed after the death of Bishop of London Gibson in 1748, and the translation of Bishop Sherlock of Salisbury to London. Sherlock served as Bishop of London from 1748 until his death in 1761 and represents the circle of church leaders in the mid-eighteenth century who were linked by the common bonds of school, university, and patronage. The eldest son of William Sherlock, dean of St. Paul's Cathedral, he was educated at Eton, where Lord Townshend, Henry Pelham, and Robert Walpole were among his friends. A graduate and later a fellow and master of St. Catharine's College, Cambridge, he was appointed master of the Temple in 1704 in succession to his father and quickly became a prominent leader in the church and at Cambridge University. Not a stranger to disputation in either the church or civil politics, he entered into the fray against the deists in 1724 and became a key spokesman in the House of Lords for the ministry of Walpole and the power of the crown. An ambitious, intelligent, and popular man, Sherlock was an active and effective bishop.[18]

Sherlock's appointment initiated a new era for the overseas imperial church. For more than a decade before his death, Gibson's influence among top civil officials in Whitehall had diminished. Sherlock, a long-time associate and friend of key government leaders, gave considerable thought to the governance of the colonial church. During the first years of his episcopacy, he was relentless in his efforts to obtain a bishop for America, a prelate who would reside permanently in the New World. Recognising the expensive, time-consuming, and less-than-efficient effort of managing congregations 3500 miles from headquarters, Sherlock wanted the office of the bishop of London relieved of the duty. This was not to be an easy assignment, for the decision was not his alone. It was both a civil and ecclesiastical matter. In 1750, the prospect of an appointment of a bishop for America was more complex and political than it had been during the previous 50 years. The issue became quickly trapped in the rhetoric of both Anglican and Congregational preachers and pamphleteers and in the crosswinds of Whitehall politics. It was shaped in no small way by the adroitness and power of nonconformist church leaders in Boston, New York, Philadelphia, and London.[19]

By upbringing and conviction Sherlock was a Tory and was willing to work with the royal family.[20] He worked for the old ideal of church and state as two different manifestations, religious and secular, of one people.[21] A realist, he also sought to allow Dissenters, although outside the national church, full political privilege, a position which was anathema to the government's political leaders. Sir Robert Walpole, Lord Townshend, and the Duke of Newcastle, seeking to stabilise the Hanoverian dynasty, appointed Whigs to bishoprics since they could be depended upon to be loyal to the crown. Sherlock was mistrusted by Hanoverian leaders who viewed him as an inveterate champion of church power, serving as a forceful spokesman for the church in the House of Lords. Although out of favour with several government leaders, he was held in high regard by the royal family and was a frequent visitor at the royal palace and with the queen.[22]

Sherlock initiated a new policy in relation to provincial church affairs seeking colonial prelates in league with Philip Yorke, first Earl of Hardwicke, and the Lord Chancellor.[23] Yorke was an experienced government leader, and working jointly with Newcastle, he had exercised extraordinary judgement in dispensing ecclesiastical patronage. His support aided Joseph Butler in his appointment as bishop of Durham, Thomas Sherlock as bishop of London, and Thomas Secker as archbishop of Canterbury.[24] Yorke sent to Sherlock for his review and consideration a plan, 'For the ecclesiastical Jurisdiction in the Plantations'. After systematic attention, Sherlock proposed to the lord chancellor that 'As the Plantations are no part of the diocese of London, nor has the Bishop of London any benefit from it, but is put to great expense about it, it is conceived to be reasonable to ease the Bishop of London of this burden that the whole shou'd not lye on him'. Sherlock proposed to divide the care of the colonial church among the English Bishops, granting to the prelate's supervision of the church in particular colonies a strategy that would relieve the bishop of London of the entire expense of overseeing the overseas church.[25] Archbishop of Canterbury Thomas Herring, however, opposed Sherlock's plan for an American episcopate and the scheme died.[26]

During the spring of 1749, discussions on an American episcopate continued between Archbishop Herring and Hardwicke. Herring suggested to Hardwicke that a settlement of bishops in the colonies without civil authority would be an important element in forging stronger ties between the colonists and the English government, and accordingly a matter worthy of the government's attention.[27] He recommended the kind of Episcopal official first suggested in the colonies by John Talbot of New Jersey in 1706 and that recalls Archbishop Ussher's 1641 plan for maintaining bishops in England at the beginning of the Puritan Revolution.[28]

By August 1749, Sherlock assessed the situation and seemed to have recognised that it was all but impossible to shift from his shoulders the

burden of the administration of the American church. Despite his pleas
the Newcastle government was reluctant to act. Sherlock wrote an angry
letter to Newcastle on 7 September 1749, declaring that 'there is not and
I think, there never was a Christian Church in the world in the condition of the Church of England is now in the Plantations; obliged to send
from one side of the world to the other to get ministers ordained to officiate in their congregations'.[29] To support his position he drafted a
memorial 'relating to Ecclesiastical Government in his Majesty's
Dominions in America'.[30] Sherlock declared that a bishop was necessary
to perform the rites of confirmation and ordination, and provide
supervision over the clergy and churches. Following in Herring's footsteps he emphasised that such a prelate would not have the civil powers
that Episcopal officers practised in England and that no bishop would
reside in New England or Pennsylvania, as a gesture to the power and
pressure of the Congregational and Presbyterian Church leaders in
those provinces.[31] Now, however, Archbishop Herring was opposed to
the plan. He and the politicians understood that the creation of an
American episcopate was a political question and that there could be
damaging domestic repercussions from an untimely agitation for a
colonial prelate that would be troublesome to both the church and the
government. Sherlock was left standing alone, abandoned by both
church and state leaders on this issue.[32]

During the following year, Sherlock made little progress promoting
the need for bishops for the colonies. Hardwicke told Newcastle, on 13
March 1749/50, that the proposal for an American bishop would be laid
before the king and Council for their consideration. The message was
clear and unchangeable, the government and the archbishop of
Canterbury were unalterably opposed to the establishment of an
American prelate. The proposal was delayed, and postponed at a meeting of the Council on 11 April 1750 and all hopes for settlement of the
longstanding matter were gone.[33]

Perhaps as a last resort and desperate effort to apply external pressure
on the government, Sherlock next sought to enlist a meeting of the
S.P.G. on 8 May 1750, to consider the question of the appointment of
an American bishop. For more than half a century, the S.P.G. had been
intermittently advocating a colonial episcopate in one form or another.
The government, which tightly controlled all state patronage including
the appointment of bishops at home, was furious that the proposal was
being considered independently, outside of civil offices. It was a potentially troublesome turn of events. Sherlock, taking charge of the
Society's proceedings, boldly urged that a letter written by him be sent

to all colonial governors soliciting their comments on the matter. Doubtless the bishop of London was aware that his leadership and the Society's action intersected and interfered with the government's supervision of the royal instructions to the provincial officials and the development of imperial policy. The project, a matter of civil and ecclesiastical significance, was abruptly suspended.

Horatio Walpole, suspecting that if the bishop of London's plan was made public the Dissenters in England would strenuously protest to the proposal, sought the advice and guidance of the Duke of Newcastle on the matter.[34] Walpole also expected that the High Church and Low Church parties within the Church of England would be hostile to the project. He believed that if the matter were brought before Parliament, the step would offer a good occasion for bringing out party differences that had been latent since the Jacobite uprising of 1745. By the end of 1750, Archbishop Herring reported that nothing was stirring for an American bishop, the two-year effort had failed despite the support for his position by proposals from Hardwicke and bishops Thomas Secker and Joseph Butler.[35]

Sherlock found it difficult to rest easy under the inaction of the government, and his discontent found ready expression in a letter of May 1751 to Dr. Philip Doddridge, a Dissenter with congenial ties to many of the latitudinarian prelates. He wrote, 'For a Bishop to live at one end of the world and his Church at another must make the office very uncomfortable for the Bishop and in a great measure useless to the people'. Sherlock's reply to the situation was to refuse to receive a commission for the exercise of colonial jurisdiction. The consequence was to prolong and increase the muddle over supervision of American church affairs that had existed since the death of Bishop Gibson.[36] It soon became apparent that the government had finished with the matter of bishops for America. In 1752, Sherlock confessed to Samuel Johnson of Stratford, Connecticut, 'I am afraid that others, who have more power and influence, do not see the thing in the light we do, and I have but little hopes of succeeding at present'.[37]

As the 1750s progressed, Sherlock became less and less able to cope with the business of the American colonies, even had he been so inclined. In 1758, his health was so bad that not only was writing out of the question, but his voice was so weak that it was all but impossible for him to dictate his letters. In these circumstances, what little business with the American colonies was carried on was conducted mainly by Dr. Samuel Nicholls, the bishop's chaplain.[38] Time had taken its toll, age and declining health made him resolute in this policy of inactivity and

Sherlock almost totally ignored the American church during his last years as bishop of London.

During the 1740s, the positions of the Congregational and Anglican adversaries sharply differed. Hobart's objections to the expansion of the English church in Connecticut were raised in a period of an increased number of Congregational ministers, who were converted to the church, and the expanding number of missionaries and missions in the colony that were sponsored by the Society. Between 1720 and 1750, the number of active Anglican parishes in Connecticut increased from one to five, with at least quarterly services held in 24 outlying communities.[39] Hobart's remarks on the nature of the ministry, however, revisited the themes that were expressed in the pamphlets of Edward Wigglesworth and Jonathan Dickinson during the 1720s and 1730s.

Bishop of London Thomas Sherlock's strong-willed efforts to persuade civil officials to appoint a colonial bishop, in the late 1740s and in 1750, was a strong commitment on his part for a more adequate supervision of the overseas church. Building on the occasional and modest efforts of his predecessors on the matter – Henry Compton, John Robinson, and Edmund Gibson – Sherlock presented his proposal at the highest level of government. The hope of colonial clergymen and the bishop of London for an American prelate remained unfulfilled.

6

Jonathan Mayhew Fears a Bishop and Challenges the Purpose of the S.P.G.

In the late 1750s further official ecclesiastical response in England to colonial Episcopal critics had been muted. Archbishop of Canterbury Thomas Herring, also the president of the S.P.G., suffered serious health problems, beginning in 1753, and never fully recovered his physical capacity. In the same year Bishop of London Thomas Sherlock, the prelate assigned with jurisdiction over the colonial church by the Board of Trade, had been incapacitated with a paralytic stroke severely limiting his official duties and he gave no further attention to American affairs.[1] As the men were appointed to office by the Crown for life, no other prelate assumed their duties.

Changed circumstances set a new course for leadership in both the church and state. Thomas Secker, bishop of Oxford, was translated on 21 April 1758 to the see of Canterbury in succession to Herring and his appointment immediately signalled the prospect of strong official interest in American affairs. As early as 1741, Secker championed the cause of an American episcopate in his celebrated Anniversary Sermon before the members of the London-based S.P.G.[2] In America, the parsons had renewed hopes that their long-time request for an American bishop would soon be fulfilled.

Secker's appointment sent two powerful and contradictory messages. For leaders of the church in the colonies there was an improved hope that the vigorous advocate for an American bishop, in 1741, would forcefully renew his effort. For Dissenters in both the colonies and England, that prospect rekindled old fears. As primate of the English church, Secker was also ex officio president of the London-based S.P.G. and a favourable example of an orthodox eighteenth-century prelate. He abhorred 'enthusiasm' and deprecated the influence and progress of Methodism, though he was receptive to its earnestness and piety.

67

His long-time support for an American prelate invited escalating rhetoric regarding that post and the purpose of the S.P.G. missionaries in the provinces.[3]

A radical Congregational minister Jonathan Mayhew led an unceasing challenge against episcopacy and the work of the S.P.G. in New England. He was the minister of the West Church in Boston and historians have called him the founder of American Unitarianism. A 1744 alumnus of Harvard, Mayhew, by 1763, was known on both sides of the Atlantic by liberal Dissenters and latitudinarian Anglicans like Bishop Benjamin Hoadly for the publication of his collection of *Seven Sermons* in 1749.[4] His direct attack on the doctrine of the Trinity stirred up much opposition from his fellow colleagues in New England. Mayhem's radical theology and liberal politics made him one of the most controversial yet respected figures in the region. He was one of the last great colonial preachers, and while trumpeting a new dawn for religious and political liberty, he led the intellectual forces for rationalism and Whiggery in his day.

As early as 1754, Mayhew began to criticise the Society for using funds to proselytise Dissenters that he said were intended for work among the Indians. Like Increase Mather, he also turned his criticism against the Church of England itself. Mayhew felt the institution was tarred with the Roman brush, echoing a familiar sixteenth-century Puritan message that 'We ought not to go wholly over to that apostate church which the scriptures sometimes intend by the name Babylon, we ought not to conform to, or symbolise with her, in any of her corruptions, and idolatrous usages; but to keep at as great a distance from them as possible, by strictly adhering to the holy scriptures in doctrine, discipline, worship and practise'.[5]

It was Mayhew's understanding, in 1758, that with the accession of Secker to the see of Canterbury, there may be an effort by London officials to appoint a bishop for the colonies. If such a turn of events were true, he felt it was a threat to the civil and religious liberties of the colonists. He immediately wrote to Thomas Hollis, a prominent London Whig, for advice and help. Mayhew also was very suspicious that Archbishop Secker and the London-based S.P.G. would terminate the charter for the Society for the Propagation of Christian Knowledge Among the Indians of North America, a Congregational missionary programme for the native Americans. His suspicions proved accurate when the Society's charter was disallowed, reinforcing Mayhew's mistrust of the Church of England.[6]

Thomas Hollis was a grandnephew of the generous benefactor of Harvard College of the same name. Trained as a lawyer, he continued the philanthropic interests of his uncle and spent hundreds of pounds a year for books which he gave to libraries in England and America.[7] Mayhew's first letter to Hollis was a grateful acknowledgement of his gift of books to the Harvard College library.[8] The tie between the two men, one a strong-willed and unorthodox Boston minister and the other an eccentric but generous philanthropist, became candid and supportive. They were intellectually compatible spirits. Both men were actively concerned with the extension and protection of civil and religious liberties. Hollis particularly favoured the writings of the seventeenth-century republicans, Sydney, Harrington, Marvell, and Milton. He edited Toland's *Life of Milton*, in 1761, and two years later Sidney's *Discourses Concerning Government with His Letters;* followed by Locke's Two Treatises on Government (1764) and Locke's Letters Concerning Toleration (1765). He remarked to Mayhew that 'Algernon Sydney, Milton, and honest Ludlow are my heroes'.[9] He sent copies of the works of these authors to Mayhew for distribution to the libraries at Harvard, Yale, and Princeton.[10] Hollis, who never held public office, considered himself a republican and a true Whig. Not an active church-man, he was suspected of atheism, although his *Memoirs* published in 1780 by the heterodox Archdeacon Francis Blackburne of Cleveland, indicate he was a man of unusual piety.

An intense phase of the Anglican controversy was launched by the recently ordained Society missionary at Christ Church in Cambridge, Massachusetts, East Apthorp. He was the son of Charles Apthorp, a prominent and wealthy Boston merchant with lucrative commercial ties that bridged the Atlantic, and had attended and graduated from Jesus College at Cambridge University. An able student, he earned the Chancellor's Prize in 1755 and was elected a fellow of his college (1758–61). Back in Massachusetts, his sermon at the opening of the recently built church on the edge of Cambridge Common and near Harvard College on 15 October, 1761, entitled *The Constitution of a Christian Church*, was a stout defence of the London Society and its efforts to evangelise the Indians.[11] His sermon was a rejoinder to Mayhew's comments on the matter and he recommended to his audi-ence that the 'ranging lawless tribes must be collected into communi-ties, and fixed to settled habitations. Thus situated, they will find the want and the benefit of arts and commerce; which should be restrained to the simpler and more necessary articles, with a strict prohibition, both of fraudulent dealing, violence, and injustice in our own traders, and of whatever commodities may vitiate their manners or extinguish the glimmering light of nature. ... Whatever the policy of the State can effect in making them men, may successfully be followed by the zeal of the Society in making them Christians'.[12] He urged the ministers of every religious group to endorse such a benevolent policy.[13] Despite Apthorp's apologia on behalf of the Society's activity among the native American population, the primary target of its work was in the Mohawk River valley of New York rather than in Massachusetts or in the New England region.

A countercharge to Apthorp's sermon in Cambridge was published by Charles Chauncy, one of the pastors of the First Church in Boston, where he was a pre-eminent leader in church affairs in New England and was ex officio a member of the Harvard Board of Overseers.[14] Welcomed into the ministry with the right hand of fellowship by Cotton Mather, Chauncy was a profound scholar, a liberal, an Arminian, and an Old Light firmly opposed to George Whitefield and the Great Awakening. His interest in the issue of episcopacy was long-standing, perhaps shaped in part by his colleague, Thomas Foxcroft, the senior minister at the First Church, who had contributed the 'Appendix' to Edward Wigglesworth's 1724 reply to John Checkley, *Sober Remarks on a Book Lately Reprinted at Boston ... In a Letter to a Friend*, regarding the legitimacy of Presbyterian ordination.[15] Chauncy may have been influenced, too, by the conversion to the Church of England, in 1732, of his brother-in-law, the attorney Addington Davenport, who was the eldest son of the magistrate, judge, member of Council, and secretary of the province of the same name, and who in turn immediately sought ordination in London. Perhaps anticipating an awkward family dispute, Chauncy immediately set to work hunting out every book he could find on the Episcopal controversy. The fruit of his research was an enormous manuscript giving a 'Compleat View of Episcopacy', which he proposed in 1734 to publish by subscription. Unlike circumstances 10 years earlier, Boston seemed little interested in the issue and the book would not appear in print until 1771.[16]

Chauncy's first public declaration of concern was his Dudleian Lecture at Harvard College delivered on 12 May 1762, *The Validity of Presbyterian Ordination*, which was a significant part of his intellectual arsenal. He presented a cogently argued challenge to Anglicans, attacking the cornerstone of his opponents' argument.[17] Chauncy emphatically proclaimed that bishops and presbyters were scripturally and historically 'officers of equal rank, who are promiscuously called either bishops or presbyters, [and] were endowed with all the ordinary powers proper to be exercised in the church of Christ, with that of ordination, as well as those teaching, baptizing and administering the Lord's supper'.[18] He argued, as had his predecessors for more than a century and a half, that ordinary pastors or presbyters had the power to ordain, refuting the notion that bishops were successors to the Apostles, declaring that the Apostles according to scriptural evidence had no successors.[19] Drawing extensively on historical scholarship, Chauncy convincingly notes that the early Church Fathers, except Ignatius, speak of bishops and presbyters in the same language, 'that the power of ordination was not deposited in the hands of bishops as distinguished from presbyters, but that bishops or presbyters, meaning by these terms one and the same order of officers, were vested with power to ordain in the church of Christ, and consequently that ordination by a council of presbyters, as practised by these churches, is valid to all the ends of the gospel ministry'.[20] By implication, Chauncy's argument suggested that ordination by bishops is neither historically valid nor necessary. Ministers could readily and legitimately fulfil the task of ordaining men for the ministry.

Both Chauncy and Mayhew drew in large measure, too, on the writings of Micaiah Towgood in advocating their anti-episcopacy arguments. Towgood, a Presbyterian minister in Exeter, England, was an accomplished if not original scholar of civil and ecclesiastical history, of Greek and Latin, and familiar with a vast number of theological writings.[21] He was also a persistent student of the scriptures. As a writer, Towgood was essentially a synthesiser of Puritan scholarship in history and theology of the period since the sixteenth-century Reformation. Towgood contributed a series of controversial publications such as *High-Flown Episcopal and Priestly Claims Examined* (London, 1737), *The Dissenting Gentleman's Third ... Letter to ... Mr. White, in Answer to His Two Defences of His Three Letters* (London, 1738), *The Dissenter's Apology* (London, 1739), *Recovery from Sickness* (London, 1742), *The Dissenting Gentleman's Answer to the Reverend Mr. White's Three Letters* (London, 1746), *An Essay Towards Attaining a True Idea of the Character and Reign of King Charles the First* (London, 1748), and *The Baptism of Infants* (London, 1750). The writings were popular with Dissenters on both sides of the Atlantic. In America it was Mayhew and Chauncy, both frequent correspondents with Towgood, who arranged for editions of his works to be published. The two men arranged for the publication of Boston editions of *The Baptism of Infants in 1765, and Recovery from Sickness* in 1768.[22] Chauncy took the lead in arranging for the publication of the fifth edition of *The Dissenting Gentleman's Answer* in 1748, and in 1768 the fourth edition of *A Dissent from the Church of England Fully Justified*.[23]

The Dissenters, of whom Towgood was a prominent spokesman for more than a generation between 1740 and 1780, expounded two pivotal doctrines: the authority of the Bible as against the authority of tradition, and the nature of the gathered Church as independent from the Establishment. Towgood asserted in the *Dissenting Gentleman's Answer* that the Church of England is a Parliamentary Church, an Erastian institution, of which the King is the supreme head. 'The Church is a mere creature of the State, and that neither the Convocation assembled, nor priests or bishops, have any power and authority to decree or repeal a single rite or ceremony, or establish a single article of faith. All authority of this kind is lodged in the King and Parliament, they only can make and unmake forms and rites of worship, prescribe to the clergy what they are to believe, and preach'.[24]

Responding to a rumour that Governor Francis Bernard and others were seeking to establish a bishop in the colonies, Mayhew wrote to Hollis requesting his assistance.[25] The Boston parson wanted to enlist the support of prominent Dissenters in England in opposition to the proposal.[26] Hollis replied to Mayhew's plea commenting that although the colonial episcopate had been discussed for a long time, that it 'is not unlikely, some time or other to take place. I do not think, however, that it will be attempted at present, but whenever it is and succeeds, I shall be heartily concerned at it'. He recommended to Mayhew Jasper Mauduit, the agent in London for the Massachusetts provincial government, as the person to orchestrate opposition to the plan with leaders among the Dissenters and at Whitehall.[27] At bottom, Mayhew's debate with Anglican apologists during the 1760s was his opposition to some of the Thirty-nine Articles, the Anglican liturgy, the activities of the S.P.G. in New England, and the rumour that Governor Francis Bernard was involved in a plan for sending a bishop to America.[28]

Rushing to defend the Society's work in the colonies was East Apthorp, the minister at Christ Church in Cambridge, who replied to the amusing but disparaging account of the ministry of Ebenezer Miller of Braintree in the *Boston Gazette* of 21 February 1763, with the tract *Considerations of the Institution and Conduct of the Society for the Propagation of the Gospel in Foreign Parts* (Boston, 1763).[29] He now argued that the fundamental purpose of the Society since its founding was to serve first the English colonists, 'to instruct our own people in the Christian Religion, and that they may live amongst them as their settled and resident ministers'.[30] Apthorp claimed that the Society's secondary, but charter-driven, purpose was to carry the gospel to all heathens who will receive it, with no specific assignment or restriction to serve the

Indians.[31] Declaring that the Society was given large latitude to govern its own affairs by its charter, he referred to the extensive work of the organisation among the Mohawk Indians in New York.[32] His defence of the S.P.G. was the strongest yet from the pen of a colonist.

Mayhew rebutted Apthorp's position and immediately offered a moderate statement of the New England position.[33] He noted that 'the constitution, worship and discipline of the Church of England [is] much less agreeable to the word of God than our own; yet he has a high veneration for many persons of that communion, as persons of great learning and wisdom, candor and piety'.[34] Observing that there was no essential theological difference between the English church and the New England churches, Mayhew admitted that the latter were more inclined to Calvinism.[35] But he argued that the Society was neglecting its missionary purpose to promote a mere party. He piercingly asserted with a sense of humour that the Society should have been called 'The Society for propagating the church of England in those parts where the administration of God's word and sacraments is provided for after the congregational and presbyterian modes'.[36] He emphasised that the New England system did not establish the Congregational Church, but only required towns to have learned and orthodox ministers of their own choice. In this regard, the laws used the word 'orthodox' to mean 'Protestant'. He did not point out that the Harvard Board of Overseers had secretly redefined 'orthodox' so as to exclude Anglicans as members. Mayhew concluded that the Anglican parishes, established in New England towns and villages by the Society and at great expense, 'have in short all the appearance of entering wedges; or rather of little lodgements made in carrying on the crusade, or spiritual siege of our churches, with the hope that they will one day submit to an Episcopal sovereign. And it will appear at least probable in the sequel that it is the true plan and grand mystery of their operations in New England'.[37] The forceful argument advanced by Mayhew declared 'that the Society have long had a formal design to root out Presbyterianism and to establish both Episcopacy and Bishops in the colonies. In pursuance of which favourite project they have in a great measure neglected the important ends of their institution ... It is hardly possible to account for the Society's conduct without supposing them to have had such a design'.[38] Furthermore, referring to recent efforts in London to appoint a bishop in the colonies and the construction of Apthorp's grand house in Cambridge, Mayhew pointedly noted that 'it is supposed by many that in a certain *superb edifice* in a neighbouring town [Cambridge], was even from the foundation designed for the Palace of one of the *humble successors* of the apostles'.[39]

At Mayhew's prompting, Hollis arranged for the tract opposing the plan for a colonial prelate to be published in London and distributed to influential officials.[40] As Mayhew had undertaken on behalf of Micaiah Towgood the publication of his works in Boston in the early 1750s, Hollis now reported in detail his arrangements for the printing in London of Mayhew's *Observations* with East Apthorp's *Considerations* annexed to it.[41] He later arranged for the London publication of Mayhew's *Defence* and sent copies to his Boston correspondent. Hollis cautioned the Boston parson that 'You are in no real danger, at present, in respect to the creation of Bishops in America, if I am rightly informed; though a matter extreamly desired by our Clergy and Prelates, and even talked of greatly, at this time, among themselves. You cannot however be too much on your guard, in this so very important affair'.[42]

Hollis dispatched to Mayhew three copies of 'a very *artful* tract ... intitled "An Answer to Dr. Mayhew's observations on the Charter and Conduct of the Society for the propagation of the Gospel in foreign parts" ... I am confident it is either written by the A[rch]B[ishop] himself or by one of his Chaplains or Dependents, with very great corrections by him'. Hollis told Mayhew that he had known Archbishop Secker for over 20 years and

> that since his elevation to the Primacy, and the observation that he left Popery unnoticed, widespreading, intolerant, overturning Popery, and yet prosecuted with bitterest severity, *Anet*, a poor old speculative Philosopher; that he shewed no hearty affection to Liberty of any sort, nor those men who loved it; that he trod with glee the mired Court paths; and juggled for Fame with his own order who yet would never grant it him, knowing him well to be an Irregular and Interloper amongst them from the medical Tribe; I had declined in my visits to him'.[43]

Mayhew informed Hollis that he had received from Israel Mauduit a copy of the *Answer to the Observations*. He noted that 'People here generally suppose, whether truly or not, that the A[rch]B[ishop] of C[an]t[erbur]y had at least a considerable hand in this *Answer*; which, I think, is a very plausible performance. It has lately been reprinted here; and my *Remarks* there on, published this Week, I send you by this opportunity'.[44] Mayhew acknowledged that he incorporated into the text Hollis's valuable suggestions. Declaring, 'it is my fixed resolution, notwithstanding many discouragements, in my little sphere to do all I can for the service of my country – Ne Republica, aut Ecclesiae

Nov-Anglicanae *aliquid detrimenti capiant*; – how little soever that may be, which is in my power'.[45]

Ever seeking new information to bolster and support his cause, Mayhew asked Hollis to send to him copies of the last two Anniversary Sermons preached before the members of the Society and to include the abstracts of the S.P.G.'s financial statements and accounts of the assignments and statements of service of its missionaries.[46] Hollis immediately sent to his Boston friend the requested materials and offered strategic advice for the next step in the challenge to the Anglican establishment. He cunningly suggested to Mayhew that 'The Society seems to me the next to be attacked, if any persons (in a tract of smallest size, pruning hard upon yourself as is the present publication, and yet harder, to strengthen, brighten, not lessen the matter and spirit of it) turning the fort of it on the *Apthorpian* and most shameful passage in their last printed account; praising the Body but lashing the Leaders; with a digression to the Arch-Leader, more or less direct, that You, an *open* man, and with a name to You, have, to pull off the mask, or endeavour it, of an Adversary who deals hard blows without a name, pretending constantly to candor, good manners, and friendliness'.[47]

Mayhew reported to Hollis that 'Mr Apthorp, the Cambridge Missionary, is lately and suddenly gone for England, and it is commonly supposed that he will not return to live in this country'.[48] Hollis suggested that Apthorp was a spy for the Archbishop of Canterbury, and that his return to England 'must have been a thorough mortification to the A[rch]B[ishop], who begat and sent him out such; and the Fathers of New England should crown with oak Leaves the Man, who, by his sole judgement and energy hath forced it'.[49] Mayhew never suspected that Apthorp was a spy writing to Hollis 'nor did I ever hear before, that he was suspected to come hither in that *honourable* Capacity. When I delivered the Discourse ... in our College Chapel, against Popery, I could scarce refrain from some strictures on *another church*, so zealously propagated among us of late years – But on the whole, thought it more advisable to refrain'.[50]

In New England, the debate drew into the arena several minor participants on the Anglican side. Arthur Browne, minister at Queen's Chapel at Portsmouth in New Hampshire since 1736, pointedly remarked that Mayhew's words were designed 'to create ill blood, and to stir up strife and contention amongst those, who generally speaking, have lived and conversed together upon very good terms, I mean churchmen and Dissenters'.[51] Furthermore, the parson added, Mayhew seeks 'if possible, to scare people from the Church, by giving a most terrible idea of it and of the bishops'.[52] In character with the rhetoric of the day, Browne proclaimed that 'These and such like were the fanatic ravings of his predecessors the Oliverian holders-forth, whose spittle he hath lik'd up, and cough'd it out again, with some addition of his own filth and phlegm'.[53]

The minister of King's Chapel in Boston, Henry Caner, endlessly refuted Mayhew's pamphlet line by line, although devoid of his adversary's style, scholarship, or reasoning.[54] Reporting to Secker in early January 1763, he declared that the position of the English church in Boston and Massachusetts was tenuous, 'We are a rope of sand; there is no union, no authority among us. We cannot even summon a convention for united council and advice, while the dissenting ministers have their monthly, quarterly, and annual associations, conventions, etc., to advise, assist and support each other in many measures which they shall think proper to enter unto'.[55]

From Lancaster in Pennsylvania, the Irish-born and Irish-educated Thomas Barton commented on the controversy and informed the Secretary of the S.P.G. that 'The establishment of Episcopacy in America has been long talked of and long expected; and I humbly beg the Honourable Society's pardon if I should take the liberty to observe that this would never, in any former time, be introduced with more success than at present. Many of the principal Quakers wish for it, in hopes it might be a check to the growth of Presbyterianism, on the other hand, would not chuse to murmur at a time when they are obliged to keep fair with the Church whose assistance they want against the combination of the Quakers, who would willingly crush them'.[56]

Ezra Stiles, the Congregational minister at Newport, Rhode Island, shared Mayhew's sentiments regarding the potential political impact of the appointment of an American bishop. He was a familiar figure with Anglicans in Connecticut and Rhode Island because he had been approached by church members in Newport in 1752 and in Stratford, Connecticut, in 1755 to serve as minister of their congregations while practising law and serving as a tutor at Yale.[57] His reluctance to accept either post was based on his sentiments 'at this time, [were] inclined to deism. I was not disposed to profess a mode of religion, which I did not believe, for the sake of a living. If Christianity was true, it was no doubt with me, whether Episcopacy and the Liturgy were a part of it. If the former rested on divine authority, the latter, I was certain, rested on human'.[58] By the summer of 1755, Stiles accepted the pastorship of the Second Congregational Church of Newport.

On 23 April 1760, Stiles delivered a sermon before a convention of the Congregational ministers of Rhode Island at Bristol entitled, *A Discourse on the Christian Union* (Boston, 1761).[59] He proposed a union of the colony's Baptist and Congregational churches,[60] as the differences between the two religious groups on doctrine, such as grace, baptism, the Lord's Supper, ordination, and polity, were minor details compared to their common agreements.[61] He further amplified that 'we agree in the sufficiency and validity of Presbyterian ordination. This was the ordination practised by the apostles, and among the Christians of the first and second centuries'.[62] He examined in some detail the ceremony of pastoral investiture, observing that 'from the beginning [it] was performed by co-ordinate presbyters or pastors; with whom the apostles left the conferring of holy orders in all the succeeding ages of the church'.[63] The Newport parson took sharp note of this different procedure with the English church, the difference being in the power and work of bishops and priests. Stiles declared that there was no scriptural source for such a practice, and that in the early church there is evidence that ordinations were performed by presbyters too.[64] Stiles concluded that 'the whole Protestant world, except the Church of England, agree in the validity of presbyterian ordination'.[65]

Stiles proclaimed in his *Discourse on the Christian Union*, 'we desire to live in peace and harmony with all – nor do we attempt to proselyte from any communion. We desire only equal Protestant liberty. And even our Episcopal brethren must confess that we treat them with much greater lenity, charity, and Christian benevolence, than they treat our congregational brethren in England'.[66] Nonetheless he felt the church posed a greater threat to liberty, both in England and in America, than any other single institution.

Stiles sensed that the Anglicans seemed to be reaching for power through the service of the S.P.G. missionaries. His fear was that when they had enough power they would achieve their long-sought ambition for the American church, to duplicate the bishops, archbishops, and all the other officers of the English establishment. If the Anglicans established a hierarchy in America, Stiles forecast that their bishops would claim superiority by divine right over denominations, which had no such pretensions. Furthermore, the bishops would expect all the rights and privileges enjoyed by English prelates, including state support and civil powers, and courts exercising jurisdiction over morals and the probate of wills. He felt that such an establishment would be a step back in the trend towards religious liberty, a movement that found the Rhode Island community in the forefront. Political freedom and religious freedom were inseparable concomitants of free inquiry and a free society.[67]

Recognising that bishops could not be established in America without the co-operation and approval of the English government, Stiles had given some thought to the prospect that the declining fortunes of the church in England would be rebuilt in America. He presumed that with a bishop in every colony they would have at their disposal many offices of the kind on which political power is built and maintained, and would curtail the freedom that would otherwise restrain them. In Maryland, Virginia, and South Carolina, Anglicans held nearly all political offices, and in the northern colonies under royal control they held most of the offices filled by appointment from London.[68]

Edmund S. Morgan has commented that the Newport parson's fears were fuelled by the British effort to stifle American commerce with the Sugar Act of 1764, and the stamp tax on legal forms, newspapers, and other documents.[69] The customs enforcement and taxation was merely the opening round of a general attack on American liberty, and Stiles was not surprised when the churchmen and Loyalists in Newport took the opportunity to strike a blow at Rhode Island liberty from within.[70] A small group of Anglicans, including some of the local customs officers together with a few renegades from other denominations, drew up a petition to the King to revoke the Rhode Island charter and establish a royal government.[71] A government that would inevitably be run by Anglicans, an unconscionable prospect in Rhode Island, where the denomination comprised only a small fraction of the population.[72]

When the Fast Day came around again in April 1764, the petition for royal government was already under way and Stiles could be more explicit about the perils to liberty than he had been the year before. Like Increase and Cotton Mather, he reminded the congregation of the dangers that New England liberty had survived in the past: in 1635 when Archbishop Laud had headed a commission to recall colonial charters and in 1685 when James II consolidated New England into one dominion under the tyrannical rule of Sir Edmund Andros. God had ultimately thwarted these efforts, said Stiles, but not before weak and corrupt men had shown themselves ready to sacrifice their country's liberties for royal favours. The same danger had now appeared in Newport.[73]

About the time that the Anglican clergy of New York and New Jersey in convention prepared their petition to the king for the appointment of an American bishop in 1765, Ezra Stiles fell into discussion with a gentleman from Massachusetts who gave him 'inside' information of affairs of church and state. The informant had told Stiles that the charters of Connecticut and Rhode Island would certainly be revoked, and that new laws would be enacted in which it was intended to remove the financial support of the Congregational ministers. With the loss of such support, the informant suggested that the Congregational parsons might be ready to consider the plan for establishing bishops in New England and the other colonies. After reordination some of the region's most distinguished ministers would be made bishops, deans, prebends, or archdeacons. Furthermore, the presentation of ministers to churches would be removed from the hands of the laity and put into the hands of the royal governor.[74]

In November 1766, a congress of Congregational ministers from Connecticut and Presbyterian ministers from New York, New Jersey, and Pennsylvania met at Elizabeth Town, New Jersey. Stiles developed the plan for the meeting which called for an annual general assembly of two delegates from each Congregational association and each presbytery, the place of meeting to rotate. The Newport parson intended that the assembly would evaluate the prospects of uniting the two churches and to advocate that cause. The assembly would 'recommend Loyalty and Allegiance to the Kings Majesty and a peaceable Submission to the public Laws and Government; and also to address his Majesty or the Kings Ministers from Time to Time with Assurances of the public Loyalty of the Churches comprehended in this Union – or with vindications of the united Denominations as a religious Body from the Aspersions with which they have been or shall be Vilified by their Episcopal Fellow Protestants, who cease not to represent us as disaffected and Enemies to the Kings Person and Government'.[75] Stiles amended the draft and deleted reference to the Episcopalians. When the congress assembled in November, he was not present. In New England the plan received little support. Connecticut Old Lights were sceptical of the scheme; they feared that the union would spur the Anglicans to new efforts. Transatlantic correspondence indicated that the English hierarchy had so far been unresponsive to the pleas by colonial parsons for a bishop. But the Newport minister's plan drew no support from a church or association in Massachusetts and Rhode Island.[76]

Stiles originally conceived the union partly as a means of protecting the apostolic Calvinist churches from attacks by the Anglicans. Yet he declared that the union should not be 'an offensive Measure to oppugnate Episcopacy'. Rather, the purpose should be to perpetuate the pure religion of Christ 'unsowered with polemical Divinity and Controversy'. The members should not devote themselves to opposing other sects, Anglican or otherwise. Never should they throw their united weight 'into any political scale whatever'.[77]

The Rhode Island parson believed that nothing should be done against the design for establishing bishops in America, but preaching the familiar Puritan doctrines. 'It will be our duty indeed to represent the Truth to our people, and write on the Episcopal Controversy. Let us do it with Candor, as we have without all Question Justice Truth Scripture and primitive Antiquity on our side. But let us not be wro't upon by political Enemies to espouse any political Measures as a Body'.[78] On these principles, Stiles opposed any formal action by the churches against the movement for a colonial bishop.

Mayhew's contribution to the long-standing criticism of the English church by Puritan and Congregational leaders crystallised the debate for the remainder of the colonial period. His pamphlets synthesised and elaborated on the issues of disagreement and formed the further discussion by both ecclesiastical and civil leaders. On the one hand, Mayhew's works raised the alarm of a possibly imminent appointment of a bishop, questioned the purpose of the missionaries of the S.P.G. in the provinces, and renewed the charges of the papist format of the Anglican liturgy. The genealogy of his arguments were in a direct line of thought from the writings of Increase and Cotton Mather, Noah Hobart, and several other prominent New England Congregational critics of the church. Mayhew believed that the possible appointment of a prelate and the agents of the S.P.G. represented a conspiracy by the English government to undermine the established church in Massachusetts and proselytise its members.

While on the other hand, the Boston minister's writings laid a solid foundation for the subsequent publications of Ezra Stiles and John and Samuel Adams. Their articles and essays shifted the direction of the controversy to an examination of the civil authority of Parliament to create a prelate, form dioceses, and impose tithes on the public to support clergymen at the expense of civil and religious liberties to others.

7
Pleas for an American Bishop in the 1760s: Archbishop of Canterbury Thomas Secker and Thomas Bradbury Chandler

After receiving news of the appointment of Thomas Secker as arch-bishop of Canterbury in 1758, clergymen in the Middle Colonies vigorously renewed an interest in an American bishop. They recalled that 17 years earlier Secker, when he was the bishop of Oxford, had strongly supported an American prelate in his Anniversary Sermon delivered before the members of the S.P.G. at St. Mary-le-Bow Church in London.[1]

Political circumstances too had changed in England with the accession of the young prince George III to the throne on 25 October 1760. He succeeded his grandfather King George II and his reign marked the beginning of a new era in England's history with a growing sense of patriotism, and a public euphoria that civil affairs would take an improved course over the previous government. This enthusiastic burst of national pride was shaped by the favourable news arriving nearly daily in London of military victories on distant battlefields – in America, the West Indies, and on the continent.[2] Accompanying the new era of leadership of the church and state was the English government's vigorous strategy to implement stronger imperial economic and military policies overseas. Not since the age of Bishop of London Henry Compton and Queen Anne, 60 years earlier, had there been a convergence of civil and ecclesiastical leadership and policies that potentially favoured the church in America and the appointment of an American prelate.

The end of warfare between France and England in 1763 also marked the close of the era of 'Salutary Neglect' by the British government towards American affairs. Faced by a large post-war debt, heavy taxes at home, and the necessity of supporting an army in America, the ministry of the Earl of Bute sought revenue from the colonies. Successive tax acts, the Sugar and Currency Acts of 1764 and the Quartering and Stamp acts of 1765, opened a new and conflicting epoch in Anglo-American relations.

A band of clergymen within easy distance of one another in Connecticut, New York, and New Jersey emerged in the 1760s, not only as the advocates of the church's interests in the region but by their publications as articulate representatives of the church at large.[3] Included in this coterie were several of the talented protégés of Samuel Johnson of Stratford, Connecticut, and the first president of King's College in New York City. He was one of the six 'Yale Apostates', of 1722, who converted from Congregationalism to the Church of England and was recognised as the 'dean' of the church in Connecticut. Among the entourage were several Yale College graduates such as Thomas Bradbury Chandler of Elizabeth Town, New Jersey, who was also a convert to the English church, and Samuel Seabury, Jr., of Burlington, New Jersey, and later of Westchester County, New York. An Englishman and Oxford University graduate Myles Cooper, Johnson's successor as president of King's College, joined the company. These four men, all strong-willed and intellectually competent, were the primary leaders of the church in the region during the 1750s, 1760s, and 1770s.

But it remains unclear if these leaders of the church decided among themselves to summon a convention of their colleagues in the Middle Colonies, in 1765, or if the task fell only on the shoulders of Chandler to initiate the call. Conventions were frequently held in Connecticut, New York, and New Jersey during the two decades before the American Revolution. In New Jersey 15 gatherings took place between 1758 and 1765.[4]

Gathered in an atmosphere of the political turmoil surrounding the implementation of the Stamp Act of 1765, the participants at the session bluntly criticised the short-sightedness of the various administrations of the English government in fulfilling the needs of the overseas national church. Since the early years of the eighteenth century, little, if any, progress had been made to strengthen the overseas church. This lamentable situation, they argued, was all the more despicable because the English church had been a vital national instrument for teaching loyalty to the crown and government to their congregations. They reminded London officials that their efforts were in contrast to the Congregational ministers who urged a separation both of church and state from England.[5] The delegates to the session presented a plan to the bishop of London, 'that the bishops to be granted are only to exercise those powers which are essential to the office with jurisdiction over none but the professors of the Church. Although this is less than could be reasonably expected in a Christian country, as we know of no instance since the time of Constantine in which bishops have not been invested with a considerable share of Civil power, yet we shall be glad to accept it, and are in hope it will be sufficient'.[6] The limited civil and ecclesiastical authority of the office was a departure from Episcopal practice in England, although the responsibilities of the proposed official followed to a letter the 1764 suggestions of Archbishop Secker in his pamphlet *An Answer to Dr. Mayhew's Observations*.[7]

Conventions of parsons in other colonies had voiced the need for an American episcopate, although with varying opinions. In Connecticut, the men pleaded for a prelate at their meetings in 1764, 1765, 1766, and 1771, but took the matter one important step further.[8] Recognising that a bishop would not be acceptable in certain provinces and doubtless with an eye to defusing, at least partially, the criticism of Congregational clergymen, the Connecticut clergymen judiciously urged that a prelate be sent to a colony outside New England. The gesture may have been a subtle tactic to urge and support the appointment of Chandler, of Elizabeth Town in New Jersey, as an American bishop.

The Massachusetts ministers, a tiny minority in an overwhelmingly Congregational colony, reported to the bishop of London, in 1768, that the state of the church in New England was as good as could be expected in the circumstances. They declared that 'all that we are able to do in these times is only to cultivate among the people committed to our care a spirit of peace and patience under the various insults to which they are exposed for refusing to join in the popular clamours that now prevail'.[9] The delegates did not mask the English church's need for a prelate in the region. They reported to the bishop of London that 'we are neither allowed to speak nor scarcely to be silent unless we join with those who we believe to be labouring in the destruction of our constitution, civil and religious. The civil Government is too weak to afford us protection; and ecclesiastical superior we have none on this side of the Atlantic, from whom we may receive timely advice or direction under our present trials'.[10]

Demonstrating an exasperation with the continuing incompleteness of the church's organisation, the Connecticut parsons in convention wrote to Bishop of London Richard Terrick during the 1771 session asking, 'What have the sons of the Church in America done, that they are treated with such neglect and overlooked by Government? An American episcopacy is essential, at least to the well-being of Religion here'.[11] Seeking further official consideration and a resolution to the dilemma, the petitioners urged Terrick to share their sentiments with

Archbishop of Canterbury Frederick Cornwallis and Lord Hillsborough, Wills Hill, Secretary of the Colonies.[12]

Renewing his interest in the affairs of the American church in 1764, Archbishop Secker published a response to Jonathan Mayhew's criticisms of the purpose of the S.P.G. missionaries in the provinces *An Answer to Dr. Mayhew's Observations on the Charter and Conduct of the Society for the Propagation of the Gospel in Foreign Parts*.[13] As the titular head of the Church of England and an accomplished preacher with a reputation as a diligent diocesan administrator, his reply was a strong and positive signal that London officials recognised the seriousness of Mayhew's charges.[14] But Secker was wearing another hat too as the president of the S.P.G. It was more than a symbolic association as the archbishop of Canterbury automatically served as head of the governing board of the organisation and had been a participating member of the body for at least three decades. On both counts, he was the ideal person to present an Anglican response to Mayhew's challenges and the pamphlets of earlier Congregational church critics.

After reading Mayhew's *Observations*, Secker recounted in his publication that the Boston minister's book was written, 'partly against the Church of England in general, partly against the conduct of the Society for the Propagation of the Gospel, in settling ministers of that Church in the Massachusetts and Connecticut; partly against appointing bishops to reside in His Majesty's American Colonies'.[15] In detail, Secker refuted the several categories of Mayhew's charges: that the Constitution and worship of the Church of England were unscriptural; that many of its clergymen were corrupt; and his criticism of the placement of S.P.G. missionaries in Massachusetts and Connecticut towns.[16] He declared that its missionaries had not been sent to New England or the other provinces 'with a formal design which they have long had, to root out Presbyterianism' and disavowed Mayhew's claim that the Society had done little to minister to convert the blacks and Indians.[17] The archbishop suggested, perhaps with his tongue in cheek, that the leaders of the S.P.G. would undoubtedly be very glad, 'if all the inhabitants of the colonies were of the Communion of the Church of England, as undoubtedly the Doctor [Mayhew] would, if they were all of his Communion, but they have sent no persons to effect this'.[18]

In response to Mayhew's assertion that the English church was maintained in communities where other churches had been settled earlier, Secker emphasised that the real conduct of the Society, in those provinces in which the church was not established and churches were not Episcopal, was to 'contribute towards supporting public worship and instruction amongst such members of the Church of England, as cannot in conscience comply with the worship and instruction of other congregations in their neighbourhood, and yet cannot wholly maintain ministers for themselves.[19] He added that the 'Missionaries are not sent to New England for the purpose of making proselytes to episcopacy'.[20]

Pressing his argument further, Secker argued that in a land where there is any pretence of toleration, the members of the church should enjoy the privilege of a complete range of its services and ministry including bishops and other necessary officers.[21] He emphasised that all members of every church are, according to the 'Principles of Liberty intitled to every Part of what they conceive to be the Benefits of it, entire and complete, so far as consists with the Welfare of Civil Government'.[22] Secker observed that members of the English church did not enjoy its 'Benefits, having no Protestant Bishop within 3,000 miles of them; a Case, which never had its Parallel before in the Christian World'.[23] He urged that two or more Bishops may be appointed for the colonial church, 'to reside where His Majesty shall think most convenient; that they may have no concern in the least with any person who do not profess themselves to be of the Church of England, but may ordain Ministers for such as do; may confirm their Children, when brought to them at a fit age for that purpose, and take such oversight of the episcopal clergy, as the Bishop of London's Commissaries in those parts have been empowered to take, and have taken, without offence'.[24] Reassuring his nonconformist readers that such colonial prelates would not enjoy the civic duties undertaken by English bishops, Secker stated 'it is not desired in the least that they should hold Courts to try Matrimonial or Testamentary Causes, or be vested with any Authority, now exercised by provincial Governors or subordinate Magistrates, infringe or diminish any Privileges and Liberties enjoyed by any of the Laity, even of our own Communion'.[25] His plan was not new and had been mooted by prominent English ecclesiastical leaders since 1750. Soon after the publication of his essay, Secker wrote to the Society's missionaries in the colonies and urged them to conciliate with Mayhew as an attempt to diminish the heat of the controversy.

Not ready to relinquish the argument, Mayhew raised his pen and replied to a critical pamphlet by his neighbour Henry Caner, minister of King's Chapel, and Secker's tract in two separate pamphlets.[26] Addressing the archbishop's *Answer*, the Boston clergyman begins by pointing out that he understood and enumerated Secker's reasons for advocating an American episcopate to be, in substance (1) 'to rule and govern well those people who are desirous to be committed to their charge', (2) 'to defend and protect both the clergy and the laity', (3) 'to unite the clergy themselves, and reduce them to order', and (4) 'to confirm new converts from schism ... in ordaining ministers from amongst themselves; in confirming weak brethren, and blessing all manner of people susceptible of such holy impressions, as are made by the imposition of the bishop's hands'.[27] Mayhew admitted that the proposal is presented from 'a more plausible and less exceptionable point of view' than he had ever seen it presented from before, for the reason that the bishops here suggested are, first, not to meddle with those not churchmen; secondly, not to have any power in matrimonial or testamentary cases, or to infringe on the functions of the governors and magistrates, or in any way diminish the powers of the laity, and lastly, not to be settled in any but Episcopal colonies.[28]

Mayhew feared the future if prelates should come to the colonies with the limited powers proposed, it was unlikely, from the nature of their relations with their English associates, that such officials would long be contented to maintain a position inferior to theirs, 'without any of their temporal power and grandieur ... and consequently wanting that authority and respect which, it might be pleaded, is needful. Ambition and Avarice, never want plausible pretexts, to accomplish their end'.[29] At all events the colonists are much safer without bishops; for, if they were once settled, 'pretexts might easily be found for increasing their power'.[30] By the establishment of bishops, the number of Anglicans might increase to such an extent as to attain a majority in the legislatures, and thereby secure, perhaps, not only an establishment of the Church of England in the colony, but also taxes for the support of bishops, test acts, ecclesiastical courts. These matters were, at this time, all the more worthy of consideration, because the colonists had already got wind of the fact that 'high-church tory-principles and maxims' had, under the new king, once more found favour since their overthrow in 1715 and 1745.[31]

Despite Mayhew's intellectual differences with his Congregational church colleagues, Samuel Hopkins (1721–1803), the distinguished theologian and reformer, declared his appreciation for the Boston minister's challenges to the presence of the English church and the missionaries of the S.P.G. in New England. He noted that Mayhew 'certainly deserves the thanks of his country for what he has done in this matter'.[32] Perhaps the most rewarding words came from the Boston ministers who voted Mayhew their thanks for the *Observations*.[33]

Mayhew's criticism of episcopacy was not limited to the Church of England. He attacked the polity and traditions of the Roman Catholic

Church in his Dudleian Lecture at Harvard in May 1765.[34] Observing that for New England Congregational ministers, their controversy with the Roman church was not merely a religious one, the Boston preacher declaimed that New England's ministers defended the worship of one God by one Mediator, Jesus Christ, 'in opposition to that of a thousand demons or idols, of the authority of the sacred oracles, in opposition to that of idle legends and traditions, and of sober reason in opposition to the grossest fanaticism'. The response of New England's clergymen was in 'defence of their laws, liberties, and civil rights as men, in opposition to the proud claims and encroachments of ecclesiastical persons, who under the pretext of religion, and saving men's souls, would engross all power and property to themselves, and reduce us to the most abject slavery'.[35] Mayhew's words were spoken soon after the close of the Seven Years' War and with the knowledge of the Catholic presence northwards in Quebec, then a part of Britain's North American empire.

The central subject on the agenda of the convention of New York and New Jersey clergymen held at Perth Amboy, in October 1765, was a discussion of the need to respond to Mayhew's criticisms of the English church. The driving force behind the meeting was Thomas Bradbury Chandler, minister of St. John's Church in Elizabeth Town, New Jersey, and a missionary of the S.P.G. since 1751. A determined strategist, he sought consensus among the ministers for the need for a colonial prelate and presented a draft text on the issue. His aim was to publish a tract that would be addressed to a larger audience than earlier pamphlets on the subject, to a reading public beyond the limited corps of interested Anglican and Dissenter ministers.

Chandler acknowledged in his tract *An Appeal to the Public* that it was written at the suggestion of his mentor, Samuel Johnson of Stratford, Connecticut, the former president of King's College in New York, and that the convention of the New York and New Jersey clergy had discussed a draft of the work and voted to publish it.[36] It was dedicated to Archbishop of Canterbury Thomas Secker, a gesture that prompted some critics to claim that Chandler was seeking the post of bishop for himself.[37] The session discussed and summarised the historical record over 65 years of repeated requests to officers of the London Society by provincial clergy meeting for a bishop.[38]

Chandler's pamphlet, *An Appeal to the Public* addressed three general themes: the origin and nature of the Episcopal office, the reasons for sending bishops to America, and the basis on which the appointment was proposed. His primary theme was that 'the Church in America, without an Episcopate, is necessarily destitute of a regular Government, and cannot enjoy the Benefits of Ordination and Confirmation'.[39] His design was to present to the 'Public, the Necessity and Importance of Episcopacy, in the Opinion of Episcopalians, and to shew the wretched Condition of the Church of England for Want of Bishops'.[40] Chandler declared that the colonial clergy could do little as a body without a bishop as the ministers were independent of each other and had no ecclesiastical superior.[41] Reciting familiar themes he indicated that a prelate was needed also for two basic reasons: for the men who needed his advice and encouragement, and for those persons who required pastoral discipline.[42] Again the complaint was presented that noted the substantial expense incurred by native colonists who travelled to London for ordination, a situation that he believed was a primary cause for the lack of clergy in the colonies.[43]

Citing three reasons why prelates had not been established in the colonies, Chandler wrote that: first, that as the country was originally settled by private adventurers chiefly of a dissenting faith, Anglican bishops had not been needed; second, that the Puritan Revolution in England in the 1640s and 1650s had kept the English government too occupied on other matters to attend to the spiritual wants of the American clergy; and third, because English civil officials were reluctant to infringe on the religious liberties of the Dissenters.[44] Now, however, after the close of the French and Indian War, he thought the time was ripe for consideration of an American episcopate.[45]

Chandler was also attempting to convince those persons who feared that the extension of Episcopal officials would be prejudicial to the integrity of their civil or religious liberty.[46] He described that the duties of an American bishop would not include any civil authority and that the office would be purely spiritual in nature and have jurisdiction only over the clergy. The prelate would not have any responsibilities over the church's lay members or the members of any other religious group.[47] Nor would the proposed officer, unlike his English counterpart, have any authority for the probate of wills, letters of guardianship and administration, or marriage licenses, nor would ecclesiastical courts be set up in America.[48] In fact Episcopal responsibilities would be limited to the ordination and governance of the clergy and the confirmation of church members.[49] Under Chandler's format, no bishop would sit in the upper house of the provincial legislature in the manner of English prelates in the House of Lords. He deftly noted that he advanced the proposal without a 'Desire to molest the Dissenters, or any Denominations of Christians, in the Enjoyment of their present religious Privileges, that we have carefully consulted their Safety and Security, and studied not to injure, but oblige them'.[50] Chandler acknowledged the intense opposition in New England and the Middle Colonies to the prospect of an Anglican bishop and observed that the sentiment 'has the Nature of Persecution, and deserves the Name' declaring that the Church of England was being unfairly punished for its adherence to traditional historical religious principles.[51] The London newspapers reported during the Stamp Act crisis of 1765 that the discontent expressed by the colonists was due in a great measure to the fear that bishops would be settled among them, a notion that Chandler rejected and asked for proof.[52] He declared that the public response to the Stamp Act was generated by an 'unconstitutional oppressive Act', an opinion expressed by many Anglican and Dissenting clergy alike.[53]

The New Jersey minister claimed that the 'sensible Dissenters' who had considered the proposed format for a bishop are not opposed to it. In England, Chandler noted, the Dissenters find that they can live with Bishops, 'the English Bishops have, for a long course of years, exercised their authority with so much mildness, tenderness and moderation, as scarcely to have afforded an instance of reasonable complaint, especially to Dissenters; and many of the latter have been so generous as to confess it'.[54] Yet he recognised that in earlier times bishops misused their power, but that fact must be understood in the context of the times. Urging that bishops be speedily appointed in the colonies, Chandler was persuaded that to delay the appointment of an American prelate might be irretrievable. He argued that if all religious groups in the colonies were to be tolerated fairly and equally then the English church was entitled to the completeness of its ministry and historical organisation.[55] If bishops were not quickly established in the colonies Chandler offered a dire prediction, he could 'forsee nothing but the ruin of the Church in this Country'.[56] Continuing his remarks, he recounted that 'The Causes indeed, which destroy it here may be local, and not immediately operate in England; but then, that Inattention and negligence in our national Superiors, which would suffer it to be destroyed in the Colonies, must have a general effect, and can produce no Good to the same Church in the Mother Country'.[57]

Chandler persuasively argued that 'Episcopacy and monarchy are, in their Frame and Constitution, best suited to each other. Episcopacy can never thrive in a Republican Government, nor Republican Principles in an Episcopal Church. For the same Reasons, in a mixed Monarchy, no Form of Ecclesiastical Government can so exactly harmonize with the State, as that of a qualified Episcopacy'.[58]

The question of how a bishop would be supported in the provinces had puzzled Dissenters and Anglicans for some time. Chandler suggested that perhaps a special tax would be levied by either Parliament or the provincial legislatures for the purpose.[59] Broaching the subject from another perspective, he discussed the history of tithes in the Church in England, suggesting that such a procedure could be considered in the colonies.[60] In the aftermath of the Stamp Act protests and in the midst of provincial objections to the Townshend duties, his timing on the matter was at best hazardous. He candidly recognised that many Americans were apprehensive about the imposition of a tax to support a prelate, explaining that in England tithes enjoyed a long-standing historical and legal precedent.[61] But Chandler noted that 'Tithes cannot be demanded by Bishops in this Country, because there are none belonging to the Church; they are demanded in England only because they are due to the church.'[62] Only an act of Parliament could extend tithes to the provinces, he remarked.[63]

Pursuing the issue further he asked, 'Shall we not be taxed in this country for the support of Bishops, if any shall be appointed?'[64] Not at all, Chandler replied, but that if a tax would be levied and a sum raised to support as many as three prelates, such a 'tax would not amount to more that four pence in one hundred pounds' and added that it would not be a hardship on the country.[65] Chandler concluded commenting that 'no tax is intended nor will be wanted' as an endowment fund had been established of the previous fifty years for such a purpose and had been supplemented with several bequests.[66] Chandler's position on a possible tax to support an episcopate was contrary to Archbishop Secker's claim three years earlier that the approval of such a levy by Parliament was impossible.[67]

The spirited defence of the English church, by a handful of the missionaries of the S.P.G., and the need for a colonial bishop by Archbishop Secker and Thomas Bradbury Chandler against Jonathan Mayhew's charges did not advance the position of any of the religious parties. No bishops were appointed to serve the church in America and the programme of the Society continued without interruption. The 80-year-old episcopacy controversy was at an impasse; despite the efforts of Secker and Archbishop of York Robert Hay Drummond to persuade high-ranking civil officials of the need for appointing a colonial prelate, they received no encouragement. The next and final round of the debate, lasting until the outbreak of the War for Independence, would be shaped not by Dissenter or Anglican ecclesiastical leaders but by radicals John and Samuel Adams in Boston and John Wilkes in London.

8
A Radical Response to a Bishop: John Adams, Samuel Adams, and John Wilkes

During the 1760s and early 1770s, the pamphlet controversy over the prospect of an American bishop, advocated most recently by Thomas Bradbury Chandler and opposed by Charles Chauncy, was dramatically transformed and brought to the attention of a wider public audience. The debate became the centre of a propaganda strategy that was designed and executed by leaders of the Sons of Liberty in Boston, Samuel and John Adams, and the radical John Wilkes in London.[1] Each of these men was an accomplished essayist and contributed essays or arranged the publication of such material in Boston, New York, Philadelphia, and London.

The long-standing and familiar plea by colonial Anglican church leaders for a bishop became absorbed in the emerging anti-imperial political rhetoric and criticism of the English policies that had been enacted following Parliament's passage of the Stamp Act in 1765 and continued until 1776. A key architect of the anti-Anglican rhetoric during the period was Samuel Adams (1722–1803), who was the son of a Boston merchant and maltster and a graduate of Harvard College in 1740. He attained an M.A. degree three years later, when he defended the thesis that it is 'lawful to resist the Supreme Magistrate, if the Commonwealth cannot be otherwise preserved' a theme that would guide his civic activity during the years ahead.[2] He was a second cousin of John Adams and burst on the political stage in the 1760s and 1770s, when he whipped up opposition to the Sugar Act (1764), the Stamp Act (1765), and the Townshend Acts (1767). In 1768 he drew up the Circular Letter to the other colonies denouncing the acts as taxation without representation.[3] With the help of John Adams and John Hancock, he was the key organiser of Boston's Sons of Liberty in 1765.[4] Adams was one of the organisers of the Non-Importation Association in

1768, and played an important role in the agitation that culminated in the Boston Massacre two years later. A member between 1765 and 1774 of the Massachusetts colonial legislature (General Court), Adams played a prominent role in public affairs until the end of the War of Independence.

Frequently employing his pen for articles in newspapers and pamphlets, Samuel Adams stirred up sentiment against the British. He helped to foment revolt through the Committees of Correspondence and his polemic was a powerful inspiration behind the Boston Massacre and the Boston Tea Party. He wrote political essays for publication in the *Boston Gazette* over more than 25 names.[5] Both John and Samuel Adams spent nearly every Sunday afternoon at printer Benjamin Edes's office assisting him in the preparation for the Monday issue of the *Boston Gazette*.[6]

A vigorous political essayist with a keen sense of historical and legal principles, John Adams (1735–1826) was a lawyer in Braintree, Massachusetts, and a graduate of Harvard College in 1755. Admitted to the bar in 1758, he first came to public notice in 1765 with his essays attacking the Stamp Act in a series of articles in the *Boston Gazette*. As a prominent Boston attorney he defended John Hancock against charges from the Customs Office in 1768 and 1769, and defended the British soldiers tried for murder in the Boston Massacre in 1770. Adams served in the Massachusetts General Court in 1770–1, the Revolutionary Provincial Congress in 1774–5, and was a Massachusetts delegate to the First and Second Continental Congresses in Philadelphia from 1774 to 1778.

The earliest indication of John Adams's sentiments regarding the English church in the colony occurred in 1764 and related to the activity of the S.P.G. in New England. In a 1764 letter to his cousin Dr. Cotton Tufts, the distinguished Boston physician, Adams objected to the presence of the Society in the region, prompted by receiving news that Archbishop of Canterbury Thomas Secker had published a reply to Jonathan Mayhew's *Observations on the Conduct of the Society*.[7] As early as in February 1756 he recorded in his diary that he was familiar with Mayhew's writings and that the Congregational minister of Boston's West Church embraced unorthodox theological doctrines.[8] At the same time Adams also recorded that he was reading *The Independent Whig* by Thomas Gordon and John Trenchard, noting in particular their critical remarks of the Episcopal office.[9] Writing to Tufts about Secker's letter, he declared that

> The Answer they say is extremely elegant, delicate, genteel and all that. If so I believe the Drs. People had an old sermon last Sunday.

The Archbishop of Canterbury has the credit of the answer. If this credit is just, the —s Genius will be roused and will produce something that Messrs. Reviewers will be puzzled to Name. I suppose you have heard or read, that they have Christened the *Observations*, the Devils Thunder Bolt, full of contents weighty and urged home.

This Controversy I hope will prevent the future Waste of the societies Money in the Maintenance of Insects that are Drones in the Cause of Virtue and Christianity, but the most active and industrious of the whole Hive in the Cause of Hierarchical Policy. [10]

John Adams delineated his views on church and state in an essay, 'Dissertation on the Canon and Feudal Law', a tract of the times and published in the *Boston Gazette* in 1765.[11] It was not a scholarly account but rather a summary of the struggle for freedom in human history and how that freedom might be preserved and maintained.[12] It was published after Adams learnt of Parliament's passage of the Stamp Act in March 1765, a statute that in his words was an 'enormous Engine, fabricated by the British Parliament, for battering down all the Rights and Liberties of America'.[13] He declared that 'Since the promulgation of Christianity, the two greatest systems of tyranny that have sprung from this original, are the canon and feudal law. The desire of dominion, that great principle by which we have attempted to account for much good and so much evil, is, when properly restrained, a very useful and noble movement in the human mind. But when such restraints are taken off, it becomes an encroaching, grasping, restless, and ungovernable power'.[14] Adams wrote that 'as long as this confederacy lasted, and the people were held in ignorance, liberty, and with her, knowledge and virtue too, seem to have deserted the earth, and one age of darkness succeeded another, till God in his benign providence raised up the champions who began and conducted the Reformation ... It was this great struggle that peopled America. It was not religion alone, as is commonly supposed; but it was a love of universal liberty, and a hatred, a dread, a horror, of the infernal confederacy before described, that projected, conducted, and accomplished the settlement of America'.[15]

A significant turning point in applying the episcopacy issue to the larger and more popular discussion of objectionable imperial policies occurred in April 1768, when Samuel Adams published three essays entitled, 'Puritan Letters', in the *Boston Gazette* under the pseudonym of 'A Puritan'.[16] He railed about bishops and popery, a long-time target of the earlier Puritan critical attacks on the Church of England. The letters, published soon after the publication of Thomas Bradbury Chandler's pamphlet *An Appeal to the Public*, which sought public support for a colonial Anglican bishopric, suggests that Adams may have been attempting to stifle the appointment of a prelate.[17] He may have also intended to merely raise the spectre of Roman Catholicism active in Boston, an argument that was likely to stir up latent popular fears.[18] The latter seems unlikely because Adams, ostensibly assessing the degree of 'Popery' that existed in various Massachusetts towns, identified communities that had active Anglican congregations and raised questions of the loyalties of the groups to American civil liberties.[19] In part, his comments were reminiscent of Increase Mather's argument that linked The Book of Common Prayer to the offensive Catholic Breviary, Missal, and Ritual on the occasion of the establishment of the first congregation in Boston in 1686.[20] This situation impelled Edward Randolph, the Customs Commissioner in Boston, in his 1689 letter to Archbishop of Canterbury William Sancroft, to write that 'Mr. Mather has published here a book called the Idolatry of ye Common Prayer worship which errudly all of us of that church obnoxious to the common people who account us popish church.'[21] David S. Lovejoy noted that this circumstance exposed the Anglicans to sustained 'malice, scorn, countless affronts, and indignities from the majority who charged them with idolatry and popery'.[22]

In the first 'Puritan Letter' Adams noted that 'I am surpriz'd to find, that so little attention is given to the danger we are in, of the utmost loss of those *religious Rights*, the enjoyment of which our good forefathers had more especially in their intention, when they explored and settled this new world. To say the truth, I have from long observation, been apprehensive, that we have above every thing else to fear is POPERY' ... 'I expect to be treated with sneer and ridicule by those artful men who have come into our country *to spy out our Liberties*; who are restless to bring us into *Bondage*, and can be successful only when the people are in a sound sleep' ... 'There is a variety of ways in which POPERY, the idolatry of Christians, may be introduced into America, which at present I shall not so much as hint at, but shall point then out hereafter in proper order. Yet, my dear countrymen – suffer me at this time, in the bowels of my compassion to warn you all, as you value your precious *civil* Liberty, and every thing you can call dear to you, to be upon your guard against POPERY ... Could our ancestors look out of their graves and see so many of *their own* sons, deck'd with the worst of *foreign Superficialities*, the ornaments of the *whore of Babylon*, how it would break their sacred Repose'.[23]

On 11 April, Adams's second 'Puritan Letter' appeared in the *Boston Gazette* stating 'that he was under a sort of constraint to mention my fears, for I did verily believe, and I do still, that much more to be dreaded from the growth of POPERY in America, than the Stamp Act or any other Acts destructive of men's *civil* rights; Nay, I could not help fancying that the Stamp-Act itself was contrived with a design only to lure the people to the habit of contemplating themselves as the slaves of men; and the transition from thence to a subjection to Satan, is mighty easy.'[24]

Following by a few weeks the publication of Samuel Adams 'Puritan Letters' an article appeared in the *Boston Gazette*, 23 May 1768, most likely by John Adams, under the penname, 'Suri Juris'. His contribution objected to Thomas Bradbury Chandler's pamphlet, *An Appeal to the Public*, supporting the appointment of an American prelate.[25] He argued that the proposal for an American episcopate was

> so flagrant an Attempt to introduce the Canon Law, or at least some of the worst Fruits of it, into these Colonies, hitherto unstained with such Pollution, uninfected with such Poison, in any Form, that every Friend of America ought to take the Alarm, Power, in any Form, and under any Limitations, when directed only by human Wisdom and Benevolence, is dangerous.[26] But the most terrible of all Power, that can be entrusted to Man, is spiritual. Because our natural Apprehensions of a Diety, Providence and future State, are so strong, and our natural Disposition to Enthusiasms and Superstition, so prevalent, that an Order of Men entrusted with the sacred Rites of Religion, will always obtain an Ascendancy over our Consciences: and will therefore be able to perswade us, (by us I mean the Body of the People) that to distinguish between the Cause of God and the Clergy, is Impiety; to speak or write freely of the Clergy is Blasphemy; and to oppose the Exorbitancy of their Wealth and Power is Sacrilege, and that any of these Crimes will expose us to eternal Misery.
>
> And whenever Conscience is on the Side of the Canon Law, all is lost. We become capable of believing any Thing a Priest shall pre-scribe. We become capable to believing, even Dr. Chandler's funda-mental Aphorisms, viz. That Christianity cannot exist without any interrupted Succession of Diocesan Bishops, and that those who deny the Succession to have been uninterrupted, must prove it to have been broken.[27]

Turning again to the role of the English church in the colonies, Samuel Adams, in March 1769, published an essay in the *Boston Gazette* under the pseudonym 'A Layman'.[28] He vigorously disputed the Reverend

Samuel Seabury's criticisms of Charles Chauncy's recent publication, *A Letter to a Friend*, that appeared in Gaines's *New York Gazette*.[29] Chauncy's publication raised questions regarding the purpose of the S.P.G. in the colonies and its financial support of its missionaries. Adams defended Chauncy's interpretation of the matter and characterised Seabury as an 'angry and railing scribbler'.

Seeking to establish a link with an influential English critic of the government's colonial policies, the 'Committee of the Sons of Liberty in the Town of Boston', on 6 June 1768, wrote to John Wilkes expressing their own growing grievances against imperial procedures. A member of Parliament and political radical, Wilkes was to colonial Americans a symbol of public challenge to English civil authority. His conflict with civil authority during the 1760s was well known in the American colonies. After 1768, American patriots carried on correspondence with Wilkes, the defender of liberty, throughout the pre-Revolutionary era.[30] The historian Pauline Maier has written that 'in the years between 1768 and 1770 no English political figure evoked more enthusiasm in America than the radical John Wilkes'.[31] Between 1768 and 1770, Wilkes challenged the authority of the Duke of Grafton, head of the government, and published freethinking parodies of the liturgy that were a feature of Wilkesite propaganda and published in both London and Boston.[32]

Professor J. C. D. Clark has remarked that Wilkes 'was steeped in a radical tradition', and came from a Dissenting family, although he outwardly conformed to the Church of England in order to participate in public life.[33] As early as 1762, Wilkes set up *The North Briton*, a newspaper that attacked, ridiculed, and abused the government of the Earl of Bute.[34] Tried and expelled from the House of Commons for publishing a seditious libel and an obscene libel, he lived mainly in Paris between 1764 and 1768. Wilkes returned to England, in 1768, in hope of securing re-election to Parliament. His successful election in Middlesex was nullified despite the fact that the winner polled considerably fewer votes than Wilkes. He became an alderman of the City of London in 1769, sheriff in 1771, and lord mayor in 1774. Wilkes's return to London from Paris was reported in the *Boston Gazette*, of 30 May 1768.

The 6 June 1768 letter from the Sons of Liberty addressed Wilkes as 'Illustrious Patriot' and concluded with five signatures of leading radical leaders, including that of John Adams. It informed him that 'The Friend of Liberty, Wilkes, Peace and good order to the number of forty-five assembled at the Whig Tavern, Boston, New England, took the first opportunity of congratulating his country, the British colonies and himself on his happy return to the land alone worthy of such an

Inhabitant.' The writers suggested that Wilkes was 'one of those incorruptible honest men reserved by heaven to bless and perhaps save a tottering Empire' and added that nothing but a common interest, and absolute confidence in an impartial and general protection, can combine so many Millions of Men, born to make laws for themselves, conscious and invincibly tenacious of their Rights.'[35]

Wilkes acknowledged to his Boston correspondents that they shared mutual concerns and he promised that 'I shall always give a particular attention to whatever respects the interests of Americans which I believe to be immediately connected with, and of essential moment to our parent country and the common welfare of this great political system'.[36] He declared that 'After the first claims of duty to England, and of gratitude to the County of Middlesex, none shall engage me more than the affairs of our Colonies, which I consider as the *propugnacula imperii*, and I know how much of our strength and weight we owe to, and derive from, them'.[37] Wilkes continued that 'The only ambition I feel is to distinguish myself as a friend of the rights of mankind, both religious and civil; as a man zealous for the preservation of this constitution and our Sovereign, *with all our laws and Native liberties that ask not his leave*, if I may use the expression of Milton'.[38] On receiving his letter, the Boston correspondents called a special meeting of the Committee of the Sons of Liberty to read it aloud. They asked and received from Wilkes permission to publish it.[39] In subsequent months, an exchange of letters continued between members of the Boston Sons of Liberty and Wilkes, including James Otis, Samuel Adams, and John Hancock.[40] Both John and Samuel Adams were elected to membership in Wilkes's Society of the Supporters of the Bill of Rights in London.[41]

During his imprisonment at the King's Bench Prison for printing 'Number 45' and the 'Essay on Woman', Wilkes wrote to the Boston Sons of Liberty on 14 April 1769, declaring that 'The cause of liberty in America as well as here shall always have in me a zealous advocate, and where my little influence extends, it shall be employed in the promotion of it.'[42] Wilkes published his first two replies to the Sons of Liberty in Boston in August 1771, as evidence to disprove charges that he was an opponent of the Americans.[43] He fervently defended his association with the colonists in the London newspaper *The Political Register* declaring, 'The cause of Liberty in America received every assistance I could give on late important occasions by the feeble production of this pen. In no other way could I be useful in prison'.[44] He pleaded with the secretary of the Sons of Liberty, William Palfrey, who was a merchant partner of John Hancock, to send him copies of the American newspapers to inform him on colonial affairs. He repeated this request regularly over the next several years.[45]

Fears of the appointment of an American prelate were recounted in the London press during the winter and spring of 1769. A correspondent writing under the pseudonym, 'Atlanticus', opposed sending a bishop to the colonies, suggesting that the Anglican ministers in America could ordain future ministers and a bishop after the manner of the first Christians and in the apostolic tradition.[46] He felt that two parties were behind the propaganda supporting an Anglican prelate, The Papists and the remains of the High Church party in the English church.[47] The prospect of the appointment of a bishop in America stirred an anonymous author to publish, in 1769, *An Alarm to Dissenters and Methodists*.[48]

Events took a new course for an American bishop in 1769, when a posthumous letter by Archbishop Secker, written on 9 January 1750–1, was published in London on 29 June.[49] The letter was a reply to Horatio Walpole's letter to Bishop of London Thomas Sherlock of 29 May 1750, but its contents, in deference to his lordship's wishes, were not made known until after his death.[50] During the following summer and autumn months, a steady stream of contributions critical of the appointment of a prelate appeared in the *London Chronicle or Universal Evening Post*, a triweekly publication of political and government information founded in 1757, and in the newspapers of Boston, New York, and Philadelphia.[51] Presumably to soften the opposition, a writer under the name, 'An Episcopal Realist', favoured the appointment of a 'Primitive or Scripture Bishop than a Church Bishop', implying a spiritual official rather than a prelate also fulfilling political duties.'[52]

Secker's argument, having been composed in the mid-course of the eighteenth-century controversy, helps the reader to appreciate the later publications that attacked and defended the plan.[53] The archbishop's suggestion was not new but argued for a colonial episcopate similar to Bishop of London Henry Compton's proposition in 1707.[54] It urged the appointment of a suffragan bishop for the provinces, an official serving under the supervision of the bishop of London and without the requirement of Parliament's approval.

Secker's purpose was to consider whether the proposal to send two or three bishops to America, to perform the Episcopal offices and to exercise such jurisdiction as had been formerly, or might be in the future, exercised by the Bishop of London's commissaries, would be reasonable and practicable. He was also seeking to determine, as Walpole seemed to apprehend, whether the power acquired by such bishops, once established, would, in the nature of things, be stretched to the extent of introducing exorbitant ecclesiastical-political innovations, thereby causing uneasiness, friction, and political adversity both in England and in the colonies.[55]

Of the 'reasonableness of the proposal abstractedly considered' Secker thought there could be no doubt. Walpole himself, he said, admitted that much, and there could have been 'scarcely a bishop of the Church of England from the [Puritan] revolution to this day who had not desired such an establishment. Any fair-minded man', he goes on, 'must see that for the necessary purposes of ordination, confirmation, and discipline, bishops are indispensable to the very existence of the Church of England in the colonies'.[56]

Having shown that the demand for American bishops was both just and reasonable, Secker's letter raised the objection that such an establishment may be attended with a dangerous increase of the church's power in the colonies. He saw no likelihood or possibility of such an event. The commissaries had neither attempted nor been able to extend their authority beyond its original limits in any of the colonies where they had been appointed; he declared 'Bishops will be still more narrowly watched by the Governors, by other Sects, by the Laity, and even the Clergy of their own Communion'.[57] The archbishop explained that there was nothing in the plan to excite any apprehension in England or the colonies. Nor had there ever been any design to tax the colonists or burden the crown for the support of the bishops to be settled in America. He reminded Walpole that an earlier effort to establish a bishopric in Virginia had failed, for the reason that it was to be funded out of the customs receipts. Secker stated that the present plan on the table had nothing of the character of a state establishment; it did not have to go to Parliament for approval, since the law permitted the ordination of suffragan bishops with only the royal assent. Therefore, the bishop of London could send suffragan bishops to the colonies created as his commissaries, but with the power to ordain, confirm, and exercise ecclesiastical jurisdiction.[58]

Finally, the archbishop proclaimed that not only was the demand for such an establishment reasonable and its aims and motives independent of any political design, but that it seemed unlikely that it could be opposed by the majority of the colonists. He suggested that, as a matter of public policy, the refusal of the request for a bishop would hurt the government more in the eyes of the Church of England than the amount of favour which the policy would secure from the Dissenters.[59] Doubtless Secker, mindful of the political consequences of his request, was stating a position Walpole felt must be taken to preserve the government's political support of Dissenters in England.

The timing of the release of the 1750 Secker letter in 1769 poses the questions: Were subsequent newspaper articles orchestrated through a connection between the Sons of Liberty in Boston and John Wilkes? Did Samuel or John Adams, or William Palfrey directly ask Wilkes to seek publication of the Secker letter in a London newspaper? I have concluded that the circumstances suggest that it is quite likely that Wilkes, a ceaseless critic of the government, was the moving force behind the publication of the article in the *London Chronicle*.[60] Wilkes had demonstrated through the years a flair for controversy and the means to promote the propaganda of a cause. He was a long-time friend of the radical English bookseller John Almon, the founder and printer of the *The Political Register* in 1767 that had published many articles generated by Wilkes that offended civil authorities.[61] It is likely too that Wilkes arranged for the publication of the following] satirical image in the *Register*, in September 1769, of an illustration that depicted 'An Attempt to Land a Bishop in America'.[62] It presented a frightened prelate ascending the shrouds, praying with clasped hands reciting a line from the Nunc Dimittis, 'Lord, now lettest thou they Servant depart in peace', two irate bully boys push *The Hillsborough* away from a Boston quay with a boat hook. On deck beside a coach are its wheels, an Episcopal crook, and mitre. On shore, a turbulent 'mob' is assembling: a man flourishes a flag with a liberty cap and motto, *Liberty & Freedom of Conscience*; two others wave copies of *Locke and Sydney on Government*; a third throws *Calvin's Works* at the bishop; a sober Quaker holds a copy of *Barclay's Apology*; and a bystander shouts, 'No Lords Spiritual or Temporal in New England'. In the foreground a monkey is about to throw a cap at the bishop. Near it lies a paper marked, 'Shall they be obliged to maintain Bishops that cannot maintain themselves'. An image that could have effectively bolstered the arguments presented by Samuel Adams's essays, 'Puritan Letters', that appeared in the *Boston Gazette* in 1768.

The next phase of the debate over an American bishop erupted from a rural corner of Yorkshire, England, and from the pen of the Reverend Francis Blackburne, archdeacon of Cleveland. It remains unclear how he was drawn into the debate on a colonial prelate, although he was no stranger to contentious argument. Perhaps the connection was made by his friend Thomas Hollis, publisher of Blackburne's *Confessional* in 1766, who urged the disputatious archdeacon to publicly comment on the subject.[63] Later Blackburn compiled and published the *Memoirs of T*[homas] *H*[ollis].[64] It also may be that as Hollis and John Adams maintained a

llustration 8.1 'An Attempt to Land a Bishop in America', *The Political Register,* September 1769, 5: facing 119.

regular exchange of correspondence, the Boston lawyer, no stranger to executing a strategy for propaganda purposes, asked Hollis to recruit an Anglican cleric to rebut Secker's posthumous letter. Another possible link was John Wilkes, whom Hollis admired, as their publications were by the same London printer and bookseller, John Almon, an association that may have cemented a bond of purpose.

Blackburne replied to Secker's letter with *A Critical Commentary* (London, 1770; Philadelphia, 1771).[65] A native of Richmond in Yorkshire and graduate of St. Catherine Hall at Cambridge University, Blackburne was a student of the liberal principles of Locke's politics from his undergraduate days. His church preferment was doubtless arrested by his principles and his decision never again to subscribe to the Thirty-nine Articles. In 1754 Blackburne started the Anti-subscription movement. Apparently Arian at heart, he opposed the need of episcopacy, confirmation, and confessions of faith. Blackburne circulated, in 1771, a petition for application to Parliament for relief from subscription to the Liturgy and Articles.[66] The petition was rejected by Parliament, though Archbishop of Canterbury Frederick Cornwallis was not averse to a revision of the Prayer Book, the bishops feared that it would disturb the peace, and wisely dropped the scheme. Since 1750 Blackburne had published essays critical of the Church's services; the theology of his college friend, Bishop William Law, on the topic of the 'sleep of the soul; and his best work, 'The Confessional, or a full and free inquiry into the right, utility, and success of establishing confessions of faith and doctrine in Protestant churches'. Thomas Hollis published the manuscript anonymously in May 1766. A lively controversy followed.

Blackburne launched his criticism of Secker's letter by suggesting that Walpole probably did not begin the discussion, since the ministers of state were not then anxious to offend the dissenting colonists.[67] The cause of the trouble must be the Bishop of London, who as diocesan of the colonial clergy of the Church of England, would understandably seek by all means in his power to improve their condition. But whoever was to blame for starting the agitation for an American bishop, Blackburne thought that all must regret the publication of Secker's letter at this late period in the debate, when the colonists should not be needlessly aggravated.[68] He rebutted Secker's arguments and suggested that the whole scheme was the outgrowth of the machinations of the S.P.G. Blackburne introduced the notion that the S.P.G. had conspired to stir up its missionaries in the colonies with a petition to English officials for bishops. He maintained that Apthorp, Chandler, and the other Anglican pamphleteers were merely instruments in the London Society's hands.

Even so ardent and powerful an advocate as Bishop Sherlock, to whom the matter owed much of the momentum and attention which it had received since 1750, argued that the archdeacon proceeded not so much from his own initiative as from the encouragement of the Society.[69]

The archdeacon declared that the motives influenced the Dissenters in England to take the side of their colonial brethren because 'They knew the hardship of the legal disabilities under which they themselves lay at home. They had good reason to believe that the influence of the established Hierarchy contributed to continue this grievance'.[70] Blackburne observed that the Dissenters in America were as yet free from the shackle of episcopacy, and that their well-being rested on maintaining the status quo. He continued that 'If Bishops were let in among them, and particularly under the notion of presiding in established Episcopal Churches, there was the highest probability they would take their precedents of Government and Discipline from the Establishment in the Mother Country, and would probably never be at rest' till they had themselves secured an establishment based on an exclusive test.[71] English Dissenters, then, knowing that their brethren across the Atlantic were of their mind, had determined to cooperate vigorously with them.

On 5 March the Boston Massacre occurred, expressing the community's resentment at the quartering of British troops in the town, during which three persons were killed and two wounded mortally. It was followed by a lull in public agitation against the British government until 27 April 1773, when the House of Commons passed the Tea Act, providing for full remission on teas exported to the American colonies.[72] The American opposition to the statute centred not upon the duty but upon the threat of monopoly. Mass meetings were held in the colonial seaport towns protesting the act. On 29 November, the Sons of Liberty in Boston branded tea importers enemies of America and pledged a boycott. On 16 December, Samuel Adams gave the signal for a disciplined group of men disguised as Mohawk Indians to board the British ship *Dartmouth* and dump all the tea into the harbour.[73] In response to this escapade, Parliament passed what were later to be known as the 'Intolerable Acts', which called for the revocation of the colonial charter of Massachusetts and the closing of the port of Boston.[74]

In late 1772 the Freeholders of Boston published *A List of Infringements and Violations of Rights complained of by the American Colonists*.[75] Among the issues in dispute was the prospect of the appointment of an Anglican bishop, noting that 'As our Ancestors came over to this country, that they might not only enjoy their civil but their religious rights, and particularly desired to be freed from Prelates, who in those times cruelly persecuted all who differed in sentiment from the established Church; we cannot see without concern the various attempts which have been made, and are now making, to establish an American Episcopate'. Declaring further that 'Our Episcopal Brethren of the colonies do enjoy, and rightfully ought ever to enjoy, the free exercise of their religion, we cannot help fearing that they who are so warmly contending for such an establishment, have views altogether inconsistent the universal and peaceful enjoyment of our Christian privileges; and doing or attempting to do anything which has even the remotest tendency to endanger this enjoyment, is justly looked upon a great grievance, and also an infringement of our rights; which is not barely to exercise, but peaceably and securely to enjoy that liberty with which Christ hath made us free'.[76]

Finally, the Freeholders stated 'that no power on earth can justly give either temporal or spiritual jurisdiction within this Province except the Great and General Court. We think therefore that every design for establishing the jurisdiction of a Bishop in this Province, is a design both against our civil and religious rights. And we are well informed that the more candid and judicious of our brethren of the Church of England in this and the other Colonies, both Clergy and Laity, conceive of the establishing of an American Episcopate both unnecessary and unreasonable'.[77]

The passage of the Quebec Act by Parliament, on 22 June 1774, provided a continuing opportunity for American radical critics to challenge English imperial policies.[78] It was intended to afford greater rights to the French inhabitants of Canada, which had come under British rule through the Treaty of Paris in 1763. The statute established a new governor and council to govern affairs in Quebec; the French civil code was officially recognised in Quebec, but English criminal law would continue to prevail in criminal matters; recognition was also given to the Roman Catholic church in Quebec: this was an important gesture because Catholics were previously ineligible for public office in the province.

The Quebec Act was not part of Lord North's colonial punitive programme, but many Americans missed the distinction and regarded the law as another 'Intolerable Act'. Opposition to the act among colonists focused on several issues, particularly New England Congregational Church leaders who feared that the Catholic Church in Quebec would extend its influence and activity southwards into their communities. The provincial suspicion of a resurgent Roman Catholic France in North

Illustration 8.2 'The Mitred Minuet', London, *The Political Register*, July 1774, 43: 312; Boston, *The Royal American*, October 1774.

America was one of the prime reasons why early in the War for Independence, the Americans would invade Quebec in an effort to end the threat. Reaction from the colonies was to expedite the opening of a Continental Congress and when the Massachusetts legislature met in Salem on 17 June 1774, Samuel Adams locked the doors and made a motion for the formation of a colonial delegation to attend the session.[79]

The First Continental Congress met in Philadelphia from 5 September to 26 October 1774 to protest the Intolerable Acts. During his time in the Congress, Samuel Adams was one of the most vocal proponents of independence. He was one of the strongest advocates of the Suffolk Resolves, drafted and adopted in early September 1774 by representatives from the towns in Suffolk county, Massachusetts, in response to the Intolerable Acts.

The Intolerable Acts and the Quebec Act raised again the prospect that the English government would appoint an American prelate. Recalling an illustration published in 1769 following the release of Archbishop Secker's letter, the July 1774 issue of *The Political Register* published a new satirical image on the same theme, entitled 'The Mitred Minuet'. Presented below, it depicts the Devil hovering over England's most influential politicians, Lord North and Lord Bute, and a group of Anglican bishops outfitted in lawn sleeves, presumably seeking together to accomplish a long time objective of establishing a colonial Anglican prelate, or approving recognition of the Roman Catholic Church in Quebec.[80] After the arrival of the publication in Boston, the engraver and silversmith Paul Revere, accurately copied the plate for publication in the October 1774, issue of the *Royal American Magazine*.[81] Perhaps the image was merely reproduced to illustrate a topic of current interest in London. It seems more likely that its appearance was to underscore the purpose and political purpose of the current sessions of the First Continental Congress in Philadelphia. The image was a visible reminder for the reader of the link between the English church and the State and the leaders responsible for developing and executing imperial policies.

9

The Controversy over a Bishop in the Colonies outside New England

From the era of Increase Mather to the age of Paul Revere, Boston was the centre of opposition to the English church in the colonies. The debate over an American bishop and the purpose of the missionaries of the S.P.G. never became vigorously declaimed intercolonial issues. There was little sustained interest in the controversies in such communities as New York, Philadelphia, Williamsburg, and Charles Town. Occasionally in the Middle Colonies, pamphlets or newspaper articles appeared from the pen of a Congregational or Presbyterian church leader warning the reader of the consequences of an Anglican prelate. But absent from such challenges was a Congregational or Presbyterian critic of the calibre of Increase or Cotton Mather, Jonathan Mayhew, or Charles Chauncy.

The situation prompts the question: Why was the issue of an American bishop of less interest and prominence in the provinces outside of New England? The answer lies in the differing social and religious characters of the Middle, Chesapeake, and Southern Colonies. Unlike Massachusetts and the other New England provinces that were peopled primarily from the Bay Colony's overflowing population, the settlers of the colonies from New York to Georgia were peoples of diverse national origins.[1] Virginia initially was the exception to this pattern of settlement. In Virginia and Maryland the English church was the dominating religious group while religious diversity was the mark of the Southern Colonies. Despite the church's official status in the two regions, no church group carried the comparable authority and influence in community affairs, as did the Congregational church in Massachusetts and Connecticut. There was no religious group in the Chesapeake and Southern Colonies that voiced opposition to the English church and its officials in a prolonged and enduring manner.

Every American colony had its own distinctive social, political, and religious history; yet for the settlers of Massachusetts and Connecticut in particular, there was a shared heritage forged by their English and early colonial experiences during the sixteenth and seventeenth centuries. A legacy that was marked in Massachusetts by such controversies and divisions as the trial of Anne Hutchinson, the exile of Roger Williams to Rhode Island, the hanging of the Quaker Mary Dyer, and the trial of the Salem witches. The first stage of the colonial Anglican controversies was initiated by Increase Mather, in 1686, on the occasion of the establishment of the first English church in Boston. At least one of his intentions was to keep the community free from differing religious practices and influences.

Despite the establishment of the Church of England in the four lower counties of New York, in North and South Carolina, and in Georgia, its membership never reached a majority of the population in these colonies.[2] The settlers of the colonies represented a variety of national backgrounds including England, Scotland, Wales, Ulster-Ireland, Sweden, France, and the German principalities. Their religious associations were no less varied and they ranged across a broad Protestant spectrum of groups from Anglican, Presbyterian, Quaker, Swedish, and German Lutheran, to Huguenot. Nearly all of the ministers in these provinces depended on their salaries paid from either the provincial purse or by the S.P.G. in London.[3]

Isolated controversies relating to the English church erupted occasionally in New York, New Jersey, and Pennsylvania. While conflicts broke out in the early decades of the eighteenth century, it was during the 1750s and 1760s that disagreements became sharper and more complicated. When New York Anglicans in the early 1750s were seeking a royal charter for the establishment of King's College, William Livingston mounted a vigorous campaign in *The Independent Reflector* objecting to granting the charter.[4] In an attempt to counter the fear of Anglican domination in religious affairs, the Reverend Ezra Stiles of Newport, Rhode Island, floated a bold but ill-fated plan in the 1760s for a Christian Union between the Congregational churches of New England and the Presbyterian churches of the Middle Colonies. In part, Stiles's plan was an effort to forestall the appointment of an American bishop, which he considered as an attempt to curtail and endanger provincial religious liberties.[5]

Soon after the publication in 1767 of Thomas Bradbury Chandler's pamphlet *An Appeal to the Public*, strongly seeking public support for the appointment of a colonial prelate, a series of articles critical of such an official appeared in the *Pennsylvania Journal and Weekly Advertizer.*[6]

Under the title of 'The Centinel', 19 of the essays appeared in the newspaper between 24 March and 28 July 1768, written by the Reverend Francis Alison with the assistance of John Dickinson and George Bryan.[7] A Presbyterian minister in Philadelphia, serving as vice provost of the College of Philadelphia and rector of the Academy, his newspaper articles retraced the comments of several earlier pamphleteers writing in opposition to the appointment of an English prelate in the provinces.

The audience for the essays remains unclear, although the message may have been directed to several groups at once. Perhaps Alison intended to communicate his words to members of Parliament in London, whose attentions to American affairs had recently been revealed to the objections of colonists to the Stamp Act and the Townshend Duties. Perhaps he was sending an alarm to the members of non-Anglican church groups in Pennsylvania and New Jersey warning them of the possibility of an Anglican bishop. If this were so, his understanding of the political strength of the English church in the region was magnified. There were only a few congregations in New York, the strongest being Trinity Church; two prominent churches in Philadelphia, Christ Church and St. Peter's; and a handful of small congregations scattered throughout the region. The area was not a strong centre of Anglican activity and it seems unlikely that the articles were intended for such a scattered and modest local audience.[8] Assessing the lack of response to the 'Centinel' articles, Chandler wrote to his long-time friend, Samuel Johnson of Stratford, Connecticut, that 'There is yet no appearance that the Pennsylvania clergy intended to bestir themselves; they have not said a word in the papers, nor wrote a line to me or the brethren this way, on the occasion; and I suspect they would let me and my Appeal and the episcopate go to purgatory before they would move a fibre of their tongues or fingers to prevent it'.[9] Three months later, again in a letter to Johnson, Chandler remarked, 'I do not choose to concern myself with the "Centinel" at present; if the clergy of Pennsylvania will not interrupt him, let him go on to the end of the chapter'.[10]

Another and more plausible explanation for Alison's 'Centinel' essays is his difficult personal and professional association with William Smith, the provost of the College of Philadelphia (now the University of Pennsylvania) since 1755. The men had been in conflict on several matters for a number of years. Perhaps the arguments were shaped by their differences in origin, age, education, religious experience, temperament, and personality. Born in 1705 in County Donegal, North Ireland, Alison was a graduate of the University of Edinburgh and trained for the ministry in the Presbyterian Church, the national church of Scotland.

While Smith, born in Aberdeen, in 1727, of parents of genteel means, was a member of the outlawed Episcopal Church of Scotland and was educated at King's College in Aberdeen. He served as a tutor in a well-to-do family on Long Island before his ordination to the Church of England ministry by the Bishop of Carlisle Richard Osbaldeston in 1753.[11] It is possible that the purpose of Alison's essays was to subvert any support by London church or civil officials for Smith's consideration for appointment as an American bishop.

As early as 1762 and 1763, conflict between the two men became public. During Smith's visit to London seeking funds for the college, he strongly opposed Alison's efforts to establish 'The Corporation for the Relief of Poor and Distressed Presbyterian Ministers and Distressed Widows and Children of Presbyterian Ministers'.[12] His resistance to the organisation was on the grounds that a collection of funds on its behalf in England was a misleading attempt to obtain monies for the general expansion of Presbyterianism in Pennsylvania.[13] The continuing discord with Smith prompted Alison to write to Ezra Stiles, the minister of the Second Congregational Church in Newport, Rhode Island, in 1764, declaring that he was 'ready to resign my place in the College and retire to the country merely through chagrin. The College is artfully got into the hands of Episcopalian Trustees'.[14] Soon afterwards Alison turned his attention to establishing and supporting several Presbyterian schools including the Newark Academy, progenitor of the University of Delaware.[15]

Smith wrote two highly critical essays disputing the 'Centinel' articles and defending the historic office of bishop.[16] Writing to Bishop of London Richard Terrick in October 1768, the Philadelphian stated that he wished Chandler had not started the bishop controversy but feels obliged to support him. The provost declared that the only opposition to a prelate came from the Presbyterians because the Lutherans and Quakers conceded that 'it is the Church's natural right'.[17] Except for Alison's essays, Chandler's latest pamphlet on the topic does not seem to have ignited much interest or support among the clergymen of any religious group in the Chesapeake and Southern colonies.

The sometimes difficult but astute Scottish-born Smith privately sought the assistance of Dr. Joseph Tucker, the dean of the Gloucester Cathedral, on behalf of a colonial bishopric. A renowned economist and authority on trade, Tucker took a keen interest in politics and trade and followed American affairs closely.[18] His pamphlets on colonial trade, commercial, and political affairs were published in England and America and he was talked of in London as a possible bishop of Albany, should a bishop be appointed to the colonies. A satirical letter appeared in *The London Chronicle* addressed 'To the R[ight] R[everend] the Lord Bishop of Albany elect', under the pseudonym of 'A Missionary Expectant', that offered congratulations. The correspondent noted, 'There are others however I find, who, considering how tender and indulgent we have been of late to the prejudices of our Colonists, have taken it for granted, that your Lordship's election, hath been made without having recourse to canonical formalities, which might at the first, give offence to the American laity, who are apt to keep a jealous look-out upon the aspiring genius of technical Ecclesiastics, such as are tenacious of old ordinals and pontificals; and these are of opinion, that your Lordship's election hath been managed by way of *conclave* (a method which naturally occur at this period) and of which nobody would be aware till the appointment should be announced in our publick prints'. The writer suggested that the next step was for the bishop to be consecrated either in England or America.[19]

Tucker maintained in various publications that a separation from the colonies was desirable, maintaining the opinion that the supposed advantage of the colonial trade to the mother country was a delusion. On the other hand, he maintained that the colonies turned loose would fall out with each other, and be glad to return to political union. The policy pleased nobody in England. With regard to current provincial politics, Smith candidly commented to Tucker that 'Silence has been my choice. I have always disliked those publications here which intended to paint the conduct of England in the light of oppression; for altho her policy, in the present instance seems greatly mistaken (as the event will probably show), yet I am persuaded that no oppression was intended, nor the consequences foreseen, or duly weighed'. Nonetheless, Smith felt any attempts to reconcile the public was a vain effort that the Ministry was short-sighted in adopting the Stamp Act to raise revenue in the colonies, and a more useful path to raise revenue would be to urge the colonists to purchase English products. The provost observed that the American people would not respond to taxation without representation in Parliament except in rejection, so the experiment to raise revenue in the provinces was not worth the risk. Smith urged the politically accomplished and well-connected Tucker to take an active interest in the issue and seek a moderate resolution on the matter.[20]

It is not known if Tucker conveyed his concerns on American church affairs to parliamentary or government officials as Smith requested; only once in his publications relating to colonial economic affairs did he refer to the episcopacy issue. Nonetheless, Tucker expressed the opinion that the Church of England in America was persecuted 'by being denied those rights [i.e., bishops] which every other sect of Christians so amply enjoys'.[21] He declared that the English church was denied full toleration as a religious body, as enjoyed by all other religious sects, with the lack of a resident bishop to perform necessary duties and that curtailing the appointment of an American prelate was 'abridging the natural rights of men'.[22] He recognised that the English church was placed in an awkward position because 'Americans have taken it into their heads to believe that an episcopate would operate as some further tie upon them not to break loose from those obligations which they owe to the Mother Country'.[23] The dean of Gloucester observed that dissenting critics and pamphleteers in America viewed the Anglican petitions for a prelate 'as an Engine, under the masque of religion, to rivet those claims [imperial], which they imagine we are forging for them'.[24]

Tucker's conclusion and suggestion was at once bold and complete. It followed along the lines of his opinion regarding the uneconomic value of the colonies to England. He declared that the mother country should give up all claims to the colonies, both civil and ecclesiastical, and let the provinces have their independence.[25] Continuing, Tucker shrewdly observed that if England severed its links to the North American colonies 'all fears and their panics [will] be at an end, then a bishop who has no more connections with England either in church or state, than he has with Germany, Sweden, or any other country, will be no longer looked upon in America as a Monster, but a Man'.[26] He concluded that such a dramatic decision and action would remove civil and ecclesiastical opposition and that the church officer appointed could be called 'from a name derived from the Greek, the Latin, or the German, that is whether he be stiled episcopus, superintendent, supervisor, overseer, etc., it matters not, provided he is invested with competent authority to ordain and confirm members of the church and to inspect the lives and morals of his own clergy'.[27]

A young graduate of the College of New Jersey (now Princeton University), William Paterson, observed the episcopacy controversy, in June 1772, and wrote on the situation to a close college mate, John MacPherson, Jr., son of a Philadelphia merchant, who was briefly visiting in London. Paterson remarked, 'That application has been made in England for an American Episcopate is known here. The newspapers are full of it. The Dissenters are so jealous of each other, it is not likely they will unite and petition against it, or if they did, it's a million to one if that would not promote rather than prevent the scheme. The Bishops and Thirty-nine Articles have been censured so severely in the University of Cambridge and the late debates in Parliament, that it is to be hoped those Reverend Fathers will find full employment at home, without intermeddling in the politicks of America. I am satisfied, that in the Colonies, few of the Church of England, except those who are stiled High-Fliers, espouse the cause, or are in the least desirous of succeeding. In the Southern Provinces, composed principally of people in communion with the Church of England, a Bishop would meet with the severest opposition'.[28]

Nonetheless, an occasional Anglican clergyman would speak on the need for an American bishop. At a convention of the clergy of New York and New Jersey at Trinity Church in New York on 19 May 1773, John Sayre delivered a sermon that renewed the discussion of episcopacy and reviewed the legitimacy of apostolic succession. A New York native and graduate of King's College, he proclaimed the traditional orthodox doctrine of the origin of the ministry reminding his audience that Christ was anointed and sent by his father into the world and that the Apostles were sent as ambassadors 'clothed with full power, to act in his name'.[29] Minister of the churches at Newburgh and Hamptonburgh, in the Hudson River valley, Sayre stated that the Apostles had authority to establish churches wherever they and their doctrine should be received and adopted. He declared that St. Paul, commissioned after the ascension of Jesus, 'ordained others, and committed unto them power to ordain elders in every city; which power ... was necessarily to remain, in succession, through every age of the world; to be exercised by persons solemnly set apart and commissioned, by the proper officers of the church; and (whatever men in this careless age may think) by none else'.[30] With political and religious controversy swirling around the Church in New York, Sayre concluded his sermon declaring that the Anglican Church was a divine institution and that the ministers must strive to preserve it from declension. He proclaimed that 'In this new world, we behold the church in an unparalleled situation; like a system without a centre ... Seeing we are persuaded in our minds, that the Government of this Zion is truly apostolical; her liturgy purely primitive, and her faith in every respect, sound, and consonant with the word of God'.[31]

Circumstances for the English churches and clergymen in Virginia and Maryland were quite different from their colleagues in the New England and Middle and Southern colonies. The church was strongest in the Chesapeake Colonies in 1775 with 95 primary and 154 secondary churches in Virginia and 55 and 28 respectively in Maryland.[32] At the time there were 120 active ministers in Virginia and 59 in Maryland.[33] In the early 1770s, the church in Virginia reflected an institution that had been shaped by its experience over the previous 150 years. Under the supervision of the London Company, it was established in 1619 by the General Assembly and in part supervised by the civil government.[34] In every parish, the vestry was the administrative and financial authority of the congregation, selecting as a rule its own members, attending to the erection and repair of churches, and assessing taxes for parochial purposes. It was also recognised as part of the civil government for the performance of certain public duties. Such lay power, authority, and influence made it awkward for an incumbent parson to counter the policies, practices, and wishes of the vestry should the incumbent minister join with his colleagues to petition the king for a bishop for Virginia.[35] Virginia clergymen were essentially quasi-Congregationalists, independent in the practice of their duties and with little supervision or intervention by the bishop of London or his provincial commissary. They grew tobacco, owned slaves, and married into the gentry. Among the 120 active clergymen residing in Virginia in 1775, 53 were native colonists, while 19 were born in England, 28 in Scotland, 4 in Ireland, and the birthplace of 20 men remains unknown.[36] Their collegiate educational experience was as diverse as their national origins, representing institutions in America, England, Scotland, and Ireland.[37] As civil events unfolded in the 1770s, a number of the ministers were revolutionary committeemen and justices of the peace. Professor Otto Lohrenz has demonstrated that this was partly due to the fact that many of the ministers were themselves planters and shared a worldview similar to the planters.[38]

The arrival of new settlers in Virginia, after 1730, brought persons affiliated with such non-Anglican religious groups as Presbyterian, Baptist, Anabaptist, and Methodist churches, religious groups that were independent in organisation and without a hierarchical structure. The congregations, not responsible to any external authority, immediately began the task of establishing a presence in their communities.

For the Virginia clergymen, there was a lack of opportunity to develop a sense of professional collegiality in the province. Commissary James Blair held several conventions of the clergy during the 1690s and early 1700s, but his leadership among his colleagues was diminished after his confrontation with Governor Francis Nicholson in 1702.[39] Many of the colony's clergymen sided with the Governor during the controversy and called into question Blair's official role and leadership. For the next four decades he turned his primary attention to serving as president of the fledgling College of William and Mary. During the eighteenth century the ministers seldom gathered, on average twice in each decade.[40] There was no opportunity for the men in the Chesapeake or Southern Colonies to meet on a regular schedule as occurred for New England Congregational ministers. As nearly all of the latter group had attended college at either Harvard or Yale, they could easily gather for informal and formal meetings at the time of their college's commencements. The Virginia clergymen did not have that kind of association with the College of William and Mary because they were alumni of colleges in other colonies, as well as in England, Scotland, and Ireland.[41]

Differing from their colleagues in the New England and Middle Colonies, the Virginia ministers demonstrated little interest for an American prelate at any time during the colonial period. The situation invites several questions for consideration. Overtures were made to Old Dominion clergymen to join with New England and Middle Colonies colleagues to support the call for an American prelate as early as 1767. Samuel Johnson of Stratford, Connecticut, former president of King's College in New York, wrote to John Camm, the Professor of Divinity at the College of William and Mary and the bishop of London's commissary in Virginia, on the subject.[42] Camm was on record indicating that bishops were needed to help bind the colonies closer to England. In a letter to Johnson, in July 1768, Thomas Bradbury Chandler expressed a more guarded view of the participation of colleagues in the southern provinces noting that 'I know not whether our being joined by the southern colonies would help forward or hasten the episcopate'.[43] It was not until 4 June 1771 that 12 ministers of more than one hundred active in Virginia met and considered the possibility of an American bishop.[44]

Commissary James Horrocks summoned the ministers to attend a regular annual meeting of the members of the Fund for the Relief of Widows and Orphans of Deceased Clergy, to be held at the College of William and Mary on 4 May. Presumably a meeting that would encourage, at least informally, a discussion among the participants of the proposal for an American prelate, but the evidence is unclear on the matter. Soon after the session he advertised in the Williamsburg newspaper that there would be a convention of the clergymen on 4 June to discuss 'the Expediency of an Application to proper Authority for an American Episcopate'.[45] The scheduled session prompted the publication of some 23 letters for and against episcopacy in the Williamsburg newspapers for the next 10 months.[46] The principal opponents to a bishop were Samuel Henley, Professor of Philosophy (1770–7), and Thomas Gwatkin, Professor of Natural Philosophy and Mathematics (1770–3) at the College of William and Mary.[47] Both men had been in the province for a short time, Henley for little more than a year and Gwatkin for about 12 months. Neither of them was a university graduate, although Gwatkin had matriculated at Jesus College, Oxford, in 1763, and was awarded a B.A. degree by decree in 1778. Henley, before his ordination in 1769, had been a minister to a dissenting congregation in Cambridge, England. Earlier in 1771, the 30-year-old Henley was a candidate for appointment as rector of Bruton Parish Church at Williamsburg, the most prominent parish in the province and historically the seat of the commissary. His candidacy prompted a vigorous challenge by lay officials regarding his orthodoxy and another candidate was selected for the post.[48] After the outbreak of the Revolution, he returned to England, taught at Harrow School, and became a distinguished classical scholar and antiquarian. Their colleagues, the president of the College (1764–71), Commissary James Horrocks, and Professor of Divinity (1749–57; 1763–72) John Camm, defended the need for a prelate. The two teams each signed their newspaper contributions as 'A Country Gentleman'.

We must ask such questions as, was the meeting called solely at the discretion of Commissary James Horrocks, or did the royal governor, Francis Fauquier, join in supporting the session? Why did so few ministers, less than one in eight of the clergy in the colony, attend the session? Did the lack of interest in the Episcopal office represent an opinion among the ministers that a bishop was not a necessary part of the church's hierarchy? Or, was support for the office curtailed because of the pressing civil issues faced by legislative officials in the 1760s and 1770s? The ministers hesitated to consider the issue for fear that civil leaders would be critical of such an issue and the meeting adjourned without further deliberation on the matter. Nonetheless, the 12 ministers in attendance agreed that the meeting was valid.

After a vigorous discussion over the efficacy of a colonial prelate, eight of the ministers in attendance at the convention were in favour of proceeding to prepare an address to the king seeking the appointment of bishops for America, while four of the attendees opposed the plan. The majority appointed a committee consisting of four members, with instructions to prepare the petition and to send a copy to every clergyman in Virginia requesting them to sign the document.[49] Assurance was given that no appeal would be sent to the king unless at least a full majority, more than 50, of the clergymen resident in Virginia had approved and signed it.[50]

In hindsight, there were two obstacles in the way of bringing bishops to Virginia. The first of these was the question of appointment of ministers to parishes. The effect that the presence of a bishop would have upon the right of a vestry to select its own minister was a moot point. This prerogative had been carefully developed and protected during the long history of the church in Virginia. It is also doubtful that the leaders among the people would accept at face value the description of a diluted episcopacy presented in the plan for an American episcopate. The General Assembly might enact laws confirming the right of the vestry to select its minister in spite of the presence of a bishop in the colony; but in their experience the king had yielded too often to the unhappy habit of disallowing laws enacted by the Virginia Assembly, when the interests of England demanded it. There would seem little reason to think that any law of the Virginia Assembly restricting the duties and privileges of bishops would be permitted to stand.

Samuel Henley and Thomas Gwatkin were two of the four clergymen who opposed the action of the majority in attendance on the grounds that an attendance of 12 ministers could not be accepted as truly representative of the whole group of parsons in the colony.[51] The two men maintained the position that the Virginia clergy should not be placed in a position that would determine the kind of episcopate that might be established in other provinces because it would violate the rights of such colonists.[52] Henley and Gwatkin also objected to the decision to address a petition to the king, declaring that because the church was established in Virginia, the endorsement of the document was required from the governor, Council, and Representatives and that the bishop of London should be informed of the proceedings.[53]

In poor health, Commissary Horrocks in the midst of the controversy decided to return to England. Some critics decried that he had sailed for England in hope of obtaining a mitre for himself. The controversy among the Virginia ministers, as sharp as any exchanges between New England Dissenters and Church of England disputants on the issue through the years, was reported in the *New York Gazette*.[54]

On receiving the news of the proceedings of the Virginia clergymen, Thomas Bradbury Chandler published *An Address from the Clergy of New-York and New Jersey to the Episcopalians in Virginia* (New York, 1771). It was endorsed by nine of the Middle Colonies' most prominent parsons including Samuel Auchmuty, Myles Cooper, John Ogilvie, Richard Charlton, Samuel Seabury, Charles Inglis, Abraham Beach, and Chandler himself.[55] The tract challenged the position of the clergy and the House of Burgesses in Virginia over the episcopacy issue and recounted the history of the attempts to obtain a colonial prelate, arguing that the church was not under adequate ecclesiastical supervision.[56] It endorsed, too, the 1767 efforts by the New Jersey, New York, and Pennsylvania clergy conventions to seek the appointment of a prelate without political powers.[57]

Chandler rhetorically inquired that as many of the members of the Virginia House of Burgesses were members of the English church that 'After such Treatment from its reputed Friends, can we wonder at the Opposition and Abuse it has received from its avowed Adversaries'?[58] Urging his Virginia colleagues to reconsider their decision, Chandler suggested that the appointment of prelates would not weaken links with Great Britain, but would allow the church to 'stand on as respectable a Footing, as other religious Societies; and that it should not be destitute of such Privileges, as are enjoyed by the most inconsiderable Sects in his Majesty's Dominions. This Church at present, in the Colonies, is in an imperfect State, wanting an essential Part of its Constitution; and whether such a State be not dishonourable to any Church or Society, let common Sense judge'.[59]

Replying promptly to Chandler's admonition, Thomas Gwatkin published *A Letter to the Clergy of New York and New Jersey, Occasioned by an Address to the Episcopalians of Virginia* (Williamsburg, 1772). He wrote that the laws of Virginia allowed that only clergymen ordained by a bishop in England could hold parishes in Virginia; and a bishop in America might ordain men by the dozen, but none of them could hold a parish in Virginia until the General Assembly changed the law.[60] He added that perhaps if the clergy of New York and New Jersey had actually known the facts about the legal establishment of the church in Virginia, they might not have been so free with their condemnation of the clergymen's lack of support for a bishop. The strength of the petition of the eight ministers in Virginia who voted to appeal to the king for a prelate was of no influence in either London or Williamsburg.

Two of the seven points presented by Gwatkin in his pamphlet contain the essence of the objections of certain persons to an American episcopate. He stated that 'Because the Establishment of an American Episcopate at this Time would tend greatly to weaken the connexion between the Mother Country and her Colonies, to continue their present unhappy Disputes, to infuse Jealousies and Fears into the Minds of Protestant Dissenters; and to give ill-disposed Persons Occasion to raise such Disturbances as may endanger the very Existence of the British Empire in America'. Furthermore, Gwatkin wrote, 'we cannot help considering it as extremely indecent for the Clergy to make such an Application without the Concurrence of the President, Council, and Representatives of this Province; an Usurpation directly repugnant to the Rights of Mankind'.[61] In fact, Gwatkin concluded that the issue could not be endorsed without the review of the colonial legislature.

In Virginia the issue was dead and the House of Burgesses adopted a resolution of thanks to the four clergymen who protested against the proposal for a bishop. Convening early in July, the Williamsburg newspaper noted that the House of Burgesses 'have also resolved the Thanks of their House be given to the Reverend Mr. Henley, the Reverend Mr. Gwatkin, the Reverend Mr. Hewitt, and the Reverend Mr. Bland, for the wise and well-timed Opposition they have made to the pernicious Project of a few mistaken Clergymen, for introducing an American Bishop; a Measure by which Disturbance, great Anxiety and Apprehension would certainly take place among his Majesty's faithful American people'.[62]

This action put an end to further consideration of a petition to the King for a bishop. No Virginia clergyman would permit his signature to remain upon the document after the House of Burgesses had spoken in such strong terms. Although the Acting Commissary of the colony, William Willie, summoned the clergy to a convention to discuss the subject on two later dates, 16 October 1771 and 20 February 1772, the parsons again did not attend the meetings.[63]

Members of the Virginia House of Burgesses were absorbed in the unfolding imperial policies and events that marked the colonial experience after 1771. In Williamsburg, the regularly published newspapers printed news of the quartering of English troops in Boston, the Boston Massacre, and Tea Party and the consequence of the Intolerable Acts for merchants, planters, and residents of the Old Dominion. Thomas Jefferson, in the summer of 1774, published for the consideration of the members of the colony's legislature, *A Summary of the Rights of British Americans*.[64] A statement of the effect of restrictive policies on colonial trade, the refusal of assent by English officials to laws passed by the House of Burgesses for trifling reasons, endeavouring to take from the people the right of representation, sending troops to the colonies, and making military superior to civil power.[65]

John K. Nelson has concluded, in his admirable study of the church in colonial Virginia, that the institution was 'indeed impaired by the absence of a bishop'.[66] The membership was denied confirmation, churches were unconsecrated, and candidates for the ministry were required to travel to London for ordination. In addition, the church was without the influence of a prelate at the highest level of provincial government. He also dismisses Rhys Isaac's argument that the episcopacy controversy in the Old Dominion was attributed to the hostile struggle over the selection of a minister for Bruton Parish, in Williamsburgh.[67] My examination of the matter concurs with Nelson's assessment, while the issue was of considerable interest in

Williamsburgh, it did not seem to have any impact in the colony beyond the town.

In Maryland, where the parsons only met twice in convention between 1730 and 1771, a committee of clergymen met at Annapolis on 14 February 1771.[68] The session cautiously petitioned the governor, to make 'an Application to the Crown for the Nomination of a Bishop in that Province, that the Students of Divinity in the American Universities may not be obliged to the Expense of a Voyage to England before they can obtain Orders; and that the Profligacies of the Clergy, too numerous in America, may not as hitherto pass unanswered'.[69] Nothing came of the petition and no further effort was initiated by the ministers on behalf of a prelate.

The final publication in the long-standing episcopacy debate came from Thomas Bradbury Chandler's pen, an historical survey of the attempt to appoint a colonial bishop throughout the eighteenth century that added no new details.[70] Chandler's most interesting observation is the recitation of extracts of sermons by English bishops before the Society calling for an American bishop. He attempted to demonstrate, from the professions of the leaders of the church, that political interests played no part in their efforts to secure bishops for America. It was not a strong argument.

Chandler's argument conceded to Francis Blackburne that 'the Members of the Church in the Colonies are likewise more connected with England than the Dissenters because they are more connected with the Head of that political Body. They are more interested in the King, and more closely connected with him, because they acknowledge and submit to his Supremacy in Ecclesiastical Matters which the Dissenters do not'.[71] He challenged Charles Chauncy's and Maicaiah Towgood's criticism of the Anglican church as a state institution, arguing that the plan for a spiritual bishop in the colonies precluded the necessity for the proposal to be reviewed by Parliament as the office would require no government financial aid. Nonetheless he declared, 'We wish however that it may be brought into Parliament so far and only so far as to be honoured with the Consent and Approbation of each Branch of the legislative Authority. But before an Episcopate can be established, or the proposed Episcopate can be altered in such a Manner as to affect the Rights of the Colonists, it *must* come before the Parliament, for nothing less, I will venture to affirm, than the Interposition of Parliament can arm it with a Force that will be regarded by the Americans in general. In either Way therefore the Dissenters are safe'.[72]

Part II A New Controversy: The Political Sentiments of the Clergymen

10
The Impact of the First Continental Congress and the Local Committees of Safety

Convening in Philadelphia in September and October 1774 as an advisory council for the colonies, the First Continental Congress considered action for recovery of rights forfeited under Parliament's repressive Coercive Acts. It eventually became the central government for the provinces, however fragmentary its powers. The creation of the Continental Association by the Congress was intended to regularise procedures against dissidents in the colonies by establishing local Committees of Safety in every county, city, and town.[1] Committees were to be elected by persons able to vote for assemblymen in each province.[2] Complaints considered by the committees were to be heard and if an accused person were found guilty the details were to be published in the local newspaper. Pauline Maier has noted that provincial conventions and local committees were allowed to establish additional regulations for executing judicial procedures.[3] Persons alleged to be Loyalists or enemies of America were 'to be complained of unto the Committee of the District or Town in which such person or persons reside'.[4]

For an observer of civil events, in the autumn of 1774, the proceedings of the Congress seemed to be set on a path that would lead the colonies to rebellion and war with England, a circumstance that indicated an uncertain and uncontrollable future for the church. The deliberations and policies adopted by the Congress generated a succession of critical essays by several prominent loyalist Anglican clergymen in the Middle Colonies and divided the opinions of members of congregations. In addition, the activity of the Congress initiated an interest in the political sentiments of the ministers by local political activists and the members of the Committee of Safety, particularly in the New England region.[5] While there was occasional interest in such views of the men in

123

the Middle, Chesapeake, and Southern Colonies, it was never as extensive or exercised at the level of intensity that occurred in the New England Colonies. For many of the S.P.G. missionaries the rapidly changing political circumstances prompted them to deviate from the instructions that they received at the time of their appointment.[6] The men were admonished to 'take special care to give no offence to the Civil Government by intermeddling in Affairs not relating to their own Calling and Function.'[7]

For the ministers who fled the colonies in 1775, 1776, and 1778, during the period of extreme activity of the local committees, it is likely that many of them sought exile rather than appear before the body, answer questions deemed of a private matter of conscience, or that were considered as inappropriate and a disclosure of their political opinions.[8] Were the ministers brought before the bodies because of their official ties to the local congregation of the English church and therefore that their political loyalties were suspect? Or were the actions due, in part, to long simmering personal animosities between a clergyman and a politically influential person or persons in the community? Or possibly, by a long-standing conflict between two or more religious groups in a town. It is clear that a variety of reasons prompted the summoning of a parson before the committee.

On 9 September 1774, delegates from the towns in Suffolk County, in which Boston was located, met in Milton and adopted the Suffolk Resolves. The resolutions were adopted by the Continental Congress that embraced the resolutions on 8 October. It was a radical statement that declared the Coercive Acts were unconstitutional and therefore not to be obeyed; urged the people of Massachusetts to form a government to collect taxes and withhold them from the royal government until the repeal of the Acts; advised the people to arm and form their own militia; and recommended stringent economic sanctions against Britain.

Several differing elements, professional and personal, brought the English ministers to the attention of the local Committees of Safety. Complaints about the men were generally based either on the content of their sermons or published material: political sentiments expressed in the pulpit and informal conversation, newspaper articles, essays, or verse. Sometimes it was as a consequence of the minister's continuing practice to offer prayers at public services on behalf of King George III, the royal family, and the English government. Occasionally it was for not fulfilling obligations imposed by either the provincial assembly or the Continental Congress to read at services of worship such as the Proclamations of official Days of Fast or the Declaration of Independence.

The first parson I have identified as exposed to systematic outcries of protesting neighbours or the local Committee of Safety was Samuel Andrews Peters, of Hebron, Connecticut. A graduate of Yale in 1757, he was suspected of informing the bishop of London and the officials of the S.P.G. on colonial political affairs. Peters was visited by members of the local Sons of Liberty on 15 August 1774, and they reviewed his papers and forced him to sign a declaration that he had not written and would not write to England on such matters.[9] Taking matters to the pulpit, he advised his congregation not to contribute aid or supplies for the relief of Boston and he was again visited on 6 September by a mob. A search of his house revealed that he had arms in his possession, and he was taken to the meeting-house green and forced to sign a declaration and confession. Soon afterwards, Peters fled to Boston and, on 25 October, sailed from Portsmouth, New Hampshire, for England.[10]

Such incidents as that encountered by Peters increased among the ministers in late 1774 and 1775, following the establishment of the Continental Association and local Committees of Safety. Nearly immediately, the two ministers in Maine, a jurisdiction of the Massachusetts Bay Colony, John Wiswall of Falmouth (present-day Portland) and Jacob Bailey of Pownalborough, encountered public harassment. The strong provisions of the Suffolk Resolves curtailing the importation and consumption of English goods or the export of colonial products to the mother country, placed the parsons in an uncomfortable position. As ministers of congregations of the Church of England, the men were recognised as agents of the Church and state as were such other imperial appointees as governors, judges, customs officers, and stamp tax collectors. For the public, there was no distinction between servants of the English state or church.

Both Wiswall and Bailey were keen observers of their communities and of emerging civil issues. The detailed accounts of their experiences, at the hands of their neighbours and the local Committee of Safety, provide a chronicle not only of their personal encounters but also the disintegration of the church in the communities they served. John Wiswall graduated from Harvard College, in 1749, and received his theological training for the Congregational ministry from the controversial liberal divine Jonathan Mayhew, the minister of Boston's West Church.[11] Prior to his Anglican ordination, Wiswall had been the Congregational minister of the Third Parish in Falmouth (1756–63). Converting to the Church of England, he travelled to London for ordination in 1763 and returned to Falmouth to serve a congregation as an S.P.G. missionary. He found that some of the leading local

Congregational laymen were determined 'to leave no stone unturn'd to prejudice their Brethren against the Church of England'. To counter their efforts, he was cautious in his preaching to avoid all possible points of controversy.[12] He found, too, that his congregation was hard pressed to pay a portion of his salary and meet the expenses of maintaining the church.[13]

On 16 September 1774, Wiswall recounted his misgivings about the course of political affairs and their impact on the church. He noted that 'The publick distractions of the Province have greatly increased, and people of every Denomination discover (it is too little to say an uneasiness) a discontent bordering upon madness on account of the late Proceedings of Parliament respecting America'. Wiswall observed that the people of his congregation 'have been quiet and peaceable, but now the leaven spreads fast among them'.[14] By November the situation had changed, and the parson refused to read from the pulpit a Fast Proclamation issued by the Massachusetts House of Representatives instead of the Royal Governor, or to take up a collection for the people of Boston suffering from the non-importation demonstrations. To do so, he said, would be to give countenance to people in rebellion.[15]

Spared from any acts of violence, Wiswall had grim premonitions, noting that 'Many of the dissenting ministers support their own popularity by encouraging the people in the tumultuous proceedings'. He believed that his role as minister was to urge his congregation's submission to authority and obedience to the laws of the colony in a quiet and peaceable manner. Such a course of action, he felt, was a means to 'check the torrent of political enthusiasm'. Wiswall noted that during these disturbing times 'even silence is now censured by the people as evidence of what they call tory principles'. He felt that as a consequence of political events he would suffer and that he already was suffering 'in my temporal interests on account of these disturbances'.[16] Yet he felt bound by his oaths of loyalty and fidelity to the Crown and church to support the position and actions of the English government.

The crisis came on 9 May 1775, when a company of country militia seized Wiswall and other leading Loyalists of the town. Brought the next day before 'a Committee or Council of War', he stated that his position had been that he had never in his sermons 'so much as glanced at the political disputes' and boldly maintained 'that not the severest punishment, not the fear of death, should tempt' him 'to violate the oath of allegiance and supremacy to King George, of canonical obedience to his diocesan, or, in conformity to the provincial congress, to deviate from the rules of the crown of England'. His position on these matters was unequivocal. The committee gave the parson his liberty on his release to remain in Falmouth, but three days later he took refuge on board HMS *Canceaux*, because of a rumour that he was to be taken into the country as a prisoner.[17]

From the ship, Wiswall sent word to his churchwardens that he would preach no more to his congregation, but if they wished to hear him they could attend his services on the *Canceaux*. None went. He wrote to a local friend in candid and heartfelt words that 'I love my Country and am willing to sacrifice every thing but a good conscience to save it from destruction'. The parson believed 'that the people are acting a very wrong part, and should they prosper in their machinations, I am determined never to join them in a rebellion'. Since the war had begun, Wiswall observed that he 'must obey God rather than man, and act agreeable to the dictates of my conscience, tho' at the hazard of every thing that is dear to me'.[18]

Wiswall sailed from Falmouth on board the *Canceaux*, on 16 May, for Boston. Hearing that his Falmouth property had been confiscated and sold for the maintenance of the rebel army, and faced with the problem of the education of his sons, he sought the assistance of the S.P.G. in sending them to England. In October, he watched a flotilla sail from Boston for the purpose of burning houses and buildings in Falmouth, and in November he heard the disquieting news that his house and church had gone up in the flames. With resignation he wrote, 'I have now no prospect left me of living in New England. And indeed the sufferings and persecutions I have undergone; together with the rebellious spirit of the people have entirely weaned my affection from my native country—the further I go from it the better'.[19]

At the end of January 1776, Wiswall sailed for England, glad to be spared the sight of the fearful punishment which he expected to be visited upon the rebellious colonies, remarking to a friend that 'You are able to judge from your own feelings what pain it must give the heart of an American to be a Spectator of the miseries which are comeing upon his countrymen, tho no more than the just punishment due for their ingratitude to the parent State and their rebellion against the best of Kings'.[20]

At Pownalborough (present-day Dresden), the missionary of the S.P.G., Jacob Bailey, was a native of Rowley in Massachusetts who graduated from Harvard College, in 1755, with a class that included his friend and occasional correspondent John Adams. After a journey to Boston in September 1774, during the period that the Continental Congress was meeting in Philadelphia, Bailey claimed that when he

returned to Maine he 'was frequently insulted and mobbed and particularly at Brunswick'.[21] When the news of Lexington and Concord
reached the Maine settlement in April 1775, he reported he was
'assaulted by a number of ruffians'.[22] Although he boasted to London
officials that none of his congregation joined the Patriot forces challenging the authority of Great Britain, the congregation seemed evenly
divided on public issues, about half of the members protested his refusal
to read the provincial Thanksgiving proclamation.[23]

On New Year's Day, 1776, a Whig meeting mischievously voted to
send for Bailey to consecrate the Liberty Pole and barely rejected a
motion that he be whipped around it, if he refused to cooperate. Later
in the spring the Whigs shot his sheep and cattle, and began again to
collect taxes from the Episcopalians to help support the Wiscasset
Congregational church.[24] A complaint against Bailey by the Committee
of Correspondence, on 24 May 1776, alleged that since 1774 Bailey had
'an undue Attachment to the Authority claimed by Great Britain over
the united Colonies' and had demonstrated that he did not support the
revolutionary movement.[25] The committee was determined that he
had 'been Guilty of a criminal Neglect in not reading Proclamations
issued by the Continental and Provincial Congresses, for days of public
fasting and Prayer … thereby throwing Contempt upon said Congresses
and virtually denying their Authority'.[26] For this Bailey was ordered to
give bond for £40 to answer to the General Court.[27] This he did, and
when further ordered to cease praying for the King, he restrained himself for a time, although he substituted a sermon that was not deroga-
tory to George III.[28]

Called again before the committee on 28 October 1776, Bailey was
to answer the charges that he had refused to read at services of worship
the Declaration of Independence, and that he had resumed his practice
of publicly praying for King George III. His long answer to the complaint is an eloquent plea for freedom of conscience. Bailey apologised
for giving offence by not reading the Declaration, but he defended
his actions by admitting that 'I was very unwilling to give any offence
by refusing to read the declaration of Independence, neither was I
desirous of bringing myself into any further trouble. But when I came
seriously to examine the solemn Oaths I had taken and the Nature of
my Subscriptions, I found I could not comply without offering great
violence to my conscience and incurring, as I apprehend, the Guilt of
Perjury'.[29] He assumed a position of passive obedience and non-resistance
declaring, 'A Church or Place of Worship ought to be sacred to Truth,
and no Minister ought to publish any Thing but what he really believes

agreeable to the Truth'.[30] He asked the members of the Committee of Safety, 'What have I done to injure the American cause? Have I taken up arms in favor of Britain? Have I gone into any publick meetings to defend or establish the pretension of either the King or Parliament? Have I prevented any one from enlisting into the service? Have I by word or writing conveyed any intelligence to the enemy? Have I ever attempted to escape out of the country, even when I have an opportunity? Or have I aided abetted or assisted the invaders of America? Why then am I charged with being an enemy to my country, what is my crime?'[31] Continuing, he declared that 'I am criminal only for acting as every honest Man ought to act in the same circumstances in rather choosing to suffer the penalty ... than to feel the Eternal reproaches of a guilty conscience'.[32] Revealing the ambiguity of his dilemma he observed 'that supposing I was really in my heart unfriendly to the Country (which I absolutely deny) it is not in my power to injure it ... I sincerely wish to see the prosperity of my Country and am willing to submit to the Authority of the present Government in all lawful and indifferent Matters; but to declare my self absolved from my former Oath of Allegiance I am convinced is neither lawful nor indifferent'.[33] Concluding, Bailey stated, 'Can any person without money, without influence, without authority, without opportunity, in such a remote corner, do any thing to obstruct the wheels of government, or to determine the operations of the war'?[34]

Sheriff Charles Cushing, a member of the Committee of Correspondence, answered Bailey on 16 November 1776, declaring that every officeholder in the colonies had taken the same oath at the accession of George III in 1760, and that according to the parson's argument, 'they all incurred the guilt of Perjury'. 'I dare say', he concluded, 'the General Court will take care that such Doctrines should not prevail – If they are Connived at the States will be Sapped – to their Foundation'.[35] The Committee embraced this opinion, found the minister to be 'a most inveterate and dangerous Enemy to the Rights and Liberties of these United States', and turned him over to the General Court. The Court was too busy to try him, and in March 1777, the Pownalborough town meeting thoroughly confused matters by striking his name from the long list of 'internal enemies' of the United States.

Bailey found that the continuing threat of persecution had discouraged his friends from helping him. Sheriff Cushing persistently threatened him with imprisonment if he conducted public or private services. In September 1778 at a settlement about 50 miles from his home, where he had gone on request to baptise the children, he was 'assaulted by a violent mob armed with clubs, axes, and other weapons', who stripped him naked in search of papers, thinking that he was trying to escape to Quebec.[36] He was presented at the next session of the Grand Jury for having preached a treasonable sermon, but its finding wasno declaration in writing of his breach of the law.

On 28 July 1778, Bailey petitioned the Council of the State of Massachusetts seeking to remove himself and family from the District of Maine.[37] He noted that he had lived in the community for three years and had not received his salary from the S.P.G.[38] Bailey stated that 'having the least prospect of getting bread for his family, and seeing nothing before him in the Eastern parts of this state but meagre famine and absolute suffering for the necessities of live, prays your Honours that he may have Liberty to depart with his family (consisting only of his wife and infant babe) to some part of Nova Scotia, and to carry what few effects he has left, the whole not amounting to one hundred dollars and consisting of a few necessary articles of furniture'.[39]

In October, the Council granted him permission to leave the State, but for lack of transportation, he was condemned to spend another winter in Maine. On a morning in June 1779, the opportunity to escape came and Bailey and his family sailed for Halifax.[40] In 1782 he moved to Annapolis, Nova Scotia, and exercised the remainder of his ministry in conflict with his fellow clergy and a life of unshakeable poverty.

The circumstances surrounding Jonathan Boucher in Annapolis, Maryland, were dramatically unlike the experiences of any of his American colleagues. Our knowledge of Boucher's experience with the committee is recounted in his 'Farewell Sermon' to his congregation that was not published until 1797.[41]

Suspicions about Boucher's political sentiments were apparent as early as 1775. When he was serving as chaplain to the Maryland provincial convention, he announced his intention of opposing the body's approval of a solemn fast day and informed the colonial officials that he would be preaching against active resistance to English policies. This turn of events prompted civil leaders to forbid him from entering his pulpit, and placed a body of armed men around it to enforce their command. Boucher later claimed that, from this time on, he believed that his life was in danger and that he never preached without a pair of loaded pistols lying on the cushion.[42]

By September, the Annapolis parson reached a decision that political circumstances prompted him to return to England. His 'Farewell Sermon' to his congregation encapsulated his political thinking and recounted for the congregation his experience of being hailed before the Committee of Safety.[43] A cogent, coherent, and emotional personal statement, the sermon is the crystallisation of Boucher's personal, educational, and political odyssey from Cumberland in England to the New World. He declared that his position in the imperial political crisis was not really open to choice, 'To choose, and, as far as we are able, to defend a cause which in our consciences we believe to be good, is not, properly speaking, a matter of choice, but of duty; and either through fear to shrink from our duty, or through any sinister views to perform it feebly, is a sin which, however small, from the commonness of the case, we may deem it, is to be dreaded and shunned more than the greatest danger'.[44] He proclaimed that his obligations as an ordained member of the Church of England, governed by law and his ordination oaths, shaped his opinion in the fast-approaching civil war and while 'Entertaining all due respect for my ordination vows, I am firm in my resolution, whilst I pray in public at all, to conform to the unmutilated Liturgy of my Church, and, reverencing the injunction of an Apostle, I will continue to *pray for the King and all that are in authority under him*; and I will do so, not only because I am so commanded, but that, as the Apostle adds, we may continue to *lead quiet* and *peaceable lives in all godliness and honesty*. Inclination, as well as duty, confirms me in this purpose. *As long as I live*, therefore, *yea*, whilst *I have my being*, will I, with Zadock the priest, and Nathan the prophet, proclaim, *God save the King*'.[45] Although a Loyalist, Boucher was not a firebrand. He wrote in May 1775, 'for my part I equally dread a Victory on either side'.[46]

Under constant surveillance by the local Committee of Safety, Boucher grew more and more unpopular and was burned in effigy.[47] Fearing the worst, he and his wife, the former Eleanor Addison, a member of a prominent Maryland family, abandoned their home and thousand-acre plantation near Alexandria on the Potomac and departed for England in September 1775, never to return again.

A no-less-compelling account of a parson's encounter with radical leaders occurred in New York City. Charles Inglis, the minister at Trinity Church, reported to London officials, in the autumn, his meetings with revolutionary officials when General George Washington arrived in the city and attended a service. Writing that before the ceremony began, 'one of the Rebel Generals called at the Rector's House and not finding him, left Word that he "came to inform the Rector that General Washington would be at Church, and would be glad if the violent Prayers for the King and Royal Family were omitted". This Message was brought to me [Inglis], and as You may suppose, I paid no Regard to it. On seeing the General not long after, I remonstrated against the Unreasonableness of his Request, which he must know the Clergy could not comply with; and told him further – "That it was not in his Power to make the Clergy depart from their Duty".[48] This Declaration drew from him an awkward Apology for his Conduct, which I believe was not authorised by Washington'.[49]

On another occasion early in the war, the Sunday morning routine of worship at Trinity Church was interrupted when, according to Inglis, he

> had proceeded some Length into the Service, a Company of about one hundred armed Rebels marched into the Church, with Drums beating, and Fifes playing – their Guns loaded and Bayonets fixed, as if going into Battle. The Congregation was thrown into the utmost Terror, and several Women fainted, expecting a Massacre was intended. I took no Notice of this, and went on with the Service; only exerted my Voice, which was in some Measure drowned by the Noise and Tumult. The Rebels stood thus in the Aisle for near fifteen Minutes; till being asked into Pews by the Sexton, they complied. Still however the People expected that when the Collects for the King and Royal Family were read, I should be fired at, as Menaces to that Purpose had been frequently flung out – the Matter however passed over without any Accident.[50]

Soon afterwards Inglis received a message from the members of the Committee of Safety that requested him 'to have the King's Arms taken down in the Churches, or else the Mob would do it, and might deface and injure the Churches. I immediately complied, people were not at Liberty to speak their Sentiments, and even Silence was construed as a Mark of Disaffection'.[51]Such turn of events encouraged Inglis to close Trinity Church and its two chapels, St. Paul's and St. George's, noting that 'even this was attended with great Hazard; for it was declaring in the strongest Manner our Disapprobation of Independency, and that under the Eye of Washington and his Army'.[52]

Remaining in the city, Inglis continued to visit the sick, baptise children, bury the dead, and 'afford what Support I could to the Remains of our poor Flock, who were much dispirited; for several, especially of the poorer Sort, had it not in their Power to leave the City'.[53] Stating that 'After we had ceased to officiate publicly, several of the Rebel Officers sent to me for the Keys of the Churches that their Chaplains might preach in them – with these Requisitions I peremptorily refused to comply; and let them know that if they would use the Churches, they must break the Gates and Doors to get in. Accordingly I took possession of all the Keys, lest the Sextons might be tampered with; for I could not bear the Thought that their Seditious and rebellious Effusions should be poured out in our Churches. When these Requisitions were repeated with Threats, my Answer was – "That I did what I Knew to be my Duty, and that I would adhere to it, be the Consequences what they would". Upon this they desisted, and did not occupy any of the Churches'.[54]

After the American forces evacuated New York City on 15 September 1776, Inglis returned to his house the next day and found that it had been 'plundered of every Thing by the Rebels. My loss amounts to near £200 this Currency, or upwards of £100 Sterling'. Now that the British were in control of the city, Inglis 'opened one of the Churches & solemnised Divine Service; when all the Inhabitants gladly attended, and Joy was lighted up in every Countenance on the Restoration of our public Worship; for very few remained but such as were Members of our Church'.[55]

Fragments of the experiences of Boucher, Inglis, Wiswall, and Bailey in 1774, 1775, 1776, and 1777 were experiencedby several other Anglican ministers in the New England and Middle colonies. Such parsons as Joshua Wingate Weeks and Edward Winslow in Massachusetts, Jeremiah Leaming in Connecticut, Thomas Barton in Pennsylvania, and John Scott in Maryland and Delaware, declared that their position on civil events were shaped by their fidelity to the oath to the crown and church undertaken at their ordinations.[56]

Reporting on the impact of the revolutionary movement on the daily routine of the ministers in New York, Charles Inglis declared that they continued to exercise their ministry, 'in Their Sermons, confirming themselves to the Doctrines of the Gospel, without touching on politics; using their Influence to allay our Heats, and cherish a Spirit of Loyalty among their People'.[57] Yet this conduct, 'however harmless, gave great offence to our flaming Patriots, who laid down as a Maxim – that those who were not for them, were against them'.[58] The parson noted that 'the Clergy were everywhere threatened; often reviled with the most opprobrious Language; sometimes treated with brutal Violence'. He claimed 'Some have been carried into distant Provinces Prisoners by armed Mobs, where they were detained in close confinement for several Weeks' and mistreated without any charges brought against them. Inglis further noted that some men had been flung into jails by committees of safety, for 'frivolous Suspicions of Plots, of which even their

Persecutors afterwards acquitted them. Some who were obliged to flee their Own Province to save their Lives, have been taken Prisoners, sent back, and are threatened to be tried for their Lives because they fled from Danger. Some have been pulled out of the Reading Desk, because they prayed for the King, and that before Independency was declared. Others have been warned to appear at Militia Musters, with their Arms – have been fined for not appearing, and threatened with Imprisonment for not paying those Fines. Others have had their houses plundered and their Desks broken open, under Pretence of their *treasonable* Papers'.[59]

Offering his understanding of the role of the laity in the revolutionary movement, Inglis is at variance with the facts in New York and all of the other colonies. One of the more interesting aspects of the revolution for the King's church was that no lay leaders stepped forward publicly to speak on its behalf. Yet Inglis remarked, perhaps only with the knowledge gleaned from peering from his pulpit at the congregation before him that 'Very few of the Laity who were respectable Men of Property, have joined in the Rebellion ... Upon the Whole, the Church of England has lost none of its Members by the Rebellion as yet – none, I mean, whose Departure from it can be deemed a Loss. On the contrary, its own Members are more firmly attached to it than ever; and even the sober and more rational among Dissenters – for they are not all equally violent and frantic – look with Reverence and Esteem on the Part which Church People have acted'.[60]

In Lancaster, Pennsylvania, Thomas Barton, a native of Ireland, graduate of Trinity College in Dublin, and brother-in-law to the scientist and astronomer David Rittenhouse, served as a British military chaplain during the French and Indian Wars. For 20 years before the outbreak of the Revolutionary War he served as an S.P.G. missionary. Prompted either by members of his congregation or the members of the local committee, he was unwilling to take the oath of allegiance to America and sought refuge behind the British lines in New York City, where he died in 1780.[61]

Writing to the secretary of the S.P.G. in March 1775, Barton remarked that 'You will not be surprised Rev. Sir, to find that in my letters to you I have dropped no Politics, when I tell you that I am no Politician. I always thought it ill became a Minister of the Gospel to set up for a Minister of State. In the present unhappy and unnatural dispute between the parent kingdom and these colonies, I foresaw that my taking an active part would do no service, but would rather injure the cause I wish to support, I mean that of Religion. I therefore consulted the interests of the Church and my own peace and quiet. Would to God a happy reconciliation would soon take place. Without this, I am afraid a glorious Empire must sink into the hands of foreigners and be lost to Britain!'[62]

More than a year later, Barton observed that the Revolutionary War had begun and the churches he served were closed, stating that 'the Fury of the Populace who would not suffer the Liturgy to be used, unless the Collects and Prayers for the King and royal family were omitted, which my conscience nor the Declaration I made and subscribed when ordained would not allow me to comply with'.[63]

A native of Cecil County, Maryland, William Edmiston of St. Thomas Parish in Baltimore County was charged by the Committee of Safety, in 1775, with teaching from the pulpit that all persons who took the British oath of allegiance and afterwards swore loyalty to the Americans were perjurers, and that all who took arms against the British were guilty of treason. Bluntly asked to recant, Edmiston refused, but he did sign a paper agreeing to desist from teaching such doctrines. His encounters with local Patriot leaders was not finished. In September 1775, he was informed that he would again be brought before the Committee of Safety. Edmiston decided to leave the province. He went to New Castle on the Delaware River, where he embarked on a ship bound for Dublin.[64]

While continuing to offer prayers on behalf of the king and royal family, Ranna Cossitt of Claremont, New Hampshire, Joshua Wingate Weeks of Marblehead, Massachusetts, and Sydenham Thorne of Delaware were brought before the local committee.[65] Although Edward Bass of Newburyport, Massachusetts, dropped the use of the collects on behalf of the royal family from services of worship, he balked at reading the Declaration of Independence to his congregation.[66]

Objections to the resolution of the First Continental Congress on the non-importation and non-consumption of English goods, and the non-exportation of colonial products to the homeland brought at least three men before the committee: John Sayre in Connecticut, Luke Babcock in New York, and William Edmiston in Maryland.[67]

In Connecticut the 38-year-old John Sayre, minister of the church at Fairfield, ran afoul of the local 'Association'. Formed after the passage of the Boston Port Act by the First Continental Congress in 1774, 'the Association' required members to pledge not to import, export, or consume British goods if grievances with England continued unredressed. Sayre informed the members of 'The Association' in print that he could not sign or endorse their statement of principles. He declared that, as a minister, he could not embrace the Association's demand not to give 'offices of humanity and hospitality' to those persons who reject the organisation's principles.[68] He continued that he looked 'on the present unnatural war, as being a judgement of God on the people of Old England, as well as on us Americans, for our many crying offences against his most holy laws, and a loud call to a sincere and immediate return to him and to our duty'.[69] Sayre claimed that he was a friend to both 'friends of America and its liberties, and the enemies of both'. As a Native American, he said, he had enjoyed its liberty and plenty and that 'it can be matter of very little importance to the community, whether I subscribe the association or not; for I am no politician; am not connected with politicians as such; and never will be either'.[70] Stating that his life was his devotion to his ministry, Sayre fulfilled that duty in Fairfield until 1779, when the British raids on the Connecticut coastal towns between 5 and 11 July by forces under William Tryon, Governor of New York, prompted him to flee to New York as a refugee, where he remained until finally moving to New Brunswick, four years later. From Flushing, New York, in 1779 Sayre wrote of all the indignities he had suffered at Fairfield in 1776. His house had been beset by 'more than 200 armed horsemen', and he had been publicly listed as an enemy to his country 'in every store, mill, mechanical shop and public house' and repeatedly in the newspapers.[71]

Providing assistance to British military forces by ministers drew the attention of the committees to William Clark in Massachusetts, Roger Viets and James Nichols in Connecticut, and James Frazer in North Carolina and Virginia. Clark, the S.P.G. missionary at Dedham, was the son of a Congregational minister and a graduate of Harvard College in 1759. He informed the officials of the London-based Society on the eve of the battles of Lexington and Concord, in 1775, that he lived in fear as 'the outrages of the Lawless' had fallen 'upon the Persons and Property of Many of the King's Loyal Subjects'. Clark stated that he had not been disturbed by the 'Sons of Sedition', but that the community was 'in a very melancholy state and apprehension of all the Horrors of a Civil War'.[72] On 6 April 1776, the General Court ordered him to be apprehended as a Loyalist. No action was taken against him at the time and he was left at large and treated no worse than any other loyal man. Yet Clark's church was stoned, and when he closed it to perform services in the private houses of the membership, it was used as a warehouse for Patriot military supplies. At Easter 1777, he explained to his congregation that the time had come and that he was giving up public services because the alternative would be to drop the prayers for the king, which he could not do as it would violate his conscience and his ordination oath.[73]

Clark's fortunes took a dramatic turn in May 1777, when two Loyalists fleeing for their lives sought his assistance. Perhaps foolishly, or possibly in keeping with the biblical command to love thy neighbour, he told them where they might be safe. 'That same Night', he reported, 'about midnight, I was assaulted by a large number ... my house ransacked, and myself us'd with indignity and insult'.[74] Brought before the local Committee on Inspection which disapproved the action of the mob, Clark was confined in a room where, to his distress, he had to look at a picture of Oliver Cromwell. He was taken to Boston for trial. Surprisingly, his lawyer left town unannounced, abandoning Clark to the mercy of the court, which without informing him of the charges against him, ordered him banished and his estate confiscated. The same day, 12 June, he was taken to the guard ship in Boston Harbour. After 10 weeks, the parson was released by the intervention of his Dedham neighbour and friend Nathaniel Ames, the Patriot physician and almanac publisher, and of several members of the General Court, who thought that he had not had a fair trial. Pending a new trial it was ordered that he should 'have leave to return to his home in Dedham, upon his giving bond to the Treasurer of this State in the sum of five hundred pounds, conditioned that he will not hold correspondence with any of the enemies of this, or the united states of America, or say or do anything to the prejudice of said states, and that he will not go more than one mile from his dwelling house'.[75] Clark was not brought to trial again, but in April 1778 the General Court gave him permission to take his family and goods to leave the colony. In June he sailed for Newport in a British transport which was visiting Boston under a flag of truce.[76]

In the night of 16 November 1776, two captured British officers, having escaped confinement, sought help at the Simsbury, Connecticut, house of Roger Viets, who fed and secreted them. The affair being discovered, Viets was committed to jail in Hartford, tried in January, by the Superior Court, and sentenced to a fine of 20 pounds and a year's additional imprisonment. The May Assembly of 1777, upon his abject confession and the petition of his people, converted the latter penalty into confinement within Simsbury's bounds for the remainder of the court-specified period; Viets had to provide a bond in the amount of £1000.[77] At the time of Viets's trial, his closest clerical neighbour, James Nichols of New Cambridge, also came before the Superior Court, charged, together with a parishioner, with treasonable practices. Although acquitted, Nichols probably was guilty. Jeremiah Leaming's conspicuous Loyalism caused him to be taken from his bed in Norwalk parsonage, on a wintry night late in 1776, and lodged for several hours in Fairfield jail, where lack of a fire caused a severe cold to settle in his hip, making him a cripple for life.

Several other ministers in Connecticut and other colonies came under similar close scrutiny by members of local committees of safety and were confined to either the immediate neighbourhood or to their houses. In Stratford, Connecticut, Ebenezer Kneeland, a Yale graduate and between 1764 and 1767 chaplain to a British regiment in America, was confined by the Committee of Safety to the limits of his parish.[78] He suffered a collapse and died on 17 April 1777. Samuel Andrews of Wallingford, placed under heavy bond, was once restricted to his house and home lot. John Rutgers Marshall of Woodbury also was 'put on the limits', to use the contemporary expression. At other times he endured physical abuse, including a most severe beating.[79]

A native of Albany and a graduate of King's College in the class of 1770, John Doty was the minister of St. George's Church in Schenectady, New York. On 14 July 1775, he was brought before a Committee of Safety where he was accused of plotting with blacks against the town.[80] Although acquitted, the young parson was later taken to Albany and charged, on 17 May 1777, with being a Loyalist.[81] Again he was released, this time through the intervention of friends, and allowed to return home. He remained there until Burgoyne's defeat in 1777, and then, with the permission of General Horatio Gates, he left for Canada. He served as chaplain to the First Battalion of Sir John Johnson's Regiment, from 1777 to 1781, and sailed for England in 1781.[82]

At Yonkers, in Westchester County, Luke Babcock, son of Chief Justice Joshua Babcock of Connecticut and a graduate of Yale in 1755, resisted the rebellion declaring in 1776 that 'I have not failed to admonish the people under my care plainly, repeatedly, and publickly for the year past that rebellion will lead its abettors to confusion in this world and everlasting destruction in the next'.[83] He was seized and taken before the New York Provincial Congress meeting at Fishkill. After the battle of Lexington, New York Patriots began exiling dangerous Loyalists to other states.[84] Babcock was ordered to be held in custody at Hartford, Connecticut. His health broken, he was released and died at Yonkers on 18 February 1777, aged 39 years.[85]

In Maryland, John Bowie, a native of the colony and educated at Marischal College in Aberdeen, Scotland, served Worcester Parish at the outbreak of the Revolutionary War. He was banished by the Committee of Safety to Frederick County, on 23 July 1776, having been implicated in a Loyalist uprising. Although confined to the county for two years, he continued to preach. Soon afterwards he took the oath of fidelity to the new state and was permitted to return to the Eastern shore, resuming his career until his death in 1801.[86] A colleague of Bowie in the province, Hugh Deane, owner of the plantation 'William Conqueror', was the loyalist minister of Copley Parish, who was wounded in a fray and was imprisoned. He died in 1777.[87]

The deliberations of the Continental Congress represented the culmination and crystallisation of nearly a century of controversies for the English church. After the sessions of the First Congress were completed in October 1774, the momentum of colonial civil affairs was set on a course towards independence. In the first instance, the long-time disputes critical of Anglican ecclesiastical polity and the church's link to English government were shaped and advanced by such Congregational church leaders as Increase and Cotton Mather, Jonathan Mayhew, and Charles Chauncy. Their arguments were further refined and recast by the essays of John and Samuel Adams in the 1760s, contributions that linked the fate of the church to the authority and power of Parliament. In league with John Wilkes, the Adams' criticism of episcopacy, the church, and Parliament was proclaimed on the pages of Boston and London newspapers.

The Congress's establishment of the Continental Association and Committees of Safety provided a framework for scrutinising and spotlighting the political sentiments of local ministers of the church. Local committees of safety did not limit their interest to the political opinions of the most prominent Anglican parsons but included all men with doubtful loyalties. From Maine to Georgia, Anglican ministers in many communities were subjected to varying degrees of interrogation and discipline by local committees. In addition congregations in cities, towns, and the countryside were exposed to the consequences of changed political circumstances. The churches were visible reminders not only of the Church of England's heritage but also of objectionable English policies: of tea, taxes, and troops. In the New England region, more than any other section of America, the presence of the church rekindled for partisans the memory of more than two centuries of Puritan and Anglican conflict. Cascading political and military events would divide and erode congregations, bewilder clergymen, diminish financial support, and terminate links between London church and civil officials. A band of parsons valiantly attempted to restrain the tide of civil events by publishing pamphlets that challenged the legitimacy of the Congress and defended imperial government.

11
Critics of the Continental Congress and *Common Sense*: Jonathan Boucher and Charles Inglis

The deliberations and decisions of the First Continental Congress meeting in Philadelphia, in September and October 1774 in retrospect, were a watershed experience for the English church. Newspapers in every provincial capital reported the proceedings and that prompted objectionable articles and essays from several leading Anglican ministers. The dramatically changed political circumstances for the institution was most recently framed by a decade of forceful colonial criticism of imperial policies: including the Stamp Act riots, the quartering of British troops, the Intolerable and Quebec Acts, the battles at Lexington, Concord, and Bunker Hill, and the publication of Thomas Paine's *Common Sense*.

Jonathan Boucher, serving St Anne's Church in Annapolis in 1770 and 1771, and Queen Anne's Parish in Prince George's County from November 1771 to September 1775, was the leading cleric in Maryland during the decade before the outbreak of the Revolutionary War. He had earned his Loyalist reputation as a preacher rather than as a pamphleteer. The audience for his Sunday morning sermons were the men of Annapolis and Maryland who led the provincial government and legislature, who directed commercial firms and managed counting houses, and who set the social fashion of the province.

Moses Coit Tyler has ranked Boucher in league with such New England Loyalist luminaries as Thomas Hutchinson and Daniel Leonard and as one of the finest spokesmen of the Loyalist writers of the period, based on his sermons and essays that were not published until 1797.[1] He is an interesting ally of the two accomplished Massachusetts leaders, although there are significant differences. Unlike the Boston Loyalist spokesmen, Boucher was not born to privilege, nor schooled in social ways by prominent parents, nor the beneficiary of a Harvard education. Nonetheless, his inclusion in such distinguished company reflects the social, economic, and geographic breadth and diversity of the Loyalist leadership.

His only work published in America was *A Letter from a Virginian to the Members of the Congress* (Boston, 1774, New York, 1774), an entreaty addressed to the delegates attending the sessions in Philadelphia during September and October 1774.[2] Acknowledging that the issues of the day indicated that the 'harmony between Great Britain and her Colonies is in danger of being destroyed', he declared, 'every man has a right to offer his advice'.[3] The parson urged the delegates to forge a resolution to the complaints of grievance with the mother country that was observant of the terms and legacy of colonial charters and in the vein of the political thought of Philip Sydney and John Locke.[4] Noting that Parliament's authority over colonial affairs was only recently challenged, Boucher recommended that the Congress's participants propose an accommodation on the issue of taxes.[5]

Boucher's further words on the course of revolutionary events were not published until 1797, when a collection of his sermons appeared in London.[6] He noted in the preface to the volume that comprised 'such Discourses as seemed to myself most likely to shew (in a way that can hardly be suspected of misrepresentation) the state of two of the most valuable Colonies, just before, and at the time of the breaking out of the troubles'.[7] Now serving as Vicar of Epson in County Surrey in England, he added that 'In transcribing these Discourses for the Press, as my own opinions and principles have undergone no change, I have made a con- science of delivering them to the public very nearly as they were deliv- ered from the pulpit. No assertion, however hazardous or hardy, has been suppressed. Many things, which though relevant and necessary at the time, are now no longer so, have notwithstanding been retained, merely for the sake of consistency'.[8] Since the late nineteenth century, Boucher's sermons have been acknowledged by scholars as a significant reflection of Loyalist ideology during the years immediately preceding the revolution.

Anne Y. Zimmer has cogently argued that although Boucher's *A View of the Causes and Consequences of the American Revolution* is of interest in evaluating his political and social thought, it must be approached with caution about supposing the sermons to be representative of his thought in the American years. The evidence indicates that the sermons are reconstructions necessitated by the loss of his papers and documents. None of this means that the sermons bear no relationship at all to Boucher's unfolding ideas between 1763 and 1775. The text he pub- lished in 1797 may very well expound, in a general way, on the content

of at least certain sermons that he delivered earlier in Maryland, particularly during the last few years of his career there. Professor Zimmer
reminds us that the sermons cannot be accepted simply as literal repro-
ductions of his American sermons, and therefore as verbatim accounts
of his earlier political thought.[9]

Remembered by historians and biographers for embracing the conservative political theory of his day, passive obedience and non-resistance,
it was merely one aspect of his informed and complicated temperament.
The parson's keen and wide-ranging intellectual interests are recounted
in the catalogue of his library that was sold at auction in London after
his wife's death in 1806.[10] An Englishmen, born in 1738 in the village
of Blencogo, in the parish of Bromfield and in the county of
Cumberland, Boucher recalled in his autobiography that his family
'lived in a state of penury and hardship as I have never since seen
equalled, no not even in parish almshouses'.[11] The recollection of his
childhood experience may have been an exaggeration of his circumstances, because his father maintained an ale house and was able to
teach his son to read, and at age six he began studying Latin at Bromfield
school.[12] Boucher's educational interests were greatly enhanced and
advanced when ten years later he became an usher at St. Bee's school
under the watchful tutelage of the Headmaster, the Reverend John
James.[13] Educated at Queen's College, Oxford, James gave influential
direction and inspiration to Boucher's academic interests. In turn, the
men became life-long friends, sharing the joys and sorrows of their personal experiences, despite living worlds apart.[14]

On the recommendation of this headmaster, Boucher had come to
America in the summer of 1759 as a tutor to a gentleman's sons at Port
Royal in Virginia.[15] Three years later he returned to London for ordination, having been assured of an appointment to the vacant Hanover
Parish in King George's County in Virginia.[16] Subsequently he removed
to the rectory of St. Mary's in Caroline County, Maryland, where he
bought a small plantation and took nearly 30 boys as pupils, 'most of
them the sons of persons of the first condition in the colony'.[17] Among
the boys he instructed was 'Jacky' Custis, the son of Martha Washington,
for whose proper training his stepfather, Col. George Washington, was
much concerned.[18]

In 1770 Boucher was appointed to the rectory of St. Anne's in
Annapolis, an appointment of considerable opportunity and prestige.
The significance of the community, Customs Officer William Eddis
declared, is that it is 'the seat of government; the public offices are here
established; and as many of the principal families have chosen this

place for their residence, there are few towns of the same size in any part of the British dominions that can boast a more polished society'.[19] Boucher also served *ex officio* as chaplain of the Lower House of the Assembly and according to his autobiographical account, *Reminiscences*, he played an influential role in shaping legislation. Doubtless, his memory inflated his political power, as he was unable, in 1773, to prevent a reduction in the provincial stipend of the clergy.[20] Nonetheless, Boucher thrived in Annapolis, as a preacher; as a friend of the governor, Robert Eden; as a member, by marriage, of a prominent Maryland family; as a patron of the local theatre; and as a member of the celebrated Homony Club.[21] He had come a long way from his village of Blencogo in Cumberland to a prestigious Annapolis pulpit.

Parson Boucher viewed all the various extralegal organisations, which the colonists devised in the 1760s and 1770s to resist the acts of Parliament, as seditious.[22] As early as 1765, he took a keen interest in the political affairs of the colonies, criticising the passage of the Stamp Act and its effects on the colonial economy, directing his observations and opinions publicly to well-placed government ministers or high-level church leaders, to whom such pleas may have raised some degree of interest. It is through his private correspondence that we comprehensively discover the range of Boucher's sentiments. Privately he expressed his concerns to his mentor, John James, headmaster of the isolated and remote school at St. Bees in Cumberland, writing that 'You can not conceive what a sad situation we are in, occasioned by this terrible Stamp Act. The troubles and alarms in England in 1745 hardly exceeded what is now to be seen or heard of, every day, all over North America'.[23] Although a clergyman, Boucher noted that 'It may not perhaps be extremely prudent in an obscure individual deeply to interest himself in public business; but as no individual whatsoever, whose understanding is not totally blind, and whose heart is still undepraved, can help seeing and owning that the Act in question is, in every sense, oppressive, impolitic and illegal, it is therefore, I think, scarce honest to be silent'.[24] The parson professed that the Americans are to be pitied as 'their best and dearest rights, which, ever Britons they are anxiously jealous of, have been mercilessly invaded by Parliament, who till now, never pretended to any such privileges; and who, even supposing they had a right to impose upon us as an internal tax, are as ignorant of the means of doing it with the ease to the people, and profit to the state, as they would be to prescribe an assessment for the inhabitants of Kamschatka'.[25]

Unhesitatingly and shrewdly Boucher complained that British officials had little information of provincial commercial affairs, and worse, took no initiative to inform themselves on such matters. He pungently observed that those colonial officials entrusted with providing such details were 'either too ignorant, or too knavish to give any to be depended upon'.[26] Four years later the parson was no less firm in supporting colonial opposition to the Townshend Acts, 'I do think the American opposition the most warrantable, generous, and manly that history can produce'.[27]

For Boucher, the weakness of government in America was part of a more general feebleness of social institutions, of which the precarious English church was an outstanding example. Where there was no loyalty to the church, he wrote, there could not be loyalty to the State. He lamented the absence of bishops in the colonies, and the poverty and indifferent discipline of the church. Americans, he remarked, were 'not sufficiently aware of the importance of externals in religion'; church services were 'narrow and contracted'; buildings, 'ordinary and mean'.[28] In the south, the discipline of the Church of England was more nearly Presbyterian than Episcopal, and the ministers had to cater to the tastes of their congregations to an undignified degree: '*Voice and action* ... almost constantly carried it'.[29] With so little attention by the State to the Church, 'it was small wonder', Boucher thought, that nothing was 'so wholly without form or comeliness, as government in America'.[30]

When the Maryland provincial convention in 1775 proclaimed a solemn fast day by way of protest, Boucher announced his intention of taking an opposing position. He informed the provincial authorities that he would be preaching against active resistance. This turn of events prompted civil officials to forbid their chaplain from entering his pulpit, and placed a body of armed men around it to enforce their command. From this time on, believing his life in danger, Boucher later claimed that he never preached without a pair of loaded pistols lying on the cushion.[31] He was under constant surveillance by the local Committee of Safety, growing more and more unpopular, and burnt in effigy.[32]

The Maryland parson bluntly attacked the resolutions of the Second Continental Congress, in 1775, with a letter published in the *New York Gazette* and addressed to the 'Deputies in Congress from the Southern Provinces'.[33] Boucher declared that the representatives of the southern colonies had been 'Sent originally as they were to mediate between us and our parent State, even the few who appointed you could and did commission you only to examine into and ascertain our alleged grievances, and to point out the best means of obtaining redress'.[34] He argued and charged that the single question before Congress was, 'whether the Parliament of Great Britain can constitutionally lay internal taxes on her colonies; and if they cannot, whether the 3d. per lb. duty on tea be a tax or not. You have been pleased very summarily to *Resolve* that they cannot'.[35] Boucher reminded the Congress 'that Resolves are not arguments; and we cannot but think it is assuming somewhat too much of the air and consequence of legal and constitutional Assemblies, thus superciliously to obtrude *Resolves* upon us, without consenting to give us any of the reasons which we are to suppose influenced you to make them. And yet from all we see of these Resolves (of which we claim a right to judge, and to be governed by or not as we think we see reason) we are free to tell you we think them unwise, and also that in their operation they will be ruinous'.[36]

Parson Boucher, ever a firm supporter of established authority, recognised that the course of events was leading to irreversible civil war. The colonies were not equipped to defend themselves against the superior forces of Great Britain's army. He cautioned the delegates from the southern colonies that the more enterprising and restless fellow colonists of the North, from New England and Boston would seize their provinces in particular. The 'Northern brethren would then become also the Goths and Vandals of America. This is not a chimerical conjecture: the history of mankind proves that it is founded in truth and the nature of things. And should the reflection chance to make any such impression on you, as we humbly think it ought, we entreat you only to remember that you are – *from the Southern Provinces*'.[37] He declared that 'Many of you, if not all, we know were educated in the bosom of the Church of England, and would of course be shocked to think that her generous polity should, for the ask only of a little paltry pre-eminence, and a few noisy huzzas to yourselves, be given up for a wild Republic of mad Independents'.[38] Pointedly acknowledging the Boston-based revolutionary leadership, Boucher rhetorically asked his readers if they had no suspicions that 'your fellow-Patriots from the north mediate a Reformation as they call it, in Church as well as in State'?[39] Englishmen, he stated, have been 'Taught by our fathers and by all our history to love and reverence the Constitution both in Church and State, under which they and we have hitherto happily lived and flourished, be not, we beg leave to entreat you, so fascinated by New England politics as to vote for destroying it, without first well knowing what we are to have in its stead'.[40]

Boucher disputed Locke himself and went about this by systematically examining Sir Robert Filmer, whom Locke had attempted to dismiss from serious consideration for all time. 'I have lately perused the book', he wrote of *Patriarcha*, 'and did not find it deserving of all that extreme contempt with which it is now the fashion to mention it'.

He was impressed with Filmer's arguments for the origin of government in the family, and for the paternal character of all authority. Furthermore, despite his 'very extravagant notions on monarchy', Filmer's essential thesis, that men are born not free, but subjects, had not been answered by Locke. When Boucher wrote that he did not believe the end of government was 'the common good of mankind', but rather 'the advancement of God's honour', he meant partly that the government ought to sanctify the laws, the traditions, the ceremonies, and usages that distinguished civilised, social man from man in a state of savagery.[41]

A skilled and eloquent wordsmith, Boucher is best known as the author of 'On Civil Liberty; Passive Obedience, and Non Resistance', which was the penultimate discourse in his work *Causes and Consequences of the American Revolution*.[42] The address has long been cited by historians of the Loyalist mind during the American Revolution for its conservative point of view. Boucher wrote the discourse in 1775, and delivered it from the pulpit of Queen Anne's Parish in Annapolis soon after, in response to a fiery Patriotic sermon delivered by Jacob Duché in Christ Church in Philadelphia on 7 July, *The Duty of Standing Fast in Our Spiritual and Temporal Liberties* (Philadelphia, 1775), a contribution which Boucher candidly found 'of a pernicious and dangerous tendency'.[43]

Not an original political theorist, Boucher was familiar with the writings of Locke and Hobbes. Jonathan C. D. Clark has noted that the Maryland minister's conservative view of the state and the individual's relationship to the established government was very much in step with the thinking of a core of Anglican leaders during the last quarter of the seventeenth century and through at least the first half of the eighteenth century, and in particular to the doctrine of divine right of kings.[44] As a scheme of political thought, it was more than an attempt to justify a particular form of monarchy; it was a genuine attempt to relate authority and liberty to Christian morality. The doctrine, that a monarch in the hereditary line of succession had a divine and indefeasible right to the kingship and authority, also implied that for a subject to rebel against him is the worst of political crimes. Where active obedience to an evil ruler is morally impossible, it held that passive obedience; the willing acceptance of any penalty imposed for non-compliance is demanded. The doctrine, especially elaborated by Tory divines in the late 1670s and early 1680s offered a view of civil society which was both authoritarian and providential. Its chief apologist was Sir Robert Filmer and his posthumously published work *Patriarcha* (1680). Boucher believed and declared that 'obedience to Government is every man's duty, because it is every man's interest; but it is particularly incumbent on Christians, because (in addition to its moral fitness) it is enjoined by the positive commands of God, and therefore, when Christians are disobedient to human ordinances, they are disobedient to God. [45] To pursue liberty, then, in a manner not warranted by law, what ever the pretence may be, is clearly hostile to liberty, and those persons who thus *promise you liberty, are themselves the servants of corruption'.*[46]

Boucher disputed Jacob Duché's statement that 'as a settled maxim, that the end of government is the common good of mankind'.[47] He embraced completely Filmer's key ideas 'that government is not of human, but divine origin; and that the government of a family is the basis, or pattern, of all other government'.[48] Boucher argued that 'it is with the most perfect propriety that the supreme magistrate, whether consisting of one or of many, and whether denominated an emperor, a king, an archon, a dictator, a consul, or a senate, is to be regarded and venerated as a vicegerent of God. ... All government, whether lodged in one or in many, is, in it's nature, absolute and irresistible'.[49] The advancing revolutionary cause prompted Boucher to pronounce that 'no government upon earth can rightfully compel any one of it's subjects to an active compliance with any thing that is, or that appears to his conscience to be, inconsistent with, or contradictory to, the known laws of God; because every man is under a prior and superior obligation to *obey God in all things'.*[50] In summation, Boucher forcefully proclaimed that 'without some paramount and irresistible power, there can be no government. In our Constitution, this supremacy is rested in the King and the Parliament, and subordinate to them, in our Provincial legislatures'.[51]

In all respects it is Boucher's 'Farewell Address' to his congregation in 1775 that neatly and elegantly encapsulates his political thinking.[52] The parson's words mirror his thinking: he was no longer mounting the pulpit to attempt with learning to persuade his congregation, since cataclysmic events and his own reflection have forced an irrevocable decision. A cogent, coherent, and emotional personal statement, Boucher tells his congregation he is leaving Annapolis, Maryland, America, and going home. He preached on the text from Nehemiah, 6:10–11: 'Afterward I came unto the house of Shemaiah, the son of Delaiah, the son of Mehetabel, who was shut in; and he said, Let us meet together in the house of God, within the temple, and let us shut the doors of the temple; for they will come to slay thee; yea, in the night will they come to slay thee. And I said, Should such a man as I flee? And who is there, who, being as I am, would go into the temple to save his life? I will not go in'.[53]

Writing to George Washington in August 1775, Boucher displayed a deep sense of betrayal and outrage. The men had been friends since the days that he served as the tutor to Washington's stepson, John Parke Custis, and despite their association events prompted them both to take different sides on civil issues. Boucher recounted to Washington that 'No Tory has yet in a single instance misused or injured a Whig merely for being a Whig ... With respect to the Whigs, however, the case has been directly the reverse; a Tory at all in the power of a Whig never escapes ill treatment merely because of his being a Tory'. Reminding Washington that 'I have at least the merit of consistency; and neither in anything in any private or public conversation, in anything I have written, nor in anything I have delivered from the pulpit, have I ever asserted any other opinions or doctrines than you have repeatedly heard me assert, in my own house or yours. You cannot say that I desired to be run down, vilified, and injured in the manner which you know has fallen to my lot, merely because I cannot bring myself to think on some political points just as you and your party would have me think. And yet you have borne to look on, at least as an unconcerned spectator, if not an abettor, whilst like the poor frogs in the fable, I have in a manner been pelted to death'.[54] Boucher harshly closed his remarks to Washington, 'You are no longer worthy of my friendship; a man of honour can no longer without dishonour be connected with you. With your cause I renounce you.'[55]

Under constant surveillance by the local Committee of Safety, Boucher grew more and more unpopular. Fearing the worst, he and his wife, the former Eleanor Addison, a member of the prominent Maryland family, abandoned their home and thousand-acre plantation near Alexandria on the Potomac and departed for England in September 1775, never to return again. Friends procured for him the curacy of Paddington on the resignation of his friend Dr. Myles Cooper, the former president of King's College in New York, and a pension from the government, while he added to his income by tutoring students and writing for journals.[56] In the autumn of 1785, he was instituted to the vicarage of Epsom, south of London, on the presentation of the Reverend John Parkhurst, the bibliographer and heir to family estates in the community. Parkhurst knew Boucher only as a clergyman who had 'distinguished himself in America during the revolution for his loyalty, and by teaching the unsophisticated doctrines of the Church of England to a set of rebellious schismatics, at the hazard of his life'.[57] Boucher continued to acquire books for his library and served the parish of Epsom for the remainder of his life.[58]

He provides us with a glimpse of his wealth in his petition to the Loyalist Claims Commission in London for loss of property. He recorded that he owned 36 slaves, employed eight white servants, and had a library estimated to be worth £500 sterling. The parson calculated his loss of property at £5645 sterling. The Commission awarded him £2,275 for relief of his losses. He received a pension of £100 sterling from the Treasury on his arrival in England in 1775, a sum that was later reduced to £60 per year.[59]

Boucher's financial circumstances, based on his wife's family's considerable wealth, set him apart from his fellow Anglican parsons. He was in the class of well-to-do Maryland planters rather than in the ranks of a modest country priest or a S.P.G. missionary living on an annual £50 stipend.

Charles Inglis

In New York City, Charles Inglis, a minister at Trinity Church, challenged a radical political polemicist from a perspective that differed from Jonathan Boucher's pulpit declarations. Irish-born and educated at Trinity College in Dublin, Inglis was the youngest son of the Reverend Archibald Inglis of Len and Kilcar in Donegal.[60] He was descended from a Scottish clerical family, his immediate ancestors for four generations having been clergymen of the Scottish Episcopal Church, outlawed since 1690. Arriving in America in 1756, the 22-year-old Inglis taught in the Free School at Lancaster, Pennsylvania, for two years before travelling to England for ordination and assignment as the S.P.G. missionary at sparsely settled Dover in Delaware.[61]

Migrating to New York in 1764, Inglis served for 12 years as the assistant minister of Trinity Church, one of the most prominent appointments in the colonial church, under the rector, Samuel Auchmuty.[62] Here he was at the centre of political and church activity within the province and the Middle Colonies. A post that gave him an advantage of frequent contact with intellectually accomplished nearby parsons like Thomas Bradbury Chandler and Samuel Seabury, and the availability of a steady stream of inter-colonial and English information published in the newspapers. Ambrose Serle, the British government's agent in New York reported to Lord Dartmouth that among the local parsons Inglis was 'the best character I know among them and of the best abilities'.[63]

During the episcopacy controversy he firmly defended the Bishop of Landaff John Ewer's *Anniversary Sermon* before the members of the

Society for the Propagation of the Gospel in London in 1767 urging the appointment of a colonial prelate.[64] But in 1774 and 1775 he was exposed to the conflicting political ideas that were debated in the provincial assembly and in Philadelphia at the First and Second Continental Congresses. The local printing presses were daily generating newspapers, tracts, and books that advocated revolutionary ideas and challenged British policies. Beginning in 1776, New York City was a battleground for the Patriot and British armies and the uncertainties of pillage and destruction caused by occupation and combat. Between 1776 and 1783, Inglis and New York would experience the unsettling rumours of imminent military action and the actual interruption of their daily life. In fact, Inglis would move his family to safety in the Highlands in the Hudson River valley 70 miles north of the city.[65]

Despite the desperate rhythms of the opening months of the war, Inglis continued his long-standing plea for a bishop, 'to make that Provision for the American Church which is necessary, and place it on at least an equal Foot with other Denominations, by granting it an Episcopate, and thereby allowing it a full Toleration'.[66] He held the opinion that if a prelate was not soon appointed 'I think there is a Moral Certainty that such another will never again offer, and I must conclude in that Case the Government is equally infatuated with the Americans at present. If fifty years a lapse without an Episcopate here, there will be no Occasion for one afterwards; and to fix one then will be as impracticable as it would be useless'.[67] He appealed to all 'judicious Persons, whether it is not contrary to sound Policy, as it certainly is to Right, Reason and Justice, that the King's loyal Subjects here, Members of the National Church, should be denied a Privilege, the want of which will discourage and diminish their Numbers, and that merely to gratify the Clamours of Dissenters, who have now discovered such Enmity to the Constitution; and who will ever clamour against any Thing that will tend to benefit or increase the Church here'.[68]

With the publication of Thomas Paine's essay *Common Sense* in Philadelphia in January 1776 the political debate over dependence or independence from England became public and bitter. Inglis was an unlikely candidate to emerge from the Revolutionary movement as a pivotal political pamphleteer. Paine had arrived in Philadelphia merely 14 months earlier from London armed with a recommendation from Benjamin Franklin.[69] The son of a poor Quaker corset maker, his education had been simple and brief, and he had been luckless in business, marriage, and in life. He was without a trace of Quaker humility, had no capacity for mystic self-surrender, and, since he fought in two wars, no absolute doctrines of non-resistance. It was a tract that enjoyed an enormous circulation, 120,000 copies being printed within three months. It boldly urged the immediate declaration of independence, not merely as a striking practical gesture that would help unite the colonies and secure French and Spanish aid, but as the fulfilment of America's moral obligation to the world. The colonies must fall away eventually, Paine said; a continent could not remain tied to an island. If now, while their society was still uncorrupt, natural, and democratic, these colonies should free themselves from a vicious monarchy, they could alter human destiny by their example.[70]

Paine's essay vulcanised public opinion: those persons who were opposed to separation from Britain made much of the generosity of the mother country towards the colonies, but the mother country at the moment was hardly acting the role of the benevolent parent. A fear was that independence might bring far greater evils: social levelling, the weakening of property rights, a mob regime, even continental anarchy. It was not at all certain that the colonists could establish stable and responsible governments to replace those that would be destroyed. The risks of a declaration of independence were vast.

But the advocates of independence from Great Britain produced even more compelling appeals to reason and to passion. The 'rights' of Americans could not, they contended, be rendered inviolate within the empire. Should Britain promise to respect them and American arms be set aside, Britain would very likely resume her tyrannical measures, perhaps at a time when America was seriously disunited and ill prepared to resist. American 'rights' would be assured under American governments; such governments, respectable, responsible, and enduring, could be established, and some sort of American union could be established as well. An independent America would be free to manufacture, and to trade as it wished with all the world. America must, cried the champions of separation, assert her independence, make an American union of American states, and seek aid and alliances in France and Spain. Samuel London, publisher of the 'open press' *New York Packet* had advertised that he would print and sell an answer to *Common Sense*. Inglis accepted the challenge and wrote in 1776 a Loyalist's response to Paine's tract.[71] He argued in *The True Interest of America Impartially Stated* (1776) that 'I find no Common Sense in this Pamphlet [Paine's], but much uncommon frenzy. It is an outrageous insult on the common sense of Americans, an insidious attempt to poison their minds, and seduce them from their loyalty and truest interest. The principles of government laid down in it are not only false, but too absurd to have entered in the head of a crazy politician before. Even Hobbes would blush to own the author for a disciple. He unites the violence and rage of a republican, with all the enthusiasm and folly of a fanatic'.[72]

The public outrage to Inglis's publication prompted a midnight mob, led by the energetic Isaac Sears and others, to seize his *The True Interest of America*.[73] Six months after the publication of the tract, Inglis reported to the Secretary of the London-based S.P.G., Richard Hind, that *Common Sense* 'was one of the most virulent, artful & pernicious Pamphlets I ever met with, and perhaps the Wit of Man could not devise one better calculated to do Mischief. It seduced thousands'.[74] He declared to the English church official that he had placed himself 'at the Risque not only of my Liberty, but of my Life, I drew up an Answer, and had it printed here, but the Answer was no sooner advertised, than the whole Impression was seized by the Sons of Liberty and burnt. I then sent a Copy to Philadelphia, where it was printed, and soon went thro a second Edition'.[75] Inglis noted that 'this Answer was laid to my Charge, and swelled the Catalogue of my Political Transgressions. In short, I was in the utmost Danger; and it is to the over-ruling Hand of Providence that I attribute my Deliverance and Safety'.[76] The parson had stoutly battled the author and pamphlet that crystallised for the public the critical and crucial revolutionary ideas of the colonial radicals but the impact, if any, of Inglis's words on the debate remains unclear. We only know with certainty that his position was finally swept away in the tide of the Revolutionary War.

Writing again to Richard Hind, the S.P.G. Secretary in London on 31 October 1776, the New York minister remarked that for the clergy the Declaration of Independence on 4 July 1776, was a watershed experience. He contended that 'The Declaration increased the embarrassment of the Clergy. To officiate publickly, and not pray for the King and Royal Family according to the Liturgy, was against their Duty and Oath, as well as Dictates of their Consciences; and yet to use the Prayers for the King and Royal Family, would have drawn inevitable Destruction on them'.[77] Inglis reported that the only course that the ministers could pursue to avoid both demands was to suspend the public worship and close their churches.[78] This was done by the clergy and without the benefit of consulting one another informally or as a result of a decision by the ministers in convention, although, he remarked, one or two churches omitted the Prayers for the King and Royal Family, and that the churches in Philadelphia remained open.[79]

Candidly disclosing to Hind his opinion regarding the origin of the war, Inglis noted that while 'civil liberty was the ostensible object [of the Revolution], the Bait that was flung out to catch the Populace at large, and engage them in the Rebellion; yet it is now past all Doubt, that an Abolition of the Church of England was one of the principal springs of the Dissenting Leaders' Conduct; and hence the Unanimity of Dissenters in this Business, their universal Defection from Government-emancipating themselves from the Jurisdiction of Great Britain, and becoming Independent, was a necessary Step towards this grand Object'.[80] A month earlier he had told Ambrose Serle, Lord Dartmouth's representative in America, that the 'controversy has been fomented by Presbyterian preachers, with a view to the extirpation of the Church of England from the colonies'.[81] An opinion that prompted Serle to record in his journal that it was 'strange, that Men, who enjoy full Liberty for the Profession of their own Principles, should have so little Decency, or even Christianity, as to be intolerant to the Religion established by that Government which has expressly provided a Toleration for their own! However, this is an argument for the full Establishment of the Church in the final Settlement of Affairs'.[82]

An astute observer of American affairs, Serle took a more detached and cautious view of the role of ministers in the political controversy, confiding to the pages of his private journal that 'One thing is very observable in the Clergy of this Country; both those of the Establishment and of the Presbyterian Interest, who take the Lead, are Fire-brands to a man, and can speak with no sort of Patience of each other. These have fomented half the present Divisions; nor is it likely that they will be quiet in future, but under a Power that may controul them both. One would think, by the Conduct of these men, that God had a great temporal Interest in this World, which wholly depended upon the management and Exaltation of their Party; and that, having so good an End, even Spite and malice might be employed as the means: But – *non tali auxilio, non defensoribus istis Deus eget*'.[83]

During the rest of the war, Inglis actively published pamphlets and proclaimed from the pulpit the sufferings and miseries of the Loyalists. In open letters under the pen name 'Papinian', which appeared in the Loyalist press, Rivington's *New York Gazette and Gaine's New York Gazette and Weekly Mercury*, he tried to persuade the Patriots of the error of their ways. Commenting on the role of clergymen, both Dissenters and Virginia Anglicans, in the course of the revolutionary movement he remarked that 'The pulpits of Dissenters universally throughout the continent, and those of a few *renegado* Churchmen to the southward, have resounded not with the gospel, but with politics not with meek lessons of peace, but with zealous exhortations to war to stimulate the lukewarm, animate the desponding, and warmly engage all in your interests'.[84] His reservations about the calibre and composition of leadership of the Congress were candidly and harshly stated, 'Republicans, smugglers, debtors and men of desperate fortunes, were the principal promoters of this unnatural rebellion'.[85] Inglis encouraged the reader of his pamphlets to determine if the members of Congress were fit to lead the country and urged them to contribute 'what you can to shake off speedily the yoke of republican tyranny, and re-unite yourselves to the parent state, from which republican ambition, phrenzy and delusion have served you'.[86]

The anniversary of the death of King Charles I provided Inglis with the opportunity to deliver a sermon at St. Paul's Chapel in New York, on 30 January 1780. He took as his text the often-used I Peter, 2:17, 'Fear God, Honour the King'. The Loyalist parson proclaimed that 'All the King's subjects are bound to Allegiance, before, or even without, any Oath for that purpose'. Inglis declared that 'if the Oath of Allegiance be broken by violating the duty to which it obligeth, it aggravates a man's guilt, by adding perjury to treason'.[87] Leaving no doubt of his position, he declaimed that 'To honour the King therefore, is not only the duty which God requires and reason approves; but it is a duty, by the discharge of which we contribute to the happiness of all our fellow subjects. For hereby we support the Constitution and Government which secure to them that happiness'.[88] The current political circumstances and war Inglis claimed 'originated from those who dishonoured the King, traduced his Government, trampled on his Authority, and imputed to him designs which had not the least foundation in truth. Imaginary dangers were pretended; the passions of the populace were inflamed to a degree of phrenzy; and every engine was enlarged to carry on the work of sedition'.[89] The parson entreated his audience to 'honour the King by faithfully adhering to, and supporting his Government'.[90]

A man of solid conviction, Inglis remained at his post until 1 November 1783, when he resigned and then sailed with his family to England with the evacuating British troops. He remarked 'when I go from America I do not leave behind me an individual against whom I have the smallest degree of resentment or ill will'.[91] After several years of intensive lobbying with church and civil officials in London as Parliament pondered legislation for the administration of Canada, Inglis finally won his reward in 1787, when he was appointed the first bishop of Nova Scotia – the first Anglican colonial bishop.[92]

The task for the clergy under the changed circumstances was to continue their ministry. Unlike their Virginia colleagues, New York parsons did not become members of the local Committees of Safety or enlist in the provincial militia. In fact, Inglis was bitterly critical of the Virginia parsons, confiding to Hind that 'For my Part I never expected much Good of those Clergy among them who opposed an American Episcopate; if such should now renounce their Alegiance and abandon their Duty, it is no more than what might naturally be looked for'.[93]

12

A Challenge to Radical Politics: Samuel Seabury, Jr., and Thomas Bradbury Chandler

Samuel Seabury, Jr., of Westchester County in New York, and Thomas Bradbury Chandler of Elizabeth Town in New Jersey, were staunch defenders of the crown and Parliament, in 1774 and 1775, against the rising radical rhetoric. Their backgrounds were strikingly similar: both men were native colonists, graduates of Yale College and nearly of the same age, Seabury was 45 and Chandler 48 years old. They were raised in families that had been members of the Congregational Church, Seabury's father was a student at Yale during the 1722 'Apostasy' of the rector, Timothy Cutler, and several tutors who converted to the English church. After completing his education at Harvard and a short stint as a Congregational minister in Maine, the senior Seabury was converted to the Anglican ministry and served as the S.P.G. missionary at New London, Connecticut. Samuel Seabury, Jr., a graduate of Yale College in 1744, spent the years 1752 and 1753 as a student at the University of Edinburgh, completing his medical training while waiting to reach the canonical age for ordination. After receiving orders Seabury was appointed by the S.P.G. in 1754 as a missionary to the English church in New Brunswick, New Jersey. Chandler converted to the English church while a student at Yale College. The junior Seabury was ordained in 1753 and Chandler had been ordained two years earlier. In 1774, the men had served for more than 20 years as missionaries of the S.P.G. for congregations in New York and New Jersey.

Convening on 5 September, radical delegates of the Congress succeeded in endorsing the Suffolk Resolves on 17 September, resolutions that had been adopted by a convention in Suffolk County, Massachusetts, on 9 September and hastily carried to Philadelphia by Paul Revere. These resolutions declared (1) that the recently adopted Coercive Acts were unconstitutional and consequently not to be obeyed; (2) urged the people of Massachusetts to form a government to collect taxes and withhold them from the royal government until the repeal of the Coercive Acts; (3) advised the people to arm and form their own militia; and (4) recommended stringent economic sanctions against Britain. Conservative delegates in attendance at the Congress unsuccessfully attempted to offset the endorsement of the Suffolk Resolves by uniting behind Joseph Galloway's 'Plan of a Proposed Union between Great Britain and the Colonies' to regulate the 'general affairs of America', with each colony continuing to govern its internal affairs.

On 14 October, the Declaration and Resolves adopted by the Congress denounced the Coercive Acts and the Quebec Act as unjust, cruel, and unconstitutional. The official statement also criticised the revenue measures imposed by the British government since 1763, the extension of vice admiralty jurisdiction, the dissolution of colonial assemblies, and the keeping of a standing army in the colonial towns in peacetime. Ten resolutions of the Congress set forth the rights of the colonists and among them to 'life, liberty and property', and, of the provincial legislatures, to the exclusive power of lawmaking, 'in all cases of taxation and internal polity', subject only to the royal veto. Thirteen Acts of Parliament since 1763 were declared to violate American rights, and economic sanctions were pledged until they were repealed. Continental Associations, closely modelled upon a Virginia Association framed between 1 and 6 August 1774, constituted a pledge by the delegates that their provinces would cease all importations from Britain effective 1 December; discontinue the slave trade; institute non-consumption of British products and various foreign luxury products; and embargo all exports to Britain, Ireland, and the West Indies effective 1 September 1775. After preparing an address to the king and to the British and American people, Congress adjourned on 26 October resolved to meet again on 10 May 1775, if by that date American grievances had not been redressed.

Soon after his return from England, Seabury took up the cause in New York of the Anglicans who were then fighting for control of the proposed King's College.[1] His several articles on the issue in newspapers launched his career as a controversialist. In view of Seabury's literary contributions to active protest of radical civil issues in the mid-1770s, it is unclear why he was so reticent to support the Anglican position for a colonial prelate in the 1760s. His biographer has remarked that Chandler sought Seabury's guidance as he prepared his pamphlet on the subject, *An Appeal to the Public*, but the Westchester parson was not forthcoming with comments, much to the annoyance of the Elizabeth Town parson.[2] But he was in attendance at the October 1766 convention of the

New York and New Jersey clergy that had the opportunity to consider and discuss Thomas Bradbury Chandler's proposed pamphlet. Published probably in November 1767, the tract brought from the pens of Presbyterians, in Philadelphia, and Congregationalists, in Boston, a series of critical articles signed 'The American Whig'. Responding to the attacks, Seabury; Myles Cooper; the president of King's College; and Charles Inglis, assistant minister at Trinity Church in New York City, published a series of rejoinders in 1767 and 1768 in the *New-York Gazette and Weekly Mercury* and signed 'A Whip for the American Whig'.[3] It is unclear which essays were published by Seabury.[4] He was not a close intimate of Chandler, Cooper, Charles Inglis, Samuel Johnson, or of other leading English church leaders. Seabury was also reluctant to join in Chandler's subsequent proposed publication, an essay in response to the collected tracts of Thomas DeLaune entitled, *A Plea for the Non-Conformists*, reprinted in New York by the Presbyterians, apparently in 1769.[5]

After the conclusion of the Congress's sessions in Philadelphia, he anonymously published three critical essays on the proceedings in November and December 1774 and January 1775. Entitled in order of publication, *Free Thoughts, on the Proceedings of the Continental Congress by A.W. Farmer* (i.e. a Westchester farmer), a second 'Farmer Letter', *The Congress Canvassed*, answered by Alexander Hamilton in *A Full Vindication of the Measures of the Congress, from the Calumnies of their Enemies.*[6] A third 'Farmer Letter' replied to Hamilton's *View of the Controversy between Great Britain and her Colonies*, in a broader treatment than in the previous publications. To this third pamphlet, Hamilton replied with *The Farmer Refuted* (1775).

Seabury's publications received little popularity in New England although they wer[e] e widely circulated in the Middle Colonies and published in England. Admitting that the colonists had grievances and that the imperial constitution was in need of reform, Seabury disputed the legitimacy and authority of the First Continental Congress that seemed to place the colonies on a path towards republicanism and independence. He was attempting pragmatically to keep the colonies loyal to the crown. With clear, precise, and forceful language and arguments, Seabury sought to convince the liberty-seeking Americans that their greatest freedom and good lay in their submitting to, and remaining under the British government, and in securing the changes they desired through peaceful and orderly appeals to that government. In the first of his essays, *Free Thoughts, on the Proceedings of the Continental Congress*, Seabury declared, 'The American Colonies are unhappily involved in a scene of confusion and discord. The bands of civil society are broken; the authority of government weakened, and in some instances taken away: Individuals are deprived of their liberty; their property is frequently invaded by violence, and not a single Magistrate has had courage or virtue enough to interpose'.[7] He had hoped that the Congress would adopt 'some prudent scheme of accommodating our unhappy disputes with the Mother-county'.[8] Seabury's essay emphasised the consequences for farmers of the Congress's adoption of the non-importation, non-exportation, and non-consumption agreements.[9] Policies that, he observed, 'intend to distress the manufacturers in Great Britain, by depriving them of employment – to distress the inhabitants of Ireland, by depriving them of flax-seed, and of a vent for their linens, – to distress the West-India people, by with-holding provisions and lumber from them, and by stopping the market for their produce'.[10] A policy from Seabury's perspective that would engender the resent of the British government against the colonies. The impact of such economic policies on the colonies would be devastating he continued, 'We have no trade but under the protection of Great Britain. We can trade no where but where she pleases. We have no influence abroad, no ambassadors, no consuls, no fleet to protect our ships in passing the seas, nor our merchants and people in foreign countries'.[11]

Prices, the Westchester clergyman and author argued at length, would inevitably rise, causing hardship for New York farmers and families, and profits for the merchants.[12] Seabury suggested that wealthy merchants had reserved enough goods to last through non-importation, and sought to ruin smaller competitors and extort huge profits from customers.[13]

Objecting strongly to these regulations, Seabury was opposed to the Committees to be appointed in each colony 'to establish such further regulations as they may think proper, for carrying their association, of which this Non-consumption agreement is a part, into execution'.[14] He declared the 'The business of the Committees so chosen is to be, to inspect the conduct of its inhabitants, and see whether they violate the Association'.[15] Opposing the process for selecting such committees, Seabury reminds his readers 'That you are Englishmen, and will maintain your rights and privileges, and will eat, and drink, and wear, whatever the public laws of your country permit, without asking leave of any illegal, tyrannical Congress or Committee on earth'.[16]

Seabury proclaimed to his readers, 'Renounce all dependence on Congresses, and Committees. They have betrayed your interests. Turn your eyes to your constitutional representatives. They are the true, and legal, and have been hitherto, the faithful defenders of your rights, and liberties. ... Your representatives know perfectly the state of the unhappy breech between our mother country and us. ... Only beseech them to heal this unnatural breech, to settle this destructive contention, that peace and quietness, and the firm protection of law, and good government, may again be our happy lot'.[17]

He magnified the power of Britain declaring, 'Can we think to threaten, and bully, and frighten the supreme government of the nation into a compliance with our demands'?[18] Supporters of Congressional measures could retort that just that had been achieved in two previous crises; but now the British were convinced that Americans were insatiable and the time had come to be firm and teach them a lesson.[19] He also emphasized the interference with people's freedom by enforcement committees noting, dramatically and colourfully, 'If I must be enslaved, let it be by a King, at least, and not by a parcel of upstart, lawless committeemen. If I must be devoured, let it be by the jaws of a lion, and not gnawed to death by rats and vermin'.[20]

In Seabury's second essay, *The Congress Canvassed*, he stated that the purpose of his work was 'to detect and expose the false, arbitrary, and tyrannical PRINCIPLES upon which the Congress acted, and to point out their fatal tendency to the interests and liberties of the colonies'.[21] The Westchester parson, in this essay addressed to the merchants of New York City, revisited several themes examined in his first publication. He challenged again the legitimacy of the Continental Congress, the process of selecting delegates from each colony, and its adoption of the Suffolk Resolves.[22] Seabury noted that the opposition of Massachusetts to the British government 'set the example to the other colonies of destroying the property of their fellow subjects, the East India company, in open defiance of the laws of the empire, to which they owed subjection, the laws of the province in which they lived, and of the general laws of humanity'.[23] He declared that the work of the Congress had been led by radical Boston political leaders, persons who had initiated the Tea Party, protested the quartering of troops, incited the mobs, and orchestrated riots.[24] Furthermore he remarked that 'It is not my design to consider intimately this adopted brat of the congress – the Suffolk resolves – Every person who wishes as reconciliation with Great Britain; who desires to continue under her dominion and protection; who hopes to enjoy the security of law and good government, and to transmit our present free and happy constitution untainted and uncorrupted to his posterity; must condemn and abhor them'. [25]

Seabury argued in detail that the merchants had illegitimately empowered New York City's delegates to Congress to speak for the entire province.[26] He asserted that the merchants, like the farmers, would also lose control of their own property. His continuing attacks on the local committees authorised by the Congress prompted an alarm that 'you are no longer your own masters: you have subjected your business, your dealings, your mode of living, the conduct and regulation of your families, to their prudence and discretion. The public laws of the province are superseded by the laws of the Congress'.[27] Seabury continued, 'You take the government of the province out of the hands of the governor, council and assembly, and the government of the city, out of the hands of the legal magistrates, and place them in a CONGRESS, a body utterly unknown in any legal sense! You introduce a foreign power, and make it an instrument of injustice and oppression'.[28]

Seabury proclaimed 'Let those, who are fond of pleading the necessities of the times, in excuse of the subversion of the laws, consider, that violent and illegal measures, even in the most necessary struggles for liberty, can never be justified, till all legal and moderate ones have failed'. Rhetorically raising the prospects that if all the complaints made against the British Parliament and Ministry are founded in fact, Seabury declared that the colonies 'have no right to proceed to such violent means of redress as the congress have directed, and you are executing, till the legal and constitutional applications of our Assembly have failed'.[29]

Alexander Hamilton, a 17-year-old student at King's College in New York, systematically rebutted Seabury's first work, *The Congress Canvassed*, with a pamphlet, *A Full Vindication of the Measures of the Congress*, which in turn invited Seabury's line by line reply in a third essay entitled *A View of the Controversy*, published in December 1774.[30] Seabury pointedly asserted again that the Congress did not have any authority to act as the colonies had not received legislative authority from Parliament. Only the British Parliament had the right to raise revenue and regulate trade in the colonies.[31] The pamphlet is a serious discussion of political and constitutional theory. While Seabury conceded that constitutional reform, including recognition of colonial control over taxation, was necessary, he asserted that the supreme authority of King and Parliament must be acknowledged. Seabury rejected the association or a union of the colonies and took an explicitly Tory view of the need to act through existing and traditional institutions such as colonial assemblies and petitions to Parliament. Again, Alexander Hamilton countered with *The Farmer Refuted*.[32]

Seabury, in January 1775, published his final essay, *Alarm to the Legislature of the Province of New York*, that was published in both New York and London, that sought an accommodation and reconciliation with Great Britain. Reflecting on the resolves of the Continental Congress the Westchester County minister urged the assembly to, 'Address yourselves to the King and the two Houses of Parliament. Let your representations be decent and firm, and principally directed to obtain a solid American Constitution; such as we can accept with safety, and Great Britain can grant with dignity'.[33] The parson's position for the Assembly was to seek a political rather than a military solution to the impasse, 'Try the experiment, and you will assuredly find that our most gracious Sovereign and both Houses of Parliament will readily meet you in the paths of peace. Only shew your willingness towards an accommodation by acknowledging the supreme legislative authority of Great Britain, and I dare confidently pronounce the attainment of whatever you with propriety can ask, and the Legislature of Great Britain with honor concede'.[34]

A keen and sharp-witted observer of political affairs, Seabury quickly challenged the drift of the radical revolutionary movement. The parson's pamphlets were much feared by the Patriots, who seized and burned or tarred and feathered copies in an attempt to stop their distribution. He was active for the Loyalist cause on several fronts; personally lobbying assembly men, he organised the largest protest meeting of Loyalists (at White Plains in April 1775), and refused to open his church on Congress-appointed fast days. Seabury was one of the signers of the White Plains protest, of April 1775, against all unlawful congresses and committees, an endorsement that publicly acknowledged his political opinions as a committed loyalist. In May 1775, Seabury informed the S.P.G. that he had 'been obliged to retire a few days from the threatened Vengence of the New England people'. Their 'Charge against the Clergy here', he continued, 'is a very extraordinary one – That they have in Conjunction with the Society and the British Ministry, laid a Plan for enslaving America. I do not think that those people who raised this Calumny believe one Syllable of it. But only intend it as an Engine to turn the popular fury upon the church; which, Should the violent Schemes of some of our eastern neighbours Succeed, will probably Fall a Sacrifice to the persecuting Spirit of Independency'.[35] For him, the controversy was based on a fundamental principle as he wrote to the Society 'That none of them [his neighbours] ever offered me any Insult, or attempted to do me any Injury that I know of.'[36]

In November 1775, he was arrested by a mob of lawless Whigs and kept in prison in Connecticut for six weeks.[37] Seabury was alleged to have authored the *Letters of a Westchester Farmer*, a charge that at the time could not be proved, he was released from custody. Returning briefly to St. Peter's Church in Westchester, he insisted on continuing with the prayers for the royal family at church services. After serving as a guide for the British army behind the lines on Long Island, his parish assignment was terminated.

For comparative purposes it should be noted that the Presbyterian Synod, which met in New York in May 1775, while it did express support for the Continental Congress and its resolutions, followed in the Anglicans' footsteps and urged loyalty to the King, disavowing any desire for separation from Britain.[38]

Ambrose Serle heard Seabury preach at St. Paul's Chapel in New York City on 19 September 1776, and afterwards dined with him at Charles Inglis's house. Lord Dartmouth's aide found Seabury to be, 'what his Writings indeed discover him, a very able and sensible Man, particularly intelligent in American Affairs, of great Wit in the Management of Controversy, and (what very rarely happens to Men of Wit) of great Candor, Modesty, and good Nature. He and Mr. Inglis have very much distinguished themselves by their Loyalty to the King, and Attachment to the British Constitution, civil & ecclesiastical; I wish I could add, that they had been as much distinguished by Encouragement as they deserve. The Misfortune has been, every Sect has received its assistance from Home, while the Religion of the State, established by mere Words, has scarce found a Toleration in Some Colonies. Till an Episcopate, founded only upon an ecclesiastical Bottom, is formed in America 'tis to be feared that the Church of England in them will dwindle to nothing'.[39]

Finally, in November 1776, after the battle of White Plains, Seabury sought refuge in New York City, which the British had taken in September.[40] He spent the rest of the war there as physician, chaplain, and champion of the Loyalist cause. In December 1776, Seabury decided to do 'Justice to the Rebels of East and West Chester' – almost none of who were Anglicans.

Delivering a sermon to His Majesty's Provincial Troops encamped at King's Bridge on the northern tip of Manhattan Island on 28 September 1777, Seabury repeated his high Tory view of kingship and Parliament. Taking as his text the popular biblical reference I Peter 2:17, 'Honor all Men. Love the brotherhood. Fear God. Honor the King', the native-born American declared that 'In the Empire to which we belong, the supreme Authority is vested in the King, the Lords and the Commons of the Realm, conjunctly called Parliament; and to the Laws of the supreme Authority absolute submission and obedience are due, both upon the principles of religion, and of good policy; otherwise the commands of God will be violated, and the Empire necessarily fall into Confusion and distress'.[41] Seabury advocated that 'in a religious view He [the King] is the Vice-gerent of God, to whom He hath committed his Sword of Justice, and his Right and Power to govern the British Empire'.[42] From a political perspective, according to Seabury, the King 'is the Power, the Glory, the Majesty of the whole People; and therefore, considered in either View, the highest Honour and Respect, that are due to any Mortal, are due to him, from every Individual who inhabits those extensive Territories that are Subject to his Command'.[43]

Seabury reminded his audience that 'we have been oppressed and harassed by Congresses, Committees and Bauditties of armed men, none of you can be ignorant. The cruel effects of their lawless tyranny many of you yet feel in the distress of your families, the destruction of your property, the imprisonment of your friends, and the banishment of your persons from your formerly peaceful and quiet dwellings. These are the proper fruits of rebellion'.[44] Declaring that the pretences of the rebellion were frivolous and groundless, Seabury added that 'Great Britain asked nothing unreasonable, nothing but what a good subject would have given unasked. The present rebellion therefore is founded on impiety, ingratitude and fathered and is supported by injustice, oppression, cruelty and tyranny'.[45] With eloquence, description, and emotion Seabury charged his audience of troops to 'a speedy end of all your Troubles, in the Suppression of this unnatural Rebellion, and in the Restoration of Peace, Order and legal Government! May he strengthen your Resolution, animate your Courage, preserve your Health, protect you in the Day of Battle and crown the Arms of our gracious Sovereign with success, giving him the Victory over all his Enemies'.[46]

Seabury and his family remained in New York City during the British occupation. His friends and fellow Loyalists who had fled to England, secured for him a gift of £50, a chaplaincy of a man-of-war, and the degree of D.D. from Oxford. In 1777 he was appointed chaplain of the provincial hospital in New York, and was transferred by the S.P.G. as missionary to Staten Island. The following year he was made chaplain of the King's American Regiment raised by the Yale-educated Colonel Edmund Fanning. Despite his political rhetoric and sympathies, Seabury did not flee the country at the close of the war but seemed effortlessly to make the transition as a citizen of the new republic. He became the minister of the congregation at Woodbury, Connecticut, and the first American Anglican consecrated as a bishop by prelates of the Scottish Episcopal church in 1784.[47] He returned to Connecticut and settled in New Haven, serving as the rector of St. James's Church. Seabury was an effective organiser and strict churchman; his efforts aided the reconstitution and reorganisation of the Episcopal church in the state and in the nation.

Serving a congregation in Elizabeth Town in New Jersey, Thomas Bradbury Chandler was a Connecticut native, a graduate of Yale in 1745, and a convert from the Congregational church during his undergraduate years. He studied theology in preparation for ordination under Samuel Johnson of Stratford, Connecticut, who later became president of King's College in New York. Chandler became one of Johnson's protégés and the men maintained a lively and frank correspondence until Johnson's death in 1772, when Chandler wrote a biography of his teacher and mentor and published it decades later.[48] His reputation, however, was enhanced among his admirers and critics by his active role in the episcopacy controversy of the 1760s and early 1770s publishing several pamphlets in support of the official.[49] A trenchant apologist on behalf of an American bishop in the 1760s, he became a staunch advocate of imperial administration in the 1770s. Chandler's essays on episcopacy were the clearest response published in answer to the criticism of Congregational church leaders. In addition, he was at the forefront of the proceedings of several conventions of the clergy during the period, sessions that sought the establishment of a prelate and created the fund for the assistance of widows and orphans of clergymen.[50] Although I have not encountered convincing biographical evidence on the matter, a question arises based on Chandler's literary productivity regarding his sense of identity. How did he consider himself as a British-American rather than merely as a native colonist? Was his turn of mind shared by many of the Anglican clergymen who faced the turmoil of the unfolding political circumstances?

Although Chandler had urged the repeal of the Stamp Act, 'finding that the evil spirit in the Colonies ... had not subsided on the repeal of it', he had undertaken to defend the government.[51] During the summer of 1774, he pseudonymously wrote *The American Querist: or Some Questions Proposed Relative to the Present Dispute Between Great Britain, and Her American Colonies.*[52] Written in a catechical format of 100 rhetorical questions, Chandler reduced the constitutional dispute between Britain and America to a single proposition: 'Whether the supreme legislative authority of every nation does not necessarily extend to all dominions of that nation; and whether any place, to which this authority does not extend, can justly be said to be a part of its dominions'.[53] His purpose was to advance the traditional ideas of political authority and civil liberty. Never subtle with his arguments, Chandler forthrightly recognised the colonists to be on 'the high road to open rebellion' and chastised self-styled Sons of Liberty and self-appointed guardians of America's welfare for their philosophical inconsistency, religious and political bigotry, and attempts to suppress freedom of speech. For Chandler the constitutional dispute between Britain and America was reduced to a single proposition: 'Whether the supreme legislative authority of every nation does not necessarily extend to all dominions of that nation; and whether any place, to which this authority does not extend, can justly be said to be a part of its dominions'.[54] The answers, he thought, were obvious to all thinking men. The publication enjoyed immediate public interest in the colonies; appearing in 11 editions in New York and reprinted in London in 1775. Condemned by the more radical segments of the population, the title page of the tenth edition proclaimed that on 8 September 1774, the pamphlet was 'in full Conclave of the Sons of Liberty in New York, committed to the Flames by the Hands of their Common Executioner; as it contains some Queries they cannot, and others they will not answer'.[55] Chandler's essay firmly placed him as an ardent Loyalist and apologist of the Crown and Parliament.

Not faltering in his drive to present and persuade his fellow colonists of the perils that would inevitably attend the forceful opposition to constituted authority, Chandler published in the late fall of 1774, soon after the adjournment of the First Continental Congress, *A Friendly Address to all Reasonable Americans*. He restated many of the themes that were discussed in Seabury's publications at the same time. His essay appeared in two editions in New York and was published the following year in both London and Dublin. Chandler propounded that any attempt 'to disturb or threaten an established government by insurrections and tumults has always been considered and treated, in every age and nation of the world, as an unpardonable crime'.[56] The Elizabeth Town parson reiterated to his audience that 'The ill consequences of open disrespect to government are so great that no misconduct of the administration can justify or excuse it'.[57] Despite the escalating turmoil of public events, he counselled his countrymen against 'being hurried Republicans' and 'hairbrained fanaticks'.[58]

Chandler was alarmed by the movement towards republicanism in the colonies, fearing dire consequences if the provinces fell under the control of 'the republican zealots and bigots of New England; whose tender mercies, when they had power in their hands, have been ever cruel towards all presumed to differ from them in matters either of religion or government'. Quakers, Baptists, Anglicans, and even those of the Dutch and German faiths had much to fear from the Quakers-hangers, who would inflict on them 'that Presbyterian yoke of bondage'.[59] His essay vigorously defended Parliament's authority to impose taxes and other policies on the colonies.[60] Defending the various imperial acts approved by Parliament in 1773 and 1774, the Tea, Intolerable and Quebec statutes, he railed against the leadership of the Boston radicals and the Suffolk Resolves that were endorsed by the Continental Congress.[61]

Striking a vigorous attack against Anglican church members throughout the colonies who supported the First Continental Congress, Chandler forcefully declared that 'you, who are members of the Church of England, it is amazing, that any of you should be so blind to your own interests, and such apostates from common sense, as to countenance and cooperate with a plan of proceedings, which, if it succeeds, will at once distress and disgrace you. You are endeavouring to provide arms for your enemies, and to put power into the hands of those who will use it against you'.[62] Continuing, he argued that 'You are setting up a sort of people for your masters, whose principles you despise, and who were always fond of subduing by the iron rod of oppression, all those, whose principles or sentiments, were different from their own. Their inveterate enmity to the Church of England has polluted the annals of British history. Their intolerance in England, toward the members of the Church, when the sovereign power was usurped by them, is recorded in characters of Blood; and the same spirit was dreadfully triumphant in New England from the first settlement of the country, till the mild disposition of Parliamentary power interposed to restrain it'.[63] Attacking the legatees of the Puritan founders of the Massachusetts colony, Chandler took aim at the implacable revolutionary political leadership from Boston and noted that 'Their descendants, who inherit their principles, are the very persons that will govern you, if the projected revolution should take place. As they have now broke loose from the authority of Parliament, which for some time past restrained them from mischief, they begin to appear in their natural colours'.[64]

Referring to the battle over episcopacy led by Boston Congregational ministers as Jonathan Mayhew and Charles Chauncy, Chandler assessed the circumstances and concluded that 'They have already resumed the old work of persecuting the Church of England, by every method in their power. The members of it are duly misrepresented, insulted and abused by them; and they have lately driven several of its clergy from their parishes and families, which are left in a state that is truly deplorable'.[65] He conclusively noted for his readers that the position of the Boston Patriots was that 'the members of the Church of England, must renounce your principles relating both to religion and government, or you can expect no quarter under the administration of such intemporate zealots'.[66]

Chandler's services and literary efforts in defence of British imperial policies and administration did not go unnoticed by officials in London. The Secretary of the Colonial Department, Thomas Pownall, a former royal governor of Massachusetts, wrote to Chandler in late 1774 that he would receive an annual stipend of £200 'from a consideration of your merit and service.' [67]

In early January 1775, Chandler published another tract in New York and that appeared later in London, an essay that challenged the accomplishments of the First Continental Congress entitled, *What Think Ye of the Congress Now?* He renewed his charges on the legitimacy, authority, and actions of the body, objected to the activities of the Sons of Liberty and the purpose of the Suffolk Resolves.[68] Chandler affirmed strongly that there was no obligation for the public to obey the charges of the congressmen because 'a very great part of the Americans are not their constituents in any sense at all, as they never voted for them, nor ever signified any approbation of their acting in behalf, and in the name, of the colonies'.[69] Berating 'the projectors of the *glorious fabric* of an independent American republic', Chandler argued that 'Rebellion and civil war are the necessary consequence of our being governed by the Congress'.[70] To his mind, the Congress, originally viewed as an object of 'curiosity', had turned out to be 'a perfect monster – a *mad, blind* monster'.[71] His stern advice was that Americans should withdraw from Congress, disband the assembly's committees, and seek repeal of the recent acts of Parliament and not move toward independence and war.

Swimming against the tide, the events at Lexington, Concord, and Bunker Hill in April 1775 were too much for Chandler; he packed his bags and departed for England the next month. He wrote to the Society in 1776 that if 'the interest of the Church of England in America had been a national concern from the beginning, by this time a general submission in the Colonies to the Mother Country, in everything not sinful, might have been expected'.[72] After a ten-year absence Chandler returned to his former parish in Elizabeth Town in 1785 and resumed his ministry.[73]

On hearing of Chandler's death in July 1790, Ezra Stiles, the president of Yale College and a contemporary of Chandler's at college, remarked that 'He was a great Reader at College, chiefly of Poetry, belle Lettres and History. A pretty good Classics Scholar, indifferent in the Sciences'.[74] He recalled that 'He conformed to the Church of England when a Senior Sophomore and became a most bigoted high Churchman, zealous for bishops, and expected to have been a bishop'.[75] Yet Stiles reported that Chandler was 'A man of good and sober Morals and much more largely read in the Fathers and ecclesiastical history than any of the American clergy of his day, but ordinary in his preaching'.[76] He bluntly characterised Chandler as 'Acrimonious, bitter and uncharitable to all Christian Sects but his own'.[77] He remembered that the Anglican parson 'Took so vigorous a part against his Country that he abdicated and went to England [and] received a Pension from the Crown', later returning from exile to settle again in Elizabeth Town.[78]

13
Quiet and Militant Patriots

Only a handful of the 311 parsons active in the colonies in 1775 were spokesmen for the Patriot cause.[1] The modest band did not include an advocate for independence comparable to their Loyalist colleagues. There was no parson contesting or contrasting the Tory opinions of Jonathan Boucher, Thomas Bradbury Chandler, Charles Inglis, or Samuel Seabury and championing the movement, nor had any of the men been a leading participant in the effort to obtain a colonial bishop. The small band of supporters of the revolutionary movement distinguished themselves either boldly on the battlefield or as attentive members of their local Committees of Public Safety. Unlike the leading Anglican Loyalists, the Patriot men were not wordsmiths publishing timely sermons or tracts on civic issues. Virginia was the seat of the largest number of Patriot ministers, while a few noted associates in Pennsylvania and the New England and Southern Colonies were in the ranks.

The number of Virginia clergy who participated actively in the revolutionary cause is impressive. In no other colony were the parsons so active and united behind the Patriots' crusade.[2] Thirteen parsons signed the Association endorsed by members of the House of Burgesses to enforce a non-importation agreement. In 20 of 60 counties in the colony, the minister of the parish or some resident minister of the church was elected by the people as a member of the County Committee for Safety.[3] Thirty clergymen served as members of the Committee in their communities.[4] In addition 23 ministers served at one time or another as Justices of the Peace in their counties.[5] After the war began all but one of the 14 army chaplains were ministers of the Anglican church.[6]

The church was strongest and long established in Virginia with 95 primary and 154 secondary congregations and 120 ministers in 1775.[7] Over more than a century and a half the English church had enjoyed a large measure of quasi-independence from London ecclesiastical authority. Contributing to this situation was the power of the local vestry, the payment of clergy salaries under the provisions of provincial statutes, and the absence of any ties to the London headquarters of the S.P.G. Yet it must be noted that many of the men were anguished by the prospect of abandoning their oath of allegiance to the Crown and Parliament undertaken at their ordination. The agony and turmoil of such a step paralysed the thinking of some men and was not easy for most of them.

The most colourful of this band was John Peter Gabriel Muhlenberg of Virginia. Born in Trappe, Montgomery County, Pennsylvania, in 1746, he cast a shadow during the Revolution that was larger than life. The eldest of 11 children of the distinguished Lutheran clergyman Henry Melchior Muhlenberg, he was also the grandson through his mother's line of the celebrated John Conrad Weiser, a capable Indian agent, sometime clergyman, and leader in the Lancaster County, Pennsylvania, German community. After learning a little Latin at the Philadelphia Academy under the supervision of William Smith, Muhlenberg and two of his brothers were sent to Halle in 1763 for further education at the Franckesche Stifungen. Four years later, growing tired of the scholastic routine, he left the university and joined the sixtieth (Royal American) Regiment of Foot, and as the secretary to one of the officers, a friend of his father, returned to Philadelphia. He was discharged from service in early 1767.[8]

Following in the footsteps of his father and grandfather, Muhlenberg prepared for the ministry under the supervision of Carl Magnus von Wrangel, provost of the Swedish churches on the Delaware River. In 1769 he became an assistant to his father and took charge of the Lutheran churches at Bedminster and New Germantown in New Jersey. Two years later he accepted a call to a German Lutheran congregation at Woodstock, Virginia. The next year, he travelled to London and was ordained an Anglican minister along with another Pennsylvanian, William White.[9] After he returned to Virginia, Muhlenberg quickly became a leader in the Woodstock community, pursuing his pastoral responsibilities as well as launching and developing a passion for a political career, an interest that would finally take his life into new directions and to national prominence. Muhlenberg was elected to the House of Burgesses in 1774 and became associated with the Revolutionary party in the legislature. Staking out his leadership position, he was made the chairman of the committee for public safety for Dunmore County.[10]

While preaching his farewell sermon, on 21 January 1776, at the English church in Woodstock with Ecclesiastes 3:1 as his text, 'To every thing there is a season, and a time to every purpose under the heaven', he called out to the dense crowd, 'There is a time to fight, and that time has now come'![11] After pronouncing the blessing, Muhlenberg, with a sharp sense of theatre, threw off his gown, showing a uniform of a Colonel of the Virginia militia.[12] He ordered the drums to beat for recruits at the church door. His rousing patriotic sermon was overtly a recruiting tool and he directly enlisted the men of his congregation. Then, when the Germans of the neighbourhood had flocked to his standard so quickly and numerously, the German Regiment of Colonel Peter Muhlenberg was among the first to be ready at the outbreak of the war of independence. He was in his element; he had found a career of action and his vocation.[13] As Colonel in charge of the Regiment, Muhlenberg gave a good account of himself at the battle of Sullivan's Island in June 1776.[14] On 21 February 1777, he was commissioned a Brigadier General in the Continental Army, and ordered north to Morristown, New Jersey. Again his brigade distinguished itself in battles at Brandywine, Germantown, and Monmouth Court House. Later he fought at Yorktown and before the war ended he was breveted major general.

Muhlenberg proved to be under fire a courageous, level-headed officer, and a strict disciplinarian. When his regiment was disbanded in 1783, he left Woodstock and moved to Philadelphia. Muhlenberg did not return to the active ministry after the war, a circumstance perhaps dictated by personal preference. Possibly this was because of the rule that a parson of the Church of England bearing arms in active service was disabled from re-entering pastoral work until the disability was removed by the bishop. If he was so inclined, the process was handicapped as there was no bishop in Virginia until 1790. More likely, as the Episcopal church had yet to find its way in the post-war era, he built on his pre-war experience in the House of Burgesses and sought a more public career. Muhlenberg thrived on an active life, one of conflict, controversy, and power, a life that centred on authority and leadership, two key elements that were missing in the colonial Anglican church.

The personal path that the Swedish Lutheran, German Lutheran, and Anglican minister and general had travelled was unconventional and remarkable. But he had paid a heavy price. His health suffered in the course of his long tour of duty, and his personal finances had been depleted. Continuing his interest in public office begun a decade earlier, Muhlenberg threw himself into the congested and turbulent arena of Pennsylvania politics. He was elected to the Supreme Executive Council of the State in 1784, and served as vice president of the Commonwealth

(1785–8) while Benjamin Franklin held the presidency. He followed this service with three terms in the U.S. House of Representatives and he was elected to the United States Senate in February 1801. He resigned the post one month later to become the collector of customs of the port of Philadelphia, a position he held until his death in 1807.[15]

Following in Muhlenberg's train, Charles Mynn Thruston, a Virginia native and student at William and Mary in 1754, took an active role in the province's revolutionary affairs. He was elected chairman of the Frederick County Committee of Safety in June 1774, and represented the county as a member of the Virginia Convention in 1775. Two years later, Thruston became a colonel of one of the 16 additional continental regiments. He was wounded and lost an arm at Amboy in March 1777.[16]

James Madison, a cousin of the author and political leader of the same name, was a graduate of the College of William and Mary in 1771, and studied law under the distinguished George Wythe in Williamsburg. He was admitted to the bar but did not enter upon practice. In 1773 he was elected professor of natural philosophy and mathematics in the college, and in 1775 he went to England for further study and ordination. As early as 1772 Madison had committed himself to a radical position in defence of political freedom that stopped narrowly short of independence.[17] While in England he denounced the English nation as 'degenerate' and 'anti-American', for 'reviling' men 'who undoubtedly are making a struggle for Liberty unparalleled in Ancient History.[18] The British government suspected that Madison was an American potential spy in England as it was reported that he was caught carrying treasonable correspondence in his shirts, in the lining of his clothes, and in his baggage.[19] But officials did not detain or charge him on any grounds.

Returning to Williamsburg and his professorship in 1776, Madison was elected president of William and Mary in 1777 and held the office until his death in 1812. Like the great majority of the clergy of the English church in Virginia, he supported the Patriot cause in the Revolution, even going so far as to speak of Heaven as a republic rather than a kingdom. He served as chaplain of the House of Delegates in 1777; on 18 August he was commissioned captain of a company of militia organised from among the students of the college, and he saw active service on several occasions during the war. For the church and clergy the war years were jarring and difficult. Madison told his cousin and namesake in 1781 that he might leave the ministry and take up the practice of law because 'Divinity and Philosophy will starve a Man in these times'.[20] For a few months before and after the Battle at Yorktown, classes at the college were suspended because the buildings were occupied first by the British and then the French and American forces. After the Revolutionary War the years were bleak and difficult for the College of William and Mary with a decline in income and attendance, requiring a reorganisation of the college.[21] In addition to guiding the college's interests, Madison was elected the first bishop of the church in Virginia and made responsible for leading that institution for several decades through similar circumstances.

While pastors Muhlenberg and Thruston provided dash, sparkle, and risk to the ranks of Virginia's clergy, there are few traces of the words of either Loyalist or Patriot preachers in the province. In part, this is attributable to the few opportunities for the parsons to bring their words from the pulpit to the printer's bench. The number of printers in colonial Virginia was always few. Accordingly, the paucity of materials makes it difficult to measure the depth and thoughtfulness of parsons on either side of the revolutionary question.

Born near Glasgow and a graduate of Glasgow College, the Reverend James Thompson came to America in 1769 to serve as a tutor to the children of Colonel Thomas Marshall, including John, the future Chief Justice of the United States Supreme Court. Thompson, who served Leed's Parish in Fauquier County, preached in all four churches in the parish until his death in 1812. Perhaps with an eye on the pulsating political affairs in the House of Burgesses in Williamsburg, Thompson took to the pulpit in June 1774 and denounced the recently imposed English taxes as destructive of American liberties and decried the economic hardships by the closing of Boston harbour. Calling on his audience to assist the New Englanders, Thompson charged that it is 'incumbent upon every one of us, as men and Christians, cheerfully to contribute according to our ability toward their relief'. The Virginia parson did not know when the political troubles effecting Boston would be felt in Virginia, yet he trumpeted a rallying-cry for military preparedness, declaring that 'I would likewise recommend to you to contribute something toward supplying the country with arms and ammunition, that if we be attacked we may be in a posture of defence'.[22]

Born in New York City in 1742, the Reverend David Griffith received his early education in America and went to England to continue his studies, completing his course in medicine in 1762.[23] In that year he passed the examination before the Company of Surgeons for appointment as a surgeon in the British army and served in that capacity in the British forces in Portugal. The length of his connection with the military forces is not known; but by 1765, he was back in America and entered into medical practice in the interior of the colony of New York. Deciding to enter the ministry, he went again to England in 1770 for holy orders. Griffith served briefly as an S.P.G. missionary at Gloucester in New Jersey before moving to Virginia the following year and becoming minister of Shelburne Parish in Loudoun County the next year.[24] Called to preach before the members of the Virginia General Convention on 31 December 1775, at Williamsburg, Griffith took as his text, Romans 13:1–2, 'Let every soul be subject unto the higher powers. For there is no power but of God: the powers that be are ordained of God. Whosoever therefore resisteth the power resisteth the ordinance of God: and they that resist shall receive to themselves damnation'.[25] The words of the letter allowed him to expand before his audience on the theme 'Passive Obedience Considered'.[26] His remarks were an antidote against the ideas of Jonathan Boucher of Maryland, whose eloquent sermons circumscribed the Tory position of civil theology. Griffith was a preacher of considerable talent and style; it is regrettable that this was his only published sermon. His words must have been pleasing to the ears of his auditors, as his prose was carefully and colourfully crafted. Summoning the Patriots to arms, Griffith declared that it was not his role to be 'a mover of sedition, or an advocate for licentiousness. It would ill become this sacred place, and the character of a minister of the gospel of Christ, to inspirit rebellion and foment disorder and confusion'. Yet his rhetoric rallied his congregation 'to remove every impediment from the progress of truth and justice to espouse the cause of humanity and the common rights of mankind'. Whether he was responding to or leading the political sentiments of his neighbours, or speaking solely for himself, we do not know. Yet Griffith continued urging action that 'the cause of truth, immutable and eternal, should engage their warmest and unremitted attention. The cause of an innocent and helpless posterity, of millions of yet unborn, plead strongly for the utmost exertion of our care and vigilance, in defence of other rights'. Drawing on history and past political conflicts, Griffith expressed 'gratitude to the memory of our ancestors [that] should inspire an awful reverence for that noble cause they have so often stood forth to defend, and which, through their glorious efforts (under God) has been, to this day, preserved'.[27] Like Muhlenberg, Griffith took his own advice and signed up as a chaplain and surgeon in the Third Virginia Regiment. He served between 1776 and 1779.[28] Retiring from the military, he became the minister of Fairfax Parish in northern Virginia and exercised a valuable leadership role in the post-war reorganisation of the church in the state.[29]

Another native parson, John Hurt, became chaplain to the Sixth Virginia Regiment. Ordained a priest in December 1774, he served briefly as a minister in Jefferson County in 1775.[30] When the regiment moved north to New Jersey he accompanied the troops. Hurt preached a stirring Patriotic sermon before the soldiers of the Fourth, Fifth, and Sixth Virginia Battalions at Chatham, New Jersey, on 20 April 1777. Despite his youth, recent ordination, and oaths of allegiance to the king, he spoke to soldiers, who at any moment expected to be called to battle in the language of a keen and sympathetic observer of the deliberations of the Continental Congress. Hurt declaimed that 'The gloomy cloud that has long been gathering and hovering over our Jerusalem, is indeed still formidable, and demands our utmost efforts to effectuate its dispersion; and this great and wished for good is in all human probability the most likely to be accomplished by firmness, unanimity, perseverance and a fixed determination strenuously to execute and defend what our Continental Congress, Provincial Assemblies, Commanding Officers, and so forth, shall wisely and prudently resolve'. Hurt persuasively argued 'that it was not through licentious opposition, or for conquest, we drew the sword, but for justice; not to introduce, but to prevent slavery; not upon a vain principle of ambition to gratify the resentment or pride of any individuals, (as many of our internal enemies have falsely asserted) but in defence of the plainest rights, and such as all mankind have ever claimed at the call of a provoked and long injured people, and that after every other method of redress had been tried in vain'.[31]

Charles Royster identifies the qualities of a wartime chaplain as one who 'could not only call for military obedience, clean living, and chaste language, but could also try to move soldiers to make Patriotism 'a constant festival of human kindness'. He has commendably referred to John Hurt as one of the most successful chaplains of the Revolution, serving in the office for ten years during and after the war.[32] Preaching to the First and Second Virginia Brigades at Valley Forge on 6 May 1778, a day set aside for acknowledging the Divine goodness and that France had recognised the United States by a treaty of alliance, Hurt said, 'Let us then consider the present duty as a point on which the fate of nations is suspended; and let us, therefore, redouble our diligence, and endeavour to acquire the highest perfection in our several duties; for the more we do for ourselves, the more reason have we to expect the smiles of Providence'. The Virginia minister believed that victory was close at hand, 'Oppression thenceforward shall be banished from the land – Peace shall till the desolated soil, and commerce unfurl her s[a]ils to every quarter of the sea-encircled globe. ... Who is there that does not rejoice that his lot has fallen at this important period; that he has contributed his assistance, and will be enrolled hereafter in the pages of history among the gallant defenders of liberty? Who is there who would exchange the pleasures of such reflections for all the ill-gotten pelf of the miser, or the dastardly security of the coward? You, my fellow-soldiers, are the hope of your country; to your arms she looks for defence, and for your health and success her prayers are incessantly offered'. He closed his battlefield sermon with an inspired Patriotic and nationalistic poem:

> Thus shall we see, and triumph in the fight,
> While malice frets, and fumes, and gnaws her
> chains, America shall blast her fiercest foes!
> Out-brave the dismal shocks of bloody war!
> And in unrival'd pomp resplendid rise,
> And shine sole empress of the Western World![33]

The leading Patriot ideologue among the Anglican clergymen throughout the colonies was an obscure man from Maryland, Isaac Campbell. At the outbreak of the Revolution he was a veteran, having served for nearly 30 years as rector of Trinity Parish in Charles County. Apart from the fact that he was born in Scotland about 1724, we know very little about his origins, education, and experience before he arrived in Maryland in 1747. We do know that he was ordained to the diaconate and priesthood on 4 and 5 July 1747, at the hands of Bishop Edmund Gibson in the chapel at Fulham Palace in London.[34] We also know that he maintained a school at his residence for many years and wrote about the nature of civil government. Our knowledge of him in this regard is based on his only surviving publication, *A Rational Enquiry into the Origin, Foundation, Nature, and End of Civil Government, showing it to be a Divine Institution*.[35]

Following the First Continental Congress sessions in Philadelphia during September and October 1774, the freemen of Charles County elected Campbell to a committee of 94 persons responsible for enforcing the non-importation and non-exportation association passed by Congress.[36] A gentleman with broad and cultivated intellectual interests, the inventory of his estate in November 1784, valued at £747.16.11, indicated that his personal library (valued at £73.11.10) included works in religion and philosophy by such authors as Aristotle, Homer, Xenophon, and Plutarch, as well as Cicero, Caesar, Ovid, and Suetonius. His philosophical works included volumes by Francis Hutcheson, Samuel Clarke, and Erasmus, Newton, Locke, and Montesquieu. Among literary figures were John Milton, Andrew Marvell, and David Hume.[37]

In his work *A Rational Enquiry*, Campbell sought to prove that all civil government was ordained by God, and to refute all arguments which claimed that civil government was founded on either the law of nature or the law of reason.[38] Although the argument of divinely sanctioned government was also employed by many Loyalists to oppose the revolutionary movement, Campbell used a different set of scriptures to validate his thesis.

Parson Campbell believed that God had initiated civil government shortly after Noah and his family had emerged from the ark. He quoted Genesis 9: 5–6 as a justification ('And surely your blood of your lives will I require: at the hand of every beast will I require it, and at the hand of man; at the hand of every man's brother will I require the life of a man. Whoso sheddeth man's blood, by man shall his blood be shed; for in the image of God made he man'.) It was then the grant of Noah and all his progeny that not only gave man the authority, but also the responsibility for punishing those who would take the life of another. Therefore, civil government was ordained by God.[39]

The Maryland parson differed significantly with his colleague Jonathan Boucher in the manner in which God's mandate for civil government was to be construed. Boucher believed that God had vested all political authority in the elite few who thus constituted the only force capable of governing according to God's will. Campbell's position was that since population was dispersed over a wide area, God must have conceived of some sort of republican scheme of government whereby a deputation of men would act for the whole in either a judicial, legislative, or executive body.[40]

Campbell justified the American Revolution by claiming that monarchy was destructive of God-given human liberty and a usurpation of the authority of legitimate government vested in all. He further reasoned that there had to be a right of revolution contained in God's delegation, since it followed that every individual who suffered monarchical institutions to continue unchallenged, rather than risk his own blood to right the usurpation and abuse they represented, must ultimately answer for his breach of covenant. The little-known Maryland cleric's philosophical position was the antithesis of the political principles and policies of the English government. When a copy of Campbell's book arrived in England, it was publicly burned because of its rampant republicanism.[41]

Though it was projected as a four-volume work, only the first volume was produced. Nothing further was published, no books, pamphlets, or sermons, and no personal papers or manuscripts of Campbell's have survived his death in 1784 to provide us with a map of his further thinking, research, and writing on the subject.

Philadelphia was the centre of Patriot support among ministers of the English church at the beginning of the Revolutionary War and with good reason. The city was the seat of the Continental Congress and the new national government. For months details of current political affairs were reported in the newspapers and gossip passed between interested parties in the taverns, coffeehouses, and on the street. Leading ministers of the church in the city played vastly differing roles during the course of the war. The three most prominent ministers of the English church in the city, Jacob Duché, William Smith, and William White, initially supported the Revolution with varying degrees of intensity. Inevitably unfolding political and military affairs prompted each man in his own manner to modify or change his position.

Duché became rector of Christ Church and St. Peter's in 1775, and was one of the most popular preachers in the city. Thirty-eight years old and the member of an old and distinguished Pennsylvania family, he was the son of Colonel Jacob Duché, a prosperous Philadelphian and a former mayor of the city. A graduate of the College of Philadelphia, he attended Cambridge University for a year before his ordination in 1759. Duché was noted in the community for his high cultivation, generous nature, and powerful and attractive preaching style. His colleague and the future first Bishop of Pennsylvania, William White, considered George Whitefield as the best reader of the Prayer Book he had ever heard, and next to Whitefield, Jacob Duché.[42] The acerbic and reticent Bostonian John Adams admiringly recorded in his Diary, on 7 September 1774, that he 'Heard Mr. Duché read Prayers. The Collect for the day, the 7th of the Month, was most admirably adapted, tho this was accidental, or rather Providential. A Prayer, which he gave us of his own Composition, was as pertinent, as affectionate, as sublime, as devout, as I ever herd offered up to Heaven. He filled every Bosom present'.[43]

At the beginning of the Revolution, Duché showed such unequivocal enthusiasm for liberty that he was made the chaplain of the Continental Congress.[44] He immediately published two eloquent Patriotic sermons, *The Duty of Standing Fast in Our Spiritual and Temporal Liberties* (Philadelphia, 1775; London, 1775), and *The American Vine* (Philadelphia, 1775), the former of which was dedicated to Washington.[45] Thomas Bradbury Chandler observed, perhaps with cutting waggishness, that Duché 'was a popular man ... fond of popularity [who] went ... with the stream'. After the Declaration of Independence, however, Duché gradually began to lose his zeal, and when General William Howe took Philadelphia and put him in jail, he experienced a complete change of heart.[46] On 8 October 1777, he wrote General George Washington a letter in which he severely criticised the Americans and predicted their defeat.[47] He advised Washington to urge Congress to recall the Declaration of Independence, and if they should refuse, to negotiate for peace at the head of his army. Washington turned this letter over to Congress, and the members of that body soon disseminated the news of their chaplain's treachery throughout the 13 colonies.[48] Those persons whose hearts had been stirred by Duché's pulpit eloquence now cursed him as a traitor.[49] In contrast, Duché's wife, her relatives, and Duché's father were all 'violent Whigs'. His brother-in-law, Francis Hopkinson, was a signer of the Declaration of Independence. The puzzling question is why Duché had changed his mind. Hopkinson attributed his brother-in-law's actions 'to the timidity of your temper, the weakness of your nerves' and adding to the litany, to 'the undue influence of those about you', implying Duché's clerical brethren.[50] Finding his professional life unendurable for him in Philadelphia, in December 1777 he fled to England.[51] Ambrose Serle wrote to Lord Dartmouth on 10 January 1778, informed him of Duché's departure for England, and tersely cited the parson as perhaps seeking 'to justify himself after doing a great deal of harm. He is thought to be a tolerable sample of American confidence and duplicity. He may perhaps be usefully employed as an Instrument upon *some* occasions, but never confidentially trusted as a Man'.[52]

The following year the Pennsylvania Assembly proscribed him and confiscated his property, but allowed his family enough money to join him in England.[53] Soon after his arrival in England his political opinion shifted again and he wrote to Washington and to many prominent Philadelphians, pleading for permission to return to America.[54] It was not until May 1792 that the exile at last came home. He served as chaplain at St. George's Fields, Lambeth Asylum, London, between 1777 and 1789, but was anxious to see his friends and native land again. He returned to Philadelphia after the laws against Loyalists had been lifted. He died in 1798, a man broken physically by the ravages of a stroke, and a convert to the teachings of Swedenborg.

Benjamin Rush noted the death of his long-time friend Duché in his Commonplace book on 2 January 1798. He summed up his career noting that Duché 'was a pleasing speaker, his voice was musical, and his action very graceful. His Sermons were elegant but declamatory and never profound'. Dr. Smith, his preceptor, said of him 'that he had never known a man before him that was the same at 36 that he was at 18 years of age'.[55]

The long-time Provost of the College of Philadelphia, William Smith, assumed a differing position. Born in Aberdeen, Scotland, he arrived in the colonies in 1751. Smith came to public attention as the 24-year-old author of the pamphlet *A General Idea of the College of Mirania* (1753) addressed particularly to the trustees nominated by the legislature to receive proposals relating to the establishment of a college in New York.[56] In it he outlined the kind of institution he thought best adapted to the circumstances of a new country. The making of good men and good citizens was to be its chief objective; history, agriculture, and religion were to be most emphasised; and it was to embrace a school to meet the needs of those who were to follow the 'mechanic profession', for whom time on the learned languages would be ill-spent. Benjamin Franklin and other Philadelphia leaders expressed an interest in his ideas and invited Smith to join the faculty of the Academy of Philadelphia.[57]

On his return to Philadelphia in May of the following year, Smith at once became a teacher of logic, rhetoric, and natural and moral philosophy in the Academy. From that time until the Revolution he was the dominant influence in its affairs. A man of considerable talents and ambitions, Smith established himself as an educational leader, a prominent figure in literary circles, and was elected a member of the American Philosophical Society. He also played a keen political hand as a friend of the Penns and a leading supporter of the proprietary interests. The Scottish divine exercised a strong role in condemning the Pennsylvania Assembly for its failure to adopt aggressive military measures during the French and Indian War, a position not inclined to endear him to the Quaker faction in the legislature.[58]

The approach of the Revolution placed him in an awkward position. Like Thomas Bradbury Chandler in New Jersey and other leaders of the English church throughout the colonies he opposed the Stamp Act 'as contrary to the faith of charters and the inherent rights of Englishmen', but he did not favour taking full steps to independence. His *Sermon on the Present Situation of American Affairs* (1775), preached before Congress, created a great sensation. It went through many editions and was translated into several languages. It was published in Philadelphia and Wilmington in the colonies, and in London and Bristol in England, and in Belfast and Dublin in Ireland. Smith eloquently declaimed opposition to recent British measures and awakened colonial Patriotism. He professed himself as 'ardently panting for a return of those Halcyon-days of harmony' and as 'animated with purest zeal for the mutual interests of Great-Britain and the Colonies'.[59] He is credited with the authorship of *Plain Truth; Addressed to the Inhabitants of America* (1776), which was also published in London and Dublin in 1776, and *Additions to Plain Truth* (1776), signed Candidus, which endeavoured to show that

'American independence is as illusory, ruinous, and impracticable, as a liberal reconciliation with Great Britain is safe, honourable, and expedient'.[60] When General William Howe was advancing on Philadelphia, Smith was among those ordered apprehended because of conduct and conversation inimical to the American cause. He gave his parole and retired to an estate named 'Barbados Island' he had purchased on the Schuylkill River. After the evacuation of the city by the British in June 1778, he returned to Philadelphia and set to work with others in an attempt to rehabilitate the College.[61]

In spite of the responsibilities that were entrusted to him and the honours he received, Smith never enjoyed the highest respect and confidence of his prominent contemporaries. While this fact may be attributed in part to political and ecclesiastical differences, it was undoubtedly due, also, to defects in Smith's character. Upon meeting him for the first time, John Adams wrote, 'He appears a plain man, tall and rather awkward, there is an appearance of art'.[62] Learned and righteous Ezra Stiles had nothing but contempt for him. 'Dr. Smith', he recorded in his diary, 'is a haughty, self-opinionated, half-learned Character'; and on another occasion, 'His moral character is very exceptional and unbecoming a Minister of Christ, and it is even a doubt whether he is a Believer of Revelation. He is infamous for religious Hypocrisy'.[63] The renowned 'bleeder', Dr. Benjamin Rush, who knew him well and attended Smith in his last illness, left a vivid portrait of him. 'Unhappily', Rush says, 'his conduct in all his relations and situations was opposed to his talents and profession. His person was slovenly and his manners awkward and often offensive in company ... he early contracted a love for strong drink and became toward the close of his life a habitual drunkard ... His temper was irritable ... and when angry he swore in the most extravagant manner. He seldom paid a debt without being sued or without a quarrel, he was extremely avaricious. ... On his death bed he never spoke upon any subject connected with religion ... nor was there a Bible or Prayer Book ever seen in his room. ... He descended to his grave ... without being lamented by a human creature. ... From the absence of all his children not a drop of kindred blood attended his funeral'.[64]

With all his faults, however, he was one of the ablest, most versatile, and most influential Pennsylvanians of his day. Rush himself admits that Smith possessed 'genius, taste, and learning'.[65] He was a clear, forceful writer and an eloquent public speaker. Notwithstanding his Loyalist tendencies, he was an ardent supporter of liberty, and his political activities, while at least influenced partly by personal motives, were in the main directed by passion for the best interests of his state and the country.

Though more interested in its temporal than in its spiritual condition, he played a significant part in the organisation of the Protestant Episcopal Church in Pennsylvania and in the new nation, the name of which he is said to have suggested.

Educated under the expert tutelage of Smith, William White was the son of a wealthy landowner and man of affairs in Philadelphia who had held various public offices both in Pennsylvania and Maryland. His father-in-law, Henry Harrison, was a former mayor of Philadelphia. White was a graduate in 1765 of the College of Philadelphia. Ordained a priest in London in 1772 he returned to America and served as the assistant minister of Christ Church when the Declaration of Independence was proclaimed, succeeding to the post of rector when the Patriot-turned-Loyalist Jacob Duché left the city for England.[66] He became the first bishop of the Episcopal church in Pennsylvania following the Revolutionary War.

No doubt, talk of political affairs was commonplace in White's household. His sister, Mary, was the wife of Robert Morris, a prominent Philadelphia shipping merchant and social leader and the financier of the Revolution. Morris had taken an active role against the Stamp Act in 1765, was a member of the Committee of Safety and the Committee of Correspondence in 1775, and a delegate to the Continental Congress. Yet the 27-year-old White astutely appeared to take little interest in politics and was reluctant to enter into public controversy. Nonetheless, he immediately and instinctively recognised the independence of the United States. The vestry of Christ Church, meeting in the evening of 4 July 1776, had perhaps made the minds of Duché and White somewhat easier when it decided that thereafter the prayers for the king would be omitted from the worship services. Soon after the Declaration of Independence was proclaimed, he took the oath of loyalty to the new state. White succeeded Duché as chaplain to the Continental Congress and subsequently to the United States Congress during the periods it met in Philadelphia, 1788 to 1789, December 1790 until its removal in 1801 to Washington.[67] During the interval between 1789 and December 1790 the national government met in New York City and Samuel Provoost served as chaplain. White seldom took a vocal part in the course of events yet by his willingness to serve the Congresses and to preach at services called on behalf of the revolutionary cause, White, however, was firmly identified with the American side. He was intimate with the early leaders of the new nation, several of the more prominent being in his congregation, and perhaps contributed to their deliberations in his understated way.

Benjamin Rush, the prominent Philadelphia physician and political activist, in a letter introduced White in 1786 to his friend Richard Price, the prominent London nonconformist minister. White was in London for his consecration as a bishop. Rush stated of White that 'In every stage of the late war he was a consistent whig. In the most doubtful stage of the war he acted as chaplain to the Congress. He is almost the only man I ever knew of real abilities and unaffected purity and simplicity of manners that had not a single enemy'.[68]

In New England, the lone highly visible Anglican clerical supporter of the Patriot interest was the 30-year-old Samuel Parker, the assistant minister at Trinity Church in Boston at the outbreak of the Revolution. A tall, powerful man, 'with a broad cheerful and rubicund face', he attracted Dissenters to his services and was acclaimed to be an excellent preacher.[69] At the time of the evacuation of Boston by British forces in March 1776, he was packing to leave with the Regulars. Andrew Eliot, the moderate Congregational minister of the New North Church and a leader in the community, called upon him and urged him to remain in the city. Eliot compassionately advised Parker that if he left the city the Anglicans would be without a shepherd, and that as the youngest of the Episcopal clergy, his political sentiments were not controversial in the community.[70] For one year the proprietors of Trinity Church invested him with the powers of the incumbent minister, in place of the absent William Walter who had fled the province. In June 1779 Parker was chosen rector in place of Walter.[71]

Immediately after the evacuation of the British troops, Trinity Church and its minister had to face the problem of the liturgy and the new state. On 18 July Parker informed the Wardens and Vestry that 'he could not with Safety perform the Service of the Church for the future as the Continental Congress had declared the American Provinces independent States'.[72] He noted that he was publicly interrupted during 'the Lord's Day preceding when reading the prayers in the Liturgy of the church for the King and had received many Threats and Menaces that he should be interrupted in the future if the Prayers for the King should be read again in the church'.[73] The wardens and vestrymen decided that it would be necessary to make such omissions, and Parker did so the next Sunday, and without their express permission went further and read the Declaration of Independence as required by the Council.[74] He was the only Anglican minister in Massachusetts to obey this order and it proved to be a course of action that engendered criticism from his ministerial colleagues.[75] During the 1780s the laymen of the church supported him for election as bishop of Massachusetts but the clergy did not.

Parker's fellow parsons were critical of his acceptance of the independence movement and reluctant to support his candidacy.[76] He was elected to succeed Edward Bass in May 1804 but served only a matter of months as he died on 6 December following a paralytic stroke.[77]

Quietly, Parker achieved other distinctions too. In 1788 he became the first Episcopal clergyman to open the Boston town meeting with a prayer and five years later he became the first minister of that denomination to deliver the election sermon. Doubtless his position in the community was shaped by his political views. Writing to his friend Samuel Peters, the exiled Connecticut parson in London in 1787, Parker candidly disclosed his opinion on matters regarding the relationship and separation of church and state. He wrote, 'I lay this down as a settled principle that the spiritual power ... derived from a spiritual ruler is not connected with or dependent upon any Civil Ruler. Where the Constitution of Church and State is so closely interwoven as in Great Britain I acknowledge it is a difficult matter to make a Distribution'.[78] Circumstances had changed significantly for the church. There were no longer any links between it and the state. There was no royal governor to intercede from time to time to halt troubles between Anglican parsons and their vestries or congregations, or between Anglicans and Dissenters, nor was there any prospect of further financial support from the London-based S.P.G., or distant supervision for the church and clergy from the bishop of London.

Unlike Parker's experience in Boston, Samuel Provoost of New York City found himself the victim of the divided political opinions of the Trinity Church congregation. Between 1769 and 1771, while serving as an assistant minister of the church his association proved to be unsteady and stormy. He did not receive his salary, a circumstance that the historian of the church attributes to the poor financial condition of the parish rather than to Provoost's political opinions.[79] While the financial circumstances of the congregation may have played a role, Provoost was an ardent Whig and his sympathy for the cause of the colonists was so marked that it brought him under condemnation by the Loyalist members of the parish, who charged him with 'endeavouring to sap the foundations of Christianity'. As a result of the non-payment of his salary and the opposition of church members, he resigned his post on 21 March 1771, and retired to East Camp in Dutchess County, New York, where he remained until 1784.[80] The controversy continued with the Trinity Church congregation after the War when, after a bitter controversy between the Whig and Loyalist membership, Provoost was elected rector in 1784.[81] His public stature was recognised and in the same year he was appointed a regent of the University of the State of New York, and in 1785, chaplain of the Continental Congress.[82]

From this relatively modest band supporting the Patriot's cause emerged a triumvirate of extraordinarily capable leaders of the post-Revolutionary War Protestant Episcopal Church in the United States of America. William White of Philadelphia, Samuel Provoost of New York City, and Samuel Parker of Boston provided exceptional leadership for the church in their respective states and nationally. White, with the assistance of Provoost, drafted the original constitution for the reformed English church that provided for defined roles for the clergy and laity. Joining a committee of William Smith of Philadelphia and Samuel Provoost of New York, White assisted a revision of the liturgy and the book of Common Prayer for American usage.[83] Consecrated a bishop with White at Lambeth Palace Chapel in London on 4 February 1787, Provoost became chaplain of the United States Senate during the period that the national government was located in New York.

By any measurement the prominence of outspoken, plain-speaking Patriot parsons of the English church were comparatively few. They were men of action and not ideas. Their pronouncements were from the pulpit and not from the pages of freshly printed pamphlets. There was no visible and sparkling wordsmith articulating the cause of the revolutionary movement. Their ranks were without a spokesman of the calibre of Thomas Bradbury Chandler or Samuel Seabury, Jr., the flamboyant bravado of Peter Muhlenberg was one of a kind and the stirring nationalistic battlefield sermons of David Griffith and John Hurt are recalled from the printed page rather than from a recording of their pulpit presence and oratory. Yet, there were several stalwart parsons who maintained Patriot sympathies and who were instrumental in continuing to serve their congregations and to publicly support the Independence movement. The band was led by William White and William Smith of Philadelphia and Samuel Parker in Boston.

14

William Knox Seeks to Establish an Ecclesiastical Imperial Policy for the American Church

After an experience of nearly 170 years in the American colonies, the status of the English church on the eve of the Revolutionary War was unsettled and imperilled. No longer was the fiery issue of episcopacy passionately argued by Congregational or Anglican wordsmiths. It was surrounded and eclipsed by new and little-understood social and political circumstances; the relative stability of earlier years was replaced by challenges to imperial authority in London and the Continental Congress in the colonies. The civil agenda was now shaped by such issues as 'no taxation without representation', or by objections to the quartering of English troops, rather than a debate that speculated on the establishment of episcopacy. The leading Congregational protagonist, Jonathan Mayhew, was dead and Charles Chauncy did not revisit the issue of bishops again after 1772. Such Anglican leaders as Thomas Bradbury Chandler and Samuel Seabury, Jr., redirected their interest from defending episcopacy to rebutting republican ideology and upholding royalist traditions and civil institutions.

Throughout the decade of protest to successive imperial policies following the introduction, in 1765, of the Stamp Act in the colonies, neither the church nor its clergymen spoke with one voice on civic issues. More congregational than Episcopal in practice, no provincial conventions of the ministers formulated, debated, or endorsed an official policy either in support or in opposition to changing political circumstances. Although Thomas Bradbury Chandler of Elizabeth Town, New Jersey, and William Smith of Philadelphia, joined the chorus of provincial critics of the Stamp Act, their actions did not generate a wide or united following among their colleagues. As a group the church neither embraced the ideological position of passive obedience and non-resistance, nor publicly supported the principles of the Declaration of Independence. Any parson who did support one position or the other was expressing his personal rather than an institutional opinion. The institution was not recognised as the English church in America but rather as the church at worship in Boston, Philadelphia, Williamsburg, Charles Town, or wherever a congregation was gathered. The ministers of the Anglican church were bluntly confronted by the shifting political rhetoric and realities of the day. As an extension of the English national church to the colonies, the institution had benefited from a century of imperial policies and administration that carried essential links to London civil and ecclesiastical officials. While some ministers of other religious groups may have shared publicly or privately political opinions similar to the Anglican parsons, no religious group maintained ties to the English government.

The provincial political issues and events in 1774, 1775, and 1776 leading to the beginning of the Revolutionary War drastically altered the careers and lives of the ministers and their families. In every colony the movement towards Independence provoked an assortment of political opinions among the men creating a crisis of loyalty. Boston was one of the earliest centres of the movement for independence in the colonies. It was the site of numerous significant protests over British regulations during the decade before the outbreak of the Revolutionary War. Violence erupted in the city over the imposition of the Stamp Act and the looting of the home of Chief Justice Thomas Hutchinson in 1765, the Boston Massacre in 1770, the Tea Party in 1773, and the Coercive Acts in 1774, all incidents which paved the way to crisis and confrontation.[1] Boston was also the stronghold of New England Loyalism and merchants were the backbone of the movement.[2] Yet while the city was the centre of Loyalism for the region, it was a minority presence.[3] The battles of Lexington, Concord, and Bunker Hill in 1775 foreshadowed the irreversible trend towards rebellion and the Declaration of Independence. Many colonists, including a number of clergymen of the English church, had hoped for reconciliation with Great Britain, but these sentiments were dashed during the next year. The long shadow of turbulent political and military events in Boston cast itself into every community in which the Anglican church was situated in New England. In each town the church's building, services and minister were daily visible reminders of English ways, ecclesiastical power and authority, and historical controversy.

On the eve of the outbreak of the American Revolutionary War, a final effort was undertaken by a second-level English civil servant to determine the state of the American church. William Knox, a clever, forceful, and rising Under-Secretary of State responsible for American affairs, undertook the study as a means for developing a more active imperial ecclesiastical policy. Born in Ireland in 1732, Knox was familiar with provincial affairs. He had served as provost marshal of the young colony of Georgia between 1756 and 1762.[4] When he returned to London, he maintained his links with the province and acted as its agent in England. For 20 years, Knox had been a discerning observer, participant, and contributor to the formulation of colonial policies.[5] His experience in Georgia and Whitehall on provincial matters was varied and frequently controversial. His printed pamphlets and numerous unpublished official memoranda strongly suggest that few people in power in Britain thought more seriously or more deeply about the controversy with the colonies at any stage of its development.

As Under-Secretary, for 12 years (1770–82), during the successive administrations of Hillsborough, Dartmouth, and Germaine, Knox played a significant role as an architect of American policy. His pen was ever in the service of official government colonial policies. With sizeable property holdings in Georgia, Knox had a vested interest in retaining the American colonies under British dominion. His first interest in provincial issues came at the close of the French and Indian War when he sent a memorial to Lord Bute recommending the creation of a colonial aristocracy, and representation of the colonies in Parliament.[6] Soon afterwards he was appointed the agent in London for Georgia and East Florida; but his commission was withdrawn by those colonies in 1765 in consequence of his publishing two pamphlets in defence of the Stamp Act, a duty that he mistakenly considered a mode of taxation least likely to meet with objection in America.[7] In 1768 Knox published *The Present State of the Nation* expressing his views on colonial policy. Immediately Edmund Burke, who was familiar with the history of the American provinces, disputed Knox's views.[8] Knox rebutted Burke's views in 1769, publishing *The Controversy between Great Britain and her Colonies Reviewed*, which also appeared in Boston.[9] He published a pamphlet in defence of the Quebec Act in 1774, a statute that was used by New England leaders to widen the breach between Great Britain and the colonies.[10] Soon afterward he drew up a project for the permanent union of the colonies and settlement with them. Lord North's conciliatory proposition of 1776 was probably based on this report.

Knox's proposed policy for the advancement of the English church in 1776 was no doubt intended as a blunt rejoinder to the Boston Congregational critics of the recent Intolerable Acts. The barrage of forceful and unrelenting challenges by the 'Black Regiment' of New England Congregational clerics to the unfolding initiatives of the

English government since the mid-1760s and the recently promulgated Suffolk Resolves hardened Knox's opinion on the inevitable drift of American affairs.[11] His interest in the affairs of the colonial church had been piqued by the petition of the New York and New Jersey clergy in convention seeking Lord Dartmouth's assistance for the appointment of an American prelate.[12] Knox's document proposing an ecclesiastical policy carried the endorsement of such Loyalists and church leaders as Thomas Bradbury Chandler, Samuel Seabury, and Charles Inglis.[13] The London-based civil servant may have considered the request for a bishop as an extraordinary opportunity to advance the church's interest while at the same time foiling the political schemes and objections of outspoken revolutionary leaders and clergymen in Boston. It was an issue that had been mooted without success for nearly a century and he may have considered that stirring again the Congregational minister's fears of a bishop would be useful. As unlikely as it may have seemed to a second-tier Whitehall official of the day, the proposal was too little and too late. Its purpose may have been altogether different, to merely antagonise further an already fractious and outspoken cadre of critics.

For Knox, the English church was an essential element of imperial policy. Nearly a decade earlier, at the bidding of Archbishop of Canterbury Thomas Secker, he published three pamphlets regarding procedures of converting and instructing Indian and Negro slaves in the American colonies.[14] His interest in American affairs was sustained through the reconstitution and reorganisation of the former English church in the 1780s.[15]

For decades, the petitions of provincial parsons and numerous conventions of the clergy had caught the attention of bishops Henry Compton and Thomas Sherlock and such civil leaders as Horace Walpole and the Duke of Newcastle. Pamphleteers like Samuel Seabury and Thomas Bradbury Chandler continued to urge publicly the appointment of an American prelate. But in late 1774 and 1775, as such prominent and forceful Loyalist parsons as Myles Cooper, Jonathan Boucher, and Chandler were beginning to appear in exile in London, the requests were no longer inoffensive petitions. English church and state officers were exposed to candid criticism on their lacklustre interest and leadership on the matter. Writing to the Society in 1776, Chandler expressed what many of his colleagues must have discussed among themselves at conventions. He bitterly noted that if 'the interest of the Church of England in America had been a national concern from the beginning, by this time a general submission in the Colonies to the Mother Country, in everything not sinful, might have been expected'.[16]

The New Jersey parson forthrightly declared that the silence of English leaders to the many colonial requests for a bishop was at bottom a betrayal of the integrity of the English church and its ministers in America. Neither the archbishop of Canterbury nor the bishop of London was active on behalf of the English church in America in the 1770s.

Knox argued that 'Although the King is graciously pleased to Instruct his Governors in the Colonies, to take care that the worship of Almighty God be duly and constantly performed, yet it does not appear that the State of Religion in the Colonies has been at any time an object of attention with the Government'.[17] He maintained that Christianity was not a political institution, 'but the mode of professing it is in all Countries prescribed by the Civil Power, and care is taken that it correspond with the Constitution of the State'.[18] He contended that as colonial civil government was under the English government, 'colonists were required to submit to the Laws and Constitution of England, as required of the inhabitants in England'. Therefore, it 'should seem proper that the mode of Religious worship established in the Colonies should be in some degree conformable to that of England'. Carrying his analysis further, Knox argued that while bishops were frequently proposed in America there were no laws in the provinces to give prelates jurisdiction or authority. He stated that 'the Laws of England would not apply to the case, and not one of the Colony Assemblies has passed an Act for the purpose, and there is no likelihood that any of them ever will'.[19] Yet Knox questioned whether the establishment of episcopacy in America was practicable and good policy and concluded 'a Dependent Church seems as necessary as dependent Governments to preserve the connection between Great Britain and her Colonies'.[20]

Besides the absence of a prelate, Knox saw other issues impeding the progress of the English church. He acknowledged the importance of American colleges preparing colonists for the ministry. Yet he noted that if a bishop was appointed in America, Great Britain would lose the advantages derived from the 'attachment to her Interest and Government', that the clergy born and educated in England and sent to America must be supposed to have carried with them.[21] He recommended that the provincial governors should undertake a survey of the colonial church. Knox was seeking such information as the legal status of the church in the provinces; the number of churches and clergy under their jurisdiction; and the number of inhabitants who professed themselves as members of the English church. To gain a more complete understanding of circumstances, Knox also urged that the government send similar queries to the missionaries of the S.P.G. The survey returns would provide information for the formulation of the government's colonial ecclesiastical policy.[22] While nothing of substance emanated from Knox's efforts, it did lead to one final effort to consider the establishment of a colonial episcopate. In 1777, the government appointed a committee of three bishops to examine the matter.[23] Their deliberations were of no consequence. The matter was dead.

Knox continued to seek new opportunities for settlement of American political affairs, and the English church was an important aspect of his draft proposals. The quality of his thought is readily apparent in his 'Considerations on the great Question, what is to be done with America'? Written no later than mid-1779, probably about the time of the appointment of the Carlisle Peace Commission in the spring of 1778, it was subsequently submitted to several members of the ministry. The document was primarily concerned with presenting Knox's 'Idea of the Constitution to be offered to the Colonies by the Supreme Legislature' as a basis for quieting fears of British intentions among the colonists, thereby 'attaching' them to Britain and 'continuing them under her Dominion'.

While seeking a political resolution to the Anglo-American controversy, Knox offered observations regarding the circumstances of the English church in the colonies. He acknowledged in forceful terms that 'Another capital Error in Our Colony system was the neglect to interweave a religious Establishment with the Civil Polity'. He continued that 'In none of the Charters or Proprietary Grants is Religion so much as mentioned and the Inhabitants are left at liberty in each Colony to adopt such mode of religious Worship as they like best. Every Man being thus allowed to be his own Pope, he becomes disposed to wish to be his own King, and so great a latitude in the choice of a religious system naturally begets republican and independent ideas in politics'. In contrast, Knox noted that 'In the Royal Governments the governors are instructed to take care that Almighty God be duly and devoutly worshipped, but no step is taken to form an established Church, nor any preference shown to the Church of England, further than the giving an allowance to one or perhaps two Ministers'.[24]

Another royal official, Lord Dartmouth's deputy Ambrose Serle, arrived in New York in 1776. He established a productive friendship with Charles Inglis, the tough-minded, scholarly, and astutely well-connected rector of Trinity Church in New York City. It was at Inglis's house that Serle on numerous occasions met Samuel Seabury, Joseph Galloway, and attorney general of New York John T. Kempe in March 1777 to discuss his plan for the establishment of the Church of England in America.[25] Conversations that also turned to political affairs – the course of the war, the prospects for peace, the terms that would be acceptable for a peace, and the nature of the political structure in America following a peace settlement.

A final burst of interest on behalf of an American episcopate occurred in early 1777. At the time, the news reaching London from the colonies reported favourable military operations by the British forces. Archbishop of York William Markham delivered the sermon at the Anniversary Meeting of the S.P.G. at St. Mary-le-Bow Church in London on 21 February and urged anew the appointment of a colonial prelate.[26] An accomplished scholar, educator, and churchman, his sermon was interpreted by opposition politicians as a bold endorsement of the government's coercive policy and he found himself at the centre of a political storm for his position and veiled threats to Dissenters.[27] However, soon afterwards a committee was appointed to study the matter but it is not known if the body met or if it presented a recommendation to civil and ecclesiastical officials.[28] The motive behind the appointment of the committee at this time is also unclear. On the one hand, it may have been a tardy effort by the government and the bishop of London or archbishop of Canterbury to correct a glaring deficiency of the colonial church. While on the other hand, it may have been a calculated strategic gesture to unsettle New England civil and Congregational crisis of episcopacy.

Charles Inglis proceeded to prepare for Serle in late August or early September 1777 a document on the state of American political and ecclesiastical affairs.[29] Serle, holding Inglis in high regard, informed Lord Dartmouth that Inglis 'in every respect is the best clerical character I have hitherto met with in this country' and a man of 'probity and honor'. Serle further commented to Dartmouth that Inglis's report was not for publication but for private information only – 'for those who are concerned in the Government of the State, and, I believe, with the sincerest Desire to convey nothing but the Truth'. Lord Dartmouth's American agent further noted that as Inglis had 'attained all he expects or indeed can attain in the Line of his Profession, [he] does not appear to have any sinister View in stating his Ideas upon the Subject'. The parson was clearly mindful of covering his tracks as Serle reported that 'the Author, unless it be necessary for the Confirmation of what he has advanced, and then he would not hesitate a Moment to vouch its Authenticity in any Mode that might be thought proper'. Serle continued that 'If your Lordship, after reading the Tract, shall consider it worthy of Lord North's attention, and if in consequence it may tend to the more happy

Establishment of church or State, I am deceived if Mr. Inglis would not esteem every end answered, for which he has taken this Trouble'. He concluded his remarks to Lord Dartmouth declaring, 'Mr. Inglis wishing for the Conveyance of a Man of War, to prevent his Paper from any Danger of falling into bad hands'.[30]

It is doubtful that Inglis executed the confidential document merely to kind-heartedly supply London civil officials with useful information on colonial political and church affairs. He was a man who clearly understood the pragmatic dynamics of power and the means to gain and exercise influence. It is likely that he had his career interests in mind as he penned each word and only London officials could help him in this regard.

As the year progressed, the government was faced with the twin tasks of supplying and supporting military operations in the colonies and quelling rising criticism of government policies at home. News from the colonies was not encouraging as General John Burgoyne's army was defeated at Saratoga on 17 October 1777, and the Franco-American alliance was formed in February 1778. The limited military achievements of the British army in the colonies throughout 1778 forced many people in Britain, in and out of government, to reconsider the underlying assumptions that had guided British policies towards the colonies since the Stamp Act critics.

Knox's report on American church and political affairs is significant on two counts. First, after nearly a century of interest by London civil officials on behalf of the extension of the church to the colonies, it was the first assessment by a high-ranking visiting English officer of the colonial affairs department. Previously royal governors and customs officers had offered comments on religious affairs to London civil and ecclesiastical officials but only within their jurisdictions. In 1776 and 1777, at a time when there was some hope among a small band of influential leaders for a reconciliation between the colonies and the English government, Knox's analysis and comments on the American situation were of import for London officers. Second, Knox's report was a confirmation and affirmation of the legitimacy of the steady stream of pleas and petitions by individual ministers and clergy conventions regarding the status and interests of colonial church affairs during the late seventeenth and throughout the eighteenth centuries. His report offered no novel or new information on the state of the church in the provinces. It merely confirmed that efforts by London imperial administrators regarding the church's colonial interests were incomplete and inadequate.

15

The State of the Clergy
in 1775 and 1783

The momentum of the proceedings of the First Continental Congress in Philadelphia, in September and October 1774, seemed to be set on a path that would lead to rebellion and war with England. For the church, it was a dire circumstance that foreshadowed an uncertain future. In addition, from Maine to Georgia, civil events would call into question the political loyalties of the church's ministers. During the previous century, rhetoric critical of the English church by Congregational Church leaders was focused on a possible prelate and the activity of the S.P.G. Now the debate was removed from an abstract discussion and became personal and sought to elicit the political opinions of the ministers of local congregations.

The creation of the Continental Association by the Congress was intended to regularise procedures against dissidents in the colonies by establishing local Committees of Safety in every county, city and town.[1] Committees were to be elected by persons able to vote for assemblymen in each province.[2] Complaints considered by the committees were to be heard and, if a person were found guilty, the details were to be published in the local newspaper. Pauline Maier has noted that provincial conventions and local committees were allowed to establish additional regulations for executing judicial procedures.[3] Persons alleged to be Loyalists or enemies of America were 'to be complained of unto the Committee of the District or Town in which such person or persons reside'.[4]

During the months between the sessions of the First Continental Congress in September and October 1774 and the battles at Lexington and Concord in April 1775, town residents began to speculate about the loyalties of the parsons, were they Patriots or Loyalists? Some of the men immediately embraced the Loyalist cause, others claimed that they were Patriots, while many men fell somewhere in between these positions.

In 1775, the momentum of political discourse in every colony was for independence from England and every clergyman had to reach a personal accommodation on the issues. Placed in a position to either violate or uphold their oaths to the crown and parliament, the men were restrained from undertaking any modification of the forms of worship, such as forsaking the prayers for the king and royal family. Several of the clergymen were harassed and ridiculed in a manner experienced by such royal officials as stamp collectors. In a few instances they became prisoners in their own houses or quickly sought refuge in exile.

In Philadelphia the celebrated physician, delegate to the Continental Congress, and keen observer of civil affairs, Benjamin Rush, identified five ranks of Loyalists early in the Revolutionary War. Included among his categories were the following: (1) those persons with an attachment to power and office; (2) persons with an association with British commerce which the war had interrupted or annihilated; (3) persons with a link to royal government; (4) persons attached to the hierarchy of the Church of England, chiefly the English ministers, particularly in the New England and Middle Atlantic states; (5) and finally persons who 'dreaded the power of the country being transferred into the hands of the Presbyterians', a motive, Rush stated, of many Quakers in Pennsylvania and New Jersey, and the English church leaders in the states where it had been established'. [5] He also observed that the population at large of the 'Untied States might have been divided nearly into three classes, viz. Tories, Whigs, and persons who were neither Whigs nor Tories. The Whigs constituted the largest class'.[6]

The prime aim of most of the men was to continue their ministry and in this respect they were like many of the clergymen in England during the Civil War and Interregnum. At that time, more than a century earlier, many men kept their livings, or died, undisturbed in their benefices. Some men, as in America later, were forced to leave their preferment for political reasons or because they could not, in good conscience, accept the Solemn League and Covenant.[7] For most colonial English ministers their political opinions were not easily formed. The choices were several: to align with either the Patriot or Loyalist cause while for many other persons the situation was complicated, confusing, and changeable, influenced by the course of political and military events. The political sentiments of the ministers were not homogeneous within a colony or region and varied in intensity from Maine to Georgia. It was a situation shaped, in part, by the differing historical experience of the church in the various colonies, by differing political circumstances, and partly by the heterogeneous social, educational, and religious backgrounds of the ministers. A wide gulf contrasted the experiences of the ministers in Massachusetts, New York, and Pennsylvania with their colleagues in Virginia and Maryland.

A large group of men did not publicly take sides on the political events, seeking, under difficult circumstances, to perform their duties, earn an income, and provide for their families. A silent minority retired from active service without leaving a trace of their political opinions. In every region, Loyalist parsons took flight during the course of the War: in New England 17, in the Middle Colonies 18, while in the Chesapeake provinces 23, and in the Southern Colonies 11 clergymen sought refuge in England, or the Maritime Provinces of Canada, or elsewhere.

From Lancaster, Pennsylvania, Thomas Barton, an S.P.G. missionary, described the complex and uncomfortable situation to the secretary of the Society in March 1775 noting that 'You will not be surprised Rev. Sir, to find that in my letters to you I have dropped no Politics, when I tell you that I am no Politician. I always thought it ill became a Minister of the Gospel to set up for a Minister of State. In the present unhappy and unnatural dispute between the parent kingdom and these colonies, I foresaw that my taking an active part would do no service, but would rather injure the cause I wish to support, I mean that of Religion. I therefore consulted the interests of the Church and my own peace and quiet. Would to God a happy reconciliation would soon take place. Without this, I am afraid a glorious Empire must sink into the hands of foreigners and be lost to Britain!'[8] In August 1775, Barton informed London officials that 'Matters have now got to such a Crisis that it is neither prudent nor safe to write or speak one's sentiments – would to God an Accommodation could take place'.[9] More than a year later, Barton reported to London officials that the churches he served were closed, stating that 'the Fury of the Populace who would not suffer the Liturgy to be used, unless the Collects and Prayers for the King and royal family were omitted, which my conscience nor the Declaration I made and subscribed when ordained would not allow me to comply with'.[10] In August 1776, the Oxford University graduate Philip Reading, who had studied theology under Barton's direction before his ordination and serving the congregations at Middletown and Appoquiniminck in Delaware, wrote to the Secretary of the S.P.G. and remarked that 'The Church of England has no longer an existence in the United Colonies of America'.[11]

No congregation or clergyman in any region escaped the ill-effects of the changing political circumstances. Nearly all congregations in the colonies were forced to suspend regular services for varying periods of time, occasionally briefly, sometimes for longer periods, and in a few instances for the entire course of the War. A situation forced, in part, by the prayers that were required in the offices of worship of the Book of Common Prayer for the king and royal family, and objected to by revolutionary authorities. During times when services were suspended, members of congregations in every colony would gather weekly for worship in the home of a member. The political sentiments of many ministers fell under the scrutinising eyes of local residents who questioned their loyalty to the independence movement.

At no time during the colonial era or under the pressing circumstances of the Continental Congress and subsequent political and military events was a strategic plan for survival debated and formulated for the church. More congregational in organisation than Episcopal in practice, the church was unable to speak in any colony with one voice on pressing civic issues. In no colony did the church take either the ideological position of passive obedience and non-resistance or the principles of the Declaration of Independence. In every instance, a parson who publicly embraced one political position or another was merely expressing his personal opinion on civic matters. Yet in each community in which a church was active, it was a prominent visible reminder of English power and controversy.

In 1775, there were 311 ministers of the English church resident in the colonies: in New England, 42 (13.5%); in the Middle Colonies, 48 (15.43%); in the Chesapeake Colonies, 179 (57.5%); and in the Southern Colonies, 42 (13.5%). At the close of the Revolutionary War, the significantly diminished ranks of clergymen numbered 141: in New England, 16 (11.34%); in the Middle Colonies, 11 (7.80%); in the Chesapeake Colonies, 102 (72.34%); and in the Southern colonies, 12 (8.51%). During the course of the war, 74 clergymen had gone into exile, 21 had moved to another state, 25 had retired, and 63 and died. The whereabouts of 11 men remains unknown.[12] By any measurement and in every region, the reduced number of ministers in 1783 underscored the weakened circumstances of the post-Revolutionary War church and its congregations in each state.[13]

The church and ministers encountered varying degrees of adversity in every region of America. In New England, particularly in Massachusetts, the seat of the most outspoken criticism of episcopacy during the colonial period and the activity of the missionaries of the S.P.G., the English church's congregations and ministers experienced the harshest consequences of the revolutionary movement. Within the region, the church encountered the severest treatment in Massachusetts and the District of Maine and less grim circumstances in New Hampshire, Rhode Island, and Connecticut.

When the British troops under the command of General Sir William Howe evacuated Boston on 17 March 1776, 18 Anglican clergymen sailed in the fleet.[14] Henry Caner, the minister of King's chapel in Boston, from 1745, fled the town for Halifax, Nova Scotia, and England with the church registers, plate, and vestments in hand.[15] It was clear for the remaining ministers in Massachusetts that they could no longer retain their positions without a change of allegiance: they had to chose whether to support the English or American cause. Table 15.1 summarises the state of the clergy in the New England Colonies in 1775 and 1783.

Table 15.1   Number of clergy in the New England colonies, 1775–83

	1775	1783	Who Fled to/moved to		Retired	Died
			England, etc.	Another state		
Massachusetts	14	4[16]	7	1	—	2
District of Maine	2	—	2	—	—	—
New Hampshire	2	—	2	—	—	—
Rhode Island	4	1	1	2	—	—
Connecticut	20	11	5	1	—	4
Total	42	16	17	4	—	6[17]

At the outbreak of the Revolution in 1775, there were 42 parsons of the church active in the New England colonies. More than 75 per cent of the men were natives of the region and 90 per cent of them were college graduates.[18] The District of Maine, which was under the supervision of the Bay Colony, and New Hampshire each included 2 parsons, Massachusetts 14, 4 in Rhode Island, and 20 in Connecticut. At the close of the war the ranks had been diminished by 62 per cent. Massachusetts could claim only 4 active ministers, none in Maine or New Hampshire, 1 in Rhode Island, while Connecticut fared the best of the New England states with 11 clergymen on duty. More than 40 per cent of the men had fled to England – 7 from Massachusetts, 2 each from Maine and New Hampshire; 5 from Connecticut, and 1 from Rhode Island. The ranks of the church's parsons had been decimated by the war and death in every former colony except Connecticut. More than one-seventh of the ministers in the region had died in the course of the Revolution. It was not until after the Civil War that the successor church, the Protestant Episcopal Church in the United States of America, would regain its stature and position in the region.[19] The men in 1775 ranged in age from 28 to 76 years old, with a median age of 39 years.[20] Eldest at 76 years old were Henry Caner, of King's Chapel in Boston, and John Beach of Newtown, Connecticut, while the youngest of the group was James Nichols, serving Goshen, Northbury, and New Cambridge (now Plymouth and Bristol), in Connecticut.

Legislation enacted by the General Court of Massachusetts, in 1777, forbade expressions in preaching or public worship that might reflect with disfavour upon the drive for independence by the colonies. It declared too that prayers could not be offered on behalf of the royal family, and a fine of £50 was to be levied on clergymen who did not abide by the law. Unwilling to bow to political pressures and circumstances and modify the liturgy or compromise their ordination oath, many left Massachusetts after local residents and officials had subjected them to bitter criticism, censure, and often restriction of their movement.

A convention of the Connecticut clergymen in September 1774 reported on the turbulent civil affairs in the colonies and the effect on the church to the S.P.G. in London. Their account declared, "That we have not made, nor are we disposed to make political matters, or any of the controversies now subsisting, our concern, or the subject of any of our letters to the Society, or any persons in England, with whom any of us have a correspondence, but adhered only to our clerical character and office'.[21] Ebenezer Dibblee, the minister at Stamford, wrote to Dr. Richard Hind, the Secretary of the S.P.G. on 29 September 1774, 'That consequences of these unhappy disputes that have arisen with our parent country, and the mode of opposition to the supposed unconstitutional acts of the British Legislature grows every day more and more serious and alarming, and bear a very threatening aspect upon the interest of religion and the well being of the Church in this province'.[22] A few days before the battles at Lexington and Concord in April 1775, Dibblee reported to the same official that 'Our duty as members of religion is now attended with a peculiar difficulty; faithfully to discharge the duties of our office, and yet carefully to avoid taking any part in these political disputes'.[23]

In Connecticut, Loyalism during the American Revolution seems to have been concentrated in the western region, especially in the Fairfield County towns of Norwalk, Stamford, Fairfield, Ridgefield, Newtown, Danbury, Greenwich, Stratford, and Redding.[24] In only a few of the western towns, however, could the Loyalists at any time muster substantial opposition to the Revolutionary spirit.

Slightly less than half the ministers of the Church in New England were serving congregations in Connecticut in 1775. Anglicanism had grown steadily since the first church had been erected in Stratford in 1723.

Between 1723 and 1770, 45 new Anglican churches had been built, 40 west of the Connecticut River, and five parishes east. Of these, 17 were primary churches served by a resident minister and 23 are classified as secondary congregations at which services were held by a visiting parson periodically, say, once a month or a quarter.[25] Twenty clergymen served the congregations in the colony in 1775. All but one of the men were native New Englanders, the sole exception was an Englishman. But unlike the experiences of the ministers in the urban centres of Boston, Philadelphia, and New York, there was no large exodus of Connecticut ministers to Nova Scotia or England during the first year or two of the war, the men remained at their posts, residing in their communities. Churches closed for a while, most no longer than one or two years and during such periods baptisms, and marriages were held either in the parsonage or at the home of a member of the parish. When the churches reopened, the ministers performed the offices of the Book of Common Prayer without the prayers on behalf of the King and royal family.[26]

At St. Paul's Church in Narragansett, Rhode Island, the Reverend Samuel Fayerweather ceased performing services on 6 November 1774, within days of the close of the First Continental Congress sessions in Philadelphia. Because a majority of the congregation were Whigs and objected to the use of the prayers for the King and the royal family, and for the success of His Majesty's armed forces, Fayerweather believed that he could not violate his ordination vows although he was known to support the American cause.[27] John Graves, minister of King's Church in Providence, apparently discontinued holding public services for the same reason in 1776. Both men continued to preach at private houses. The Patriots in the colony, as in Massachusetts, had passed a decree on 4 May 1776, forbidding the use of the King's name in all Rhode Island proceedings including church services. In July 1776 a fine was set for £100 on anyone preaching or praying for the royal family.[28]

Rhode Island became the first American colony to renounce allegiance to King George III on 4 May 1776. Newport, the capital, was the centre for the administration of customs and the court of vice admiralty, and was occupied by the British troops between December 1776 and October 1779. The city was the only centre of Loyalism in Rhode Island, and, as in Boston, the merchants were the key element in the group, yet a minority faction.[29] George Bissett, the minister of Trinity Church, continued to hold worship services until 25 October 1779, when he fled with the evacuation of the British troops. Soon afterwards a mob entered the church building and the royal arms were removed and taken to the battery for use in target practice.[30]

Table 15.2   Number of clergy in the Middle Colonies, 1775–83

	1775	1783	Who Fled to/Moved to England, etc.	Another State	Retired	Died
New York	20	4	8	3	—	5
New Jersey	11	4	6	—	1	—
Pennsylvania	12	3	5	1	2	1
Delaware	5	—	—	3	—	2
Total	48	11	19	7	3	8[31]

Table 15.2 summarises the state of the clergy in the Middle Colonies in 1775 and 1783. Circumstances for the church and ministers in the Middle Colonies of New Jersey, Pennsylvania and Delaware were similar to those in the New England region. But the situation was quite different in New York City where the English army and naval forces were headquartered from 1776 to 1783. In 1775, there were 48 ministers serving congregations and the 2 Anglican-related colleges in the area: 20 in New York, 11 in New Jersey, 12 in Pennsylvania, and 5 in Delaware. At the close of hostilities in 1783 there were only 12 ministers active in the region – 4 each in New York and New Jersey, 3 in Pennsylvania, and none in Delaware. The pre-Revolutionary War church had suffered a loss of 77 per cent of its ministers. As in New England, the post-war church, the Episcopal Church, would suffer the consequences of the dislocations of men and support for several generations.

At the beginning of the Revolutionary War there were 20 ministers serving the churches and King's College in New York. Thirteen of the men were native colonists, while 2 had been born in Great Britain, and 1 each in Scotland and Ireland, the origins of 4 are unknown. Six of the ministers were graduates of Yale, 5 were alumni of King's (New York), and 2 men were graduates of Cambridge, and 1 each were graduates of Harvard, Philadelphia, Oxford, and St. Andrews.[32] The birthplaces of the men serving the region in 1775 were more diverse than that for their New England colleagues with 25 of the 48 men native colonists.[33]

The age of the men ranged from 72 years to 24 years, with a median age of 40 years. Richard Peters of Christ Church in Philadelphia was the eldest, while the King's College graduate in New York City, John Vardill, remaining in London after ordination, was the youngest.[34]

The Middle Colonies were the scene of numerous military actions between British and American forces during 1776, 1777, and 1778. For more than two years the shifting tide of pivotal battles in the region marked the church and its ministers. Several victories by the British army and navy on Long Island, Manhattan, and in New Jersey, created a stronghold for the English until the end of the war. But the course of events presented a range of changed circumstances for the ministers. Myles Cooper, the president of King's College, fled to England in 1775, as did seven other men soon afterwards, while Samuel Seabury, Charles Inglis, John Doty, and Epinetus Townsend all served their congregations and as chaplains to Royal Regiments.[35] But Ephraim Avery, serving congregations at Rye and Bedford in Westchester County, had his horses seized and property plundered by a mob. After suffering a stroke his health declined, his life and career scarred by civil strife, he committed suicide on 5 November 1776.[36] A neighbouring minister, Luke Babcock at Yonkers, was seized by a mob and summoned to appear before the New York Provincial Congress meeting in Fishkill. He was held in custody in Hartford, Connecticut, where his health broke down. Returning to Yonkers he died 14 February 1777, at the age of 39 years.[37] At Albany, Harry Munro was imprisoned as a Loyalist in 1776, and on his release fled for protection to the British army in Canada, and was appointed deputy chaplain to the Fifty-third and Thirty-first Regiments.

Congregations remained active although the membership was usually politically divided in Queens on Long Island, on Staten Island, in Westchester County, in Albany, and on both Phillipsburg and Van Cortlandt Manors.

Among the 11 New Jersey clergymen, Thomas Bradbury Chandler and Samuel Cooke fled the colony in 1775, first to New York and then to England.[38] While Jonathan Odell, the loyalist poet of the American Revolution and a grandson of Jonathan Dickinson, the first president of the College of New Jersey (Princeton University), and Samuel Cooke, George Panton, and John Preston served as British Army chaplains. Isaac Browne, a physician, fled behind British lines in 1776, served as a chaplain to New York Volunteers and fled to Nova Scotia in 1783. One clergyman suffered a bout of insanity between 1776 and 1780 but he suddenly recovered in the latter year. Two other men closed their churches in 1776 rather than modify the liturgy and the prayers for the king, resuming their duties following the peace. More than half of the 11 Anglican ministers in New Jersey at the outbreak of the Revolution remained in their parishes or served as chaplains in the American army. Five parishes remained active during the years between 1775 and 1783.

In Pennsylvania the 5 active Loyalist ministers fled the colony while 4 men continued to provide services throughout the war. Daniel Batwell, English-born and a graduate of Corpus Christi College in Oxford University, had been serving congregations at York, Huntington, and Carlisle since 1773. He was given the alternative by authorities under the terms of a resolve by Congress of 27 December 1777, of taking the oath of allegiance to the State of Pennsylvania or removing behind the British lines. He chose the latter, because, he declared, that he had already suffered much for speaking his loyal principles; that a loaded musket was levelled at him with threats of violence, and that he was thrown into the river by the mob and imprisoned for five months.[39]

While in Delaware 3 of the 5 ministers held services during the course of the war.

Table 15.3   Number of clergy in the Chesapeake colonies, 1775–83

	1775	1783	Who fled to/ moved to England, etc.	Who fled to/ moved to another state	Retired	Died
Maryland	59	35	11	3	5	13
Virginia	120	67	12	5	15	25
Total	179	102	23	8	20	38[40]

Table 15.3 summarises the state of the clergy in the Chesapeake Colonies in 1775 and 1783. The annals of the church in the Chesapeake Colonies differs from the historical accounts of the other provinces. It is a difference driven in Virginia by its long history of beneficent royal government after 1624 and in Maryland by the need of the proprietor to address the policies of the Council of Trade and Plantations. In Virginia the church was established in 1619 under the auspices of the London Company of Virginia but not until 1702 in Maryland, ten years after the implementation of royal government and objections by Quakers. At the beginning of the eighteenth century the number of religious groups in Maryland reflected the proprietor's interest in peopling the colony and welcoming settlers of diverse national and religious backgrounds. Because the church was established in both colonies the ministers were not associated with the S.P.G. Their stipends were payable in tobacco allotments determined by law and administered by the vestry of the local congregation.

At the beginning of the Revolutionary War there were 179 parsons active in the region – 59 in Maryland and 120 in Virginia.[41] In Maryland among the native colonists there were the following: Maryland, 13,

Pennsylvania and Virginia, 4 each, Connecticut and New Jersey, 1 each; other national origins included England, 13, Scotland, 9, Ireland, 3, and 11 unknown.[42] In the Old Dominion the origins of the parsons included the following: native born, Virginia, 42, Connecticut and Pennsylvania, 3 each, New York and Maryland, 2 each, New Jersey, 1; other national origins included Scotland, 28, England, 19, Ireland, 4, and 16 unknown.[43] The ministers in the Chesapeake Colonies ranged in age from 24 to 79 years old, with a median age of 37 years. Patrick Henry of St. Paul's parish in Hanover County, Virginia was the eldest, while John Leland, Jr., of Wicomico Parish in Northumberland County, Virginia, and Christopher Todd of Brunswick Parish in Stafford County, Virginia, were the youngest at 23 years. In 1783 the ranks had diminished to 103 ministers in both states – 35 in Maryland and 67 in Virginia. Among the 179 ministers in 1775, 23 were exiled, 8 men moved to another state, 23 retired, and 38 died.

The support of the Virginia clergymen ranged across a broad spectrum of political sentiments, from active and passive Loyalists to active and passive Patriots. A situation shaped in part by the many men that had deeply embedded roots, with a network of family and social connections. Many of the men had married into the gentry and some of them were also planters.[44]

At the outbreak of the Revolutionary War, there were 120 ministers and 95 primary and 26 secondary congregations in the Old Dominion.[45] Despite its legal foundation, long history, and reliance on English and Scottish officials and friends for its supply of ministers, the clergy corps were not active in seeking the appointment of a bishop or strong advocates of British policies. Twenty-five of the men became members of their county's Committee of Public Safety and 13 served as chaplains in either the Virginia militia or the Continental Army.[46]

The political sympathies of the Maryland parsons seem to have been rather neatly divided; 22 of the ministers have been identified as Loyalists and 21 as Patriots.[47] For the remaining 15 ministers their opinions on political affairs are unknown. In 1775 all 44 parishes had incumbents, many also had curates; five years later only 21 had rectors. The intervening years had taken a heavy toll on the ranks of the church's leadership.[48]

In July 1776 the Virginia Convention addressed issues relating to the established church and made changes in the Prayer Book of the Church of England in Virginia by eliminating from the Daily Offices reference to the King and royal family and inserting prayers for the Magistrates of the Commonwealth.[49] The revised liturgy implored God to bless the efforts of the revolutionary Virginians.[50] Apart from the action of a handful of Loyalist clergy in refusing to use the amended Prayer Book, no protest either of clergy or people seems to have been made to these changes, much to the surprise of Lord Dunmore, who wrote to Lord Germain, Secretary of State for the colonies. He was of the opinion that the action of the Convention in striking the prayers for the King from the Prayer Book was so serious a matter that it would shock the majority of the people back into allegiance to their King.[51] In May 1777 the new Virginia legislature ruled that each free adult male was to abjure his allegiance to the king and to swear true fidelity to the Commonwealth. Within a month after notification, each county court was to appoint certain of its justices to tender the test to the county's inhabitants including the clergy.

The weakness of Loyalism in Virginia may not be a paradox at all as Virginia was a homogeneous society in the sense of being free from serious internal division. There was no equivalent of the split between the Hutchinsons and Olivers and the Adamses and Otises in Massachusetts. Whichever way Virginians and the ministers of the English church went in the Revolutionary struggle, the great majority would go in the same direction. For the parsons, however, the motivating force may not have been generated from the fountain of Republican ideology as much as from the reality of preserving their incomes and protecting their personal wealth and property. Apart from leading merchants, the outstanding Loyalists included the president of the College of William and Mary, the Reverend John Camm, and two members of the faculty, the Reverend Thomas Gwatkin and the Reverend Samuel Henley, all British immigrants.

As the revolutionary era opened in Maryland, taxes continued to be collected for the support of the clergy and the construction, expansion, or repair of church buildings.[52] As vacancies occurred in parishes through the death of ministers, replacements were made. It was not until after delegates were appointed to the Continental Congress in 1774 and a Provincial Convention began to raise a militia that several clergymen determined that political circumstances were beyond reconciliation between Great Britain and the colonies. During the last months of 1775, 7 of the 59 parsons left their Maryland livings for England.[53] Anglicans in Maryland were merely one religious group among many, including Catholics, Presbyterians, Quakers, German Reformed, and Lutherans. Established by law, the church provided the proprietor with more than 40 livings for patronage.

Circumstances for the church in Maryland changed when the Provincial Convention on 25 May 1776, took up matters on ecclesiastical affairs and 'Resolved that every Prayer and Petition for the King's Majesty, in the Book of Common Prayer and the administration of the Sacraments, and other rites and ceremonies of the church ... be hense forth omitted in all Churches and Chapels in this Province, until our unhappy differences are ended'.[54] Unlike the situation in Massachusetts, Connecticut, and New York, the clergymen were saved from individually wrestling with the issue of including or deleting the prayers for the Royal family and the British government as the provincial assembly relieved them from that burden.[55]

When the Declaration of Rights was promulgated by the Maryland Provincial Convention on 3 November 1776, it preserved to the Church all of its property: The churches, chapels, glebes, and all other property belonging to the church of England, ought to remain to the church of England forever'.[56] The clergy who remained at their posts and performed their duties were to continue to receive their stipend. Although the property of the church was preserved by the legislature, there are few records of vestry meetings in Maryland parishes between 1776 and 1780 to disclose the management of churches.[57] Possibly the wardens and vestrymen of the several parishes considered the Bill of Rights of 1776 was deficient, for the new legislature enacted a law in 1779 which gave the vestries title to their property. It was this statute which allowed the church to reorganise itself as an independent body during the 1780s.[58]

Although the Church of England was legally established in the Southern Colonies of North and South Carolina and Georgia, it was a minority institution in the religiously diverse provinces and that status remained during the colonial era. During the several waves of immigration to the region, New England Puritans to Dorchester in South Carolina, Scotch-Irish Presbyterians, Quakers, German-Lutherans, and Baptists, who had settled in the backcountry, the three colonies each developed a distinctive religious character.[59] The foundation of the church in the region was the consequence of relentless leadership by several hard-driving imperial officers with the provincial legislatures. Its establishment was a hollow victory as it came in every instance after vigorous objections and divisive debate by representative spokesmen of the nonconformist community. In North Carolina, the English church saw its most rapid expansion after its establishment in 1765 during the years of support of Governor William Tryon.[60] Just as it was finally becoming a viable force in the colony, the independence movement removed the government financial support and divided the political loyalties of the ministers.[61]

Table 15.4   Number of Clergy in the Southern Colonies, 1775–83

	1775	1783	Who Fled to/ Moved to England, etc. Another State	Who Fled to/ Moved to England, etc. Another State	Retired	Died
North Carolina	14	3	4	1	2	4
South Carolina	22	7	7	1	—	7
Georgia	6	2	4[62]	—	—	—
Total	42	12	15	2	2	11[63]

Table 15.4 summarises the state of the clergy in the Southern Colonies in 1775 and 1783.

On the eve of the battles of Lexington and Concord, there were 42 ministers in the Southern Colonies: 14 in North Carolina, 22 in South Carolina, and 6 in Georgia. The origins of the men were varied and included native colonists from Virginia and South Carolina, 2 each; Pennsylvania, Maryland, North Carolina, 1 each; and foreign born from England, 13; Scotland, 6; Wales, 3; German provinces, 2; Ireland, and the Leeward Islands, 1 each; and the origins of 9 men is unknown.[64] The men ranged in age from Alexander Garden, Jr., of St. Thomas and St. Denis Parish, in Berkeley County, South Carolina, at 71 years, to Nathaniel Blount, of Beaufort Parish, in Beaufort County, North Carolina, at 26 years.[65]

The flow of immigration into the backcountry of North Carolina had brought many Quakers, Presbyterians, Moravians, and Baptists. In 1775, there were only 12 Anglican ministers in the colony, and unlike the clergymen in the other colonies, few of the North Carolina ministers were college graduates.[66]

The church in the region was drastically weakened during the war by the reduction in the number of ministers, the closing and damage to churches, and the disestablishment of the church. The English church had been established in South Carolina since 1706.[67] Until 1759, when the provincial government assumed the obligation, the S.P.G. provided the annual salaries for its missionaries.[68] Now each congregation had to raise funds to meet expenses for the parson's salary and the maintenance of the fabric and church buildings. The annals of the Church of England in Georgia was modest compared to the account in South Carolina. In part this was due to the recent establishment of the colony, the sparseness of its population, and the religious diversity of its settlers. Despite the fact that the church was established in the province and that the colony had been divided into 12 parishes after 1765, the majority of Georgians were Dissenters by the outbreak of the Revolution.[69]

In 1783 the clergy ranks had been significantly thinned in the region: there were only three ministers in North Carolina, seven in South Carolina, and two in Georgia. From the region 15 parsons sought refuge in England: 4 each from North Carolina and Georgia, and 7 from South Carolina. Death claimed the lives of 11 men from the Southern Colonies and 2 had retired.

The action of the provincial congress at Hillsborough in drafting the North Carolina State constitution of 1776 symbolised not only the transition from colony to commonwealth but also new circumstances for the church. The principle of separation of church and state was affirmed, but religious tests for office holding were imposed. Following the sentiments of the citizens, the constitution provided that no active clergyman might be a member of the Assembly or the Council, and that no one church should ever be established, nor any persons compelled to attend church services or pay for a glebe, church, or minister unless he voluntarily agreed to do so. Ministers of all denominations were granted the right to solemnise marriages.[70] Protection in property rights was provided for the former established church by granting that all glebes, churches, lands, and so forth 'heretofore purchased ... shall be and remain forever to the Use and Occupancy of that religious Society, Church, Sect, Denomination' which possessed them.[71] All arrears in salaries or other claims due the clergy up to 18 December 1776 were validated and were to be paid.[72] Even though the church was now disestablished, it was not the intention of the makers of the constitution that the Anglican faith should become the target of economic reprisal, but only that all other faiths should now be placed on an equal footing with it.[73]

Civil and military affairs bluntly reshaped their careers and lives of the 311 ministers residing in America in 1775. Immediately the men found themselves placed in an awkward and vulnerable position, a consequence of serving an English institution. Many ministers in every colony found their political sentiments under popular scrutiny. Local residents were challenging imperial policies and administration, indeed all matters English, including tea, taxes, troops, and the church. As local leaders of the church they faced an uncertain future and inevitable financial hardship. Among the ranks of ministers were men who had served their congregations for only a few years while others had been active for 20, 30, 40, and in rare instances for 50 years.

In every colony the clergymen faced financial hardship. When the institution was disestablished under the provisions of new state constitutions, the men lost their stipends: it occurred in 1775 in South Carolina, in 1776 in Maryland and North Carolina, in 1777 in New York and Georgia, and in 1786 in Virginia. No congregation of the church was independent of financial support from one of the two colonial legislatures, the London-based Society, or the English Treasury. At once it became necessary for members of congregations to voluntarily raise the funds to meet the expenses of maintaining the minister and church property. While the S.P.G. officials accepted the responsibility to continue the salaries of its missionaries that remained in America during the war years, the men frequently did not receive payment for two or three years. A special fund was established in London in the winter of 1776 seeking 'Subscriptions for the Relief of the Clergy of the Church of England in North America'.[74] Contributions were received from the bishops of London and Winchester, the archbishops of Canterbury and York, and other ecclesiastical dignitaries, as well as from such political leaders as Augustus Henry Fitzroy, the Duke of Grafton; Charles Townshend; and Wills Hill, the Earl of Hillsborough.[75] Quickly a sum of £775.5 was contributed, increasing over the next few months to a total of £6,416.16.1.[76] It was reported in July 1776 that funds had been distributed to those colonial ministers who had taken refuge in England and men who remained in America.[77]

16

The English Church, a Cause of the American Revolution

Forty years after the first battles of the Revolutionary War, John Adams, the second president of the United States, with intensity and clarity, recalled in a 2 December 1815 letter to Jedidah Morse, minister of the First Congregational Church of Charlestown, Massachusetts, that the episcopacy controversy was one of the causes of the Revolution.[1] He remarked to the annalist of the American Revolution that the objection was not only to the office of bishop, but also to the authority of parliament, 'If Parliament could tax us, they could establish the Church of England'.[2] Furthermore, Adams argued, that if left unchecked Parliament could appoint bishops, create provincial dioceses, establish tithes, restrain Dissenters, and impose penalties on liberty and property.[3]

On another occasion, writing to Hezekiah Niles, founder and publisher of *Niles' National Register* on 13 February 1818, Adams commented on the important role that Jonathan Mayhew exercised in reviving New England animosities against tyranny in church and state.[4] Recalling the bishop debate defended by Archbishop Secker, East Apthorp, and Henry Caner, Adams stated, 'If any gentleman supposes the controversy to be nothing to the present purpose, he is grossly mistaken. It spread a universal alarm against the authority of parliament. It excited a general and just apprehension that bishops and diocese and churches, and priests and tythes, were to be imposed on us by parliament'. Continuing, he declared that 'It was known, that neither king, nor ministry, nor archbishops, could appoint bishops in America without an act of parliament; and if parliament could tax us, they could establish the Church of England, with all its creeds, articles, tests, ceremonies and tythes, and prohibit all other churches, as conventicles and schism shops'.[5]

The Massachusetts sage, however, did not disclose to his two correspondents that he had played a key role during the 1760s and 1770s in

211

changing the issue from a limited ecclesiastical matter for a particular religious group to a civil argument. Adams's essays and newspaper articles between 1764 and 1775 firmly placed the Episcopal subject among the colonial radical complaints of imperial policies. He argued that, should a bishop be established, the office would become a potential threat to civil and religious liberties in America, a contention that was enlarged and presented by Samuel Adams's essays in the *Boston Gazette*.

A visiting English civil servant, Ambrose Serle, echoed the observation of John Adams that religious issue was one of the causes of the American Revolution. A protégé and Under-Secretary of William Legge, the second earl of Dartmouth and the Secretary of State for the colonies, Serle was a shrewd, intelligent, and calculating deputy.[6] Arriving in New York in 1776, he vigilantly gathered and interpreted details on civil and religious affairs during the months leading up to the first battles of the war. Serle developed a network of resourceful informants who fed him a steady stream of intelligence regarding American political, military, and church affairs, details that he immediately forwarded to Lord Dartmouth. Between 1776 and 1778 he accompanied the British army through the middle colonies and gleaned from a variety of sources including churchmen and Loyalist public officials, valuable information on civil matters.

Serle particularly noted that both religious leaders and issues were a significant feature of the revolutionary movement. He reported to Lord Dartmouth on 8 November 1776 that 'Among the causes of the present civil war, there is one, which though now overlooked as a matter of inferior magnitude, has operated as much as any to the general distraction, and may probably hinder more than any, all the endeavours for peace and reconciliation'.[7] Not limited to one sect or another, he commented that the preachers of all denominations were participating in the political debate.[8] The London official concisely expressed that 'I could not have believed but from ocular demonstration and other indisputable evidence, that so many warm teachers could have been found any where for public inflammation, or that these could so universally have forgotten, that some of the first principles of their profession are peace, love, and goodwill towards all men'.[9] This circumstance of 'religious contention and disorder', Serle noticed, was based 'in the defective Constitution of our colonial policy. Every church has its pretensions to take the lead, because nothing truly decisive has been done to give any one a real superiority'.[10] The Under-Secretary of State remarked that 'The Congregationalists, on the other hand plead numbers, and look with a kind of envious disdain upon the Episcopalians in all their pretensions of precedency. These latter are, as your lordship knows, for the most part Calvinists with respect to discipline, and of course have a pretty strong inclination to every sort of democracy'.[11] Serle concluded that 'I look upon both sides as equally removed from the question, and believe, from what I have seen and heard, that under the notion of godliness, so much evident hypocrisy and wickedness are not to be found in all the world, as in our colonies of North America'.[12]

In step with the opinion of Adams that the issue of an Anglican prelate was a cause of the American Revolution, Professor J. C. D. Clark has forcefully argued that it was a war of religion.[13] He concludes that it was a conflict anchored in longstanding differences between religious groups, in particular Anglicans, Presbyterians, Congregationalists, and Baptists, regarding ecclesiastical polity, theology, and political authority.[14] Clark acknowledges that within each group underlying differences occurred on these issues in England and America.[15] I have confined my attention in this book to analysing the experience of the colonial English church as central to the unfolding sagas of a proposed episcopate, ecclesiastical polity, and political independence.

For nearly a century before the Declaration of Independence was proclaimed in July 1776 in Philadelphia, the church was embroiled in disputes, primarily in Boston, with occasional rumblings of complaint in other New England and Middle Colonies. The presence of the church in New England, the role of the missionaries of the S.P.G. in the region, and subsequent resistance to an Anglican bishop, were all factors that contributed to the church as a cause of the Revolution. It was a lineage traced in part to the Puritan and Anglican debates regarding the Episcopal office in sixteenth-century England, to the revocation of the Massachusetts Bay Colony Charter in 1684, and the granting of a royal charter and appointment of a royal governor, Edmund Andros, in 1686.

After the founding of the S.P.G. in 1701, a steady stream of ministers began to serve congregations in the New England and Middle Colonies during the first two decades of the eighteenth century. Individually and in convention the men began a ceaseless stream of correspondence with the bishop of London and the Society urging the appointment of a bishop. A prelate was sought to complete the structure of the church's historic ministry and to perform such services as the ordination of candidates for the ministry, confirmation of members, and to supervise the clergymen. Discussions on the appointment of an American bishop had proceeded to such an encouraging point that Bishop of London Henry Compton, the Society, and Queen Anne approved the purchase of a house for a prelate in Burlington, New Jersey, by Governor Robert Hunter in October 1712.[16]

For the remainder of the colonial period other issues surfaced that opposed the presence of the church, particularly in Massachusetts. The Anglican congregations and ministers in the colony mounted a campaign during the first two decades of the eighteenth century for church members to be relieved from paying those town taxes, as in Newbury, that supported the Congregational church and minister.[17] It was an effort continued after 1725 by Timothy Cutler and Samuel Myles, rectors respectively of Christ Church and King's Chapel in Boston that pressed London officials for support and relief.[18] In Connecticut, the English clergymen may have urged English leaders to seek the revocation of the colony's charter in hope that a new document would be more favourable to the church.[19] While in New York and New Jersey, ministers may have sought a prelate to counter the strength of the Dutch Reformed, Presbyterian, and Quaker groups in the royal colonies. Without the residential attendance of a supervising bishop, a handful of church leaders asserted leadership to define and defend the historical nature of the church and its priesthood and episcopacy.

Between the early 1720s and the early 1750s the arguments over a possible bishop and the purpose of the missionaries of the S.P.G. underwent a process of distillation and formulation. The debate focused on the historical validity of the ministerial orders, initiated by John Checkley, and answered by such Congregational ministers as Edward Wigglesworth, Jonathan Dickinson, and Noah Hobart. A main feature of the published exchanges was the marshalling of evidence, or lack of it, on the historical origins of the priesthood and bishops during the eras of the Apostolic and Early Church.

In the 1750s and 1760s the radical Congregational minister of Boston's West Church, Jonathan Mayhew, fused anew the two key arguments that had propelled resistance to the church since 1686: the validity and need for bishops in America, and the role of the S.P.G. in the provincial communities. Mayhew, like Increase and Cotton Mather two and three generations earlier, sensed that the presence of the English church in New England communities represented a plot by London officials to erode the strength and membership of the non-Anglican churches. In retrospect, his tracts shaped the discussion on the subjects by both ecclesiastical and civil leaders for the remainder of the colonial period. Mayhew launched on the subjects that drew into the arena on behalf of the Anglicans, Archbishop of Canterbury Thomas Secker, in London, and Thomas Bradbury Chandler in Elizabeth Town, New Jersey, and the Boston Congregationalist Charles Chauncy.

The final era for the discussion of the heated issue over the appointment of an American bishop and the role of the S.P.G. and the English
church in the colonies began soon after the government of George
Grenville and Parliament adopted the Stamp Act in March 1765, to take
effect on 1 November.[20] It was an act that extended to the colonies duties
long levelled in the mother country.[21] In Boston and other colonial urban
centres the statute led to popular opposition and challenges to colonial
policies that persisted with increasing activity to the American
Revolutionary War. In Braintree, John Adams, and in Boston, Samuel
Adams were instrumental in formulating provincial objections to the
tax.[22] The instruments drafted by both men objected to such details of
the law as the power of the Vice-Admiralty Court to hear cases by the
judge alone, without a jury. Their works vigorously protested the legitimacy of a tax that was to be levied on the provincial public with neither
representation nor consent. The impact of the Stamp Act in Boston influenced and transformed the nature and significance of the Anglican drive
for a prelate and the presence of the English church in the provinces.

An important feature of the statute that neither John nor Samuel
Adams referred to appears in an early section of the law. The Act
included that among the written instruments required to pay a stamp
tax were the official documents used in Ecclesiastical Courts under the
authority and supervision of a bishop.[23] Such ecclesiastical proceedings
as citations (a summoning to court, a process of a spiritual court), mon-
itories (warnings from a judge; information on scandals and abuses; a
letter of admonition that served as a warning), sentences of excommu-
nication and so forth were under the provisions of the statute.[24] The
terms of the legislation required that a duty was to be imposed 'For
every skin or piece of vellum or parchment, or sheet or piece of paper,
on which shall be ingrossed, written, or printed, any monition, libel,
answer, allegation, inventory or renunciation in ecclesiastical matters in
any court of probate, court of the ordinary, or other court exercising
ecclesiastical jurisdiction within the said colonies and plantations, a
stamp duty of one shilling per sheet'.[25]

Grenville, who was, at the time of drafting the legislation, serving as
the first Lord of the Treasury and Chancellor of the Exchequer, was told
that no 'such courts were established in America, replied that at some
future period it was very possible that they might be, and that then it
would be proper that those instruments should pay the stamp duty'.[26]
His remark assumes importance in light of the discussions that occurred
with the ministry by Archbishop of Canterbury Thomas Secker and

Archbishop of York Robert Hay Drummond in 1763 and 1764 urging the appointment of an American prelate.[27] The coinciding circumstances suggest that Grenville maintained a favourable prospect for the appointment of a colonial bishop. But from another perspective it is possible that the Government included the tax on ecclesiastical judicial procedures to incite critics of a proposed American Episcopal officer.

Summarising the status of a prelate for the colonies, Archbishop Secker commented in a letter to Samuel Johnson of Stratford, Connecticut, 31 July 1766, 'It is very probable, that a bishop or bishops would have been quietly received in America before the Stamp Act was passed here. But it is certain, that we could get no permission here to send one. Earnest and continued endeavours have been used with our successive ministers, but without obtaining more than promises to consider and confer about the matter; which promises have never been fulfilled. The king hath expressed himself repeatedly in favour of the scheme and hath proposed, that if objections are imagined to lie against other places, a Protestant bishop should be sent to Quebec, where there is a popish one, and where there are few Dissenters to take offence'.[28]

The strongest colonial opposition to an Anglican bishop came in Boston after 1765, when John and Samuel Adams in alliance with John Wilkes in London, brought the subject to the leading radical Whig newspaper in the provinces, *The Boston Gazette*. The arguments of the two Adams cousins had a long genealogy, traceable to the resistance that erupted as soon as the first Anglican church appeared in Boston in 1686. The progenitor of the movement was Increase Mather, minister of the Old North Church in Boston and President of Harvard College. John and Samuel Adams's essays signalled a dramatic shift in the disputes over episcopacy and the purpose of the S.P.G. in the colonies that guided public discourse on the subjects until the outbreak of the Revolutionary War. The topics were no longer controversies addressed by clergymen holding differing views of the ministry and church, but became a civil issue anchored in the complex and evolving arguments in opposition to imperial policies and the authority of Parliament.

A 28-year-old Harvard College graduate, Elbridge Gerry, a member of the Marblehead committee of safety and was under the influence of Samuel Adams. On 10 November 1772, he sought to encourage Adams to enlist the Massachusetts Congregational clergy to supplement and proclaim from their pulpits objections to various English imperial policies.[29] Gerry's goal was to collar the ministers' longstanding fears over the establishment of an Anglican bishop, a fear that he embraced too.[30] Sending Anglican bishops to the colonies, Gerry wrote to Adams, was a part of the large-scale plot by the English government to 'plunder unguarded America.' The prelates would demand their 'ungodly Mode of Tythes,' and by doing so, deprive the colonists of their property.[31] Not only was Gerry concerned about bishops, but he also saw the issue as a part of the encroaching nature of power in general and the centralisation of power by Britain and her royal officials in particular.[32] He was firmly opposed to the English government's efforts to pay judges from custom receipts which would place them out of reach of public control, to send bishops to America, and to enlarge the royal and civil establishment in the colonies.[33]

Alice M. Baldwin has noted that many of the Congregational ministers in New England kept alive the spirit of resistance of the acts of Great Britain between 1765 and 1774.[34] Perhaps the call on the services of the Congregational ministers to publicly support radical colonial policies was to place them in sharp contrast with the suspected Loyalist political opinions of English church ministers. It was a situation that could be exploited by local radicals eager to prosecute the American cause. For the Anglican ministers there was no escaping the public scrutiny of local critics of imperial policies. As representatives of the English church the men were visible targets for anti-English attacks.

Melded into the continuing stream of protesting radical political rhetoric, the criticisms of the provincial English church was allied with the objections to the Stamp Act (1765), the Townshend Acts (1767), the Quartering of British troops in Boston (1765), the Boston Massacre (1770) and Tea Party (1773), and the Quebec Act and Intolerable Acts (1774). At once the church, by the very nature of its English origins, was a cause of the American Revolution and a victim of radical political events. Following the beginning of the Revolutionary War churches were closed for either brief or extended periods of time, the membership of congregations declined, and the ranks of clergymen diminished by exile, retirement, and death.

In the eyes and rhetoric of radical leaders, the church was an institution dependent on the political, ecclesiastical, and financial resources of London officials and agencies. The Church of England in America and its ministers, including native colonists, were required to submit and adhere to the polity and practices of the institution: ordination by an Anglican prelate and use of the Book of Common Prayer for services and sacraments and its canon law. Furthermore, the church's identity was linked to the royal coat of arms that were prominently displayed in the churches of the provincial capitals and major seaport towns. As local representatives of the English state church, of which King George III served as the Defender of the Faith, the loyalty of many of the parsons was challenged by energetic and vocal Patriots. In many communities of the New England and Middle Colonies, the Anglican clergyman became as revered and welcome as the stamp tax collector, customs officer, admiralty judge, and royal governor.

Ironically, it was the church's association with the English government that fostered its initial extension to the American colonies in the seventeenth century and that in the 1760s and 1770s exposed the institution and its ministers to challenges of conspiratorial activity and questionable loyalties. The overseas development of the church was provided in the royal charters granted to the Virginia Company of London, to proprietors, and in the commissions and instructions granted to governors. At various periods during the colonial era the church was legally established in Virginia, Maryland, New York, North and South Carolina, and Georgia. During the 1670s, 1680s, and 1690s, the Board of Trade and Plantations pursued a policy to place English congregations in the urban centres of Boston, Newport, New York, Philadelphia, and Charles Town.[35] Between 1607 and 1783, the destiny of the church in America was intimately linked to the policies and leadership of the English government and church.

In company with the effect of the Declaration of Independence and Revolutionary War on the ranks of English clergymen, congregations in all of the colonies encountered difficulty. Churches in the leading urban centres and provincial capitals of Boston, New York, Philadelphia, and Williamsburg fared unevenly by events. For the three Boston churches the consequences of political affairs and the war differed. Two of the three churches were served by great-grandsons of Increase Mather, and both men were converts from the Congregational Church ministry. At Christ Church (The Old North Church), Mather Byles, Jr., was a Loyalist while his cousin, William Walter, holding a similar political opinion, served as minister at Trinity Church since 1767. In company with Henry Caner the minister of King's Chapel, the men fled Boston with the evacuation of the British in March 1776, seeking refuge initially in Halifax, Nova Scotia, and later in London.

King's Chapel, the first Anglican congregation established in New England and the centre of Increase Mather's objectionable censure in the 1680s and 1690s, was the most prominent of the three churches. It had been the place for worship by successive royal governors and other high-ranking civil officials as well as for prominent local merchants. Members of its congregation attempted to keep it open during the war and sought to hold joint services with Trinity Church.

But the latter church was unwilling to do so, perhaps because of King's Chapel's long-time association with imperial officers.[36] King's Chapel closed its doors in 1776 and services were suspended until 1782 when James Freeman was appointed a 'reader' in the absence of an ordained clergyman. A graduate of Harvard College in 1777, his background was in the Congregational Church but he was having doubts about the validity of the doctrine of the Trinity. After publicly discussing his objections on the theological issue in a series of sermons, the congregation agreed in June 1785 to amend the Anglican Book of Common Prayer along Unitarian principles as suggested by Freeman, eliminating most references to the Trinity. The change represented a drastically new direction for worship at the church but the revisions were not undertaken with the intention of withdrawing from the Episcopal religious group. Matters were further complicated when Freeman applied for ordination from the recently consecrated Bishop of Connecticut, Samuel Seabury. His disavowal of the doctrine of the Trinity prevented his ordination. But on 18 November 1787, Freeman was ordained a minister in the name of the congregation by the Senior Warden of King's Chapel, and with the ceremony the first Anglican congregation in New England became the first Unitarian church in the world.[37]

A fire stemming from a Revolutionary War battle destroyed Trinity Church in New York City in 1776 and a new building was not erected in its place until 1790. The Christopher Wren-styled Christ Church in Philadelphia survived the war unscathed, with services conducted throughout the war years, served by the Reverend William White, a key architect of the reconstitution and reorganisation of the post-war church. Within its walls in the 1780s were held the several proceedings that led to the establishment of the Protestant Episcopal Church in the United States of America.[38]

St. Anne's Church in Annapolis, Maryland, served by Loyalist Jonathan Boucher until he fled to England in 1775, the building was razed in the same year to make way for a larger church. But the bricks and timber that were stored for the new church were commandeered by the Committee of Safety of the provisional government and used to build forts at the mouth of the Severn River to protect the city against attacks by the enemy. It was not until 1792 that a new church was finally constructed and opened.

The members of the Virginia House of Burgesses and such leaders of the independence movement as George Washington, Thomas Jefferson, and Patrick Henry occasionally worshipped at Bruton Parish Church in Williamsburg. But in 1780 the capital of the new state was removed to

Richmond and the church's membership declined and the building fell into disrepair, not to be restored until the twentieth century.

The impact of the Declaration of Independence and the Revolutionary War on the colonial church was devastating: it was disestablished in the states in which it had been privileged before the war.[39] In every province, churches closed for varying periods of time, membership declined, and the ranks of ministers were diminished by exile, retirement, and death and were not replaced.[40] The three colonial collegiate institutions associated with the church and established and guided under the leadership of Anglican clergymen during the colonial period were forced to close. In New York, King's College closed, the college buildings were commandeered by a local Committee of Safety in 1775 and soon afterwards by the British troops as a hospital. Instruction continued for the remainder of the war in a private house because New York remained in British hands until November 1783.[41] The College of Philadelphia met similar difficulty with a local Committee of Safety and suspended instruction entirely in the spring of 1777, its buildings used first at a Continental army barracks and then as a British hospital but reopened in September 1778 after the British troops evacuated the city.[42] In Williamsburg the College of William and Mary suspended instruction for only a few months before and following the siege of Yorktown in 1781.[43] King's College was re-chartered by the legislature of New York in 1784 as Columbia College and in Pennsylvania the College of Philadelphia was re-chartered in 1791 by the legislature under the name of the Trustees of the University of Pennsylvania.[44]

In a profound sense the seventeenth- and eighteenth-century debates with the church represented a continuing clash in America of a divisive issue within the Church of England. A conflict between the inheritors and custodians of Puritan ideas and practices of church and state in Old and New England with ministers who embraced Anglican traditions and practices. On the one hand, the Puritan descendants recalled the religious persecutions of their forefathers in sixteenth- and seventeenth-century England. While on the other hand, the presence of the English church, attended by royal government officials and prominent merchants, represented the anglicisation process that had gradually occurred in the colonies since about 1690.[45]

Ironically, it was the English church's association with the government that fostered its extension to the American colonies in the seventeenth century and exposed it in the next century to challenges of conspiracy and questionable loyalties. At its founding in America the church was an element of imperial policy, featured in the charters granted to colonisation companies and proprietors and detailed in the instructions to royal governors. Beginning in the 1670s and 1680s and 1690s, the establishment of the church in the provinces became a cornerstone of the anglicisation policies formulated by the Council of Trade and Plantations.[46] The church's fate was shadowed and sealed by the Declaration of Independence on 4 July 1776. Radical civil affairs transformed the public experience of the English congregations and ministers. The churches were closed for brief or extended periods of time during the war, the membership of congregations declined, and the ranks of clergymen diminished by exile, retirement, and death. In addition, the nearly 180-year chronicle of the church in America had come to an abrupt end. At once the Anglican church, by the very nature of its Englishness, was one of the causes of the American Revolution and also a victim of the turn of radical political events. The clergymen's required ordination oaths of fealty to the Crown and Parliament were critical and objectionable popular issues that defined the institution's position in revolutionary America.

Appendix I

Political Sentiments of Colonial Clergymen of the Church of England during the American Revolutionary War: 1775–83

The statistical data regarding the political sentiments of the ministers of the King's Church active during the American Revolution has been compiled from my database 'The Colonial American Clergy of the Church of the England, 1607–1783 (www.jamesbbell.com)'. It is a biographical resource of the 1280 men who were associated with the church in the mainland American provinces. The information has been culled from many sources including the several volumes of Frederick Lewis Weis, the Fulham Palace Papers of the bishops of London, and the records of the Society for the Propagation of the Gospel in Foreign Parts. In addition, details have been gathered from the published records of the alumni of colleges and universities in Colonial America, England, Scotland, Ireland, and elsewhere. Particularly helpful for determining the political sentiments of the men have been Clifford K. Shipton's volumes of *Sibley's Harvard Graduates*; Franklin Bowditch Dexter's *Biographical Sketches of the Graduates of Yale College*; Gregory Palmer, ed., *A Bibliography of Loyalist Source Material in the United States* (Westport, 1982); Gregory Palmer, *Biographical Sketches of Loyalists of the American Revolution* (Westport, 1984); Peter Wilson Coldham, *American Loyalist Claims* (Washington, DC, 1980), John K. Nelson, *A Blessed Company: Parishes, Parsons, and Parishioners in Anglican Virginia, 1690–1776* (Chapel Hill, 2001), Nancy L. Rhoden, *Revolutionary Anglicanism: The Colonial Church of England Clergy during the American Revolution* (Basingstoke, 1999).

Other invaluable resources have been G. MacLaren Brydon, 'The Clergy of the Established Church in Virginia and the Revolution' *Virginia Magazine of History and Biography*, XLI (1933), 11–23; 123–43; 231–43; 297–309; and William Warren Sweet, 'The Role of the Anglicans in the American Revolution', *Huntington Library Quarterly*, XI (1947–48),

51–70. The numerous excellent articles of Professor Otto Lohrenz that have appeared in historical journals have revised and expanded our understanding of several Virginia clergymen during the Revolutionary War era. Also, Joan R. Gundersen's, *The Anglican Ministry in Virginia, 1723–1766: A Study of a Social Class* (New York, 1989); Susan L. Patterson, 'Biographical Sketches of Anglican clergymen trained at the College of William and Mary, 1729–1776: A Study of James Blair's Plan and its Results', unpublished M.A. thesis, College of William and Mary, 1972; Nelson W. Rightmyer's, *Maryland's Established Church* (Baltimore, 1956); Carol Van Voorst's, *The Anglican Clergy in Maryland, 1692–1776* (New York, 1989); Frederick Dalcho, *An Historical Account of the Protestant Episcopal Church, in South Carolina* (Charleston, 1820), and S. Charles Bolton, *Southern Anglicanism, the Church of England in Colonial South Carolina* (Westport, 1982).

The following list includes men who resided in the mainland American colonies during all or part of the period between 1 January 1775 and 31 December 1783 and were ordained ministers of the Church of England. The vast majority of the men were active ministers serving congregations in their provinces. A small number of them were either retired or had pursued other fulltime careers such as schoolteachers. As is noted, a number of them fled into exile rather than to serve their congregations during the Revolutionary War era. It should be noted that John Vardill, a New York native and graduate of King's College, is listed as a Loyalist although he lived in London from 1774 when he sought ordination until his death in 1811.

The list of ministers is arranged alphabetically by geographical regions – New England, Middle, Chesapeake, and Southern colonies. The number of men represented in each region and denoting a percentage of the total is respectively 42 (13.50%), 48 (15.43%), 179 (57.55%), and 42 (13.50%), a total of 311 clergymen.

I have included the men who served congregations in Maine with the clergymen of Massachusetts because politically the District of Maine was under the jurisdiction of the Massachusetts government.

It has been relatively easy to tabulate for a handful of men their political sentiments as either 'Active Loyalists' or 'Active Patriots'. For those persons who have been noted as holding either 'Moderate' or 'Passive' political opinions, the classification process has been more subjective and daunting based on whatever evidence has been found. In addition, for a large group of men no evidence has surfaced to indicate their political opinions during the Revolutionary War and I have noted that circumstance as 'Political Opinions Unknown'.

New England

New Hampshire: 2

	Loyalists				Patriots			
	Active	Moderate	Passive	Fled	Active	Moderate	Passive	Political opinion unknown
Moses Badger	x	—	—	x	—	—	—	—
Ranna Cossitt	x	—	—	x	—	—	—	—
Total	2	—	—	2	—	—	—	—

Massachussetts: 16

	Loyalists				Patriots			
	Active	Moderate	Passive	Fled	Active	Moderate	Passive	Political opinion unknown
Jacob Bailey	x	—	—	x	—	—	—	—
Edward Bass	—	—	—	—	—	x	—	—
Gideon Bostwick	—	—	x	—	—	—	—	—
Mather Byles, Jr.	x	—	—	x	—	—	—	—
Henry Caner	x	—	—	x	—	—	—	—
William Clark	x	—	—	—	—	—	—	—
Nathaniel Fisher	—	x	—	—	—	—	—	—
Stephen Lewis	—	—	—	—	—	x	—	—
William McGilchrist	—	—	x	—	—	—	—	—
Samuel Parker	—	—	—	—	—	x	—	—
Winwood Serjeant	x	—	—	x	—	—	—	—
John Troutbeck	x	—	—	x	—	—	—	—
Joshua W. Weeks	x	—	—	x	—	—	—	—
Edward Winslow	x	—	—	x	—	—	—	—

(Contd.)

Massachussetts: 16 (*Contd.*)

	Loyalists				Patriots			
	Active	Moderate	Passive	Fled	Active	Moderate	Passive	Political opinion unknown
William Walter	x	—	—	x	—	—	—	—
John Wiswall	x	—	—	x	—	—	—	—
Total	10	1	2	9	—	3	—	—

Rhode Island: 4

	Loyalists				Patriots			
	Active	Moderate	Passive	Fled	Active	Moderate	Passive	Political opinion unknown
George Bisset	x	—	—	x	—	—	—	—
Samuel Fayerweather	—	—	x	—	—	—	—	—
John Graves	—	—	—	—	—	—	—	—
William Wheeler	—	—	x	—	—	—	—	—
Total	1	—	2	1	—	—	—	—

Connecticut: 20

	Loyalists				Patriots			
	Active	Moderate	Passive	Fled	Active	Moderate	Passive	Political opinion unknown
Samuel Andrews	x	—	—	—	—	—	—	—
John Beach	—	x	—	—	—	—	—	—
Richard S. Clarke	—	—	—	—	—	—	—	x
Ebeneser Dibblee	—	—	x	—	—	—	—	—
Daniel Fogg	—	—	x	—	—	—	—	—
William Gibbs	—	—	—	—	—	—	—	x
Matthew Graves	—	x	—	x	—	—	—	—

(*Contd.*)

Connecticut: 20 (*Contd.*)

	Loyalists				Patriots			
	Active	Moderate	Passive	Fled	Active	Moderate	Passive	Political opinion unknown
Bela Hubbard	—	x	—	—	—	—	—	—
Abraham Jarvis	—	—	x	—	—	—	—	—
Ebenezer Kneeland	—	x	—	—	—	—	—	—
Jeremiah Leaming	—	x	—	—	—	—	—	—
Richard Mansfield	x	—	—	x	—	—	—	—
John R. Marshall	—	—	—	—	—	—	—	x
Christopher Newton	—	—	—	—	—	—	—	x
James Nichols	—	x	—	—	—	—	—	—
Samuel A. Peters	x	—	—	x	—	—	—	—
John Sayre	—	—	x	x	—	—	—	—
James Scovill	—	x	—	x	—	—	—	—
John Tyler	x	—	—	—	—	—	—	—
Roger Viets	—	x	—	x	—	—	—	—
Total	4	8	4	6	—	—	—	4

New York: 20

	Loyalists				Patriots			
	Active	Moderate	Passive	Fled	Active	Moderate	Passive	Political opinion unknown
Samuel Auchmuty	x	—	—	—	—	—	—	—
Ephraim Avery	—	—	—	—	—	—	—	x
Luke Babcock	x	—	—	—	—	—	—	—
John Beardsley	x	—	—	x	—	—	—	—
Joshua Bloomer	—	—	—	—	—	—	—	x

(*Contd.*)

New York: 20 (*Contd.*)

	Loyalists				Patriots			Political opinion unknown
	Active	Moderate	Passive	Fled	Active	Moderate	Passive	
John Bowden	—	—	—	—	—	x	—	—
Richard Charlton	—	—	—	—	—	—	—	x
Myles Cooper	x	—	—	x	—	—	—	—
Leonard Cutting	—	—	—	—	—	—	—	x
John Doty	x	—	—	x	—	—	—	—
Charles Inglis	x	—	—	x	—	—	—	—
Benjamin Moore	—	—	—	—	—	x	—	—
Harry Munro	x	—	—	x	—	—	—	—
John J. Oehl	—	—	—	—	—	—	—	x
Bernard Page	—	—	—	—	—	—	—	x
Samuel Provoost	—	—	—	—	x	—	—	—
Samuel Seabury	x	—	—	—	—	—	—	—
John Stuart	x	—	—	x	—	—	—	—
Epenetus Townsend	x	—	—	x	—	—	—	—
John Vardill	x	—	—	x	—	—	—	—
Total	11	—	—	8	1	2	—	6

New Jersey: 11

	Loyalists				Patriots			Political opinion unknown
	Active	Moderate	Passive	Fled	Active	Moderate	Passive	
William Ayres	—	—	—	—	—	—	—	x
Abraham Beach	x	—	—	—	—	—	—	—
Robert Blackwell	—	—	—	—	x	—	—	—

(*Contd.*)

New Jersey: 11

	Loyalists				Patriots			
	Active	Moderate	Passive	Fled	Active	Moderate	Passive	Political opinion unknown
Isaac Brown	x	—	—	x	—	—	—	—
Thomas B. Chandler	x	—	—	x	—	—	—	—
Samuel Cooke	x	—	—	x	—	—	—	—
William Fraser	—	x	—	—	—	—	—	—
Jonathan Odel	x	—	—	x	—	—	—	—
Uzal Ogden	x	—	—	x	—	—	—	—
George Panton	x	—	—	x	—	—	—	—
John Preston	x	—	—	—	—	—	—	—
Total	8	1	—	6	1	—	—	1

Pennsylvania: 12

	Loyalists				Patriots			
	Active	Moderate	Passive	Fled	Active	Moderate	Passive	Political opinion unknown
Thomas Barton	x	—	—	x	—	—	—	—
Daniel Batwell	x	—	—	x	—	—	—	—
Thomas Coombe	x	—	—	x	x	—	—	—
George Craig	—	—	—	—	—	x	—	—
William Curie	—	—	—	—	—	—	—	x
Jacob Duché	x	—	—	x	x	—	—	—
T. F. Illing	—	—	—	—	—	—	—	x
Alexander Murray	x	—	—	x	—	—	—	—
Richard Peters	—	—	—	—	—	—	—	x

(*Contd.*)

Pennsylvania: 12 (*Contd.*)

	Loyalists				Patriots			
	Active	Moderate	Passive	Fled	Active	Moderate	Passive	Political opinion unknown
William Smith	—	—	—	—	—	x	—	—
William Stringer	—	—	—	—	—	—	—	x
William White	—	—	—	—	x	—	—	—
Total	5	—	—	5	3	2	—	4

Delaware: 5

	Loyalists				Patriots			
	Active	Moderate	Passive	Fled	Active	Moderate	Passive	Political opinion unknown
Samuel Magaw	—	—	—	—	—	x	—	—
Philip Reading	—	x	—	—	—	—	—	—
Aeneas Ross	—	—	—	—	—	x	—	—
Sydenham Thorn	x	—	—	—	—	—	—	—
Samuel Tingley	—	—	x	—	—	—	—	—
Total	1	1	1	—	—	2	—	—

Chesapeake Colonies

Maryland: 59

	Loyalists				Patriots			
	Active	Moderate	Passive	Fled	Active	Moderate	Passive	Political opinion unknown
Henry Addison	x	—	—	x	—	—	—	—
Bennet Allen	x	—	—	x	—	—	—	—
John Andrews	—	—	—	—	—	x	—	—
William Barroll	x	—	—	—	—	—	—	—

(*Contd.*)

Maryland: 59 (*Contd.*)

	Loyalists				Patriots			
	Active	Moderate	Passive	Fled	Active	Moderate	Passive	Political opinion unknown
Hamilton Bell	—	—	—	—	—	x	—	—
Hamilton Bell, Jr.	—	—	—	—	—	x	—	—
Jeremiah Berry	—	—	—	—	x	—	—	—
Bartholomew Booth	—	—	x	—	—	—	—	—
Jonathan Boucher	x	—	—	x	—	—	—	—
John Bowie	x	—	—	—	x	—	—	—
Thomas Braithwaite	—	—	—	—	—	—	—	x
Thomas Brown	x	—	—	—	—	—	—	—
Richard Brown	—	—	—	—	—	—	—	x
Isaac Campbell	—	—	—	—	x	—	—	—
Thomas Chase	—	—	—	—	x	—	—	—
Thomas Claggert	—	—	—	—	—	—	x	—
Hugh Deane	x	—	—	—	—	—	—	—
William Edmiston	x	—	—	x	—	—	—	—
John Eversfield	x	—	—	—	—	—	—	—
Henry Fendall	x	—	—	x	—	—	—	—
Edward Gantt	—	—	—	—	—	—	x	—
Thomas Gates	—	—	—	—	x	—	—	—
George Goldie	—	—	—	—	—	—	—	x
John Gordon	—	—	—	—	x	—	—	—
George Gowndrel	—	—	—	—	—	—	—	x
William Hanna	—	—	—	—	x	—	—	—
Walter H. Harrison	—	—	—	—	x	—	—	—

(*Contd.*)

Maryland: 59 (*Contd.*)

	Loyalists				Patriots			
	Active	Moderate	Passive	Fled	Active	Moderate	Passive	Political opinion unknown
Jacob H. Hindman	—	—	—	—	—	—	—	x
Thomas Hopkinson	—	—	—	—	—	—	—	x
Philip Hughes	—	x	—	—	—	—	—	—
Samuel Keene	—	—	—	—	x	—	—	—
Francis Lauder	—	—	—	—	—	x	—	—
Thomas Lendrum	—	x	—	—	—	—	—	—
David Love	x	—	—	x	—	—	—	—
Robert McCormick	—	—	—	—	—	—	—	x
James McGill	—	—	—	—	—	—	—	x
Daniel McKinnan	x	—	—	x	—	—	—	—
John McPherson	—	—	—	—	—	x	—	—
Walter Magowan	—	—	—	—	—	x	—	—
Joseph Messenger	x	—	—	—	—	—	—	—
George Mitchell	—	—	—	—	—	—	—	x
John Montgomery	x	—	—	—	—	—	—	—
Hugh Neill	—	—	x	—	—	—	—	—
John Patterson	x	—	—	x	—	—	—	—
Thomas Read	—	—	—	—	—	x	—	—
Robert Reade	—	—	—	—	—	—	—	x
John Rosse	x	—	—	—	—	—	—	—
John Scott	x	—	—	x	—	—	—	—
Samuel Sloane	—	—	—	—	—	—	—	x
John Stephen	x	—	—	—	—	—	—	—
Moses Tabbs	—	—	—	—	—	—	—	x

(*Contd.*)

Maryland: 59 (*Contd.*)

	Loyalists				Patriots			
	Active	Moderate	Passive	Fled	Active	Moderate	Passive	Political opinion unknown
William Thomson	—	—	—	—	—	x	—	—
Thomas Thornton	—	—	—	—	x	—	—	—
Joseph Threlkeld	—	—	—	—	—	—	—	x
Philip Walker	x	—	—	x	—	—	—	—
William West	—	—	—	—	x	—	—	—
Alexander Williamson	—	—	x	—	—	—	—	—
James Wilner	—	—	—	—	x	—	—	—
George Worseley	—	—	—	—	—	—	—	x
Total	19	2	3	10	12	8	2	13

Virginia: 120

	Loyalists				Patriots			
	Active	Moderate	Passive	Fled	Active	Moderate	Passive	Political opinion unknown
William Agar	x	—	—	x	—	—	—	—
John Agnew	x	—	—	x	—	—	—	—
Robert Andrews	—	—	—	—	x	—	—	—
William Andrews	x	—	—	x	—	—	—	—
Isaac Avery	—	—	—	—	x	—	—	—
Thomas Baker	—	—	—	—	—	—	—	x
Alexander Balmaine	—	—	—	—	x	—	—	—
Robert Barret	—	—	—	—	—	x	—	—
Benjamin Blagrove	—	—	—	—	x	—	—	—

(*Contd.*)

Virginia: 120 (*Contd.*)

	Loyalists				Patriots			
	Active	Moderate	Passive	Fled	Active	Moderate	Passive	Political opinion unknown
William Bland	—	—	—	—	x	—	—	—
John Bracken	—	—	—	—	—	x	—	—
John Braidfoot	—	—	—	—	x	—	—	—
John Brander	—	—	—	—	—	—	—	x
Clement Brooke	—	—	—	—	x	—	—	—
John Bruce	x	—	—	—	—	—	—	—
John Brunskill, III	—	—	—	—	—	—	x	—
Robert Buchan	—	—	—	—	—	—	—	x
John Buchanan	x	—	—	—	—	—	—	—
Henry J. Burges	—	—	—	—	x	—	—	—
John Cameron	—	—	—	—	—	x	—	—
John Camm	x	—	—	—	—	—	—	—
Ichabod Camp	x	—	—	x	—	—	—	—
Archibald Campbell	—	—	—	—	—	x	—	—
Jesse Carter	—	—	—	—	—	—	—	x
Charles Clay	—	—	—	—	x	—	—	—
John Cordell	—	—	—	—	x	—	—	—
William Coutts	—	—	—	—	—	—	x	—
James Craig	—	—	—	—	—	x	—	—
James Craig	—	—	—	—	x	—	—	—
Alexander Cruden	x	—	—	x	—	—	—	—
David Currie	—	—	—	—	—	x	—	—

(*Contd.*)

Virginia: 120 (*Contd.*)

	Loyalists				Patriots			
	Active	Moderate	Passive	Fled	Active	Moderate	Passive	Political opinion unknown
Townsend Dade	—	—	—	—	x	—	—	—
Joseph Davenport	—	—	—	—	x	—	—	—
Price Davies	—	—	—	—	—	x	—	—
Thomas Davis, Sr.	—	—	—	—	x	—	—	—
Thomas Davis, Jr.	—	—	—	—	x	—	—	—
Archibald Dick	—	—	—	—	—	x	—	—
Robert Dickson	—	—	—	—	—	—	—	x
John Dixon	x	—	—	—	—	—	—	—
William Douglas	x	—	—	—	—	—	—	—
Hancock Dunbar	—	—	—	—	—	—	—	x
William Duncan	x	—	—	x	—	—	—	—
William Dunlap	—	—	—	—	x	—	—	—
Arthur Emmerson	—	—	—	—	—	x	—	—
William Fanning	—	—	—	—	x	—	—	—
Thomas Fielde	x	—	—	—	—	—	—	—
James M. Fontaine	—	—	—	—	x	—	—	—
Isaac Giberne	—	—	—	—	x	—	—	—
George Goldie	—	—	—	—	—	—	—	x
Alexander Gordon	x	—	—	—	—	—	—	—
Spence Grayson	—	—	—	—	x	—	—	—
David Griffith	—	—	—	—	x	—	—	—
George Gurley	—	—	—	—	x	—	—	—

(*Contd.*)

Virginia: 120 (*Contd.*)

	Loyalists				Patriots			
	Active	Moderate	Passive	Fled	Active	Moderate	Passive	Political opinion unknown
Thomas Gwatkin	x	—	—	x	—	—	—	—
Lewis Gwilliam	—	—	—	—	—	—	x	—
Thomas Hall	x	—	—	x	x	—	—	—
Arthur Hamilton	—	—	—	—	x	—	—	—
William Harrison	x	—	—	—	x	—	—	—
Samuel Henley	x	—	—	x	—	—	—	—
Patrick Henry	—	—	—	—	—	x	—	—
James Herdman	x	—	—	—	—	—	—	—
John W. Holt	—	—	—	—	x	—	—	—
William Hubbard	—	—	—	—	x	—	—	—
John Hurt	—	—	—	—	x	—	—	—
Devereux Jarrett	—	—	—	—	—	x	—	—
Thomas Johnston	—	x	—	—	—	—	x	—
Edward Jones	—	—	—	—	—	—	x	—
Emmanuel Jones, Jr.	x	—	—	—	—	—	—	—
Emmanuel Jones III	—	—	—	—	—	—	—	x
John Jones	—	—	—	—	—	—	—	x
Rodham Kenner, Jr.	—	—	—	—	—	—	—	x
Samuel Klug	—	—	—	—	x	—	—	—
William Leigh	—	—	—	—	x	—	—	—
John Leland	—	—	—	—	—	x	—	—
John Leland, Jr.	—	—	—	—	—	x	—	—
Patrick Lunan	—	—	—	—	—	—	—	x

(*Contd.*)

Virginia: 120 (*Contd.*)

	Loyalists				Patriots			
	Active	Moderate	Passive	Fled	Active	Moderate	Passive	Political opinion unknown
Thomas Lundie	—	—	—	—	x	—	—	—
John Lyon	x	—	—	—	—	—	—	—
John Lyth	—	—	—	—	x	—	—	—
Samuel McCroskey	—	—	—	—	x	—	—	—
Christopher MacRae	x	—	—	—	—	—	—	—
Fitzhugh McKay	—	—	—	—	x	—	—	—
Archibald McRobert	—	—	—	—	x	—	—	—
James Madison	—	—	—	—	x	—	—	—
Nathaniel Manning	—	—	—	—	—	x	—	—
James Marye, Jr.	—	—	—	—	—	x	—	—
Lee Massey	—	—	—	—	x	—	—	—
John Matthews	—	—	—	—	—	—	—	x
Mathew Maury	—	—	—	—	x	—	—	—
Andrew Moreton	—	—	—	—	—	—	—	x
Peter Muhlenberg	—	—	—	—	x	—	—	—
William Nixon	—	—	—	—	—	—	—	x
James Ogilvie	x	—	—	x	—	—	—	—
William Peazley	—	—	—	—	—	—	—	x
Thomas Price	x	—	—	—	x	—	—	—
John H. Rowland	x	—	—	x	—	—	—	—
John H. Saunders	—	—	—	—	x	—	—	—
James Scott	—	—	—	—	—	x	—	—
Benjamin Sebastian	—	—	—	—	x	—	—	—

(*Contd.*)

Virginia: 120 (*Contd.*)

	Loyalists				Patriots			
	Active	Moderate	Passive	Fled	Active	Moderate	Passive	Political opinion unknown
Miles C. Selden	—	—	—	—	x	—	—	—
William Selden	—	—	—	—	—	x	—	—
James Semple	—	—	—	—	—	x	—	—
Samuel Shield	—	—	—	—	—	x	—	—
Henry Skyren	—	—	—	—	—	x	—	—
Adam Smith	—	—	—	—	x	—	—	—
Thomas Smith	—	—	—	—	x	—	—	—
James Stevenson	—	—	—	—	—	x	—	—
William Stuart	—	—	—	—	x	—	—	—
Daniel Sturges	—	—	—	—	—	x	—	—
James Thompson	—	—	—	—	—	x	—	—
Charles M. Thruston	—	—	—	—	x	—	—	—
Christopher Todd	—	—	—	—	—	—	—	x
Jacob Townshend	x	—	—	—	—	—	—	—
William Vere	—	—	—	—	—	x	—	—
Abner Waugh	—	—	—	—	x	—	—	—
Alexander White	—	—	—	—	x	—	—	—
Thomas Wilkinson	—	—	—	—	—	—	—	x
William Willie	—	—	—	—	—	—	—	x
Francis Wilson	—	—	—	—	—	x	—	—
John Wingate	—	—	—	—	—	—	x	—
Total	25	1	—	11	49	25	6	18

North Carolina: 14

	Loyalists				Patriots			
	Active	Moderate	Passive	Fled	Active	Moderate	Passive	Political opinion unknown
John Alexander	x	—	—	—	—	—	—	—
Nathaniel Blount	—	—	—	—	—	x	—	—
Thomas Burges, Sr.	—	—	—	—	—	—	x	—
Charles Cupples	—	—	—	—	x	—	—	—
Daniel Earle	—	—	—	—	x	—	—	—
Hezekiah Ford	x	—	—	—	—	—	—	—
James Frazer	x	—	—	x	—	—	—	—
John McClean	x	—	—	x	—	—	—	—
William McKenzie	x	—	—	x	—	—	—	—
George Meiklejohn	x	—	—	—	x	—	—	—
Charles Pettigrew	—	—	—	—	—	x	—	—
James Read	x	—	—	—	—	—	—	—
Charles E. Taylor	—	—	—	—	x	—	—	—
John Wills	—	x	—	x	—	—	—	—
Total	7	1	—	4	4	2	1	—

South Carolina: 22

	Loyalists				Patriots			
	Active	Moderate	Passive	Fled	Active	Moderate	Passive	Political opinion unknown
Benjamin Blackburn	—	—	—	—	—	—	—	x
John Bullman	x	—	—	x	—	—	—	—
Robert Cooper	x	—	—	x	—	—	—	—

(*Contd.*)

South Carolina: 22 (*Contd.*)

	Loyalists				Patriots			
	Active	Moderate	Passive	Fled	Active	Moderate	Passive	Political opinion unknown
Edward Ellington	—	—	—	—	—	—	—	x
Alexander Findlay	—	—	—	—	—	—	—	x
James Foulis	x	—	—	x	—	—	—	—
Alexander Graham, Jr.	—	—	—	—	—	—	—	x
William E. Graham	—	—	—	—	—	—	—	x
James Harrison	—	—	—	—	—	—	—	x
Samuel Hart	—	—	—	—	—	—	—	x
Edward Jenkins	—	—	—	—	—	—	—	x
John Lewis	—	—	—	—	x	—	—	—
Samuel F. Lucius	—	—	—	—	—	—	—	x
Charles F. Moreau	—	—	—	—	—	—	—	x
Offspring Pearce	—	—	—	—	x	—	—	—
William Percy	—	—	—	—	x	—	—	—
Henry Purcell	—	—	—	—	x	—	—	—
Robert Purcell	x	—	—	x	—	—	—	—
Robert Smith	—	—	—	—	x	—	—	—
James Stuart	x	—	—	x	—	—	—	—
Paul Turquand	—	—	—	—	—	x	—	—
Samuel F. Warren	—	—	—	—	x	—	—	—
Total	5	—	—	5	6	1	—	10

Georgia: 6

	Loyalists				Patriots			
	Active	Moderate	Passive	Fled	Active	Moderate	Passive	Political opinion unknown
James Brown	—	—	—	—	—	—	—	x
John Holmes	x	—	—	x	—	—	—	—
John Rennie	—	—	—	—	—	—	—	x
James Seymour	x	—	—	x	—	—	—	—
Haddon Smith	x	—	—	x	—	—	—	—
John Stewart	—	—	—	—	—	—	—	x
Total	3	—	—	3	—	—	—	3

Grand total: 311 ministries

	Loyalists				Patriots			
	Active	Moderate	Passive	Fled	Active	Moderate	Passive	Political opinion unknown
	101	15	12	71	76	45	9	59

Appendix II

A Summary of the Birthplaces, Birth Years, and Colleges Attended by Colonial American Church of England Clergymen, 1775

Table I A Birthplaces of New England men

	NH	Mass	Conn	RI	NY	Eng	Scot
Maine	—	2	—	—	—	—	—
New Hampshire	—	1	1	—	—	—	—
Massachusetts	2	6	1	—	—	4	1
Rhode Island	—	2	—	—	—	1	1
Connecticut	1	1	15	—	2	1	—
Total	3	12	17	—	2	6	2

Table I B A summary of the men's birth years by decades

	1700–9	1710–19	1720–9	1730–9	1740–9	Unknown
Maine	—	—	—	2	—	—
New Hampshire	—	—	—	—	2	—
Massachusetts	1	2	2	4	4	1
Rhode Island	—	—	1	1	1	1
Connecticut	1	4	1	8	5	1
Total	2	6	4	15	12	3

Table I C A summary of colleges attended

	Harvard	Yale	Oxford	King's	Other	Unknown
Maine	2	—	—	—	—	—
New Hampshire	1	—	—	—	1 Rhode Island	—
Massachusetts	8	2	2	—	—	2
Rhode Island	2	—	—	—	1 Aberdeen	1
Connecticut	2	15	—	1	1 Philadelphia	1
Total	15	17	2	1	3	4

Table II A   Birthplaces of Middle Colonies men

	NY	NJ	Pa	Conn	Eng	Scot	Ire	Other
New York	6	—	1	3	2	1	3	1 each Mass., R.I., Palatine, and unknown
New Jersey	1	2	—	3	1	3	—	1 unknown
Pennsylvania	—	—	3	—	2	4	2	1 unknown
Delaware	1	—	3	—	1	—	—	—
Total	8	2	7	6	6	8	5	6

Table II B   A summary of the men's birth years by decades

	1700–9	1710–19	1720–9	1730–9	1740–9	1750–9	Unknown
New York	1	—	3	6	6	2	2
New Jersey	1	1	2	1	6	—	—
Pennsylvania	1	1	3	3	2	1	1
Delaware	—	1	1	1	2	—	—
Total	3	3	9	11	16	3	3

Table II C   A summary of colleges attended

	Harvard	Yale	King's	New Jersey	Philadelphia	Oxford
New York	1	3	8	—	1	1
New Jersey	—	3	—	2	—	1
Pennsylvania	—	—	—	—	3	1
Delaware	—	—	1	—	1	1
Total	1	6	9	2	5	4

	Cambridge	Dublin	St. Andrews	Aberdeen	Glasgow	Other
New York	1	2	1	—	—	2 unknown
New Jersey	1	—	—	2	—	2 none
Pennsylvania	—	2	—	3	1	1 Leyden, 1 unknown
Delaware	—	—	—	—	—	2 unknown
Total	2	4	1	5	1	8

Table III A   Birthplaces of Chesapeake colonies men

	Conn	NY	NJ	Penn	Mary	Va	Eng	Scot	Ire	Unknown
Virginia	3	2	1	3	2	42	19	28	4	16
Maryland	1	—	1	4	13	4	13	9	3	11
Total	4	2	2	7	15	46	32	37	7	27

Table III B   A summary of the men's birth years by decades

	1690–9	1700–9	1710–19	1720–9	1730–9	1740–9	1750–9	Unknown
Virginia	1	3	6	12	22	42	7	27
Maryland	—	3	5	6	12	18	2	13
Total	1	6	11	18	34	60	9	40

Table III C   A summary of colleges attended

	Yale	King's	Coll. of NJ	Phil	W and M	Log	Oxf	Unknown
Virginia	2	—	2	3	30	—	6	46
Maryland	—	1	3	7	3	1	7	21
Total	2	1	5	10	33	1	13	67

	Camb	Edin	St.Andr	Aber	Glasg	Dublin	Halle
Virginia	6	3	1	12	5	3	1
Maryland	2	1	—	9	2	2	—
Total	8	4	1	21	7	5	1

Table IV A   Birthplaces of Southern Colonies men

	PA	MY	VA	NC	SC	ENG	SCOTS	IRE	Un known	Other
North Carolina	1	1	2	1	—	2	3	1	3	—
South Carolina	—	—	—	—	1	12	2	—	5	2 Germany
Georgia	—	—	—	—	1	2	1	—	1	1 Leewards
Total	1	1	2	1	2	16	6	1	9	3

Table IV B   A summary of the men's birth years by decades

	1700–9	1710–19	1720–9	1730–9	1740–9	1750–9	Unknown
North Carolina	—	1	—	3	3	3	4
South Carolina	1	—	2	7	6	—	6
Georgia	—	—	—	—	4	2	—
Total	1	1	2	10	13	5	10

Table IV C   A summary of colleges attended

	Phil.	Oxf.	Camb.	Aberd.	Edin.	Glas.	St.Andr.	Unknown
North Carolina	1	—	—	1	1	—	1	10
South Carolina	—	7	4	2	—	1	—	8
Georgia	—	2	—	2	—	—	—	2
Total	1	9	4	5	1	1	1	20

Table V A   Grand total of birthplaces

Colony	Number
New Hampshire	3
Massachusetts	13
Rhode Island	1
Connecticut	27
New York	10
New Jersey	3
Pennsylvania	16
Delaware	—
Maryland	16
Virginia	48
North Carolina	1
South Carolina	2
Georgia	—
England	64
Scotland	54
Ireland	13
Other	Provinces of today's Germany, 3; Leeward Islands, 1
Unknown	36
Total	311

Table V B   Grand total of the men's birth years by decades

1690–9	1700–9	1710–19	1720–9	1730–9	1740–9	1750–9	Unknown	Total
1	12	21	33	69	101	20	54	311

Table V C   A grand total of colleges attended

Colleges	Number
Aberdeen	32
Cambridge	14
College of New Jersey (Princeton)	7
College of Philadelphia (Pennsylvania)	17
College of Rhode Island (Brown)	1
College of William and Mary	33
Dublin	9
Edinburgh	5
Glasgow	8
Halle	1
Harvard	16
King's	11
Leyden	1
Log	1
Oxford	28
Yale	25
St. Andrew's	3
None	3
Unknown	96
Total	311

Notes

Prologue

1. Jonathan Boucher, *A View of the Causes and Consequences of the American Revolution in Thirteen Discourses, Preached in North America Between the Years 1763 and 1775, with an Historical Preface* (London, 1797, New York, 1967 edition): xxiv–xxv.
2. *The Works of John Adams, Second President of the United States* (Boston, 1856). Charles F. Adams, ed. X: 185–8. The most recent edition of *The Papers of John Adams* published by the Massachusetts Historical Society has not reached the date of this letter, 2 December 1815.
3. J. C. D. Clark, *The Language of Liberty, 1660–1832: Political Discourse and Social Dynamics in the Anglo-American World* (Cambridge, 1994): xi–xii.
4. James B. Bell, *The Imperial Origins of the King's Church in Early America, 1607–1783* (London, 2004).
5. Clark, *The Language of Liberty*, 4.
6. Ibid., 41.
7. In addition, this book complements and supplements my earlier study, *Imperial Origins of the King's Church*, an examination of the structural transfer of the Church of England and its establishment in the colonies. It is a study that considered the roles exercised on the church's behalf by the Council of Trade and Plantations, the bishop of London, the royal governors and deputies of the London prelate and the activity and financial support of the Society for the Propagation of the Gospel.
8. Bell, *Imperial Origins of the King's Church*, 3–9.
9. Ibid., 10–47.
10. Ibid., 198–200.
11. Ibid., 30–2.
12. Ibid., Chap. 13.
13. The following are key works that address the subject: Francis L. Hawks, *Collections of the Protestant Episcopal Historical Society for the Year 1851* (New York, 1851); Francis L. Hawks and William S. Perry, *Documentary History of the Protestant Episcopal Church in the United States of America* (New York, 1863–64); William S. Perry, *History of the American Episcopal Church* (Boston, 1885); Alfred Lyon Cross, *The Anglican Episcopate and the American Colonies* (New York, 1902); Claude H. Van Tyne, *The Causes of the American Revolution* (Cambridge, 1922); William W. Manross, *History of the American Episcopal Church*, Third edition (New York, 1959); Bernard Knollenberg, *Origin of the American Revolution: 1759–1766* (New York, 1960); Carl Bridenbaugh, *Mitre and Sceptre; Transatlantic Faiths, Ideas, Personalities, and Politics 1689–1775* (New York, 1962); Raymond W. Albright, *History of the Protestant Episcopal Church* (New York, 1964); Frederick V. Mills, Sr., *Bishops by Ballot: An Eighteenth-Century Ecclesiastical Revolution* (New York, 1978); John F. Woolverton, *Colonial Anglicanism in North America* (Detroit, 1984);

Patricia U. Bonomi, *Under the Cope of Heaven: Religion, Society, and Politics in Colonial America* (New York, 1986).

14. David Ramsay, *The History of the American Revolution* (London, 1793). II: 312–13.
15. Ibid., 313.
16. Ibid.
17. Ibid.
18. John C. Miller. *Origins of the American Revolution* (Stanford, 1959): 186–97.
19. Knollenberg, *Origin of the American Revolution*, 76–86.
20. Stephen Taylor, 'Whigs, Bishops and America: The Politics of Church Reform in Mid-Eighteenth-Century England', *The Historical Journal*. 30 (1993): 338.

1 The Seeds of Discord: An English Church Established in Boston

1. *The Works of John Adams, Second President of the United States* (Boston, 1856). Charles F. Adams, ed. X: 185–8. The most recent edition of *The Papers of John Adams* published by the Massachusetts Historical Society has not reached the date of this letter, 2 December 1815.
2. Ibid., 185
3. Ibid.
4. Ibid.
5. Ibid.
6. James Grahame, *The History of the United States of North America*, Second edition (Philadelphia, 1848) II: 457–9.
7. Council of Trade and Plantations also known at various periods as Committee of Trade and Plantations, Lords of Trade and Plantations, and Board of Trade and Plantations.
8. B. R. Burg, *Richard Mather* (Boston, 1982): 7, 20, 40; B. R. Burg, *Richard Mather of Dorchester* (Lexington, 1976): 23.
9. Larzer Ziff, ed., *John Cotton and the Churches of New England* (Cambridge, 1968): 136–8, 175–6; Everett Emerson, *John Cotton*, Revised edition (Boston, 1990): 6; Larzer Ziff, *The Career of John Cotton: Puritanism and the American Experience* (Princeton, 1962); Charles E. Hambrick-Stowe, *The Practice of Piety: Puritan Devotional Disciplines in Seventeenth-Century New England* (Chapel Hill, 1982).
10. Chapter 2.
11. *A.P.C.E.Col.Ser., 1680–1720*: 435–6. *Cal.S.P.Col.Ser., 1677–1680*: 121–2. For a discussion of the relationship between the church and state see Richard Hooker, *Of the Laws of Ecclesiastical Polity: Books VI, VII, VIII*, P. G. Stanwood, ed. (Cambridge, 1981): 315–31.
12. I am grateful to Dr. R. A. Beddard of Oriel College in Oxford University for bringing to my attention an unpublished 1688 letter of John Evelyn to an unnamed prelate. It may have been written to his good friend William Sancroft, Archbishop of Canterbury. Evelyn discussed in the letter many matters of state and proposed a colonial bishop for the American provinces. British Library, MSS Tanner 447, fos. 69 and 70.
13. I have discussed the origins of imperial policies and procedures regarding the extension of the English church overseas in Chapter 2 of my *Imperial Origins*.

14. `J. C. D. Clark, *The Language of Liberty, 1660–1832: Political Discourse and Social Dynamics in the Anglo-American World* (Cambridge, 1994): 245–6.

15. Henry W. Foote, *Annals of King's Chapel from the Puritan Age of New England to the Present Day* (Boston, 1882) I: 58–83.

16. For a more detailed analysis of the establishment of the congregation in Boston and the roles played by Randolph and Andros, see my discussion in *Imperial Origins*: Chapter 3.

17. Increase Mather, *A Narrative of the Miseries of New-England, by Reason of an Arbitrary Government Erected there under Sir Edmund Andros* (London, 1688; Boston, 1689, 1775); *The Revolution in New England Justified and the People there Vindicated* (Boston, 1691).

18. Robert M. Middlekauff, *The Mathers. Three Generations of Puritan Intellectuals, 1596–1728* (New York, 1971): 87.

19. Stephen Foster, *The Long Argument: English Puritanism and the Shaping of New England Culture, 1570–1700* (Chapel Hill, 1991).

20. Julius Herbert Tuttle, 'The Libraries of the Mathers', *P.A.A.S.* 20 (1911): 268–356. William Prynne. *Sixteen Quaeres Proposed to Our Lord Prelates* (Amsterdam, 1637); [David Calderwood]. *The Pastor and Prelate, or Reformation and Conformitie Shortly Compared by the Word of God, by Antiquity and the Proceedings of the Ancient Kirk* (Leyden, 1628) and also his *The Presbyterian Government is Divine; Reasons to Prove that it is Unlawful to Hear the Ministers of England; and That King may Abrogate Prelacy Without any Violation of his Oath* (n.p., n.d.).

21. Clark, *Language of Liberty, 1660–1832*: 47.

22. Thomas J. Holmes, *Increase Mather: A Bibliography of his Works* (Cleveland, 1931) I: 46.

23. *Diary of Cotton Mather: Mass.Hist.Soc.Coll.* Seventh series (Boston, 1911) VII: 133–4.

24. William Henry Whitmore, ed. *The Andros Tracts, The Prince Society* (Boston, 1870) II: 211.

25. Increase Mather, *A Brief Discourse Concerning the Unlawfulness of the Common Prayer Worship. And of Laying the Hand on, and Kissing the Booke in Swearing* (Boston, 1686): 2.

26. Ibid., 4.

27. Ibid., 14.

28. Ibid., 15.

29. Ibid.

30. Ibid., 17–18.

31. Holmes, *Increase Mather*, I: 56–7.

32. Tuttle, 'Libraries of the Mathers', 283.

33. 'C. D'., *New-England's Faction Discovered; or A Brief and True Account of Their Persecution of the Church of England; the Beginning and Progress of the War with the Indians; and other Late Proceedings There, in a Letter from a Gentleman of that Country to a Person of Quality. Being an Answer to a Most False and Scandalous Pamphlet Lately Published; Intituled, News from New England &c.* (London, 1690): 8–9.

34. John Williams, *A Brief Discourse Concerning the Lawfulness of Worshipping God by the Common Prayer. Being in Answer To a Book. Entituled, A Brief Discourse Concerning the Unlawfulness of the Common-Prayer Worship. Lately Printed in*

New-England, Let all Things Be Done Decently, and in Order, I. Cor. 14. 40 (London, 1693).

35. Increase Mather, *Some Remarks, on a Pretended Answer, to a Discourse Concerning the Common-Prayer Worship. With an Exhortation to the Churches in New-England, to Hold Fast the Profession of Their Faith without Wavering* (Boston, 1713): 1.

36. Increase Mather, *A Testimony Against Several Prophane and Superstitious Customs Now Practised by some in New-England, The Evil Whereof is Evinced from the Holy Scriptures, and from the Writings both of Ancient and Modern Divines* (London, 1687; Boston, 1688).

37. As quoted in Holmes, *Increase Mather*, II: 569.

38. Cotton Mather, *The Serviceable Man. A Discourse Made Unto the General Court of the Massachusetts Colony, New England, At the Anniversary Election* (Boston, 1690): 31.

39. K. G. Davies, 'The Revolutions in America', in Robert Beddard, ed. *The Revolutions of 1688* (Oxford, 1991): 256–60.

40. David S. Lovejoy, *The Glorious Revolution in America* (New York, 1972): 348.

41. 'Episcopal Ministers Address', *Mass.Hist.Soc.Coll.* Third series (Boston, 1838) VII: 192–5.

42. Kenneth Silverman, *Selected Letters of Cotton Mather* (Baton Rouge, 1971): 216.

43. Gordon S. Wood, *The Radicalism of the American Revolution* (New York, 1992): 61–2, 109, 174–6. Gordon S. Wood, 'Conspiracy and the Paranoid Style: Causality and Deceit in the Eighteenth Century', *W.M.Q.*, Third series XXXIX (1982): 401–1. Bernard Bailyn, *The Ideological Origins of the American Revolution* (Cambridge, 1967): 94–5. G. B. Warden, *Boston, 1689–1776* (Boston, 1970): 241–64.

2 Discord Enlarged: The Society for the Propagation of the Gospel

1. James B. Bell, *The Imperial Origins of the King's Church in Early America, 1607–1783* (London, 2004): 47–53, 71–3.

2. Ibid., 26–9. *Archives of Maryland, Proceedings and Acts of the General Assembly of Maryland, April 1684–June 1692* (Baltimore, 1894): 425–30.

3. *Proceedings and Acts of the General Assembly of Maryland, April 26, 1700–May 3, 1704* (Baltimore, 1904): 91–8, 265–73, 418–20.

4. Bell, *Imperial Origins of the King's Church*, 28.

5. Ibid., 84–5. *E.R.S.N.Y.* (Albany, 1901) I: 1073–9.

6. *E.R.S.N.Y.*, VI: 4177.

7. John Miller, *New York Considered and Improved, 1695* (New York, 1970 edition). Earlier editions of the book had been published in London, 1843, Cleveland, Ohio, 1845, and in New York, 1862.

8. Ibid., 74–81. The King's Farm was a tract of land on lower Manhattan Island granted to Trinity Church by Governor Fletcher. The property was intended to provide income for the maintenance of the church which was organized in 1697. A portion of land became the original campus of King's College in 1754 (now Columbia University). Trinity church continues to own vast

stretches of the original grant making it the wealthiest congregation of the Episcopal church in the United States. See Bell, *Imperial Origins of the King's Church*, 33–4.

9. *Calendar of State Papers, Colonial Series, America and West Indies, 15 May 1696–31 Oct. 1697*, J. W. Fortescue, ed. (London, 1904): 84, 86–7, 93.
10. Bell, *Imperial Origins of the King's Church*, 24–5.
11. James B. Bell, Colonial American Clergy of the Church of England Database, www.jamesbbell.com.
12. William W. Manross, *A History of the American Episcopal Church*. Third edition (New York, 1959): 121.
13. M. Eugene Sirmans, *Colonial South Carolina: A Political History, 1663–1763* (Chapel Hill, 196): 75–100.
14. Bell, *Imperial Origins of the King's Church*, 38–40.
15. Sirmans, *Colonial South Carolina*, 75–6.
16. Ibid., 87–8.
17. Ibid., 89.
18. Nicholas Trott, *The Laws of the British Plantations in America, Relating to the Church and Clergy, Religion and Learning* (London, 1721): 5–22. F.P.P., IX: 3–16, South Carolina Church Act, 1706.
19. Sirmans, *Colonial South Carolina*, pp. 87–9.
20. Mattie Erma Edwards Parker, ed., *North Carolina Charters and Constitutions, 1578–1698* (Raleigh, 1963): 76–104.
21. Ibid., 109–240.
22. *C.R.N.C.*, I: 543–5.
23. Ibid., 604.
24. Ibid., 601–2.
25. Ibid.
26. Ibid., 571–3.
27. Hugh Talmage Lefler, 'The Anglican Church in North Carolina: The Proprietary Period', in *The Episcopal Church in North Carolina, 1701–1959*, Lawrence Foushee London and Sarah McCulloh Lemmon, eds (Raleigh, 1985): 8.
28. Ibid.
29. *C.R.N.C.*, I: 787–90.
30. *C.R.N.C.*, II: 207–13.
31. Ibid., 207.
32. *C.R.N.C.*, V: 107, 116.
33. Ibid., 228–30, 233–4, 257–8, 261.
34. Ibid., 1006–7, 1009–11, 1019–20, 1024, 1080, 1082, 1036, 1097, VI: 358, 468, 891.
35. *C.R.N.C.*, VII: 88.
36. *C.R.N.C.*, VI: 1235, VII: 920, IX: 928.
37. Lefler, 'The Anglican Church in North Carolina', 24–5; *C.R.N.C.*, XI: 1011, Article XXXIV of the state constitution.
38. For details regarding the financial support of Anglican congregations during the colonial era see my *Imperial Origins of the English Church*, 74–104.
39. Clifford K. Shipton, *Sibley's Harvard Graduates* (Boston, 1937) V: 47–52.
40. Sydney E. Ahlstrom, *A Religious History of the American People* (New Haven, 1972): 224–5.
41. Bell, *Imperial Origins of the King's Church*, 7–9.

42. John K. Nelson, *A Blessed Company: Parishes, Parsons, and Parishioners in Anglican Virginia, 1690–1776* (Chapel Hill, 2001): 282–9.

43. Ibid., 282–3.

44. Ibid., 284.

45. Ibid., 287.

46. Edward Carpenter, *The Protestant Bishop: Being the Life of Henry Compton, 1632–1713, Bishop of London* (London, 1956): 270–2.

47. Ethyn Williams Kirby, *George Keith (1638–1716)* (New York, 1942): 122–6. On George Keith's visit to America, his role in the Quaker schism in Pennsylvania, and his attack on Cotton Mather, see Jon Butler, 'Gospel Order Improved: The Keithian Schism and the Exercise of Quaker Ministerial Authority in Pennsylvania', *W.M.Q.* Third Series 31 (1974): 430–52.

48. George Keith, *A Journal of Travels from New-Hampshire to Caratuck, on the Continent of North America* (London, 1706): 5.

49. George Keith, *The Doctrine of the Holy Apostles & Prophets the Foundation of the Church of Christ, As it was Delivered in Sermon at Her Majesties Chappel, at Boston in New-England, the 14th of June 1702* (Boston, 1702).

50. Keith, *A Journal of Travels*, 5–6.

51. Increase Mather, *Some Remarks on a Late Sermon, Preached at Boston in New England, by George Keith M. A. Shewing That his Pretended Good Rules in Divinity, Are Not Built on the Foundation of the Apostles & Prophets* (Boston, 1702).

52. Ibid., 2–4, 14–15. The Second Commandment: 'Thou shalt not make to thyself any graven image, nor the likeness of any thing that is in heaven above, or in the earth beneath, or in the water under the earth. Thou shalt not bow down to them, nor worship them; for I the Lord thy God am a jealous God, and visit the sins of the fathers upon the children unto the third and fourth generation of them that hate me, and shew mercy unto thousands in them that love me, and keep my commandments'.

53. George Keith, *A Reply to Mr. Increase Mather's Printed Remarks on a Sermon Preached by G. K. at Her Majesty's Chappel in Boston, the 14th of June, 1702, In Vindication of the Six Good Rules in Divinity There Delivered. Which He hath Attempted (though Very Feebly and Unsuccessfully) to Refute* (New York, 1703).

54. Keith, *A Journal of Travels*, 6.

55. For an analysis of the structure and purposes of these meetings see my *Imperial Origins of the English Church*, Chap. 8.

56. Bell, Colonial American Clergy of the Church of England Database, www.jamesbbell.com.

57. Lambeth Palace Library, S.P.G. Papers, vol. XII: 180–3, John Talbot to the Secretary, Philadelphia, 1 September 1703.

58. Lambeth Palace Library, Archbishops of Canterbury MSS. vol. 930: no. 38, Henry Dodwell to Thomas Tenison, 29 August 1700.

59. Lambeth Palace Library, Archbishops of Canterbury MSS. vol. 711. no. 18, Bishop of London's Paper about a suffragan bishop for the plantations, Dec. 1707.

60. Carpenter, *Henry Compton*, 279. Bell, *Imperial Origins of the English Church*, Chap. 11.

61. Carpenter, *Henry Compton*, 279–80.

62. Sir Robert Phillimore, *The Ecclesiastical Law of the Church of England*. Second edition by Sir W. G. F. Phillimore (London, 1895) I: 77.
63. MSS, Historical Society of Pennsylvania, The Rev. William Becket to Dr. David Humphreys, Lewes, Delaware, 13 March, 15 March, 1727/28.
64. Frank J. Klingberg, *Carolina Chronicle: The Papers of Commissary Gideon Johnston, 1707–1716* (Berkeley, 1946): 121.
65. Ibid.

3   A Handmaiden for Episcopacy: John Checkley of Boston

1. Carl Bridenbaugh, *Cities in the Wilderness: The First Century of Urban Life in America, 1625–1742* (New York, 1964) I: 143.
2. G. B. Warden, *Boston, 1689–1776* (Boston, 1970): 36.
3. Bridenbaugh, *Cities in the Wilderness*, 289.
4. Ibid., 79.
5. Warden, *Boston*, 89.
6. Clifford K. Shipton, *Sibley's Harvard Graduates* (Cambridge, 1933) IV: 120–37, VI: 439–67.
7. Walter Muir Whitehill, *Boston: A Topographical History* (Cambridge, 1963): 37.
8. Clifford K. Shipton, *Sibley's Harvard Graduates* (Cambridge, 1933) VI: 127.
9. J. C. D. Clark, *The Language of Liberty, 1660–1832: Political Discourse and Social Dynamics in the Anglo-American World* (Cambridge, 1994): 5.
10. Charles Leslie, *The Religion of Jesus Christ the Only True Religion, or a Short and Easie Method with the Deists, Wherein the Certainty of the Christian Religion is Demonstrated by Infallible Proof from Four Rules, Which are Incompatible to any Imposture That Ever Yet Has Been, or That Can Possibly Be. In a Letter to a Friend* (Boston, 1719).
11. Robert D. Cornwall, 'The Search for the Primitive Church: The Uses of the Early Church Fathers in the High Anglican Tradition, 1680–1745', *Anglican and Episcopal History (formerly the Historical Magazine of the Protestant Episcopal Church* 59 (1990): 307.
12. Ibid., 315.
13. [John Checkley], *Choice Dialogues, Between a Godly Minister and an Honest Countryman, Concerning Election and Predestination* (Boston, 1720).
14. John Checkley, *A Modest Proof of the Order and Government Settled by Christ and His Apostles in the Church. A Discourse Shewing Who is a True Pastor of the Church of Christ* (Boston, 1723).
15. Ibid., ii.
16. Ibid.
17. Ibid., ii–iii.
18. Ibid., iii.
19. Ibid., v.
20. Edward Wigglesworth, *Sober Remarks on a Book Lately Reprinted at Boston, Entituled, A Modest Proof of the Order & Government Settled by Christ and His Apostles in the Church. In a Letter to a Friend* (Boston, 1724).
21. Ibid., 71.
22. Ibid., 75.

23. Jonathan Dickinson, *A Defence of Presbyterian Ordination. In Answer to a Pamphlet, Entitled, A Modest Proof, of the Order and Government Settled by Christ, in the Church* (Boston, 1724).

24. Ibid., 8, 42. [John Checkley], *A Defence of a Book Lately Re-Printed at Boston, Entitled, A Modest Proof, &c. In a Reply to a Book Entitled, Sober Remarks on A Modest Proof, &c. [By Edward Wigglesworth], With Strictures on John Dickinson's Defence of Presbyterian Ordination. Also Animadversions Upon [Thomas Walter's] Essay Upon the Paradox, Infallibility Many Sometimes Mistake. [And] The Ruling and Ordaining Power of Congregational Bishops or Presbyters Defended* [By Thomas Foxcroft] (Boston, 1724). [John Checkley], *A Letter to Jonathan Dickinson* [Boston, 1725].

25. Anonymous, *A Brief Account of the Revenues, Pomp, and State of the Bishops, and Clergy in a Letter &c.* (Boston, 1725): 1, 3.

26. Ibid., 4.

27. Ibid., 5–10.

28. Ibid., 11–12.

29. Perry Miller, *The New England Mind: From Colony to Province* (Cambridge, 1962): 468–74. Checkley did not abandon his argument with the conclusion of his trial. He arranged to have his eloquent statement of defence delivered at his proceedings published in London. Presumably he was unable to enlist a Boston printer to do the job. Familiar with the intricacies of the English law, Checkley skilfully argued his case in *The Speech of Mr. John Checkley upon His Tryal, at Boston in New England for Publishing the Short and Easy Method with the Deists: To which was added, A Discourse concerning Episcopacy; In Defence of Christianity, and the Church of England against the Deists and the Dissenters. To which is added: The Jury's Verdict; His Plea in Arrest of Judgement; and the Sentence of the Court* (London, 1730).

30. Miller, *The New England Mind*, 474–5.

31. Jonathan Dickinson, *The Scripture-Bishop, or the Divine Right of Presbyterian Ordination & Government Considered in a Dialogue Between Praeleticus and Eleutherius* (Boston, 1732).

32. James Wetmore, *Eleutherius Enervatus or An Answer to a Pamphlet, Intituled, the Divine Right of Presbyterian Ordination, &c. Argued. Done by Way of Dialogue between Eusebius and Eletherius, Together with Two Letters upon this Subject, some Time agoe Sent to the Supposed Author of That Pamphlet* (New York, 1733).

33. Ibid., 5; Clark, *Language of Liberty*, 33–4.

34. Arthur Browne, *The Scripture-Bishop, or the Divine Right of Presbyterian Ordination and Government Consider'd in a Dialogue Between Praeleticus and Eleutherius, Examined in Two Letters to a Friend* (No place, 1733). John Beach, *A Vindication of the Worship of God According to the Church of England, from the Aspersions Cast upon It By Mr. Jonathan Dickinson, in a Sermon Preached at Newark, June 2, 1736, and by J. G. Being a Letter to the Members of the Church of England at Newark* (New York, 1736): 3; 4–5. John Beach, *An Appeal to the Unprejudiced. In Supplement to the Vindication of the Worship of God According to the Church of England, From the Injurious and Uncharitable Reflections of Mr. Jonathan Dickinson* (Boston, 1737).

35. Jonathan Dickinson, *The Scripture-Bishop Vindicated. A Defence of the Dialogue Between Praeleticus and Eleutherius, upon the Scripture-Bishop, or the Divine*

Right of Presbyterian Ordination and Government. Against the Exceptions of a Pamphlet Intituled, The Scripture-Bishop Examin'd. In a Letter to a Friend (Boston, 1733).

36. Samuel Johnson, *A Letter from A Minister of the Church of England to His Dissenting Parishioners. Containing a Brief Answer to the Most Material Objections Against the Establish'd Church That Are to be Found in De Laune's Plea, The Answer to the Bishop of Derry, The Plain Reasons for Separating, &c. and Together with Plain Reasons for Conformity to the Church of England* (New York, 1733).

37. Ibid., 4.

38. Samuel Johnson, *A Second Letter from a Minister of the Church of England to His Dissenting Parishioners, In Answer to Some Remarks made on the Former, by one J. G.* (Boston, 1734); *A Third Letter from a Minister of the Church of England to the Dissenters, Containing Some Observations on Mr. J. G'.s Remarks on the Second* (Boston, 1737).

39. John Graham, *Some Remarks upon a late Pamphlet Entitled, A Letter from a Minister of the Church of England, to His Dissenting Parishioners. Shewing how far the Book is From Answering the Titles and how Remote the Matters of Fact Therein Mentioned, are from the Truth; Together with a Brief Indication of the Presbyterians from those Reproaches Therein Cast upon Them* ([Boston], 1733); *Some Remarks upon a Second Letter from the Church of England Minister, to His Dissenting Parishioners* (Boston, 1736).

40. F.P.P., 40:1, Rev. Samuel Johnson to John Arnold, 4 December 1735, Stratford, Connecticut.

41. Beilby Porteus, *The Works of Thomas Secker, LL.D., Late Lord Archbishop of Canterbury, to which is prefixed a Review of His Grace's Life and Character* (London, 1771) I: ii–xv.

42. Ibid., V: 88.

43. Ibid., V: 108–9.

44. The sermon is conveniently printed in Frank J. Klingberg, *Anglican Humanitarianism in Colonial New York* (Philadelphia, 1940): 211–33.

4 The English Origins of a Colonial American Controversy

1. Several studies of the proposal for establishing a colonial Anglican episcopate offer differing perspectives of the issue. The primary works are Alfred Lyon Cross, *The Anglican Episcopate and the American Colonies* (New York, 1902); Carl Bridenbaugh, *Mitre and Scepter: Transatlantic Faiths, Ideas, Personalities, and Politics, 1689–1775* (New York, 1962); and Frederick V. Mills, Sr., *Bishops by Ballot: An Eighteenth-Century Ecclesiastical Revolution* (New York, 1978). Yet each of these still-useful studies did not consider the historical origins of the debate within the context of the Church of England's post-Reformation history. See also William Nelson, *The Controversy over the Proposition for An American Episcopate, 1767–1774. A Bibliography of the Subject* (Paterson, NJ, 1909). Henry W. Foote, *Annals of King's Chapel* (Boston, 1882, 1896). Edmund Slafter, *John Checkley* (Boston, 1897). Philip Davidson, *Propaganda and the American Revolution 1763–1783* (Chapel Hill, 1941). Norman Sykes,

Edmund Gibson, Bishop of London, 1669–1748 (London, 1926): 143–5, 166–75, 390–1.

2. Jonathan Mayhew, *Observations on the Charter and Conduct of the Society for the Propagation of the Gospel in Foreign Parts; Designed to Shew Their Non-Conformity to Each Other. With Remarks on the Mistakes of East Apthorp, M. A., Missionary at Cambridge, in Quoting and Representing the Sense of the Said Charter, &c. As also Various Incidental Reflections Relative to the Church of England, and the State of Religion in North-America, Particularly in New England* (Boston, 1763): 103.

3. Bernard Bailyn, ed. *Pamphlets of the American Revolution, 1750–1776* (Cambridge, 1965): 60.

4. James Tunstead Burtchaell, *From Synagogue to Church: Public Services and Offices in the Earliest Christian Communities* (Cambridge, 1992).

5. I am particularly indebted to Paul F. Bradshaw's, *The Anglican Ordinal, Its History and Development from the Reformation to the Present Day* (London, 1971): 8.

6. Ibid., 9.

7. Ibid., 10.

8. Ibid.

9. Ibid., 13–14.

10. Ibid. 19–36. Diarmaid MacCulloch, *Thomas Cranmer: A Life* (London, 1996): 460–1.

11. Bradshaw, *Anglican Ordinal*, 37–40; Peter Lake, *Moderate Puritans and the Elizabethan Church* (Cambridge, 1982): 21–2, 49–53, 108–12.

12. Lake, *Moderate Puritans*, 46–7, 77–92. On this issue I am also indebted to A. F. Scott Pearson, *Thomas Cartwright and Elizabethan Puritanism, 1535–1603* (Gloucester, 1966 printing): 85–104; and Patrick Collinson, *The Elizabethan Puritan Movement* (London, 1967): 123–4.

13. Lake, *Moderate Puritans*, 74–5.

14. Bradshaw, *Anglican Ordinal*, 40–1.

15. Ibid., 43–54.

16. Ibid., 55–7.

17. W. B. Patterson, *King James VI and I and the Reunion of Christendom* (Cambridge, 1997): 280–90.

18. Nicholas Tyacke, 'Puritanism, Arminianism and Counter-Revolution', in Conrad Russell, ed., *The Origins of the English Civil War* (London, 1973): 119–43.

19. Ibid., 159–166. William Prynne and John Bastwick, *A New Discovery of the Prelates Tyranny, in Their Late Prosecutions of Mr. W. Pryn* (n.p. 1641). John Bastwick, *A Declaration Demonstrating and Infallibly Proving that all Malignants, Whether They be Prelates, Popish Cavaliers, with All Other Ill Affected Persons, are Enemies to God and the King, etc.* (London, 1643): 56.

20. Bradshaw, *Anglican Ordinal*, 61–2.

21. Ibid., 62.

22. James Ussher, *The Reduction of Episcopacy into the Form of Synodical Government, Received in the Antient Church, Proposed in the Year 1641. As an Expedient for the Prevention of those Troubles, which Afterwards did Arise about the Matter of Church Government, Episcopal and Presbyterial Government Conjoyned. Proposed Now Again Anno 1703, for Removing the Difference in the*

Church of Scotland (Edinburg, 1703); W. M. Abbott, 'James Ussher and "Ussherian" episcopacy, 1640–1655: the primate and his *Reduction manuscript'*, *Albion* 22 (1990): 237–59.

23. Bradshaw, *Anglican Ordinal*, 62–4.
24. On this controversy I am grateful to Professor J. C. D. Clark for bringing to my attention J. S. Morrill, 'The Church in England, 1642–9', in John Morrill, ed., *Reactions to the English Civil War, 1642–1649* (London, 1982): 89–114; idem, 'The Attack on the Church of England in the Long Parliament, 1640–1642', in Dereck Beales and Geoffrey Best, eds, *History, Society and the Churches: Essays in Honor of Owen Chadwick* (Cambridge, 1985): 105–24; Paul Christianson, 'The Causes of the English Revolution: A Reappraisal', *Journal of British Studies* 15 (1976) pp. 40–75.
25. John Spurr, *The Restoration of the Church of England, 1646–1689* (New Haven, 1991): 3–4.
26. Ibid., 7.
27. Ibid., 5–7.
28. Ibid., 3–4.
29. Norman Sykes, *From Sheldon to Secker. Aspects of English Church History, 1660–1768* (Cambridge, 1959): 8; Spurr, *Restoration of the Church of England*, 12–28.
30. Spurr, *Restoration of the Church of England*, 15.
31. John Gauden, *The Loosing of St. Peter's Bands; Setting Forth the True Sense and Solution of the Covenant in Point of Conscience, so far as it Relates to Episcopacy* (London, 1660).
32. Spurr, *Restoration of the Church of England*, 24–8.
33. Ibid., 32. Christopher Hill, *Puritanism and Revolution* (London, 1962): 199–214.
34. John Miller, *Charles II* (London, 1991): 55–64, 76–81, 98–100. Ronald Hutton, *Charles the Second, King of England, Scotland, and Ireland* (Oxford, 1989): 180–4. R. Buick Knox, *James Ussher, Archbishop of Armagh* (Cardiff, 1967): 124–45.
35. Spurr, *Restoration of the Church of England*, 32–3.
36. Ibid., 36.
37. Bradshaw, *Anglican Ordinal*, 65. Spurr, *Restoration Church of England*, 1–28.
38. Bradshaw, *Anglican Ordinal*, 65–7. Spurr, *Restoration Church of England*, 29–42.
39. Bradshaw, *Anglican Ordinal*, 95–6.
40. Ibid., 96. Spurr, *Restoration Church of England*, 42–51.
41. Bradshaw, *Anglican Ordinal*, 98–9. Spurr, *Restoration Church of England*, 77–104.
42. N. H. Keeble and J. H. Lloyd Thomas, eds, *The Autobiography of Richard Baxter* (London, 1974): 177–85.
43. Richard Baxter, *A Treatise of Episcopacy; Confuting by Scripture, Reason, and the Churches Testimony, that Sort of Diocesan Churches, Prelacy, and Government, which Casteth out the Primitive Church Species* (London, 1681), and *The True History of Councils Enlarged* (London, 1682).
44. N. H. Keeble, *Richard Baxter: Puritan Man of Letters* (Oxford, 1982): 117–18.
45. Ibid., 118–19.
46. Clare Jackson, *Restoration Scotland, 1660–1690: Royalist Politics, Religion and Ideas* (Woodbridge, Suffolk, 2003): 104–10.
47. Ibid., 109.

48. Ibid., 110–13.
49. Ibid., 120–1.
50. Ibid., 123–62.
51. Ibid., 53–4, 76.

5 Noah Hobart Decries Anglican Expansion: Thomas Sherlock Proposes an American Bishop

1. Noah Hobart, *Ministers of the Gospel Considered as Fellow Labourers; A Sermon Delivered at the Ordination of the Reverend Noah Welles at Stamford, Dec. 31, 1746* (Boston, 1747): 9–10.
2. Franklin B. Dexter, ed. *The Literary Diary of Ezra Stiles* (New York, 1901) I: 425.
3. Edmund S. Morgan, *The Gentle Puritan: A Life of Ezra Stiles, 1727–1795* (New Haven, 1962): 17–18.
4. Dexter, *Literary Diary of Ezra Stiles*, 20.
5. Ibid., 21–2.
6. Nelson Rollin Burr, *The Story of the Diocese of Connecticut: A New Branch of the Vine* (Hartford, 1962): 47–61.
7. Hobart, *Ministers of the Gospel*, 24–6.
8. Ibid., 26.
9. James B. Bell, 'Anglican Clergy in Colonial America Ordained by Bishops of London', *P.A.A.S.*, 83 (1973): 157.
10. Wetmore, *A Vindication of the Professors of the Church of England in Connecticut. Against the Invectives Contained in a Sermon Preached at Stamford by Mr. Noah Hobart, Dec. 31, 1746. In a Letter to a Friend ...* (Boston, 1747): 29.
11. Ibid., *Postscript* [James Wetmore]. Edward Weston, *The Englishman Directed in the Choice of His Religion, Reprinted for the Use of English Americans, with a Prefatory Address Vindicating the King's Supremacy and Authority of Parliament, in Matters of Religion, and Thereby Demolishing All the Pleas of Dissenters for Separation, According to the Concessions of the Dissenting Gentleman's Answer to the Rev. Mr. White's Letters. Pages 3, and 53. Being Also a Justification of the Church of England Against the Misrepresentation of that Answer* (Boston, 1748): 5–6.
12. Noah Hobart, *A Serious Address to the Members of the Episcopal Separation in New-England. Occasioned by Mr. Wetmore's Vindication of the Professors of the Church of England in Connecticut* (Boston, 1743): 41.
13. Ibid., 48–57.
14. Ibid., 64.
15. Ibid., 65.
16. Ibid., 78, 57–61, 137.
17. F.P.P., IV: 161–2, Address of the Clergy of Massachusetts, Connecticut, and Rhode Island to King George I, Newport, Rhode Island, 21 July 1725; Stephen Taylor, 'Whigs, Bishops and America: The Politics of Church Reform in Mid-Eighteenth-Century England', *The Historical Journal* 36:2 (1993): 337–8.
18. Edward Carpenter, *Thomas Sherlock, 1678–1761, Bishop of Bangor, 1728; of Salisbury, 1734; of London, 1748* (London, 1936): Chaps 1–4.
19. J. C. D. Clark, *English Society, 1660–1832: Religion, Ideology, and Political Politics during the Ancien Regime* (Cambridge, 2000): 348–85.

20. *O.D.N.B.*
21. Carpenter, *Thomas Sherlock*, 24–96, 263–64.
22. Ibid., 38.
23. Ibid., 193. Cross, *The Anglican Episcopate*, 113–14. Bridenbaugh, *Mitre and Sceptre*, 90–2. For an interpretation of the issue in the context of the dynamics of English politics of the period and differing from Bridenbaugh's account see Taylor, 'Whigs, Bishops and America: The Politics of Church Reform in Mid-Eighteenth-Century England': 333–51. For an examination of the administrative policies and procedures of the various bishops of London for the colonial church, see the Prologue and Chapter 6 of my book *The Imperial Origins of the English Church in Early America, 1607–1783* (London, 2004).
24. George Harris, *The Life of Lord Chancellor Hardwicke* (London, 1847) II: 370, III: 520.
25. Carpenter, *Thomas Sherlock*, 194–5.
26. Ibid., 163–90, 194–6.
27. Ibid., 199. Bridenbaugh, *Mitre and Sceptre*, 92–3.
28. John Spurr, *The Restoration Church of England, 1646–1689* (New Haven, 1991): 26.
29. Carpenter, *Thomas Sherlock*, 202.
30. Ibid., 204–5. For the full text see Thomas Bradbury Chandler, *A Free Examination of the Critical Commentary on Archbishop Secker's Letter to Mr. Walpole. Which is Added an Appendix, a Copy of Bishop Sherlock's Memorial* (New York, 1774): 103–22.
31. Carpenter, *Thomas Sherlock*, 204–8.
32. Taylor, 'Whigs, Bishops and America', 352.
33. Carpenter, *Thomas Sherlock*, 204–8.
34. Cross, *The Anglican Episcopate*, 331–2.
35. Carpenter, *Thomas Sherlock*, 208–10. Stanley Nider Katz, *Newcastle's New York: Anglo-American Politics, 1732–1753* (Cambridge, 1968): 207–8.
36. Carpenter, *Thomas Sherlock*, 210–20.
37. Ibid., 220.
38. Cross, *The Anglican Episcopate*, 128.
39. Burr, *Story of the Diocese of Connecticut*, 11–62.

6   Jonathan Mayhew Fears a Bishop and Challenges the Purpose of the S.P.G.

1. Edward Carpenter, *Thomas Sherlock, 1678–1761* (London, 1936): 325.
2. The sermon is conveniently printed in Frank J. Klingberg, *Anglican Humanitarianism in Colonial New York* (Philadelphia, 1940): 213–33.
3. Leslie W. Barnard, *Thomas Secker: An Eighteenth-Century Primate* (Sussex, 1998): 23–39.
4. Jonathan Mayhew, *Seven Sermons upon the Following Subjects: The Difference Betwixt Truth and Falsehood, Right and Wrong. The Natural Abilities of Men for Discerning these Differences. The Right and Duty of Private Judgement. Objections Considered. The Love of God. The Love of Our Neighbour. The First and Great*

Commandment, &c. (Boston, 1749). Charles W. Akers, *Called unto Liberty. A Life of Jonathan Mayhew, 1720–1766* (Cambridge, 1964): 76–7.

5. Jonathan Mayhew, *A Discourse on Rev. XV. 3d. 4th. Occasioned By the Earthquakes in November 1755* (Boston, 1755): 46.

6. Akers, *Jonathan Mayhew*, 173. Clifford K. Shipton, *Sibley's Harvard Graduates* (Boston, 1960) XI: 455.

7. Akers, *Jonathan Mayhew. 1720–1766*, 139–40. Caroline Robbins, 'The Strenuous Whig, Thomas Hollis of Lincoln's Inn', *W.M.Q.* Third Series VII (1950): 406–53. Caroline Robbins, *The Eighteenth-Century Commonwealthman* (Cambridge, 1959): 260–8. William H. Bond, *Thomas Hollis of Lincoln's Inn: A Whig and His Books* (Cambridge, 1990).

8. Bernard Knollenberg, 'Thomas Hollis and Jonathan Mayhew: Their Correspondence, 1759–1766', *Mass.Hist.Soc.P.* (Boston, 1956) 69: 109–10.

9. Ibid., 116. See the following for an account of the wide-ranging contents of Hollis's library collection: Seamus Deane, ed. 'A Catalogue of the Very Valuable and Highly Interesting United Libraries of Thomas Hollis, Esq. and Thomas Brand Hollis, Esq., Including likewise the Theological and Political Library of the Late John Disney', *Sale Catalogues of Libraries of Eminent Persons* (London, 1973).

10. Akers, *Jonathan Mayhew*, 140–6.

11. East Apthorp, *The Constitution of a Christian Church Illustrated in a Sermon at the Opening of Christ Church in Cambridge on Thursday 15 October 1761* (Boston, 1761).

12. Ibid., 24.

13. Ibid., 24–5.

14. See Charles H. Lippy, *Seasonable Revolutionary: The Mind of Charles Chauncy* (Chicago, 1981); John Corrigan, *The Hidden Balance: Religion and the Social Theories of Charles Chauncy and Jonathan Mayhew* (Cambridge, 1987).

15. Edward Wigglesworth, *Sober Remarks on a Book Lately Reprinted at Boston, Entituled, A Modest Proof of the Order & Government Settled by Christ and His Apostles in the Church. In a Letter to a Friend* (Boston, 1724).

16. Shipton, *Sibley's Harvard Graduates* (Boston, 1942) VI: 447–8. Charles Chauncy, *A Complete View of Episcopacy, as Exhibited from the Fathers of the Christian Church, Until the Close of the Second Century* (Boston, 1771): 46.

17. Charles Chauncy, *The Validity of Presbyterian Ordination; Asserted and Maintained. A Discourse Delivered at the Anniversary Dudleian Lecture at Harvard College in Cambridge, New England, May 12, 1762* (Boston, 1762).

18. Ibid., 28–9.

19. Ibid., 30–73.

20. Ibid., 68, 73.

21. James Manning, *A Sketch of the Life and Writings of the Rev. Micaiah Towgood* (London, 1792).

22. Ibid., 20, 50–1.

23. Ibid., 32.

24. Micaiah Towgood, *The Dissenting Gentleman's Answer, to the Reverend Mr. White's Three Letters; in Which Separation from the Establishment is Fully Justified; the Charge of Schism is Refuted and Retorted; and the Church of England*

and the Church of Jesus Christ, are Impartially Compared, and Found to be Constitutions of a Quite Different Nature (New York, Boston, 1748): 7.

25. Shipton, *Sibley's Harvard Graduates* XI: 452. Akers, *Jonathan Mayhew*: 76–7. Bernard Bailyn, *Faces of Revolution: Personalities and Themes in the Struggle for American Independence* (New York, 1990): 125–36.
26. Knollenberg, 'Thomas Hollis and Jonathan Mayhew: Their Correspondence, 127–31.
27. Ibid., 131.
28. Akers, *Jonathan Mayhew*, 159.
29. East Apthorp, *Considerations of the Institution and Conduct of the Society for the Propagation of the Gospel in Foreign Parts* (Boston, 1763).
30. Ibid., 10–11. Jonathan Mayhew, *Observations on the Charter and Conduct of the Society for the Propagation of the Gospel in Foreign Parts; Designed to Shew Their Non-Conformity to Each Other. With Remarks on the Mistakes of East Apthorp, M. A., Missionary at Cambridge, in Quoting and Representing the Sense of the Said Charter, &c. As also Various Incidental Reflections Relative to the Church of England, and the State of Religion in North-America, Particularly in New England* (Boston, 1763).
31. Apthorp, *Considerations of the Institution*, 11–12.
32. Ibid., 15–17.
33. Jonathan Mayhew, *Observations on the Charter*.
34. Ibid., 100.
35. Ibid., 71.
36. Ibid., 30.
37. Ibid., 57.
38. Ibid., 103.
39. Ibid., 105.
40. Knollenberg, 'Hollis and Mayhew Correspondence', 137, 142–4.
41. Ibid., 145. Caroline Robbins, 'The Strenuous Whig', 434–5.
42. Knollenberg, 'Hollis and Mayhew Correspondence', 142.
43. Ibid., 145–6. Peter Annet (1693–1769) was an English deistic writer and author of *Tracts of a Certain Free Enquirer* (1761).
44. Knollenberg, 'Hollis and Mayhew Correspondence', 149, 153.
45. Ibid., 150.
46. Ibid., 154.
47. Ibid., 156.
48. Ibid., 159.
49. Ibid., 165.
50. Ibid., 169.
51. [Arthur Browne], *Remarks on Dr. Mayhew's Incidental Reflections Relative to the Church of England, as Contained in his Observations on the Charter, and Conduct of the Society &c. By a Son of the Church of England* (Portsmouth, 1763): 25–8, 4. Akers, *Jonathan Mayhew*, 185–6.
52. [Browne], *Remarks on Dr. Mayhew's Incidental Reflections*, 5.
53. Ibid., 24.
54. [Henry Caner], *A Candid Examination of Dr. Mayhew's Observations on the Charter and Conduct of the Society for the Propagation of the Gospel in Foreign Parts. To Which is Added, A Letter to a Friend; Containing a Short Vindication of the said Society Against the Mistakes and Misrepresentations of the said Doctor in His Observations on the Conduct of the Society. By One of its Members* (Boston, 1763).

55. *Mass.Hist.Soc.Coll.* 74 (1918): xxv.
56. SPG MSS. Series B., vol. 21, Rev. Thomas Barton to Secretary Daniel Burton, 16 November 1764, Lancaster, Pennsylvania.
57. Edmund S. Morgan, *The Gentle Puritan: A Life of Ezra Stiles, 1727–1795* (New Haven, 1962): 109–10.
58. Abiel Holmes, *The Life of Ezra Stiles* (Boston, 1798): 35–6.
59. Ibid., 40–1.
60. Ezra Stiles, *A Discourse on the Christian Union; the Substance of Which was Delivered before the Reverend Convention of the Congregational Clergy in the Colony of Rhode Island, Assembled at Bristol, April 23, 1760* (Boston, 1761).
61. Morgan, *The Gentle Puritan*, 204–9.
62. Stiles, *Christian Union*, 1–50.
63. Ibid., 30.
64. Ibid., 32–3.
65. Ibid., 33–7.
66. Franklin B. Dexter, ed. *The Literary Diary of Ezra Stiles* (New York, 1901) I: 125.
67. Stiles, *Christian Union*, 36.
68. Morgan, *The Gentle Puritan*, 210–17.
69. Ibid., 220–1.
70. Ibid., 221.
71. Ibid.
72. Ibid., 216–19.
73. Ibid., 219–21.
74. Ibid., 221–5.
75. Ibid., 240–1.
76. Ibid., 245–6.
77. Ibid., 246.
78. Ibid., 248–9.

7 Pleas for an American Bishop in the 1760s: Archbishop of Canterbury Thomas Secker and Thomas Bradbury Chandler

1. Thomas Secker, *A Sermon Preached before the Incorporated Society for the Propagation of the Gospel in Foreign Parts, at their Anniversary Meeting in the Parish Church of St. Mary-le-Bow, On Friday, February 20,1740–1* (London, 1741).
2. Paul Langford, *A Polite and Commercial People: England, 1727–1783* (Oxford, 1992): 340–7.
3. Bruce E. Steiner, *Samuel Seabury: A Study in the High Church Tradition* (Athens, Ohio, 1971): 110–26.
4. James B. Bell, *The Imperial Origins of the King's Church in Early America, 1607–1783* (London, 2004): 111–12, 119–20.
5. F.P.P., VI, 156–7, Clergy of New York and New Jersey to Bishop Richard Terrick, Perth Amboy, 2 Oct. 1765.
6. Ibid.
7. Thomas Secker, *An Answer to Dr. Mayhew's Observations on the Charter and Conduct of the Society for the Propagation of the Gospel in Foreign Parts* (London, 1764; Boston, 1764): 59–60.

8. F.P.P., II, 296–7, Clergy of Connecticut to Bishop Richard Terrick, New Haven, 14 Sept. 1764; ibid., 300–1, Hebron, 6 June 1765; ibid., 308–9, Stratford, 8 Oct. 1766; ibid., 317, 19 May 1771.

9. F.P.P., VI, 68–9. Clergy of Massachusetts and Rhode Island to Bishop Richard Terrick, Boston, 22 September 1768.

10. Ibid.

11. F.P.P., I: 317, Clergy of Conn. To Bishop Richard Terrick, 24 May 1771.

12. Ibid.

13. Secker, *An Answer to Dr. Mayhew's Observations.* John S. Macauley and R. W. Greaves, eds, *The Autobiography of Thomas Secker, Archbishop of Canterbury* (Lawrence, 1988): 48. Beilby Porteus, *A Review of the Life and Character of the Right Rev. Dr. Thomas Secker, Late Lord Archbishop of Canterbury.* Fifth edition (London, 1797): 58–62.

14. *O.D.N.B.*

15. Secker, *An Answer to Dr. Mayhew's Observations*: 3.

16. Ibid., 3–8.

17. Ibid., 10–11; 36–49.

18. Ibid., 9.

19. Ibid., 12–13.

20. Ibid., 13.

21. Ibid., 59–67.

22. Ibid., 59.

23. Ibid.

24. Ibid., 59–60.

25. Ibid., 60.

26. Henry Caner, *A Candid Examination of Dr. Mayhew's Observations on the Charter and Conduct of the Society for the Propagation of the Gospel in Foreign Parts. Interspers'd with a Few Brief Reflections Upon Some Other of the Doctor's Writings. To which is Added A Letter to a Friend, Containing a Short Vindication of the Said Society, Against Mistakes and Misrepresentations of the Doctor in His Observations on the Conduct of that Society. By One of its Members* (Boston, 1763). Jonathan Mayhew, *A Defence of the Observations on the Charter and Conduct of the Society for the Propagation of the Gospel in Foreign Parts Against an Anonymous Pamphlet Falsely Intitled A Candid Examination of Dr. Mayhew's Observations, &c., and also Against the Letter to a Friend Annexed Thereto, said to Contain a Short Vindication of Said Society. By One of its Members (Boston, 1763);* and *Remarks on An Anonymous Tract, Entitled An Answer to Dr. Mayhew's Observations on the Charter and Conduct of the Society for the Propagation of the Gospel in Foreign Parts. Being a Second Defence of the said Observations* (Boston, 1764, London, 1765). Akers, *Jonathan Mayhew,* 186–95.

27. Mayhew, *Remarks on An Anonymous Tract,* 56–7.

28. Ibid., 57–8.

29. Ibid., 60.

30. Ibid., 62.

31. Ibid., 62–7.

32. Samuel Hopkins, *An Enquiry Concerning the Promises of the Gospel* (Boston, 1765): vi.

33. Akers, *Jonathan Mayhew,* 187–8, *Boston Gazette,* 17 October 1763.

34. Jonathan Mayhew, *Popish Idolatry. A Discourse Delivered in the Chapel of Harvard College in Cambridge, New England, May 8, 1765. At the Lecture Founded by the Honourable Paul Dudley, Esquire* (Boston, 1765).

35. Ibid., 48–9. Pauline Maier, 'The Pope at Harvard: The Dudleian Lectures, Anti-Catholicism, and the Politics of Protestantism', *Mass.Hist.Soc.P.* XCVII (1985) 21–4. Francis D. Cogliano, *No King, No Popery: Anti-Catholicism in Revolutionary New England* (Westport, 1995): 9, 41–55.

36. *An Appeal to the Public in Behalf of the Church of England in America. Wherein the Original Nature of the Episcopal Office are Briefly Considered, Reasons for Sending Bishops to America are Assigned, the Plan on Which it is Proposed to Send Them is Stated, and the Objections Against Sending Them are Obviated and Confuted. With an Appendix, Wherein is Given Some Account of An Anonymous Pamphlet.* (New York, 1767): ix.

37. Chandler, *An Appeal to the Public*: title page. On the matter of Chandler's possible interest in a mitre, he joins a number of men of whom it was rumoured by either friends or foes during the seventeenth and eighteenth century that they were seeking appointment as a colonial bishop. Included in the band were Alexander Murray of Virginia in the 1670s, Jonathan Swift of Ireland in the early 1700s, Samuel Johnson of Stratford, Connecticut, in the 1730s and 1740s, and William Smith of Pennsylvania, Josiah Tucker of England, and Chandler in the 1760s and early 1770s.

38. For a summary discussion of the convention proceedings see Frederick V. Mills, Sr., 'The Internal Anglicans Controversy Over an American Episcopate, 1763–1775', *H.M.P.E.C.*, 44 (1975): 259–60.

39. Chandler, *An Appeal to the Public*, 26.

40. Ibid., 26–7.

41. Ibid., 28–9.

42. Ibid., 32–3.

43. Ibid., 34–8, 35.

44. Ibid., 47–8.

45. Ibid., 54.

46. Ibid., 76–7.

47. Ibid., 95.

48. Ibid., 79, 95.

49. Ibid., 79.

50. Ibid.

51. Ibid., 82.

52. Ibid., 89.

53. Ibid.

54. Ibid., 90.

55. Ibid., 116–17.

56. Ibid., 113.

57. Ibid., 113–14.

58. Ibid., 115.

59. Chandler's suggestion that a tax might be levied to meet the expense of maintaining one or more bishops in America prompted a critical letter of reply from 'Atlanticus', in the *London Chronicle*, 25–28 June 1768. The correspondent remarked that 'the legislature of Great Britain will hardly for their gratification impose so ungrateful a tax and burden upon a most Christian

people ... who hold the form of Prelatic government to be unscriptural and unlawful'.

60. Chandler, *An Appeal to the Public,* 97–108.
61. Ibid., 97–9.
62. Ibid.
63. Ibid., 105.
64. Ibid., 107.
65. Ibid.
66. Ibid., 108. Bequests had been received for the support of an American bishop from Archbishop of Canterbury Thomas Tenison, £1,000; Sir John Trelawny, £1,000; Lady Elizabeth Hastings, £500; Bishop of Durham Joseph Butler, £500; Bishop of Gloucester Martin Benson, £200; Bishop of London Richard Osbaldeston, £500; and Mr. Paul Fisher of Clifton, near Bristol, £1,000.
67. Secker, *An Answer to Dr. Mayhew's Observations,* 63–4.

8 A Radical Response to a Bishop: John Adams, Samuel Adams, and John Wilkes

1. This pivotal and illuminating aspect of the controversy has not previously received attention in the works of such scholars of the subject as Alfred Lyon Cross, *The Anglican Episcopate and the American Colonies* (New York, 1902); Carl Bridenbaugh, *Mitre and Sceptre: Transatlantic Faiths, Ideas, Personalities, and Politics, 1689–1775* (New York, 1962); Jack M. Sosin, 'The Proposal in the Pre-Revolutionary Decade for Establishing Anglican Bishops in the Colonies', *J.Eccl.H.* 23 (1962): 76–84; William Allen Benton, *Whig-Loyalism: An Aspect of Political Ideology in the American Revolutionary Era* (Madison, NJ, 1969); Frederick V. Mills, Sr., *Bishops by Ballot: An Eighteenth-Century Ecclesiastical Revolution* (New York, 1978); or Nancy L. Rhoden, *Revolutionary Anglicanism: The Colonial Church of England Clergy during the American Revolution* (London, 1999). Peter M. Doll, *Revolution, Religion, and National Identity: Imperial Anglicanism in British North America, 1745–1795* (Madison, 2000). Pauline Maier, *From Resistance to Revolution: Colonial Radicals and the Development of American Opposition to Britain, 1765–1776* (New York, 1972): 163–4.
2. H. Trevor Colbourn, *The Lamp of Experience: Whig History and the Intellectual Origins of the American Revolution* (Chapel Hill, 1965): 73–7.
3. William M. Fowler, Jr., *Samuel Adams: Radical Puritan* (New York, 1997): 78–80.
4. Ibid., 57–71.
5. Philip Davidson, *Propaganda and the American Revolution, 1763–1783* (Chapel Hill, 1941): 242.
6. Ibid., 227.
7. Thomas Secker, *An Answer to Dr. Mayhew's Observations on the Charter and Conduct of the Society for the Propagation of the Gospel in Foreign Parts.* (London, 1764; Boston, 1764). Jonathan Mayhew, *Observations on the Charter and Conduct of the Society for the Propagation of the Gospel in Foreign Parts; Designed to Shew Their Non-Conformity to Each Other. With Remarks on the Mistakes of East Apthorp, M. A., Missionary at Cambridge, in Quoting and Representing the Sense of the Said Charter, &c. As also Various Incidental Reflections Relative to the*

Church of England, and the State of Religion in North-America, Particularly in New England (Boston, 1763).

8. *The Adams Papers, Diary and Autobiography of John Adams*, L. H. Butterfield, ed. (Cambridge, 1961) I: 6.

9. Ibid.

10. *Adams Family Correspondence*, L. H. Butterfield, ed. (Cambridge, MA, 1963) I: 19–20. John Adams to Dr. Cotton Tufts, 9 April 1764.

11. John Adams, 'Dissertation on the Canon and Feudal Law', *Boston Gazette*, 12, 19 Aug., 21 Oct. 1765; *Papers of John Adams*, Robert J. Taylor, ed. (Cambridge, 1977) I: 103–28. The essay was reprinted in England three times before the War for Independence. See too the discussion on Canon Law in J. C. D. Clark, *The Language of Liberty, 1660–1832: Political Discourse and Social Dynamics in the Anglo-American World* (Cambridge, 1994): 167–80.

12. Page Smith, *John Adams* (New York, 1962) I: 78–9.

13. *Boston Gazette*, 12 Aug. 1765.

14. Ibid.

15. Ibid.

16. *Boston Gazette*, 4, 11, 18 April, 1768.

17. Thomas Bradbury Chandler, *An Appeal to the Public in Behalf of the Church of England in America. Wherein the Original Nature of the Episcopal Office are Briefly Considered, Reasons for Sending Bishops to America are Assigned, the Plan on Which it is Proposed to Send Them is Stated, and the Objections Against Sending Them are Obviated and Confuted. With an Appendix, Wherein is Given Some Account of an Anonymous Pamphlet* (New York, 1767).

18. Fowler, *Samuel Adams*, 80.

19. *Boston Gazette*, 11 April 1768.

20. Increase Mather, *A Brief Discourse Concerning the Unlawfullness of the Common Prayer Worship. And of Laying the Hand On and Kissing the Booke in Swearing [Cambridge, 1686]: 2; A Testimony Against Several Prophane and Superstitious Customs Now Practiced by Some in New-England, The Evil Whereof is Evinced from the Holy Scriptures, and from the Writings both of Ancient and Modern Divines* (London, 1687, Boston, 1688, probably a shadow of the London edition).

21. Bodleian Library, University of Oxford, Tanner MSS 27: 29, Edward Randolph to Archbishop of Canterbury, William Sancroft, Boston, 28 May 1689.

22. David S. Lovejoy, *The Glorious Revolution in America* (Middletown, 1972): 325.

23. *Boston Gazette*, 4 April 1768. Adams probably had in mind the increased number of Anglican ministers and congregations in the colony since 1686 and the recent conversion of two of Increase Mather's grandsons from the ministry of the Congregational Church to the English Church, William Walter and Mather Byles, Jr.

24. *Boston Gazette*, 11 April 1768.

25. The essay is conveniently found in *The Papers of John Adams*, Robert J. Taylor, ed. (Cambridge, Mass., 1977) I: 211–14.

26. John Adams, 'Dissertation on the Canon and Feudal Law', *Boston Gazette* 12, 19 Aug., 30 Sept., 21 Oct. 1765. It was reprinted in the *London Chronicle* in corresponding installments, 23, 28 Nov., 3, 26 Dec. 1765, under a title furnished by Thomas Hollis, 'A Dissertation on the Feudal and the Canon Law'. *The Adams Papers, Diary and Autobiography of John Adams*, L. H. Butterfield, ed. (Cambridge, 1961) I: 258. Hollis in 1768 reprinted the essays as part

of a collection he called *The True Sentiments of America ... Together with a Dissertation on the Canon and the Feudal Law*, Ibid., II: 361–2.

27. *The Papers of John Adams*, I: 213–14.

28. *Boston, Gazette*, 27 March 1769.

29. Charles Chauncy, *A Letter to a Friend, Containing Remarks on Certain Passages in a Sermon Preached by the Right Reverend Father in God, John Lord Bishop of Landaff, Before the Incorporated Society for the Propagation of the Gospel in Foreign Parts, at Their Anniversary Meeting in the Parish Church of St. Mary-le-Bow, February 20, 1767. In Which the Highest Reproach is Undeservedly Cast upon the American Colonies* (Boston, 1767).

30. Worthington C. Ford, ed., 'John Wilkes and Boston', *Mass.Hist.Soc.P.* 47 (1914): 191–216. Maier, *From Resistance to Revolution*, 162–4.

31. Ibid., 163–4.

32. Ibid., 310–11. *A New Form of Prayer, and Thanksgiving for the Happy Deliverance of John Wilkes, Esq.* (London, 1768); a fourth edition was published in Boston, 1769, as *Britannia's Intercession for the Deliverance of John Wilkes, Esq.*

33. J. C. D. Clark, *English Society, 1660–1832: Religion, Ideology and Politics During the Ancien Regime* (Cambridge, 2000): 365–8; Caroline Robbins, *The Eighteenth-Century English Commonwealthman* (New York, 1968): 324–8.

34. Peter Shaw, *American Patriots and the Rituals of Revolution* (Cambridge, 1981): 48–73. John Sainsbury, *Disaffected Patriots; London Supporters of Revolutionary America, 1769–1782* (Montreal, 1987): 15–17.

35. *Papers of John Adams*, I: 214–16, Committee of the Boston Sons of Liberty to John Wilkes, Boston 6th June 1768; the additional signatories were Benjamin Kent, Thomas Young, Benjamin Church, Jr., and Joseph Warren; Audrey Williamson, *Wilkes: 'A Friend of Liberty'* (London, 1974): 190–1. Maier, *From Resistance to Revolution*, 165–6.

36. British Museum Additional MS 30870, fo. 46; *Mass.Hist.Soc.P.*, 47: 192–3, John Wilkes to Boston Committee Sons of Liberty, King's Bench Prison, 19 July 1768; Williamson, *Wilkes*, 191. Sainsbury, *Disaffected Patriots*: 32–4.

37. *Mass.Hist.Soc.P.*, 47: 192.

38. *Complete Prose Works of John Milton* (New Haven, 1962) III: 347, *Eikonoklastes*.

39. *Papers of John Adams*, I: 220–3, Committee of the Boston Sons of Liberty to John Wilkes, Boston, 5 Oct. 1768.

40. Williamson, *Wilkes*, 192; Peter D. G. Thomas, *John Wilkes: A Friend to Liberty* (Oxford, 1996): 161; John Almon, *The Correspondence of the Late John Wilkes with His Friends, from the Original Manuscripts, in which are Introduced Memoirs of His Life* (London, 1805) V: 252–69; Arthur M. Schlesinger, *Prelude to Independence: The Newspaper War on Britain, 1764–1776* (New York, 1957): 35–7. British Library, Additional Manuscripts, 30870, fols. 45, 46, 75–6, 222–3.

41. Schlesinger, *Prelude to Independence*, 35.

42. John Wilkes to William Palfrey, King's Bench Prison, 14 April 1769, *Col. Soc.Mass.P.*, 37: 413.

43. Ibid., 412.

44. Ibid.

45. Ibid., John Wilkes to William Palfrey, King's Bench Prison, 14 April, 413; 24 July 1769: 414; *Mass.Hist.Soc.P.*, 47: 196–8, 200–2, 208, 210; *Col.Soc.Mass.P.*, John Wilkes to William Palfrey, Princes Court, near Storey's Gate, Westminster, 24 July 1770: 418. On the occasion of William Palfrey's visit to

London, Samuel Adams wrote a letter of introduction on his behalf to John Wilkes, Harry Alonzo Cushing, ed., *The Writings of Samuel Adams* (New York, 1906) II: 100–1. John Wilkes's brother-in-law, George Hayley, was the commercial agent in London for John Hancock and William Palfrey, Sainsbury, *Disaffected Patriot*, 26. William Palfrey was born in Boston in 1741 and died at sea in December 1780. He was active in the movements that preceded the Revolutionary War and visited England in 1771 and again in late 1774 and early 1775. Maier, *From Resistance to Revolution*, 243. Palfrey may have carried with him to England portions or all of John Adams's 'Novanglus, or, A History of the Dispute with America, from its Origin in 1754, to the Present Time; Written in 1774', letters published in the *Boston Gazette* as the first edition was published in London by John Almon in 1775, *Papers of John Adams*, II: 24–32, 45–54. Palfrey served as an aide to General George Washington from March till April, 1776, when he was appointed paymaster-general with the rank of lieutenant colonel. In November 1780, he was appointed consul general in France by a unanimous vote of Congress, and embarked in a ship for that country, which was never heard of after she left the capes.

46. *The London Chronicle*, 4–7 February 1769.
47. Ibid., 14–16 February 1769.
48. Ibid., 6–9 May 1769, *An Alarm to Dissenters and Methodists* (London, 1769).
49. *The London Chronicle*, 29 June 1769. Thomas Bradbury Chandler, *A Free Examination of the Critical Commentary on Archbishop Secker's Letter to Mr. Walpole. To which is Added an Appendix, a Copy of Bishop Sherlock's Memorial* (New York, 1774): 103–22.
50. Walpole's letter is conveniently found in Cross, *Anglican Episcopate*, 324–30.
51. *The London Chronicle*, 15–17 August; 2–5; 14–16; 21–23 September 1769.
52. Ibid., 24 October 1769.
53. Cross, *Anglican Episcopate*, 186–9. Bridenbaugh, *Mitre and Sceptre*: 270. Mills, *Bishops by Ballot*, 27–8.
54. See earlier, Chap. Two.
55. For a discussion of the commissary's office and its application in the colonies see James B. Bell, *The Imperial Origins of the King's Church in Early America, 1607–1783* (London, 2004): 58–73.
56. Beilby Porteus, *The Works of Thomas Secker* (London, 1811), *A Letter to the Right Honourable Horatio Walpole, esq.; Written Jan. 9, 1750/1, by the Right Reverend Thomas Secker ... Concerning Bishops in America* (London, 1769) VI: 492–7.
57. Ibid., 497–9.
58. Ibid., 501–3.
59. Ibid., 503–9.
60. Frederick Seaton Siebert, *Freedom of the Press in England, 1476–1776* (Urbana. Ill., 1952): 5, 8, 356–9, 362, 372. George Rudé, *Wilkes and Liberty: A Social Study of 1763 to 1774* (Oxford, 1962): 155–7.
61. Seibert, *Freedom of the Press*, 386–9; Almon became sympathetic to the American cause, *Adams Papers*, II: 224; Clark, *Language of Liberty*, 327.
62. 'An Attempt to Land a Bishop in America', *The Political Register*, September 1769 (London, 1769). v: facing 119.
63. Robbins, *The Eighteenth Century Commonwealthman*, 260–70, 324.
64. Francis Blackburne, compiler, *Memoirs of T. H.* (London, 1780). 2 vols.

65. Francis Blackburne, *A Critical Commentary on Archbishop Secker's Letter to the Right Honourable Horatio Walpole, Concerning Bishops in America* London, 1770, Philadelphia, 1771). Walpole (1678–1757), usually called Horace, was a younger brother of Sir Robert Walpole.
66. Clark, *English Society, 1660–1832*: 371–4; Robbins, *The Eighteenth Century Commonwealthman*, 324–8.
67. Blackburne, *A Critical Commentary on Archbishop Secker's Letter*, 5.
68. Ibid., 5–7.
69. Ibid., 38–9.
70. Ibid., 48.
71. Ibid., 48–9.
72. Fowler, *Samuel Adams*, 100–12. Hiller B. Zobel, *The Boston Massacre* (New York, 1970).
73. Fowler, *Samuel Adams*, 113–24.
74. Ibid., 125–7.
75. *A List of Infringements and Violations of Rights Complained of by the American Colonists from the Votes and Proceedings of the Freeholders and Other Inhabitants of the Town of Boston in New England, Just Published by Order of the Town* (Boston, 1772). Cushing, *Writings of Samuel Adams*, II: 350–69. *London Chronicle*, 1–3 July 1773. Fowler, *Samuel Adams*, 119–20.
76. Cushing, *Writings of Samuel Adams*, II: 367–8.
77. *Ibid.*, 368.
78. For a discussion of the development, implementation, and controversy surrounding the Quebec Act see Peter M. Doll, *Revolution, Religon, and National Identity: Imperial Anglicanism in British North America* (Madison, 2000): 92–154.
79. Fowler, *Samuel Adams*, 130.
80. *The Political Register*, July 1774, vol. 43: 312. See also the British Museum, *Catalogue of Satires* (London, 1935). Vol. 5: 166, that describes in detail the meaning and characters of the print. A copy of the image was also published in *The Hibernian Magazine*, Dublin, Ireland, November 1774, Vol. 4: 680.
81. A Boston publication, *The Royal American* had a circulation of about 1,000 copies, Clarence S. Brigham, *Paul Revere's Engravings* (New York, 1969): 106, 124–5.

9 The Controversy over a Bishop in the Colonies outside New England

1. J. C. D. Clark, *The Language of Liberty, 1660–1832: Political Discourse and Social Dynamics in the Anglo-American World* (Cambridge, 1994): 60–1, 205–17, 307.
2. James B. Bell, *The Imperial Origins of the English Church in Early America: 1607–1783* (London, 2004): 26–40.
3. Ibid., 74–104.
4. David C. Humphrey, *From King's College to Columbia, 1746–1800* (New York, 1976): 36–54.
5. Edmund S. Morgan, *The Gentle Puritan: A Life of Ezra Stiles, 1727–1795* (New Haven, 1962): 231–54.
6. Thomas Bradbury Chandler, *An Appeal to the Public in Behalf of the Church of England in America. Wherein the Original Nature of the Episcopal Office are*

Briefly Considered, Reasons for Sending Bishops to America are Assigned, the Plan on Which it is Proposed to Send Them is Stated, and the Objections Against Sending Them are Obviated and Confuted. With an Appendix, wherein is Given Some Account of an Anonymous Pamphlet (New York, 1767).

7. The articles have been reprinted in Elizabeth I. Nobakken, ed., *The Centinel: Warnings of a Revolution* (Newark, Del., 1980): 19–20. John Dickinson (1732–1808), a leading opponent of the Stamp Act and subsequent imperial policies, published in December 1767, 'Letters from a Pennsylvania Farmer' in the *Pennsylvania Chronicle*. The role of George Bryan (1731–91) in the publication of the 'Centinel' articles is more difficult to determine. He was a prominent Philadelphia merchant, politician, jurist, and Presbyterian.
8. Ibid., 53–70.
9. Herbert and Carol Schneider, eds, *Samuel Johnson President of King's College: His Career and Writings* (New York, 1929) I: 437.
10. Ibid., 444.
11. James B. Bell, Colonial American Clergy of the Church of England, 1607–1783 Database at www.jamesbbell.com.
12. Ann D. Gordon, *The College of Philadelphia, 1749–1779: Impact of an Institution* (New York, 1989): 95–8.
13. Elizabeth A. Ingersoll, 'Francis Alison: American Philosophe, 1705–1799', PhD dissertation, University of Delaware, 1974: 279–80.
14. Thomas Firth Jones, *A Pair of Lawn Sleeves: A Biography of William Smith, 1727–1803* (Philadelphia, 1972): 70; Gordon, *College of Philadelphia*: 98–9.
15. Ingersoll, 'Francis Alison: American Philosophe', 509–33.
16. Nobakken, *The Centinal*: 'Anti-Centinel', No. 1, 16 June; No. 2, 29 Sept. 1768, 191–200.
17. F.P.P., VIII: 40–1, William Smith to Bishop Richard Terrick, Philadelphia, 22 October 1768.
18. *O.D.N.B.*
19. The London Chronicle, 6–8 June 1769, 'A Missionary Expectant'.
20. Albert F. Gegenheimer, *William Smith, Educator and Churchman, 1727–1803* (Philadelphia, 1943): 159.
21. Josiah Tucker, *Four Tracts together with Two Sermons on Political and Commercial Subjects* (Gloucester, 1774): 214.
22. Ibid., 214–15.
23. Ibid., 215.
24. Ibid.
25. Ibid.
26. Ibid.
27. *The London Chronicle*, 6–8 June 1769.
28. W. Jay Mills, ed. *Glimpses of Colonial Society and the Life at Princeton College, 1766–1773, by One of the Class of 1763* (Philadelphia, 1903): 96.
29. John Sayre, *A Sermon Preached Before the Convention of the Clergy of the Provinces of New York and New Jersey, on Wednesday the 19th Day of May, 1773. In Trinity Church, in the City of New York* (New York, 1773).
30. Ibid., 9.
31. Ibid., 14–16.
32. Bell, *Imperial Origins of the King's Church*, 198–200.
33. See Appendix II, Table III-A.

34. Bell, *Imperial Origins of the King's Church*, Chap. 2, for a discussion of the establishment of the church in Virginia.

35. Ibid., chapter 10 for an examination of the duties and powers of the vestry in governing and managing parish affairs.

36. See Appendix II, Table III-A.

37. The American colleges attended were Yale, 2; College of New Jersey, 2; College of Philadelphia, 3, College of William and Mary, 30; English Universities, Oxford, 6; Cambridge, 6; Scottish Universities, Aberdeen, 12; Edinburgh, 3; Glasgow, 5; St. Andrews, 1; Ireland, Trinity College, Dublin, 3; Unknown, 46; See Appendix II, Table III-C.

38. Otto Lohrenz, 'The Advantage of Rank and Status: Thomas Price, A Loyalist Parson of Revolutionary Virginia', *The Historian* 60 (1998): 561–77, and his 'The Reverend Abner Waugh: The "Best Dancer of the Minuet in the State of Virginia"', *The Kentucky Review* 15 (2003): 28–40.

39. Bell, *Imperial Origins of the King's Church*, 72–3.

40. Ibid., 110–14.

41. Ibid., 144–6, 195–6.

42. Johnson suggested in his 10 April 1767 letter to Camm that three American bishops were necessary, one each in Virginia, at Albany, New York, and in the Caribbean Islands. Schneider, *Samuel Johnson*, I: 398–9. The episcopacy controversy is outside of the scope of John K. Nelson's excellent study, *A Blessed Company: Virginia, 1690–1776* (Chapel Hill, 2001).

43. Schneider, *Samuel Johnson*, I: 444.

44. Clark, *Language of Liberty*, 342.

45. *Virginia Gazette* (Purdie and Dixon) 9 May 1771. For an excellent evaluation of the Virginia controversy see George MacLaren Brydon, *Virginia's Mother Church and the Political Conditions under which it Grew* (Philadelphia, 1952). I: 341–64.

46. George W. Pilcher, 'Virginia Newspapers and the Dispute Over the Proposed Colonial Episcopate, 1771–1772', *The Historian*, XXIII (1960): 98–113, and his 'The Pamphlet War on the Proposed Virginia Anglican Episcopate, 1767–1775', *H.M.P.E.C.*, 30 (1961): 266–79.

47. Clark, *Language of Liberty*, 344–5.

48. Ibid., 345–6.

49. Frederick V. Mills, Sr., 'The Internal Anglican Controversy Over an American Episcopate: 1763–1775', *H.M.P.E.C.*, 44 (1975): 268–71.

50. F.P.P., XIV: 213–14, James Horrocks to Bishop Richard Terrick, [London] 8 October 1771.

51. *Virginia Gazette* (Purdie and Dixon), 6 June 1771; Ray Hiner, Jr., 'Samuel Henley and Thomas Gwatkin; Partners in Protest', *H.M.P.E.C*, 37 (1968): 39–50.

52. Thomas Gwatkin, *A Letter to the Clergy of New York and New Jersey, Occasioned by an Address to the Episcopalians of Virginia* (Williamsburg, 1772): 7.

53. Ibid.

54. *New-York Gazette*, June, July, August, 1771.

55. Thomas Bradbury Chandler, *An Address from the Clergy of New-York and New Jersey to the Episcopalians in Virginia, Occasioned by Some Late Transactions in that Colony Relative to an American Episcopate* (New York, 1771): 58.

56. Ibid., 2.

57. Ibid., 10–34.
58. Ibid., 7.
59. Ibid., 55.
60. Gwatkin, *A Letter to the Clergy of New York and New Jersey*, 10–12.
61. Ibid., 7.
62. *Virginia Gazette* (Purdie and Dixon), 18 July 1771.
63. Brydon, *Virginia's Mother Church*, I: 355–7.
64. Thomas Jefferson, *A Summary View of the Rights of British America. Set Forth in Some Resolutions Intended for the Inspection of the Present Delegates of the People of Virginia Now in Convention (Williamsburgh, 1774)*.
65. *The Papers of Thomas Jefferson*, Julian P. Boyd, ed. (Princeton, 1950) I: 121–37.
66. John K. Nelson, *A Blessed Company: Parishes, Parsons, and Parishioners in Anglican Virginia, 1690–1776* (Chapel Hill, 2001): 294.
67. Rhys Isaac, *The Transformation of Virginia, 1740–1790* (Chapel Hill, 1982): 181–205, 209–40.
68. Bell, *Imperial Origins of the King's Church*, 111.
69. *Virginia Gazette* (Purdie and Dixon), 28 Mar. 1771.
70. Thomas Bradbury Chandler, *A Free Examination of the Critical Commentary on Archbishop Secker's Letter to Mr. Walpole. Which is Added an Appendix, a Copy of Bishop Sherlock's Memorial* (New York, 1774).
71. Ibid., 30.
72. Ibid., 36.

10 The Impact of the First Continental Congress and the Local Committees of Safety

1. I am indebted for these summary details to Pauline Maier's study, *From Resistance to Revolution: Colonial Radicals and the Development of American Opposition to Britain, 1765–1776* (New York, 1991 edition): 281–7.
2. Ibid., 281.
3. Ibid.
4. Ibid., 281–2.
5. For a discussion of the work of the Committees of Safety see Alexander Clarence Flick, *Loyalism in New York During the American Revolution* (New York, 1901, 1969 edition): 58–272; Robert McCluer Calhoon, *The Loyalists in Revolutionary America, 1760–1781* (New York, 1973): 295–305.
6. University of Oxford, Bodleian Library, Gough Pamphlets, No. 1673 (42), Instructions for the Clergy Employ'd by the Society, no place, no date.
7. Ibid.
8. A scholarly study of the persons summoned before Committees of Safety in each of the colonies, ministers, lawyers, merchants, public officials, and so forth would be useful. During 1775, 20 English ministers went into exile in England, in 1776, 6, and in 1777, 14, or a total of 40 of the 67 men who left the country between 1775 and 1786. This information is culled from James B. Bell, Colonial American Clergy of the Church of England Database, www.jamesbbell.com.
9. Sheldon S. Cohen, *Connecticut Gadfly Loyalist: The Reverend Samuel Peters* (Hartford, 1976): 14–15.

10. Ibid., 15–23.
11. Clifford K. Shipton, *Sibley's Harvard Graduates* (Boston, 1960) XI: 440–72.
12. Ibid., XII: 524.
13. S.P.G. MSS. Series A. John Wiswall to S.P.G., 8 May 1765.
14. John Wiswall, Journal, Acadia University Library: 23. Leventhal and Mooney, 'Bibliography of Loyalist Source Material', Part I. *P.A.A.S.* 85 (1975): 81.
15. Ibid.
16. Shipton, *Sibley's Harvard Graduates* XII: 524.
17. Ibid., 525–6.
18. Calvin R. Batchelder, *History of the Eastern Diocese* (Claremont, 1876) I: 61.
19. Wiswall, Journal: 39.
20. Wiswall, Journal, 15 Jan. 1776. While never really happy in London, Wiswall served as a chaplain in the Royal Navy for most of the war. His life and career in a shambles, the education of his sons uncertain, and his links to family and friends in Massachusetts severed, Wiswall petitioned in 1783 the Loyalist Claims Commission seeking redress for his loss of income and personal property. Wiswall was granted a stipend of £60 a year. Estimating his losses at £1,010 sterling, he was awarded £265 sterling by the commission. Gregory Palmer, *Biographical Sketches of Loyalists of the American Revolution* (Westport, 1984): 943.
21. Clifford K. Shipton, *Sibley's Harvard Graduates* (Boston, 1965) XIII: 531.
22. Ibid.
23. Ibid.
24. Ibid.
25. James Phinney Baxter, ed., *Documentary History of the State of Maine* (Portland, 1910). Second Series. 14:349.
26. Ibid., 349.
27. Ibid., 349–50.
28. Shipton, *Sibley's Harvard Graduates* (Boston, 1965) XIII: 532.
29. Baxter, ed., *Documentary History of the State of Maine*, 14:390.
30. Ibid., 391.
31. Ibid., 393.
32. Ibid.
33. Ibid.
34. Ibid.
35. Ibid., 397. Leventhal and Mooney, 'A Bibliography of Loyalist Source Material in the United States', *P.A.A.S.* Part IV. 90 (1980): 127–8, 130–3.
36. William S. Bartlet, *The Frontier Missionary* (Boston, 1853): 122. Leventhal and Mooney, 'Loyalist Source Material', *P.A.A.S.* Part I. 85 (1975): 407.
37. Baxter, ed., *Documentary History of the State of Maine*. 16:42–3.
38. Ibid., 43.
39. Ibid.
40. Bartlet, *The Frontier Missionary*, 129.
41. Jonathan Boucher, *A View of the Causes and Consequences of the American Revolution; in Thirteen Discourses, Preached in North America between the Years 1763 and 1775* (London, 1797), 1967 reprint): 561–96.
42. Jonathan Bouchier, *Reminiscences of an American Loyalist, 1738–1789* (Boston, 1925): 113.
43. Ibid., 104–8.

44. Boucher, *Causes*, 581.
45. Ibid., 588.
46. Wallace Brown, *The King's Friends: The Composition and Motives of the American Loyalists Claimants* (Providence, 1965): 173.
47. Ibid., 106–8.
48. S.P.G. MSS, Vol. B. 2, No. 68, Charles Inglis to Richard Hind, Secretary, New York, 31 October 1776.
49. Ibid.
50. Ibid.
51. Ibid.
52. Ibid.
53. Ibid.
54. Ibid.
55. Ibid.
56. For each of the men see their entries in James B. Bell, Colonial American Clergy of the Church of England Database, 1607–1783, www.jamesbbell.com. For Weeks, see Shipton, *Sibley's Harvard Graduates* XIV: 356–60; Winslow, Shipton, *Sibley's Harvard Graduates* IX: 102–6; SPG MSS. B., Vol. 21, Rev. Thomas Barton to Dr. Richard Hind, 25 November 1776, Lancaster, PA.
57. S.P.G. MSS, Vol. B. 2, No. 68, Charles Inglis to Richard Hind, Secretary, New York, 31 Oct. 1776.
58. Ibid.
59. Ibid.
60. Ibid.
61. Bell, Colonial American Clergy.
62. SPG MSS. B., Vol. 21, Rev. Thomas Barton to Secretary Richard Hind, 1 March 1775, Lancaster, PA.
63. SPG MSS. B., Vol. 21, Rev. Thomas Barton to Dr. Richard Hind, 25 November 1776, Lancaster, PA.
64. Finding his way to London, Edmiston, claimed his annual income was £350 sterling and became a beneficiary of the Archbishop of Canterbury's fund for distressed clergy. Filing a petition with the Loyalist Claims Commission he declared that he owned 500 to 600 acres in Cecil County and 550 acres in Baltimore County. These properties were later granted by the Legislature to his wife and children who remained in Maryland. Edmiston estimated the value of the land and property awarded to his family at £3,250 sterling and asked the Commissioners to determine his personal loss. Edmiston received a pension of £120 per year and £1,000 sterling for his losses. Rodney K. Miller, 'The Political Ideology of the Anglican Clergy', *H.M.P.E.C.* 45 (1976): 227–36.
65. See Bell, Colonial American Clergy; for Weeks; Shipton, *Sibley's Harvard Graduates* XIV: 356–60.
66. Shipton, *Sibley's Harvard Graduates* XI: 345–52.
67. See Bell, Colonial American Clergy.
68. John Sayre, *From the New-York Journal, Mr. Holt* (Philadelphia, 1776): 3.
69. Ibid., 4.
70. Ibid., 5–6.
71. Before his death in June 1784 Sayre filed a petition with the Loyalist Claims Commission in London seeking reimbursement for the loss of property valued at £1,300 sterling. Sayre was awarded £460 sterling compensation.

Among the losses noted by Sayre was his remarkable library containing 600 volumes. Palmer, *Biographical Sketches of Loyalists*, 765.

72. S.P.G. MSS. Series B., Vol. 27, William Clark to S.P.G., Dedham, 15 April 1775.
73. William Stevens Perry, *Historical Collections Relating to the American Colonial Church* (Privately printed, 1873) III: 591–2. Leventhal and Mooney, 'Loyalist Source Material', *P.A.A.S.* Part I. 85 (1975): 102, 124, 294. Part V. 90 (1980): 138.
74. S.P.G. MSS. Series B., Vol. 22, William Clark to S.P.G., Dedham, 5 Jan. 1778.
75. *Acts and Resolves of the Province of Massachusetts Bay* (Boston, 1918): 20: 99.
76. By 1783 Clark was in London and petitioned the Loyalist Claims Commission for compensation. He recounted his experiences at Dedham, estimating his losses of salary and property at £1,200 sterling. The commissioners awarded him an annual stipend of £60 sterling. Palmer, *Biographical Sketches of Loyalists*, 158–9.
77. Bruce E. Steiner, *Connecticut Anglicans in the Revolutionary Era: A Study in Communal Tensions* (Hartford, 1978): 56–7.
78. Bell, Colonial American Clergy.
79. Steiner, *Connecticut Anglicans in the Revolutionary Era*, 57.
80. *Minutes of the Albany Committee of Correspondence, 1775–1778; Minutes of the Schnectady Committee, 1775–1779*, Alexander C. Flick, ed. (Albany, 1925) II: 1020–1.
81. Ibid., 1099.
82. For his services the S.P.G. granted him a pension of £50 per year and the British Treasury awarded him an annual stipend of £40. Petitioning the Loyalist Commission, he claimed personal losses of £250 sterling and received compensation of £75, Palmer, *Biographical Sketches of Loyalists*, 230.
83. S.P.G. Mss, Series B. Vol. 3, No. 21, Luke Babcock to S.P.G., Yonkers, 22 March 1776.
84. Philip Ranlet, *The New York Loyalists* (Knoxville, 1986): 159.
85. Bell, Colonial American Clergy.
86. Ibid.
87. Ibid.

11   Critics of the Continental Congress and *Common Sense*: Jonathan Boucher and Charles Inglis

1. Moses Coit Tyler, *The Literary History of the American Revolution, 1763–1776* (New York, 1897) I: 316–28.
2. Jonathan Boucher, *A Letter from a Virginian, to the Members of the Congress to be Held at Philadelphia, on the First of September, 1774* (Boston, 1774, New York, 1774).
3. Ibid., 3–4.
4. Ibid., 4. J. C. D. Clark, *The Language of Liberty, 1660–1832: Political Discourse and Social Dynamics in the Anglo-American World* (Cambridge, 1994): 92.
5. Boucher, *A Letter from a Virginian*, 13, 20–9.
6. Jonathan Boucher, *A View of the Causes and Consequences of the American Revolution; in Thirteen Discourses, Preached in North America between the Years 1763 and 1775; With an Historical Preface* (London, 1797).

7. Ibid., xxviii.
8. Ibid., lxxxv.
9. Anne Y. Zimmer, *Jonathan Boucher: Loyalist in Exile* (Detroit, 1984): 338.
10. *A Catalogue of the Very Valuable and Extensive Library of the late Rev. Jonathan Boucher, M.A., F.R.S.* (London, 1806). Numbering 305 pages, the catalogue enumerates more than 8,600 titles in Boucher's collection, many of which were multiple volumes. I am grateful to J. C. D. Clark for bringing to my attention this important publication. It remains uncertain how many, if any, of the volumes were a part of his library in America. Several months after Boucher fled the country, his attorney advertised in the *Maryland Gazette*, 5 June 1777, that his library was for sale and possibly all or a portion of the materials he acquired in the course of his residence in Virginia and Maryland was sold at that time. But it is unclear if the sale ever took place because a number of imprints in Boucher's collection were purchased by the Bodleian Library, Oxford, in 1836. The collection had been formed from Boucher's library by the Rev. Charles Godwyn (1700–70), a Fellow of Balliol College, and included about 300 tracts in 41 volumes relating to American affairs and the War of Independence. The collection suggests materials that could only have been acquired in America during the colonial and Revolutionary War period. Depending on the outcome of a Maryland sale of Boucher books and pamphlets, if any, it is possible that Boucher's 1806 library numbered about 15,000 volumes significantly surpassing the libraries accumulated by any other minister of the colonial King's church. For example, the well-read Thomas Bradbury Chandler's distinguished library, which was sold when he died in 1790, numbered slightly more than 600 volumes. Boucher's library must rank as one of the largest, if not the largest, collection of books in colonial America, outstripping the number of titles in the collections of such bibliophiles as Cotton Mather, William Byrd II of Virginia, Thomas Prince of Boston, and James Logan of Philadelphia. Boucher's collection compares favourably with several college libraries: Harvard in 1723 claimed 3,000 volumes, and in 1764, 5,000; Yale in 1742 had a library of 2,600 volumes, while Princeton in 1761 had a collection of 1,261 volumes.
11. Jonathan Bouchier, ed., *Reminiscences of an American Loyalist, 1738–1789. Being the Autobiography of the Revd. Jonathan Boucher, Rector of Annapolis in Maryland and afterwards Vicar of Epsom, Surrey, England* (Boston, 1925): 9. Anne Young Zimmer and Alfred H. Kelly, 'Jonathan Boucher: Constitutional Conservative', *Journal of American History* 58 (1972): 897–922. Michael D. Clark, 'Jonathan Boucher: The Mirror of Reaction', *Huntington Library Quarterly* 33 (1969): 19–32. Robert McCluer Calhoon, *The Loyalists in Revolutionary America, 1760–1781* (New York, 1973): 218–33. Philip Evanson, 'Jonathan Boucher: The Mind of An American Loyalist', *Maryl.Hist.Mag.*, 52 (1963): 123–36. I am indebted to Anne Y. Zimmer's excellent biography, *Jonathan Boucher: Loyalist in Exile* (Detroit, 1984): 17–34.
12. Bouchier, *Reminiscences*, 9–10.
13. Ibid., 20–3. Zimmer, Boucher: 36–7.
14. See in *passim* the rich collection of letters from Jonathan Boucher to the Rev. John James and others, *Maryl.Hist.Mag.* Vols. 7 (1912), 8 (1913), 9 (1914), 10 (1915). See also the correspondence between Boucher and his teacher in Margaret Evans, ed. *Letters of Richard Radcliffe and John James of*

Queen's College, Oxford, 1755–1783 (Oxford, 1888): *Passim.* Zimmer, *Boucher,* 36–7.

15. Bouchier, *Reminiscences,* 23–7. Zimmer, *Boucher,* 37–43.

16. Bouchier, *Reminiscences,* 30; 40. Zimmer, *Boucher,* 43–8.

17. Bouchier, *Reminiscences,* 41. Zimmer, *Boucher,* 48–9.

18. Bouchier, *Reminiscences,* 48; 59. Zimmer, *Boucher,* 78–81.

19. William Eddis, *Letters from America,* Aubrey C. Land, ed. (Cambridge, 1969): 13. Zimmer, *Boucher,* 86–90.

20. Bouchier, *Reminiscences,* 92. Zimmer, *Boucher,* 123–30.

21. Thomas J. Wertenbaker, *The Golden Age of Colonial Culture,* Second edition (New York, 1949): 85–104. Zimmer, *Boucher,* 91–104.

22. Zimmer, *Boucher,* 160–79.

23. *Maryl.Hist.Mag.,* 7 (1912): 295. Jonathan Boucher to [Rev. John] James, St, Mary's, 9 December 1765.

24. Ibid.

25. Ibid.

26. Ibid., 296.

27. *Maryl.Hist.Mag.,* 8 (1913): 44. Jonathan Boucher to the Rev. John James, 25 July 1769.

28. Boucher, *A View of the Causes,* 232.

29. Bouchier, *Reminiscences,* 102.

30. Ibid., xliv.

31. Bouchier, *Reminiscences,* 113.

32. Ibid., 106–8.

33. Ibid., 130–6.

34. Ibid., 131.

35. Ibid.

36. Ibid.

37. Ibid., 132–3.

38. Ibid., 133.

39. Ibid.

40. Ibid., 133–4.

41. See Robert Filmer, *Patriarcha and Other Political Works of Sir Robert Filmer.* Peter Laslett, ed. (Oxford, 1949). Peter Laslett, 'Sir Robert Filmer: The Man versus the Whig Myth', *W.M.Q.* Third Series 5 (1948): 523–46. J. C. D. Clark, English Society, 1660–1832: *Religion, Ideology, and Politics during the Ancien Regime,* Second edition (Cambridge, 2000): 431–3.

42. Boucher, *A View of the Causes,* 495–560.

43. Ibid., 496.

44. Clark, *English Society,* 105–23.

45. Boucher, *A View of the Causes,* 507–8.

46. Ibid., 510. Zimmer, *Boucher,* 195–226.

47. Boucher, *A View of the Causes,* 512.

48. Ibid., 530.

49. Ibid., 534.

50. Ibid., 545.

51. Ibid., 546. Boucher wrote a broadside attempting to demonstrate the illegality of the revolutionary movement in Maryland, entitled 'Queries Addressed to the People of Maryland, which consisted of thirteen rhetorical questions

concerning the behaviour of the committees of safety and the provincial convention'. See Rodney K. Miller, 'The Political Ideology of the Anglican Clergy', *H.M.P.E.C.* 45 (1976): 229.

52. Boucher, *A View of the Causes*, 561–96.
53. Ibid., 553.
54. Ibid., 554.
55. Ibid., 554–5.
56. Evans, ed., *Letters of Richard Radcliffe and John James*, xvii.
57. Zimmer, *Boucher*, 230–1.
58. Zimmer, *Boucher*, 227–46.
59. Gregory Palmer, *Biographical Sketches of Loyalists of the American Revolution* (Westport, 1984): 80. Herbert Leventhal and James E. Mooney, 'A Bibliography of Loyalist Source Material in the United States', *P.A.A.S.* Part I. 85 (1975): 213, 271, 441. Part IV. 90 (1980): 118–19, 140–3, 154. Zimmer, *Boucher*, 342–4.
60. Brian C. Cuthbertson, *The First Bishop: A Biography of Charles Inglis* (Halifax, Nova Scotia, 1987): 2.
61. John Wolfe Lydekker, *The Life and Letters of Charles Inglis. His Ministry in America and Consecration as First Colonial Bishop, from 1759 to 1787* (London, 1936): 1–7. A useful compilation of many documents relating to Inglis's career, the book does not note either his associations with Ambrose Serle and Lord Dartmouth or examine his political opinion. James B. Bell, 'Anglican Clergy in Colonial America Ordained by Bishops of London', *P.A.A.S.* 84 (1975): 134. Cuthbertson, *Inglis*, 5–17.
62. Cuthberston, *Inglis*, 19–32.
63. B. F. Stevens, *Facsimiles of Manuscripts in European Archives relating to America, 1773–1783* (London, 1895): 24. No. 2045.
64. John Ewer, *A Sermon Preached before the Incorporated Society for the Propagation of the Gospel in Foreign Parts, at Their Anniversary Meeting in the Parish Church of St. Mary-le-Bow, On Friday February 20, 1767* (New York, 1768); Charles Inglis, *A Vindication of the Bishop of Landaff's Sermon from the Gross Misrepresentations and Abusive Reflections Contained in Mr. William Livingston's Letter to His Lordship; with Some Additional Observations on Certain Passages in Dr. Chauncey's Remarks, &c.* (New York, 1768).
65. Cuthbertson, *Inglis*, 37.
66. S.P.G. MSS, Vol. B. 2, No. 68, Charles Inglis to Richard Hind, Secretary, New York, 31 October 1776.
67. Ibid.
68. Ibid.
69. *The Papers of Benjamin Franklin*, William B. Willcox, ed. (New Haven, 1978) 21: 325–6.
70. Thomas Paine, *Common Sense; Addressed to the Inhabitants of America*. Third edition (London 1776): 26. Harvey J. Kaye, *Thomas Paine and the Promise of America* (New York, 2005): 51.
71. Cuthbertson, *Inglis*, 41–4.
72. [Charles Inglis], *By an American. The True Interest of America Impartially Stated, in Certain Strictures on a Pamphlet Entitled Common Sense* (Philadelphia, 1776): vi.
73. Cynthia Dubin Edelberg, *Jonathan Odell: Loyalist Poet of the Revolution* (Durham, 1987): 26.

74. S.P.G. MSS, Vol. B. 2, No. 68, Charles Inglis to Richard Hind, Secretary, New York, 31 October 1776.
75. Ibid.
76. Ibid.
77. Ibid.
78. Ibid.
79. Ibid.
80. Ibid.
81. Ibid.
82. Edward H. Tatum, Jr., ed., *The American Journal of Ambrose Serle, Secretary to Lord Howe, 1776–1778* (San Marino, 1940): 115–16.
83. *Ibid.*, 131. Serle's Latin quotation, meaning 'God needs neither such help as that, nor any defending', is an alteration of a line from Virgil's *Aeneid*, Book 2, line 521–2. The poet wrote, '*Non tali auxilio nec defensoribus istis tempus eget; non, si ipse meus nunc adforet Hector*'. I am grateful to Robert East Mooney for this detail.
84. Charles Inglis, *Letters of Papinian: in Which the Conduct, present State and Prospects, of the American Congress, are Examined* (New York, 1779; London, 1779): 22.
85. Ibid., 107.
86. Ibid., 130.
87. Charles Inglis, *The Duty of Honoring the King, Explained and Recommended: in a Sermon Preached in St. George's and St. Paul's Chapels, New York, on Sunday, January 30, 1780, Being the Anniversary of King Charles I* (New York, 1780): 14.
88. Ibid., 20.
89. Ibid., 25.
90. Ibid., 28.
91. B. F. Stevens, *Facsimiles of Manuscripts in European Archives relating to America, 1773–1783* (London, 1895): 24. Number 2067. Lydekker, in his *Life and Letters of Charles Inglis*, makes no reference to the clergyman's dramatic effort to supply political and church intelligence to officials in London.
92. Inglis filed a petition with the Loyalist Claims Commission seeking compensation for losses of property valued at £7,909 and was awarded £4,135 sterling. He received a pension of £200 sterling. Palmer, *Biographical Sketches of Loyalists*, 442–3. Leventhal and Mooney, 'A Bibliography of Loyalist Source Material', *P.A.A.S.* Part I, 85 (1975): 108, 169, 209, 212, 215, 229, 231, 233–4, 238, 241, 272, 276, 414; Part IV, 90 (1980): 118, 126, 134, 137, 140–4.
93. S.P.G. MSS, Vol. B. 2, No. 68, Charles Inglis to Richard Hind, Secretary, New York, 31 October 1776.

12   A Challenge to Radical Politics: Samuel Seabury, Jr., and Thomas Bradbury Chandler

1. See the excellent discussion of the controversy over the establishment of a charter for King's College in *The Independent Reflector, or Weekly Essays on Sundry Important Subjects More Particularly Adapted to the Province of New York*, Milton Klein, ed. (Cambridge, 1963). David C. Humphrey, *From King's College to Columbia, 1746–1800* (New York, 1976): 35–54.

2. Thomas Bradbury Chandler, *An Appeal to the Public in Behalf of the Church of England in America. Wherein the Original Nature of the Episcopal Office are Briefly Considered, Reasons for Sending Bishops to America are Assigned, the Plan on Which it is Proposed to Send Them is Stated, and the Objections Against Sending Them are Obviated and Confuted. With an Appendix, Wherein is Given Some Account of an Anonymous Pamphlet* (New York, 1767). Bruce E. Steiner, *Samuel Seabury: A Study in the High Church Tradition* (Athens, Ohio, 1971): 108–9.

3. Steiner, *Samuel Seabury*, 110.

4. Ibid., 110–23.

5. Ibid., 124. Thomas DeLaune, *A Plea for the Non-Conformists, Shewing the True State of Their Case: in a Letter to Dr. Benjamin Calamy. Added, A Parallel Scheme of the Pagan, Papal, and Christian Rites and Ceremonies: and a Narrative of the Sufferings Underwent by Thomas De Laune, With a Preface by D. De Foe* (Boston, 1763, Ballston, N.Y., 1800).

6. A. W. Farmer [Samuel Seabury, Jr.,] *Free Thoughts, on the Proceedings of the Continental Congress, Held at Philadelphia Sept. 5, 1774: Wherein Their Errors are Exhibited, Their Reasoning Confuted, and the Fatal Tendency of Their Non-Importation, Non-Exportation, and Non-Consumption Measures, are Laid Open to the Plainest Understanding; and the Only Means Point Out for Preserving and Securing Our Present Happy Constitution: In a Letter to the Farmers and Other Inhabitants of North America in General, and to Those of the Province of New-York in Particular* (New York, 1774); *The Congress Canvassed: or, An Examination into the Conduct of the Delegates at Their Grand Convention, Held in Philadelphia Sept. 1, 1774, Addressed to the Merchants of New-York* (New York, 1774, London 1775); *A View of the Controversy Between Great-Britain and Her Colonies: Including a Mode of Determining Their Present Disputes, Finally and Effectually; and of Preventing All Future Contentions. In A Letter to the Author of A Full Vindication of the Measures of the Congress, from the Calumnies of Their Enemies* (New York, 1774). Steiner, *Samuel Seabury*, 129–47.

7. [Seabury], *Free Thoughts, on the Proceedings of the Continental Congress*, 3.

8. Ibid.

9. Ibid., 4.

10. Ibid., 4–6.

11. Ibid., 9.

12. Ibid., 9–10.

13. Ibid., 11–12.

14. Ibid., 17.

15. Ibid., 18.

16. Ibid., 19.

17. Ibid., 23.

18. Ibid., 6.

19. Ibid., 8.

20. Ibid., 18.

21. [Seabury], *The Congress Canvassed*, 13.

22. Ibid., 5–6.

23. Ibid., 6.

24. Ibid., 6–7.

25. Ibid., 13.

26. Ibid., 8–9.
27. Ibid., 16.
28. Ibid., 20.
29. Ibid., 24.
30. Alexander Hamilton, *A Full Vindication of the Measures of the Congress from the Calumnies of Their Enemies; In Answer to A Letter Under the Signature of A. W. Farmer. Whereby His Sophistry is Exposed, His Cavils Confuted, His Artifices Detected, and His Wit Ridiculed; in a General Address to the Inhabitants of America, and a Particular Address to the Farmers of the Province of New-York, Magna est & Praevalebit. Truth is Powerful, and Will Prevail* (New York, 1774). J. C. D. Clark, *The Language of Liberty, 1660–1832: Political Discourse and Social Dynamics in the Anglo-American World* (Cambridge, 1994): 102.
31. [Samuel Seabury], *A View of the Controversy Between Great Britain and Her Colonies*, 14–15. Steiner, *Samuel Seabury*, 150–1.
32. Alexander Hamilton, *The Farmer Refuted; or A More Imparted and Comprehensive View of the Dispute Between Great-Britain and the Colonies, Intended as a Further Vindication of the Congress: In Answer to a Letter from A. W. Farmer, Intitled A View of the Controversy Between Great-Britain and Her Colonies: Including a Mode of Determining the Present Disputes Finally and Effectively, &c.* (New York, 1775).
33. [Samuel Seabury], *An Alarm to the Legislature of the Province of New York, Occasioned By Present Political Disturbances, in North America, Addressed to the Honourable Representatives in General Assembly Convened* (New York, 1775; London, 1775): 13.
34. Ibid. Steiner, *Samuel Seabury*, 151–3.
35. S.P.G. MSS B-II, 648–50, the Rev. Samuel Seabury to Secretary Richard Hind, 30 May 1775.
36. Ibid.
37. Steiner, *Samuel Seabury*, 158–64.
38. Leonard J. Trinterud, *The Forming of an American Tradition* (Philadelphia, 1949): 246–9.
39. Edward H. Tatum, Jr., ed., *The American Journal of Ambrose Serle, Secretary to Lord Howe, 1776–1778* (San Marino, 1940): 116–17.
40. Steiner, *Samuel Seabury*, 166–71.
41. Samuel Seabury, *St. Peter's Exhortation to Fear God and Honor the King, Explained and Inculcated: In a Discourse Addressed to His Majesty's Provincial Troops, in Camp at King's Bridge, On Sunday the 28th September 1777* (New York, 1777): 16. Steiner, *Samuel Seabury*, 171.
42. Seabury, *St. Peter's Exhortation to Fear God and Honor the King*, 16.
43. Ibid., 16–17.
44. Ibid., 19.
45. Ibid., 20.
46. Ibid., 22–3. At the close of the war Seabury claimed a loss of £ 50 and received £30 sterling compensation from the Loyalist Claims Commission. Palmer, *Biographical Sketches of Loyalists*, 768–9.
47. James B. Bell, *The Imperial Origins of the King's Church in Early America, 1607–1783* (London, 2004): 204–5.
48. Thomas Bradbury Chandler, *The Life of Samuel Johnson, D. D., The First President of King's College in New-York* (New York, 1805).

49. Thomas Bradbury Chandler, *An Appeal to the Public in Behalf of the Church of England in America. Wherein the Original Nature of the Episcopal Office are Briefly Considered, Reasons for Sending Bishops to America are Assigned, the Plan on Which it is Proposed to Send Them is Stated, and the Objections Against Sending Them are Obviated and Confuted. With an Appendix, Wherein is Given Some Account of an Anonymous Pamphlet* (New York, 1767); *The Appeal Defended: or the Proposed American Episcopate Vindicated, in Answer to the Objections and Misrepresentations of Dr. Chauncy and Others* (New York, 1769); *The Appeal Farther Defended, In Answer to the Farther Misrepresentations of Dr. Chauncy* (New York, 1771). Wallace Brown, *The King's Friends: The Composition and Motivation of the American Loyalist Claimants* (Providence, 1965): 119.
50. Bell, *Imperial Origins of the Imperial Church*, 120–4; 176–82.
51. Chandler, *An Appeal to the Public*, 89.
52. [Thomas Bradbury Chandler], *The American Querist: or Some Questions Proposed Relative to the Present Dispute Between Great Britain, and Her American Colonies. By a North American* (New York, 1774; Boston, London, 1775).
53. Ibid., 6.
54. Ibid.
55. [Chandler], *The American Querist*, Tenth edition (New York, 1774): Title page.
56. Thomas Bradbury Chandler, *A Friendly Address to All Reasonable Americans, on the Subject of Our Political Confusions; in Which the Necessary Consequences of Violently Opposing the King's Troops and of a General Non-Importation are Fairly Stated* (Boston, 1774, New York, 1774; 1775; London, 1775; Dublin, 1775): 5.
57. Ibid.
58. Ibid.
59. Ibid., 49–53.
60. Ibid., 10–14.
61. Ibid., 14–23.
62. Ibid., 49.
63. Ibid., 49–50.
64. Ibid., 50.
65. Ibid.
66. Ibid.
67. E. B. O'Callaghan, ed., *Documents Relative to the Colonial History of the State of New York* (Albany, 1857) VIII: 569.
68. Thomas Bradbury Chandler, *What think Ye of the Congress Now? or an Enquiry, How Far the Americans are Bound to Abide by and Execute the Decisions of the Late Congress* (New York, 1775; London, 1775): 4, 22.
69. Ibid., 6.
70. Ibid., 40.
71. Ibid., 48.
72. Brown, *The King's Friends*, 121.
73. For an account of Chandler's flight to New York and London, and for his years in residence in England see, Frank Gavin, 'The Rev. Thomas Bradbury Chandler in the Light of his (unpublished) Diary, 1775–1785', *C.Hist.* I (1932): 90–106. For his contributions to the Royalist cause Chandler was awarded by the Crown in 1775 an annual pension of £200. Gregory Palmer, *Biographical Sketches of Loyalists of the American Revolution*

(Westport, 1984): 148. Herbert Leventhal and James E. Mooney, 'A Bibliography of Loyalist Source Material', *P.A.A.S.* Part I. 85 (1975): 163, 169, 171, 213–14. Part IV. 90 (1980): 126, 140–1.
74. *The Literary Diary of Ezra Stiles, D.D., LL.D.* Franklin Bowditch Dexter, ed. (New York, 1901) III: 398.
75. Ibid.
76. Ibid.
77. Ibid.
78. Ibid.

13   Quiet and Militant Patriots

1. See Appendix I for a summary account by colony of the known wide-ranging political opinions of the ministers active between 1775 and 1783.
2. G. MacLaren Brydon, 'The Clergy of the Established Church in Virginia and the Revolution', *V.M.H.B.* 41 (1933): 12–13. For a minister to continue to serve his parish he was required to take the oath of allegiance to the Commonwealth. There were also nine other clergymen who resigned their parishes in 1776 and 1777 without appearing to have accepted other assignments. They may have been Loyalists who unwilling to accept the new government withdrew from their parishes, and perhaps returned to England.
3. Ibid., 16–17.
4. George MacLaren Brydon, *Virginia's Mother Church and the Political Conditions under which it Grew* (Philadelphia, 1952) II: 43.
5. I am grateful to Professor Otto Lohrenz for calling to my attention this important detail.
6. Brydon, 'The Clergy of the Established Church in Virginia and the Revolution', 16. The lone exception was a German Lutheran minister for a German-speaking regiment.
7. James B. Bell, *The Imperial Origins of the King's Church in Early America, 1607–1783* (London, 2004): 198–202. Appendix I.
8. William Germann, 'The Crisis in the Early Life of General Peter Muhlenberg', *P.M.H.B.* 37 (1913): 298–392, 450–70. Edward W. Hocker, *The Fighting Parson of the American Revolution; a Biography of General Peter Muhlenberg, Lutheran Clergyman, Military Chieftan, and Political Leader* (Philadelphia, 1936): 7–27. Henry Augustus Muhlenberg, *The Life of Major General Peter Muhlenberg of the Revolutionary Army* (Philadelphia, 1849): 13–29.
9. James B. Bell, 'Anglican Clergy in Colonial America Ordained by Bishops of London'. *P.A.A.S.* 83 (1973): 151. Thomas Nelson Rightmyer, 'The Holy Orders of Peter Muhlenberg', *H.M.P.E.C.* 30 (1961): 183–97.
10. Brydon, *Virginia's Mother Church*, II: 93–8. Hocker, *The Fighting Parson*, 44–8. Muhlenberg, *Peter Muhlenberg*, 50–61.
11. Germann, 'Muhlenberg', *P.M.H.B.* 37 (1913): 469. Joel T. Headley, *Chaplains and Clergy of the Revolution* (New York, 1864): 121–6. Hocker, *The Fighting Parson*, 61–3. Muhlenberg, *Peter Muhlenberg*, 50–4.
12. Brydon, 'The Clergy of the Established Church in Virginia and the Revolution', *V.M.H.B.* 41 (1933), 242–3.

13. Germann, 'Muhlenberg', *P.M.H.B.* 37 (1913): 469. Hocker, *The Fighting Parson,* 65–75.
14. For Muhlenberg's military career see the 'Orderly Book of General John Peter Gabriel Muhlenberg, March 26–December 20, 1777', *P.M.H.B.* 33 (1909): 257–8, 454–74; 34 (1910): 21–40, 166–89, 336–60, 438–77; 35 (1911): 59–89, 156–87, 290–303. Muhlenberg, *Peter Muhlenberg,* 54–136.
15. *D.A.B.; A.N.B.;* Hocker, *The Fighting Parson,* 126–77. Muhlenberg, *Peter Muhlenberg,* 307–34.
16. Brydon, 'The Clergy of the Established Church in Virginia and the Revolution', 302–3. Brydon, *Virginia's Mother Church* II: 422–3.
17. Charles Crowe, 'Bishop James Madison and the Republic of Virtue', *Journal of Southern History.* 30 (1964): 59–60.
18. Ibid., 60.
19. Franklin B. Wickwire, *British Subministers and Colonial America* (Princeton, 1966): 168–9. *A.N.B.*
20. William T. Hutchinson, ed. *The Papers of James Madison* (Chicago, 1962) II: 294.
21. Brydon, *Virginia's Mother Church* II: 475–8. Brydon, 'The Clergy of the Established Church in Virginia and the Revolution', 239–40.
22. William Meade, *Old Churches, Ministers and Families of Virginia* (Philadelphia, 1857) II: 219.
23. James B. Bell, Colonial American Clergy of the Church of England, 1607–1783, Database at, www.jamesbbell.com.
24. Brydon, 'The Clergy of the Established Church in Virginia and the Revolution', 140. G. MacLaren Brydon, 'David Griffith, 1742–1789, First Bishop Elect of Virginia', *H.M.P.E.C.* 9 (1940): 194–230.
25. For a convenient reprint of Griffith's sermon with critical commentary see George MacLauren Brydon, *H.M.P.E.C.* 44 (1975): 77–93. Brydon, *Virginia's Mother Church* II: 384, 435, 464.
26. J. C. D. Clark, *The Language of Liberty, 1660–1832: Political Discourse and Social Dynamics in the Anglo-American World* (Cambridge, 1994): 123–4.
27. David Griffith, *Passive Obedience Considered: in a Sermon Preached at Williamsburgh, December 31st, 1775* (Williamsburgh, [1776]): 24–5. William Sydnor, 'Doctor Griffith of Virginia: Emergence of a Church Leader, March 1779–June 3, 1786', *H.M.P.E.C.* 45 (1976): 5–24; 'Doctor Griffith of Virginia: The Breaking of a Church Leader, September 1786–August 3, 1789', ibid., 113–32.
28. For David Griffith's military career I am indebted to William Sydnor's excellent article 'David Griffith – Chaplain, Surgeon, Patriot', *H.M.P.E.C.* 44 (1975): 247–56. Charles Royster, *A Revolutionary People at War: The Continental Army and American Character* (Chapel Hill, 1979): 17–18, 161–74.
29. Brydon, 'David Griffith, 1742–1789. First Bishop-Elect of Virginia', *H.M.P.E.C.* 9 (1940): 194–230. Brydon, *Virginia's Mother Church* II: 438, 461–5.
30. Bell, Colonial American Clergy of the Church of England.
31. John Hurt, *The Love of Our Country. A Sermon Preached before the Virginia Troops in New Jersey* (Philadelphia, 1777): 14–15.
32. Royster, *A Revolutionary People at War,* 163.
33. Ibid., 250–1.

34. Bell, 'Anglican Clergy in Colonial America Ordained by Bishops of London', 118.

35. Isaac Campbell, *A Rational Enquiry into the Origin, Foundation, Nature, and End of Civil Government, showing it to be a Divine Institution* (Annapolis, 1787). The only known copy is deposited in the collections of the Maryland Historical Society in Baltimore. The very bottom of the page carrying the publication date has been torn away. The publication is not identified in any of the standard bibliographies. See James F. and Jean H. Vivian, 'The Reverend Isaac Campbell: An Anti-Lockean Whig', *H.M.P.E.C.* 39 (1970): 71.

36. Vivian, 'The Reverend Isaac Campbell', 74.

37. Ibid., 75.

38. Ibid., 81.

39. Ibid., 85.

40. Rodney K. Miller, 'The Political Ideology of the Anglican Clergy', *H.M.P.E.C.* 45 (1976): 235.

41. Ibid., 236.

42. Bird Wilson, *Memoir of the Life of the Right Reverend William White* (Philadelphia, 1839): 28. Edward Duffield Neill, 'Rev. Jacob Duché, the First Chaplain of Congress', *P.M.H.B.* 2 (1878): 58–73.

43. Butterfield, Lyman H., ed., *The Adams Papers, Diary and Autobiography of John Adams* (Cambridge, 1961) II: 126–7. Adams later remarked that he had heard no preachers in Philadelphia 'like ours in Boston, excepting Mr. Duché'. Ibid., II: 149.

44. Neill, 'Jacob Duché', 64–7. Headley, *Chaplains and Clergy*, 83–8. Kevin J. Dellape, 'Jacob Duché: Whig-Loyalist'? *Pennsylvania History* 62 (1995): 293–305.

45. *The Papers of George Washington*, W.W. Abbott, ed., *Revolutionary War Series* (Charlottesville, 1985) 1: 246–47.

46. Neill, 'Jacob Duché', 69.

47. *The Papers of George Washington*, Philander D. Chase, ed., *Revolutionary War Series* (Charlottesville, 2001) 11: 430–6, 497.

48. Ibid., 527–8.

49. *The Papers of George Washington*, Philander D. Chase, ed., *Revolutionary War Series* (Charlottesville, 2002) 12: 341; 13: 363–4. *The Papers of Thomas Jefferson*, Julian P. Boyd, ed. (Princeton, 1950 to the present, the volumes are still being published) II: 37–9. Neill, 'Jacob Duché', 69–70.

50. Neill, 'Jacob Duché', 70.

51. Wallace Brown, *The Good Americans: The Loyalists in the American Revolution* (New York, 1969): 74–6.

52. B. F. Stevens, *Facsimiles of Manuscripts in European Archives relating to America, 1773–1783* (London, 1895): 24. No. 2075.

53. The Loyalist Claims Commission granted Duché an annual pension of £130. He filed a claim for £2000 for losses and the Commission awarded him £496 sterling. Gregory Palmer, *Biographical Sketches of Loyalists of the American Revolution* (Westport, 1984): 236. Herbert Leventhal and James E. Mooney, 'A Bibliography of Loyalist Source Material in the United States', *P.A.A.S.* Part I. 85 (1975): 271–2, 293, 295, 298, 300. Part IV 90 (1980): 140–2, 157.

54. *The Writings of George Washington,* John C. Fitzpatrick, ed. (Washington, 1933) 27: 91–2.
55. *The Autobiography of Benjamin Rush. His 'Travels Through Life' together with his Commonplace Book for 1789–1803.* George W. Corner, ed. (Princeton, 1948): 240.
56. William Wilson Manross, *A History of the American Episcopal Church* Third edition (New York, 1959): 130–2. Thomas F. Jones, *A Pair of Lawn Sleeves: A Biography of William Smith, 1727–1803* (Philadelphia, 1972): 1–42.
57. Before entering on his duties Smith returned to London in 1753 for ordination. Bell, 'Anglican Clergy in Colonial America Ordained by Bishops of London', 151. Frank Gegenheimer, *William Smith: Educator and Churchman, 1727–1803* (Philadelphia, 1943): 43–50.
58. Gegenheimer, *William Smith,* 124–82.
59. William Smith, *A Sermon on the Present Situation of American Affairs. Preached in Christ Church, June 23, 1775. At the Request of the Officers of the Third Battalion of the City of Philadelphia, and District of Southwark* (Philadelphia, 1775; Wilmington, 1775; London, 1775; Bristol, 1775; Belfast, 1775; Dublin, 1775): i–ii.
60. [Attributed to William Smith], *Plain Truth; Addressed to the Inhabitants of America, Containing Remarks on a Late Pamphlet, Entitled Common Sense. By Candidus* (Philadelphia, 1776; London, 1776; Dublin, 1776): Title page. The essay has also been attributed to James Chalmers, for a discussion on the matter see William D. Andrews, 'William Smith', *Dictionary of Literary Biography, Colonial American Writers, 1735–1781,* Emory Elliott, ed. (Detroit, 1984). 31: 220.
61. Ann D. Gordon, *The College of Philadelphia, 1749–1779: Impact of an Institution* (New York, 1989): 251–95.
62. *Diary and Autobiography of John Adams,* Lyman H. Butterfield, ed. (Cambridge, 1961) 2: 118.
63. *The Literary Diary of Ezra Stiles, D.D., LL.D. President of Yale College,* Franklin Bowditch Dexter, ed. (New York, 1901) II: 338, 528.
64. *The Autobiography of Benjamin Rush,* George W. Corner, ed.: 262–5.
65. Ibid., 263.
66. Manross, *History of the American Episcopal Church,* 180, 187–8.
67. *D.A.B.; A.N.B.;* Headley, *Chaplains and Clergy,* 171–4.
68. *Letters of Benjamin Rush,* L. H. Butterfield, ed. (Princeton, 1951) I: 408.
69. Clifford K. Shipton, *Sibley's Harvard Graduates* (Boston, 1972) XVI: 77.
70. Ibid.
71. Ibid., 78. Lorenzo Sabine, *Biographical Sketches of Loyalists of the American Revolution* (Boston, 1864) II: 147–8.
72. Andrew Oliver and James Bishop Peabody, eds, *The Records of Trinity Church, Boston, 1728–1830, Publications of The Colonial Society of Massachusetts* (Boston, 1980). LV: 170.
73. Ibid. Leventhal and Mooney, 'Loyalist Source Material', Part I. *P.A.A.S.,* 85 (1975): 103.
74. Oliver and Peabody, *The Records of Trinity Church,* 171.
75. Shipton, *Sibley's Harvard Graduates* XVI: 78.
76. Ibid., 82–3.
77. Ibid., 83.

78. Ibid., 81–2.
79. Morgan Dix, *The Parish of Trinity Church in the City of New York* (New York, 1898) I: 330.
80. Ibid., II: 36–8.
81. Ibid., II: 2–19; 245–54.
82. E. Clowes Chorley, 'Samuel Provoost, First Bishop of New York', *H.M.P.E.C.* 2 (1933): 9–11.
83. Manross, *History of the American Episcopal Church*, 195–6.

14   William Knox Seeks to Establish an Ecclesiastical Imperial Policy for the American Church

1. Pauline Maier, *From Resistance to Revolution: Colonial Radicals and the Development of American Opposition to Britain, 1765–1776* (New York, 1974): 51–64; 194–5; 276–7.
2. Wallace Brown, *The King's Friends: The Composition and Motivation of the American Loyalist Claimants* (Providence, 1965): 21–3.
3. Ibid., 36.
4. Leland J. Ballot, *William Knox: The Life and Thought of an Eighteenth-Century Imperialist* (Austin, 1977): 3–16; 17–41.
5. Ibid., 71–184.
6. William Knox, *A Letter to a Member of Parliament, wherein the Power of the British Legislature and the Case of the Colonists are briefly and impartially considered* (London, 1765).
7. William Knox, *The Claims of the Colonies to an Exemption from Internal Taxes Imposed by Authority of Parliament, Examined: In a Letter from a Gentleman in London, to his Friend in America* (London, 1765). Ballot, *William Knox*, 69–77. Edmund S. Morgan, *Benjamin Franklin* (New Haven, 2002): 152–65.
8. Burke published in 1757 *An Account of the European Settlements in America, A Chronicle of the Western Hemisphere from the Age of Exploration and Discovery to the Mid-Eighteenth Century* (London, 1757).
9. William Knox, *The Controversy Between Great Britain and Her Colonies Reviewed; the Several Pleas of the Colonies, in Support of Their Right to All The Liberties and Privileges of British Subjects, and to Exemption from the Legislative Authority of Parliament, Stated and Considered; and the Nature of Their Connection with, and Dependence on, Great Britain, Shewn upon the Evidence of Historical Facts and Authentic Records* (London, 1769, Boston, 1769).
10. William Knox, *The Justice and Policy of the Late Act of Parliament for Making More Effectual Provision for the Government of the Province of Quebec Asserted and Proved: and the Conduct of Administration Respecting that Province Stated and Vindicated* (London, 1774).
11. Bernard Bailyn, *The Ordeal of Thomas Hutchinson (Cambridge, 1974): 304.*
12. *The Manuscripts of the Earl of Dartmouth, Historic Manuscript Commission Report. Fourteenth Report* (London, 1895) II: 219.
13. Ibid.
14. William Knox, *Three Tracts Respecting the Conversion and Instruction of the Free Indian and Negro Slaves in the Colonies. Addressed to the Venerable Society for the Propagation of the Gospel in Foreign Parts* (London, 1768).

15. Knox continued his interest in the fortunes of the American colonial church until at least the late 1780s when he published *Observations Upon the Liturgy. With a Proposal for its Reform, upon the Principles of Christianity, as Professed and Taught by the Church of England; and an Attempt to Reconcile the Doctrines of the Angels'Apostacy and perpetual Punishment, Man's Fall and Redemption, and the Incarnation of the Son of God, to Our Conceptions of the Divine Nature and Attributes. By a Layman of the Church of England, Late an Under Secretary of State. To Which is Added, The Journals of the American Convention, Appointed to Frame an Ecclesiastical Constitution, and Prepare a Liturgy for the Episcopal Churches in the United States* (London, 1789).

16. E. Alfred Jones, *The Loyalists of New Jersey: Their Memorials, Petitions, Claims, Etc. From English Records* (Newark, 1927): 42.

17. Staffordshire County Record Office. Stafford, England, Manuscripts of the Earl of Dartmouth, William Knox to Lord Dartmouth, ca. 1774–78, endorsed on verso, 'Mr. Knox on the State of Religion in America'.

18. Ibid.

19. Ibid.

20. Ibid.

21. Ibid.

22. Ibid.

23. British Library, Stowe Mss. 119, fo. 164.

24. Jack P. Greene, ed. 'William Knox's Explanation for the Revolution', *W.M.Q.* Third Series 30 (1973): 303.

25. Edward H. Tatum, Jr., ed. *The American Journal of Ambrose Serle, Secretary to Lord Howe, 1776–1778* (San Marino, 1940): 202, 204.

26. Frances Maseres, an article published in the *Political Advertiser*, 27 March 1778, and reprinted in *Occasional Essays on Various Subjects, Chiefly Political and Historical: Extracted Partly from the Publick Newspapers* (London, 1809): 28–9. William Markham, *A Sermon Preached before the Incorporated Society for the Propagation of the Gospel in Foreign Parts; at the Anniversary Meeting in the Parish Church of St. Mary-le-Bow, on Friday February 21, 1777* (London, 1777): xxiv.

27. Ibid., xiv–xxiv.

28. British Library, Stowe Mss. 119, fo. 164.

29. Tatum, *The American Journal of Ambrose Serle*, 115, 145, 152, 167,170, 172–3, 190–1, 193, 196, 198–9, 209–10, 236–7, 268, 280.

30. B. F. Stevens, *Facsimile of Manuscripts in European Archives Relating to America, 1773–1783* (London, 1895) 24: Number 2067.

15   The State of the Clergy in 1775 and 1783

1. I am indebted for these summary details to Pauline Maier's study, *From Resistance to Revolution: Colonial Radicals and the Development of American Opposition to Britain, 1765–1776* (New York, 1991 edition): 281–7.

2. Ibid., 281.

3. Ibid.

4. Ibid., 281–2.

5. George W. Corner, ed., *The Autobiography of Benjamin Rush* (Philadelphia, 1948): 117–18.

6. Ibid., 119.
7. See Anne Whiteman, 'The Restoration of the Church of England', in *From Uniformity to Unity 1662–1962*. Geoffrey F. Nuttall and Owen Chadwick, eds (London, 1962): 35–6.
8. SPG MSS. B., Vol. 21, Rev. Thomas Barton to Secretary Richard Hind, 1 March 1775, Lancaster, Pennsylvania.
9. SPG MSS. B., Vol. 21, Rev. Thomas Barton to Dr. Richard Hind, 24 August 1775, Lancaster, Pennsylvania.
10. SPG MSS. B., Vol. 21, Rev. Thomas Barton to Dr. Richard Hind, 25 November 1776, Lancaster, Pennsylvania.
11. SPG MSS. B., Vol. 21, Rev. Philip Reading to Dr. Richard Hind, 25 August 1776, Appoquiniminck, Delaware.
12. See Appendix I.
13. James B. Bell, *The Imperial Origins of the King's Church in Early America* (London, 2004): 200–9.
14. Henry Wilder Foote, *Annals of King's Chapel from the Puritan Age of New England to the Present Day* (Boston, 1896) II: 305.
15. Ibid., 345–6.
16. Massachusetts gained one clergymen during the course of the war when British military chaplain Stephen Lewis decided to support the patriot cause and served as minister of Christ Church in Boston.
17. This information has been gathered from two sources: Appendix I, an individual account of the political opinions of the ministers by colony and my Colonial American Clergy of the Church of England database, a resource of biographical details, at www.jamesbbell.com.
18. See Appendix II, Table I A. Connecticut was the birthplace of 17 men; Massachusetts, 12; New Hampshire, 3; New York, 2; England 6 and Scotland 2. The ministers were primarily educated at the two leading New England colleges: Yale, 17; Harvard, 15; Oxford, 2; and 1 each at King's in New York, Rhode Island in Providence, Philadelphia, and Aberdeen. The colleges attended, if any, by 4 persons are unknown.
19. Bell, *Imperial Origins of the King's Church*, 203–9.
20. See Appendix II, Table I B. Their births by decades ranged from: 1700–9, 2; 1710–19, 6; 1720–9, 4; 1730–9, 15; 1740–9, 12; with 3 persons whose dates of birth are unknown.
21. Kenneth Walter Cameron, ed., *The Church of England in Pre-Revolutionary Connecticut* (Hartford, 1976): 192.
22. Francis L. Hawks and William Stevens Perry, eds, *Documentary History of the Protestant Episcopal Church in the United States of America* (New York, 1864) II: 197.
23. Ibid., 198.
24. Robert A. East, *Connecticut's Loyalists* (Chester, 1974): 14–15. David H. Villers, '"King Mob" and the Rule of Law: Revolutionary Justice and the Suppression of Localism in Connecticut, 1774–1783', in *Loyalists and Community in North America*, Robert M. Calhoon, Timothy M. Barnes, and George A. Rawlyk. eds (Westport, 1994): 17–30; Brown, *King's Friends*, 69–70.
25. Bell, *Imperial Origins of the King's Church*, 199.
26. Cameron, *The Church of England in Pre-Revolutionary Connecticut*, 200.
27. Ibid., 358, 403, 414–16.
28. Ibid., 48.

29. Brown, *King's Friends*, 45.
30. Wilkins Updike, *History of the Episcopal Church in Narragansett Rhode Island* (New York, 1847): 403.
31. See Appendix I for an individual account by colony of the political opinions of the ministers of the region who were serving congregations between 1775 and 1783.
32. The data for this statistical information is drawn from my 'The Colonial American Clergy of the Church of England Database' comprising biographical information relating to the 1,280 men who were associated with the English church between 1607 and 1783.
33. See Appendix II, Table II A. The places of birth of the men included New York, 8; Pennsylvania, 7; Connecticut, 6; New Jersey, 2; and Massachusetts, and Rhode Island, 1 each. Scotland was the homeland for 8 men; England, 6; Ireland, 5; and 1 from the Palatinate, and one minister whose origin in a German state is unknown. The colleges attended by the men included the following: King's in New York, 9; Yale, 6; Philadelphia, 5; Princeton, 2; Harvard, 1; Oxford, 4; Cambridge, 2; Trinity College in Dublin, 4; Aberdeen 5, St. Andrews, Glasgow, and Leyden 1 each, 2 who did not attend college, and information for 5 men is unknown. See Appendix II, Table II C.
34. See Appendix II, Table II B. The decades of their births ranged from: 1700–9, 3; 1710–19, 3; 1720–9, 9; 1730–9, 11; 1740–9, 16; and 1750–9, 3, and 2 are unknown.
35. For biographical details on each man see Bell, Colonial American Clergy of the Church of England Database.
36. Ibid.
37. Ibid.
38. For a description of the impact of the Revolutionary War on the ministers and congregations see Nelson R. Burr, *The Anglican Church in New Jersey* (Philadelphia, 1954): 373–415.
39. E. Alfred Jones, *The Loyalists of New Jersey* (Newark, 1927): 23.
40. See Appendix I for an individual account by colony of the political opinions of the ministers of the region who were active between 1775 and 1783. I am grateful to Professor Otto Lohrenz for his assistance on identifying the political sentiments of the Chesapeake Colonies ministers. Particularly helpful were his numerous publications detailed in the Bibliography, and his The Virginia Clergy and the American Revolution, 1774–1799, unpublished Ph.D. dissertation, University of Kansas, Lawrence, Kansas, 1970. See too, Sandra Ryan Dresbeck, The Episcopalian Clergy in Maryland and Virginia, 1765–1805, unpublished Ph.D. dissertation, University of California at Los Angeles, 1976.
41. At least 38 of the 59 Maryland men were college graduates, representing such colleges on both sides of the Atlantic as Oxford, 7; Cambridge, 2; Aberdeen, 9; Glasgow, 2; Edinburgh and Dublin, 1 each; Philadelphia, 7; Princeton, 3; Log, 1; King's (New York), 1; and William and Mary, 3. See Appendix II, Table I C.
42. See Appendix II, Table I A. The data for this statistical information is drawn from my 'The Colonial American Clergy of the Church of England Database'.
43. See Appendix II, Table I A. By decades their births stretched from the turn to the mid-eighteenth century: 1690–99, 1; 1700–9, 3; 1710–19, 6; 1720–9,

12; 1730–9, 22; 1740–9, 42; 1750–9, 7; and 27 persons whose dates of birth are unknown.

44. Otto Lohrenz, 'The Advantage of Rank and Status: Thomas Price, A Loyalist Parson of Revolutionary Virginia', *The Historian* 60 (1998): 561–77, and his 'The Reverend Abner Waugh: "Best Dancer of the Minuet in the State of Virginia"', *The Kentucky Review* 15 (2003): 28–40.

45. Bell, *Imperial Origins of the King's Church*, 199–200; Appendix II Table III A.

46. Brown, *The Good Americans*, 235.

47. See Maryland section of Appendix I.

48. Rightmyer, *Maryland's Established Church*, 118–19; Appendix I.

49. George MacLaren Brydon, *Virginia's Mother Church and the Conditions under which it Grew* (Richmond, 1952) II: 386.

50. Ibid., 395.

51. Ibid., 416–17.

52. Rightmyer, *Maryland's Established Church*, 117.

53. The men were Henry Addison, Bennett Allen, Jonathan Boucher, William Edmiston, Henry Fendall, John Ross, and Philip Walker. The controversial Allen was born in 1737 at Hereford, England, the son of a clergyman. He was a graduate and later fellow of Wadham College, Oxford. In Maryland he held the parish in Frederick from 1768 to 1777 although he was seldom in residence. Allen retained a succession of curates to perform the required duties while he lived in the urbane surroundings of Philadelphia. He owed his Maryland post to the patronage of Lord Baltimore and in turn Allen stoutly defended his lordship against paternity charges with the publication of a poem. Allen is also remembered for killing Lloyd Dulany in a duel in London on 18 June 1782. *Maryl.Hist.Mag.* 39 (1944): 66–71. William Edmiston, a graduate of the College of Philadelphia in 1759 served as a Presbyterian minister before his Anglican ordination in 1766. He served as a curate under Allen between 1770 and 1775. Little is known about the origins and education of Henry Fendall, John Ross, and Philip Walker. Fendall and Walker seemed to have died ca. 1775 and 1776. Rightmyer, *Maryland's Established Church*, 209–10, 217.

54. Rightmyer, *Maryland's Established Church*, 116. Peter Force, *American Archives*, Fourth Series. V: 1598.

55. Robert J. Brugger, *Maryland: A Middle Temperament* (Baltimore, 1989): 122.

56. Rightmyer, *Maryland's Established Church*, 117; *Proceedings of the Convention of the Province of Maryland, Held at the City of Annapolis, on Wednesday the Fourteenth of August, 1776* (Annapolis, [1776]): 60–1.

57. Rightmyer, *Maryland's Established Church*, 118. A useful study would be to examine the surviving church registers in Maryland and each of the other colonies to determine, insofar as possible, the number of church services, baptisms, marriages, and burials conducted for each congregation during the period between 1776 and 1783.

58. Rightmyer, *Maryland's Established Church*, 118.

59. For a discussion of the establishment and development of the church in North Carolina, South Carolina, and Georgia see my *Imperial Origins of the King's Church*. Chap. 3.

60. *C.R.N.C.*, VII: 88; VI: 1235; VII: 920; IX: 298.

61. Alice Elaine Mathews, *Society in Revolutionary North Carolina* (Raleigh, 1976): 68.

62. James Brown was licensed in 1779 to serve in Georgia, he appears later as a loyalist refugee in the Bahamas.
63. See Appendix I for an individual account by colony of the political opinions of the ministers of the in the region serving congregations between 1775 and 1783.
64. See Appendix II, Table IV A.
65. See Appendix II, Table IV B. The decades of the men's births were as follows: 1700–09, 1; 1710–19, 1; 1720–9, 2; 1730–9, 10; 1740–9, 13; 1750–9, 5, with data for 10 men unknown. The collegiate institutions attended by the men also reflected their national origins: College of Philadelphia, 1; Oxford, 9; Cambridge, 4; Aberdeen 5; and one each at Glasgow, Edinburgh, and St. Andrews, while the college experience, if any, for 20 men is unknown. See Appendix II, Table IV C.
66. Bell, *Imperial Origins of the King's Church*, 196.
67. Nicholas Trott, *The Laws of the British Plantations in America, Relating to the Church and Clergy, Religion and Learning* (London, 1721): 5–22. F.P.P., IX: 3–16, South Carolina Church Act, 1706.
68. Bell, *Imperial Origins of the King's Church*, 92.
69. Kenneth Coleman, *Colonial Georgia: A History* (New York, 1976): 230–4.
70. Hugh Talmage Lefler, 'The Anglican Church in North Carolina: The Royal Period', in *The Episcopal Church in North Carolina, 1701–1959*. Lawrence Foushee London and Sarah McCulloh Lemmon, eds (Raleigh, 1985): 24–5. *C.R.N.C.*, XI: 1011, Article XXXIV of the State Constitution.
71. *C.R.N.C*, XI: 1011, Article XXXIV of the State Constitution.
72. Ibid.
73. William S. Powell, *North Carolina through Four Centuries* (Chapel Hill, 1989): 185–8.
74. *London Chronicle*, 27–29 February 1776.
75. Ibid.
76. Ibid., 29 February–2 March, 21–23 March, 30 March–2 April, 23–27 July 1776. The value of £775.5.0 has increased to £77,516.14 in 2006, the equivalent of $155,032.28. for £6,416.16.1the value has increased to £7,750,784.17 in 2006, or the equivalent of $15,501,568.
77. Ibid., 23–27 July 1776.

16 The English Church, a Cause of the American Revolution

1. *The Works of John Adams, Second President of the United States* (Boston, 1856). Charles F. Adams, ed. X: 185–8. The most recent edition of *The Papers of John Adams* published by the Massachusetts Historical Society has not reached the date of this letter, 2 December 1815. Jedidiah Morse, *Annals of the American Revolution; or a Record of the Causes and Events which Produced, and Terminated in the Establishment and Independence of the American Republic* (Hartford, 1824, 1968 edition): 197–200; Adams extended his comments on this issue in subsequent letters of 5, 22 December 1815, 1, 20 January, 1816: 200–17.
2. *Works of John Adams*, 185.
3. Ibid.

4. Morse, *Annals of the American Revolution*, 221.
5. Ibid., 222.
6. Edward H. Tatum, Jr., ed. *The American Journal of Ambrose Serle, Secretary to Lord Howe, 1776–1778* (San Marino, 1940): xi–xii.
7. B. F. Stevens, *Facsimiles of Manuscripts in European Archives relating to America, 1773–1783* (London, 1895). 24: No. 2045.
8. Ibid.
9. Ibid.
10. Ibid.
11. Ibid.
12. Ibid.
13. J. C. D. Clark, *The Language of Liberty, 1660–1832: Political Discourse and Social Dynamics in the Anglo-American World* (Cambridge, 1994): 297–303.
14. Ibid., 303–11, 351–81.
15. Ibid., 311–51.
16. Mary Lou Lustig, *Robert Hunter, 1666–1734: New York Augustan Statesman* (Syracuse, 1983): 109–10. John Romeyn Brodhead, *Documents Relative to the Colonial History of the State of New York* (Albany, 1855) V: 316–17. Governor Hunter reported to the Secretary of the S.P.G, 10 May 1714, that £226.7.5 had been spent on renovations for the house. By 1740 the premises were not used, and on 28 June 1748 it burnt to the ground, a total loss. George Morgan Hills, *History of the Church in Burlington, New Jersey* (Trenton, 1876): 104–8, 113, 256, 265–6.
17. William Stevens Perry, *Historical Collections Relating to the American Colonial Church* (Hartford, 1873) III: 93–4, 97–8, 99–113.
18. *Ibid.*, 191–200, 202, 205–9.
19. Edmund S. Morgan and Helen M. Morgan, *The Stamp Act Crisis: Prologue to Revolution* (Chapel Hill, 1995): 15–16.
20. 'An act for granting and applying certain stamp duties, and other duties, in the British Colonies and plantations in America, towards further defraying the expenses of defending, protecting, and securing the same; and for amending such parts of the several acts of parliament relating to the trade and revenues of the said colonies and plantations, as direct the manner of determining and recovering the penalties and forfeitures therein mentioned'. *The Statues at Large* (5 Geo. III. C. XII) (Cambridge, 1765): 179–204. For two excellent analyses of the English side of this issue see: P. D. G. Thomas, *British Politics and the Stamp Act Crisis: The First Phase of the American Revolution, 1763–1767* (Oxford, 1975), and Paul Langford, *The First Rockingham Administration, 1765–1766* (Oxford, 1973).
21. Langford, *The First Rockingham Administration*, 76.
22. Harry Alonzo Cushing, *The Writings of Samuel Adams* (New York, 1904) I: 1–73. *The Papers of John Adams*, Robert J. Taylor, ed. (Cambridge, 1977) I: 129–43.
23. Frances Manserve, opposition to a bishop, in *Occasional Essays on Various Subjects, Chiefly Political and Historical: Extracted Partly from The Publick Newspapers* (London, 1809): 25.
24. Ibid.
25. *The Statues at Large* (5 Geo. III. C. XII): 180.
26. Manserve, *Occasional Essays on Various Subjects*, 25.

27. Stephen Taylor, 'Whigs, Bishops and America: the Politics of Church Reform in Mid-Eighteenth-Century England', *The Historical Journal*, 36 (1993): 333.

28. Herbert and Carol Schneider, eds, *Samuel Johnson President of King's College: His Career and Writings* (New York, 1929) III: 286–7.

29. Alice M. Baldwin, *The New England Clergy and the American Revolution* (New York, 1928): 117. George A. Billias, *Elbridge Gerry, Founding Father and Republican Statesman* (New York, 1976): 23–4. Cushing, *Works of Samuel Adams*, II: 348–52. G. B. Warden, *Boston, 1689–1776* (Boston, 1970): 210–11, 255–64.

30. Billias, *Elbridge Gerry*, 23–4.

31. Clifford K. Shipton, *Sibley's Harvard Graduates* (Boston, 1970) XV, 240.

32. Billias, *Elbridge Gerry*, 24.

33. Ibid., 30.

34. Baldwin, *The New England Clergy*, 120–1.

35. James B. Bell, *The Imperial Origins of the King's Church in Early America, 1607–1783* (London, 2004): 30–40.

36. Henry Wilder Foote, *Annals of King's Chapel: From the Puritan Age of New England to the Present Day* (Boston, 1896) II: 306–7. Andrew Oliver and James Bishop Peabody, eds, *The Records of Trinity Church, Boston, 1728–1830* (Boston, 1980) I: 168–72.

37. Foote, *Annals of King's Chapel*, 378–95; David Robinson, *The Unitarians and Universalists* (Westport, Conn., 1985): 259.

38. Frederick V. Mills, Sr., *Bishops by Ballot: An Eighteenth-Century Ecclesiastical Revolution* (New York, 1978): 264–87.

39. Bell, *Imperial Origins of the King's Church*, 203–9.

40. Ibid.

41. Ibid., 566. David C. Humphrey, *From King's College to Columbia, 1746–1800* (New York, 1976): 269-82. John F. Roche, *The Colonial Colleges in the War for American Independence* (Millwood, N.Y., 1986): 71–2, 83–5.

42. Cremin, *American Education*, 566. Ann D. Gordon, *The College of Philadelphia, 1749–1779. Impact of an Institution* (New York, 1989): 251–80.

43. Lawrence A. Cremin, *American Education: The Colonial Experience, 1607–1783* (New York, 1970): 565–6. Roche, *Colonial Colleges*, 63–4, 75–6, 119–20, 133–5.

44. Roche, *Colonial Colleges*, 148–53, 165–6, 168–71, 182.

45. Bell, *Imperial Origins of the King's Church*, 3–57, 142.

46. Ibid., 3–57.

Bibliography

Abbreviations

A.Epis.Hist.	*Anglican and Episcopal History*
A.N.B.	*American National Biography*
A.P.C.E.Col.Ser.	*Acts of the Privy Council of England Colonial Series*
C.Hist.	*Church History*
C.R.Ga.	*Colonial Records of Georgia*
C.R.N.C.	*Colonial Records of North Carolina*
C.R.S.C.	*Colonial Records of South Carolina*
Col.Soc.Mass.P.	*Colonial Society of Massachusetts Publications*
D.A.B.	*Dictionary of American Biography*
D.N.B.	*Dictionary of National Biography*
E.R.S.N.Y.	*Ecclesiastical Records of the State of New York*
F.P.P.	*Fulham Palace Papers*
H.L.Q.	*Huntington Library Quarterly*
H.M.P.E.C.	*Historical Magazine of the Protestant Episcopal Church*
J.A.Hist.	*Journal of American History*
J.Eccl.H.	*Journal of Ecclesiastical History*
Maryl.Hist.Mag.	*Maryland Historical Magazine*
Mass.Hist.Soc.Coll.	*Massachusetts Historical Society Collections*
Mass.Hist.Soc.P.	*Massachusetts Historical Society Proceedings*
O.D.N.B.	*Oxford Dictionary of National Biography*
P.A.A.S.	*Proceedings of the American Antiquarian Society*
P.M.H.B.	*Pennsylvania Magazine of History and Biography*
S.R.N.C.	*State Records of North Carolina*
S.P.G.	*Society for the Propagation of the Gospel in Foreign Parts*
V.M.H.B	*Virginia Magazine of History and Biography*
W.M.Q.	*William and Mary Quarterly*

Manuscript sources

London
British Library
MSS Stowe, 119, folio 164. Appointment of a Committee of Three Bishops.

Lambeth Palace Library
MSS. Fulham Palace Papers. 42 vols. Letters and Papers of the Bishops of London and Colonial American clergymen, 1628–1783.
MSS. 1123. American Colonies: Correspondence to and from the Archbishops of Canterbury.
—— Part I. 1725–1754. II. 1755–1760. III. 1760–1763.
MSS. 1729, 184–247ff. A transcription of an unfinished autobiography by Thomas Secker, Archbishop of Canterbury (1758–1768); dated August, 1766.

MSS. S.P.G. Papers. 17 vols. Minutes, financial records, and correspondence from 1701–11, 1737–50 of the Society. Also includes some later correspondence of the archbishops of Canterbury relating to American affairs, particularly to documents relating to the conferring of the episcopate on the Protestant Episcopal Church in the United States after the Revolutionary War.

MSS. Archbishops of Canterbury, vol. 711, No. 18. Bishop of London's Paper about a Suffragan bishop for the Plantations, December 1707.

MSS. Archbishops of Canterbury, vol. 930: No. 38. Henry Dodwell to Thomas Tenison, 29 August 1700.

Oxford
Rhodes House Library
Archives of the Society for the Propagation of the Gospel in Foreign Parts, London.

MSS. S.P.G. A. Copies of Letters to and from Missionaries in America, 1702–36. 26 vols.

MSS. S.P.G. B. Letters to and from Missionaries in America, 1702–84, 25 vols.

MSS Box B-26. Maine, New Hampshire and Vermont.

MSS S.P.G. C/Am.

—— C/Am.1 New York and New Jersey 1707–30.

—— C/Am.2 New York and New Jersey 1730–91.

—— C/Am.3 Connecticut 1635–1796.

—— C/Am.4 Pennsylvania 1703–84.

—— C/Am.5 Massachusetts 1712–1812.

—— C/Am.6 Maine, New Hampshire, Vermont, 1755–1811.

—— C/Am.7 Southern Colonies: Maryland, Virginia, North Carolina, South Carolina, Georgia, East Florida, 1712–45.

—— C/Am.8 Southern Colonies: Maryland, Virginia, North Carolina, South Carolina, Georgia, East Florida, 1759–84.

—— C/Am.9 Rhode Island 1658–1800.

—— C/Am.10 Virginia and Pennsylvania Deeds 1691–1767.

—— C/Am.12 Letters sent to America 1731–34.

—— C/Am.13 Bills of Exchange and Receipts.

MSS S.P.G. Journals: Minutes of the Society's Meetings, 1701–84. 23 vols.

Journal Appendix A, Documents 1701–1810.

Journal Appendix B, Documents 1701–11.

MSS S.P.G. Minutes of the Meetings of the Standing Committee, 1710–84. 49 vols.

S.P.G. Anniversary Sermons and Annual Reports, 1701–89. 11 vols.

Stafford
Staffordshire County Record Office
MSS. Earl of Dartmouth, William Knox to Lord Dartmouth, ca. 1774–78, endorsed on verso, 'Mr. Knox on the State of Religion in America'.

Philadelphia
Historical Society of Pennsylvania
MSS. The Rev. William Becket to Dr. David Humphreys, Lewes, Delaware, 13 March, 15 March 1727/28.

Wolfville, Nova Scotia
Acadia University Library
MSS. John Wiswall, Journal

Newspapers
Boston Gazette
London Chronicle
Virginia Gazette (Purdie & Dixon)

Unpublished dissertations

Dresbeck, Sandra Ryan. 'The Episcopalian Clergy in Maryland and Virginia, 1765–1805', unpublished Ph.D. dissertation, University of California at Los Angeles, 1976.

Ingersoll, Elizabeth A. 'Francis Alison: American Philosophe, 1705–1779', unpublished Ph.D. dissertation, University of Delaware, 1974.

Kinlock, Hector H. 'Anglican Clergy in Connecticut, 1701–1785', unpublished Ph.D. dissertation, Yale University, 1959.

Lohrenz, Otto. 'The Virginia Clergy and the American Revolution', unpublished Ph.D. dissertation, University of Kansas, 1970.

Printed sources

Acts of the Privy Council of England, Colonial Series. I, II. London, 1908.

Acts and Resolves of the Province of Massachusetts Bay, 20. (Boston, 1918).

Adams, Charles F., ed. *The Works of John Adams, Second President of the United States*. Vol. X. Boston, 1856.

Adams, Henry. History of the United States of America during the First Administration of Thomas Jefferson. I. New York, 1921.

Ahlstrom, Sydney E. A Religious History of the American People. New Haven, 1972.

Akers, Charles W. Called unto Liberty: A Life of Jonathan Mayhew, 1720–1766. Cambridge, 1964.

Albright, Raymond W. *A History of the Protestant Episcopal Church*. New York, 1964.

Almon, John. *The Correspondence of the Late John Wilkes with His Friends, from the Original Manuscripts, in which are Introduced Memoirs of His Life*. London, 1805.

Anonymous. *A Brief Account of the Revenues, Pomp, and State of the Bishops, and Clergy in a Letter &c*. Boston, 1725.

Apthorp, East. *The Constitution of a Christian Church Illustrated in a Sermon at the Opening of Christ Church in Cambridge on Thursday 15 October 1761*. Boston, 1761.

—— *Considerations on the Institution and Conduct of the Society for the Propagation of the Gospel in Foreign Parts*. Boston, 1763.

—— *A Review of Mr. Mayhew's Remarks on the Answer to his Observations on the Charter and Conduct of the Society for the Propagation of the Gospel in Foreign Parts*. London, 1765.

Bailyn, Bernard. *Pamphlets of the American Revolution: 1750–1776*. I. Cambridge, 1965.

—— *The Ideological Origins of the American Revolution*. Cambridge, 1967.

—— *Faces of Revolution: Personalities and Themes in the Struggle for American Independence*. New York, 1990.

Baldwin, Alice M. *The New England Clergy and the American Revolution*. Durham, 1928.

Ballot, Leland J. *William Knox: The Life and Thought of an Eighteenth-Century Imperialist*. Austin, 1977.

Barnard, Leslie W. *Thomas Secker: An Eighteenth Century Primate*. Sussex, 1998.

Bartlet, William S. *The Frontier Missionary; A Memoir of the Life of the Rev. Jacob Bailey*. Boston, 1853.

Bastwick, John. *A Declaration Demonstrating and Infallably Proving that all Malignants, Whether They be Prelates, Popish Cavaliers, with All Other Ill Affected Persons, Are Enemies to God and the King, etc.* London, 1643.

Batchedler, Calvin R. *A History of the Eastern Diocese*. I. Claremont, 1876.

Batwell, Daniel. *A Sermon Preached at York-Town, before Captain Morgan's and Captain Price's Companies of Rifle-Men. On Thursday, July 20, 1775. Being the Day Recommended by the Honorable Continental Congress for a General Fast throughout the Twelve United Colonies of North America*. Philadelphia, 1775.

Baxter, Richard. *A Treatise of Episcopacy; Confuting by Scripture, Reason, and the Churches Testimony, that Sort of Diocesan Churches, Prelacy, and Government, which Casteth out the Primitive Church Species*. London, 1681.

—— *The True History of Councils Enlarged*. London, 1682.

Beach, John. *A Vindication of the Worship of God According to the Church of England, from the Aspersions Cast upon It By Mr. Jonathan Dickinson, in a Sermon Preached at Newark, June 2, 1736, and by J. G. Being a Letter to the Members of the Church of England at Newark*. New York, 1736.

—— *An Appeal to the Unprejudiced. In Supplement to the Vindication of the Worship of God According to the Church of England. From the injurious and Uncharitable Reflections of Mr. Jonathan Dickinson*. Boston, 1737.

—— *The Duty of Loving our Enemies. A Sermon Preached at Boston, September 24, 1738*. Boston, 1739.

—— *An Attempt to Vindicate Scripture Mysteries, Particularly, The Doctrine of the Holy Trinity, The Atonement of Christ, and the Renovation of the Holy Ghost; Also, of the Eternity of the Future Punishments: With some strictures upon what Mr. J. Taylor hath advanced upon those Points. In a Sermon, Preached before the Clergy of the Church of England, in Connecticut, at their annual Convention, at New Haven, June 4th, 1760*. New Haven, 1760.

—— *A Calm and Dispassionate Vindication of the Professors of the Church of England, against the Abusive Misrepresentation and Falacious Argumentations of Mr. Noah Hobart, in his late Address to them*. Boston, 1749.

—— *A Continuation of the Calm and Dispassionate Vindication of the Professors of the Church of England, against the Abusive Misrepresentations and Fallacious Argumentations of Mr. Noah Hobart, in his Second Address to them*. Boston, 1751.

—— *A Friendly Expostulation, With all Persons concern'd in publishing A late Pamphlet, Entitled, The Real Advantages which Ministers and People may enjoy, especially in the Colonies, by conforming to the Church of England*. New York, 1763.

Bell. James B. 'Anglican Clergy in Colonial America Ordained by Bishops of London'. *P.A.A.S.* 83 (1973).

—— *The Imperial Origins of the King's Church in Early America, 1607–1783*. London, 2004.

Bennett, J. H. 'English Bishops and Imperial Jurisdiction 1660–1725'. *H.M.P.E.C.* 32 (1963).

Benton, William Allen. *Whig-Loyalism: An Aspect of Political Ideology in the American Revolutionary Era*. Madison, NJ, 1969.

Berry, Joseph B. *History of the Diocese of Massachusetts, 1810–1872*. Boston, 1959.

Billias, George A. *Elbridge Gerry, Founding Father and Republican Statesman*. New York, 1976.

Blackburne, Francis. A Critical Commentary on Archbishop Secker's Letter to the Right Honourable Horatio Walpole, Concerning Bishops in America. London, 1770.

—— Compiler, *Memoirs of T. H.* 2 vols. London, 1780.

Bolton, S. Charles. *Southern Anglicanism: The Church of England in Colonial South Carolina.* Westport, 1982.

Bond, William H. *Thomas Hollis of Lincoln's Inn. A Whig and His Books.* Cambridge, 1990.

Bonomi, Patricia U. *Under the Cope of Heaven: Religion, Society, and Politics in Colonial America.* New York, 1986.

Boucher, Jonathan. *A Letter from a Virginian to the Members of the Congress to be held at Philadelphia, on the First of September, 1774.* New York, 1774.

—— *A View of the Causes And Consequences of the American Revolution: in Thirteen Discourses, Preached in North America between the Years 1763 and 1775: With an Historical Preface.* London, 1797.

—— *A Catalogue of the Very Valuable and extensive Library of the late Rev. Jonathan Boucher, M.A., F.R.S.* London, 1806.

Bouchier, Jonathan, ed. *Reminiscences of an American Loyalist, 1738–1789. Being the Autobiography of the Revd. Jonathan Boucher, Rector of Annapolis in Maryland and afterwards Vicar of Epsom, Surrey, England.* Boston, 1925.

Boyd. Julian P., ed. *The Papers of Thomas Jefferson.* II. Princeton, 1950.

Bradshaw, Paul F. *The Anglican Ordinal. Its History and Development from the Reformation to the Present Day.* London, 1971.

Bridenbaugh, Carl. *Cities in the Wilderness: 1625–1742.* I. New York, 1964.

—— *Mitre and Sceptre: Transatlantic Faiths, Ideas, Personalities, and Politics 1689–1775.* New York, 1962.

Brodhead, John Romeyn, ed. *Documents Relative to the Colonial History of the State of New York.* V. Albany, 1855.

Brown, Wallace. *The King's Friends. The Composition and Motives of the American Loyalist Claimants.* Providence, 1965.

Brown, Wallace. *The Good Americans. The Loyalists in the American Revolution.* New York, 1969.

Brown, William Cabell. 'Draft for the Creation of a Bishoprick in Virginia'. *V.M.H.B.* 36 (1928).

Browne, Arthur. *The Scripture-Bishop, or the Divine Right of Presbyterian Ordination and Government Consider'd in a Dialogue Between Praeleticus and Eleutherius, Examined in Two Letters to a Friend.* Boston?, 1733.

Browning, Andrew. *Thomas Osborne, Earl of Danby and Duke of Leeds, 1632–1712.* Glasgow, 1951.

Brugger, Robert J. *Maryland: A Middle Temperament.* Baltimore, 1989.

Brydon, G. MacLaren, 'David Griffith, 1742–1789. First Bishop-Elect of Virginia'. *H.M.P.E.C.* IX (1940).

—— 'The Clergy of the Established Church in Virginia and the Revolution'. *V.M.H.B.* 41 (1933).

—— 'New Light upon the History of the Church in Colonial Virginia'. *H.M.P.E. C.* 10 (1941).

—— *Virginia's Mother Church and the Political Conditions under which It Grew.* 2 vols. Richmond and Philadelphia, 1947, 1952.

Burg, B. R. *Richard Mather*. Boston, 1982.
—— *Richard Mather of Dorchester*. Lexington, Kentucky, 1976.
Burr, Nelson R. *The Story of the Diocese of Connecticut: A New Branch of the Vine.* Hartford, 1962.
Burtchaell, James Tunstead. *From Synagogue to Church: Public Services and Officers in the Earliest Christian Communities.* Cambridge, 1992.
Butler, Jon. *Awash in a Sea of Faith: Christianizing the American People.* Cambridge, 1990.
Butterfield, Lyman H., ed. *Letters of Benjamin Rush.* I. Princeton, 1951.
—— Editor. *The Adams Papers, Diary and Autobiography of John Adams.* II. Cambridge, 1961.
—— Editor, *Adams Family Correspondence.* I. Cambridge, 1963.
'C. D.' *New-England's Faction Discovered; or A Brief and True Account of Their Persecution of the Church of England; the Beginning and Progress of the War with the Indians; and other Late Proceedings There, in a Letter from a Gentleman of that Country to a Person of Quality. Being an Answer to a Most False and Scandalous Pamphlet Lately Published; Intituled, News from New England & c.* London, 1690.
[Calderwood, David]. *The Pastor and the Prelate, or Reformation and Conformatie shortly compared by the Word of God, by Antiquity and the Proceedings of the Ancient Kirk.* Leyden, 1628.
—— *The Presbyterian Government is Divine; Reasons to Prove that it is Unlawful to hear the Ministers of England; and That King may Abrogate Prelacy Without any Violation of his Oath.* Place?, ca. 1615.
Calendar of State Papers, Colonial Series, 1677–1680 (London, 1896).
Calendar of State Papers, Colonial Series, 1710–11 (London, 1924).
Calhoon, Robert McCluer. *The Loyalists in Revolutionary America, 1760–1781.* New York, 1973.
Cameron, Kenneth Walter, ed. *The Church of England in Pre-Revolutionary Connecticut.* Hartford, 1976.
Campbell. Isaac. *A Rational Enquiry into the Origin, Foundation, Nature, and End of Civil Government, showing it to be a Divine Institution.* Annapolis, 1787.
[Caner,Henry], *A Candid Examination of Dr. Mayhew's Observations on the Charter and Conduct of the Society for the Propagation of the Gospel in Foreign Parts. To Which is Added, A Letter to a Friend; Containing a Short Vindication of the said Society Against the Mistakes and Misrepresentations of the said Doctor in His Observations on the Conduct of the Society. By One of its Members.* Boston, 1763.
Carpenter, Edward. *Thomas Sherlock, 1678–1761, Bishop of Bangor, 1728; of Salisbury, 1734; of London, 1748.* London, 1936.
—— *The Protestant Bishop: Being the Life of Henry Compton, 1632–1714, Bishop of London.* London, 1956.
Champion, J. A. I. *The Pillars of Priestcraft Shaken: The Church of England and its Enemies, 1660–1730.* Cambridge, 1992.
Chandler, Thomas Bradbury. *An Appeal to the Public in Behalf of the Church of England in America. Wherein the Original Nature of the Episcopal Office are briefly considered, Reasons for sending Bishops to America are Assigned, the Plan on which it is proposed to send them is stated, and the objections against sending them are obviated and confuted. With an Appendix, wherein is given some account of an anonymous pamphlet.* New York, 1767.

—— *An Address from the Clergy of New York and New Jersey to the Episcopalians in Virginia, Occasioned by Some Late Transactions in that Colony Relative to an American Episcopate.* New York, 1771.

—— *The Appeal Farther Defended, In Answer to the Farther Misrepresentations of Dr. Chauncy.* New York, 1771.

—— *An Appendix to the American Edition of the Life of Archbishop Secker: containing His Grace's Letter to the Revd. Macclanechan, on the Irregularity of his Conduct; with an Introductory Narrative.* New York, 1774.

—— *A Free Examination of the Critical Commentary on Archbishop Secker's Letter to Mr. Walpole. Which is Added an Appendix, a Copy of Bishop Sherlock's Memorial.* New York, 1774.

—— [Chandler, Thomas Bradbury]. *The American Querist: or Some Questions Proposed Relative to the Present Dispute Between Great Britain, and Her American Colonies. By a North American.* New York, 1774; London, 1775.

—— *A Friendly Address to All Reasonable Americans, on the Subject of Our Political Confusions; in Which the Necessary Consequences of Violently Opposing the King's Troops and of a General Non-Importation are Fairly Stated.* New York, 1774; 1775; London, 1775; Dublin, 1775.

—— *What think Ye of the Congress Now? or an Enquiry, How Far the Americans are Bound to Abide by and Execute the Decisions of the Late Congress.* New York, 1775; London, 1775.

—— *The Life of Samuel Johnson, D. D., the First President of King's College in New York.* New York, 1805.

Chauncy, Charles. *The Validity of Presbyterian Ordination: Asserted and Maintained. A Discourse Delivered at the Anniversary Dudleian Lecture at Harvard College in Cambridge, New England, May 12, 1762.* Boston, 1762.

—— *A Letter to a Friend, Containing Remarks on Certain Passages in a Sermon Preached by the Right Reverend Father in God, John Lord Bishop of Landaff, Before the Incorporated Society for the Propagation of the Gospel in Foreign Parts, at Their Anniversary Meeting in the Parish Church of St. Mary-le-Bow, February 20, 1767. In Which the Highest Reproach is Undeservedly Cast upon the American Colonies.* Boston, 1767.

—— *A Complete View of Episcopacy, as Exhibited from the Fathers of the Christian Church, Until the Close of the Second Century.* Boston, 1771.

[Checkley, John]. *Choice Dialogues, Between a Godly Minister and an Honest Countryman, Concerning Election and Predestination.* [Boston, 1720].

—— *A Modest Proof of the Order and Government Settled by Christ and His Apostles in the Church. A Discourse Shewing Who is a True Pastor of the Church of Christ.* Boston, 1723.

—— [Checkley, John]. *A Defense of a Book Lately Re-Printed at Boston, Entitled, A Modest Proof, of the Order and Government Settled by Christ and His Apostles in the Church In a Letter to a Friend. In a Reply to a Book Entitled, Sober Remarks on A Modest Proof, &c. [By Edward Wigglesworth], With Strictures on John Dickinson's Defence of Presbyterian Ordination. Also Animadversions Upon [Thomas Walter's] Essay Upon the Paradox, Infallibility Many Sometimes Mistake. [And] The Ruling and Ordaining Power of Congregational Bishops or Presbyters Defended* [By Thomas Foxcroft]. Boston, 1724.

—— [John Checkley], *A Letter from the Author of the Postscript of the Defence of a Book Entitled, A Modest Proof of Church Government &c.; Jonathan Dickinson, Author of the Remarks on that Postscript.* [Boston, 1725].

—— *Short and Easy Method with the Deists: To which was added, A Discourse concerning Episcopacy; In Defence of Christianity, and the Church of England against the Deists and the Dissenters. To which is added: The Jury's Verdict; His Plea in Arrest of Judgment; and the Sentence of the Court.* London, 1730.

Chorley, E. Clowes. 'Samuel Provoost, First Bishop of New York'. *H.M.P.E.C.* 2 (1933).

Christianson, Paul. 'The Causes of the English Revolution: A Reappraisal', *Journal of British Studies.* 15 (1976).

Clark, J. C. D. *Revolution and Rebellion: State and Society in England in the Seventeenth and Eighteenth Centuries.* Cambridge, 1986.

—— *The Language of Liberty: 1660–1832.* Cambridge, 1994.

—— *English Society, 1660–1832: Religion, Ideology, and Political Politics during the Ancien Regime.* Cambridge, 2000.

Clark, Michael D. 'Jonathan Boucher: The Mirror of Reaction'. *H.L.Q.* 33 (1969).

Clarke, Samuel. *The Scripture-Doctrine of the Trinity ... Wherein all the Texts in the New Testament Relating to that Doctrine and the Passages in the Liturgy of the Church of England, Are Collected, Compared, and Explained* (London, 1712).

Cohen, Sheldon S. *Connecticut's Loyalist Gadfly: The Reverend Samuel Andrew Peters.* Hartford, 1976.

Cogliano, Francis D. *No King, No Popery: Anti-Catholicism in Revolutionary New England.* Westport, 1995.

Colburn, H. Trevor. *The Lamp of Experience: Whig History and the Intellectual Origins of the American Revolution.* Chapel Hill, 1965.

Coldham, Peter Wilson. *American Loyalist Claims.* Washington. DC, 1980.

Coleman, Kenneth. *Colonial Georgia: A History.* New York, 1976.

Collier, Jeremy. *An Ecclesiastical History of Great Britain, Chiefly of England: From the First Planting of Christianity in this Island with a Brief Account of the Affairs of Religion in Ireland.* London, 1714.

Collinson, Patrick. *The Elizabethan Puritan Movement.* London, 1967.

Colonial Records of North Carolina. Raleigh, 1886–90.

Corner, George W., ed. *The Autobiography of Benjamin Rush. His 'Travels Through Life' Together with his Commonplace Book for 1789–1813.* Princeton, 1948.

Cornwall, Robert D. 'The Search for the Primitive Church: The Uses of the Early Church Fathers in the High Anglican Tradition, 1680–1745'. *A.Epis.Hist.* 59 (1990).

Cotton, John, *The Keys of the Kingdom of Heaven, and Power there of, According to the Word of God, By that Learned and Judicious Divine, Mr. John Cotton, Teacher of the Church at Boston in New-England, Tending to Reconcile some Present Differences about Discipline* (London, 1644).

Cremin, Lawrence A. *American Education: The Colonial Experience, 1607–1783.* New York, 1970.

Cross, Alfred Lyon. *The Anglican Episcopate and the American Colonies.* Cambridge, 1902.

Cushing, Harry Alonzo. *The Writings of Samuel Adams.* II. New York, 1906.

Cuthebertson, Brian. *The First Bishop: A Biography of Charles Inglis.* Halifax, 1987.

Davidson, Philip. *Propaganda and the American Revolution, 1763–1783.* Chapel Hill, 1941.

Davies, Samuel. *Religion and Patriotism, the Constituents of a good Soldier. A Sermon preached to Capt. Overton's Independent Company of Volunteers, Raised in Hanover County, Virginia, August 17th, 1755.* Philadelphia, 1755.

Deane, Seamus, ed. 'A Catalogue of the very valuable and highly interesting united libraries of Thomas Hollis, Esq. and Thomas Brand Hollis, Esq., including likewise the Theological and Political Library of the late John Disney', *Sale Catalogues of Libraries of Eminent Persons*. London, 1973.

Dellape, Kevin J. 'Jacob Duché: Whig-Loyalist'? *Pennsylvania History*. 62 (1995).

DeMond, Robert O. *The Loyalists in North Carolina during the Revolution*. Durham, 1940.

Dexter, Franklin B., ed. *The Literary Diary of Ezra Stiles*. I. New York, 1901.

Dickinson, Jonathan. *A Defence of Presbyterian Ordination. Answer to a Pamphlet, Entitled, A Modest Proof, of the Order and Government Settled by Christ, in the Church*. Boston, 1724.

—— *The Scripture-Bishop, or the Divine Right of Presbyterian Ordination & Government Considered in a Dialogue Between Praeleticus and Eleutherius*. Boston, 1732.

—— *The Scripture-Bishop Vindicated. A Defence of the Dialogue Between Praeleticus and Eleutherius, upon the Scripture-Bishop, or the Divine Right of Presbyterian Ordination and Government. Against the Exceptions of a Pamphlet Intituled, The Scripture-Bishop Examin'd. In a Letter to a Friend*. Boston, 1733.

Dix, Morgan. *A History of the Parish of Trinity Church in the City of New York*. 4 vols. New York, 1898–1906.

[Dodwell, Henry]. *A Vindication of the Deprived Bishops, Asserting Their Spiritual Rights Against a Lay Deprivation, Against the Charge of Schism, as Managed by the Late Editors of an Anonymous Baroccian MS., etc.* London. 1692.

[Dodwell, Henry]. *A Defence of the Vindication of the Deprived Bishops In a Reply to Dr. Hody and Another Author ... By the Author of the Vindication*. London, 1695.

Doll, Peter M. *Revolution, Religion, and National Identity: Imperial Anglicanism in British North America, 1745–1795*. Madison, 2000.

Duché, Jacob. *The Life and Death of the Righteous. A Sermon Preached at Christ-Church, Philadelphia, On Sunday, February the 13th, 1763, at the Funeral of Mr. Evan Morgan*. Philadelphia, 1763.

—— *The Duty of Standing Fast in Our Spiritual and Temporal Liberties. A Sermon, Preached in Christ Church, July 4th, 1775, Before the First Battalion of the City and Liberties of Philadelphia*. London, 1775.

—— *Discourses On Various Subjects*. 2 vols. London, 1779.

Dunton, John. 'John Dunton's Journal in Massachusetts, 1686' *Mass.Hist.Soc.Coll.* Second Series. 2 (1846).

East, Robert A. *Connecticut's Loyalists*. Chester, 1974.

Ecclesiastical Records of the State of New York. Albany, 1901–16.

Eddis, William. *Letters From America*. Aubrey C. Land, ed. Cambridge, 1969.

Edelberg, Cynthia Dubin. *Jonathan Odell, Loyalist Poet of the American Revolution*. Durham, 1987.

Einstein, Lewis. *Divided Loyalties: Americans in England During the War of Independence*. London, 1933.

Eliot, Andrew. 'Remarks upon the Bishop of Oxford's Sermon'. *Mass.Hist.Soc.Coll.* Second Series. II (1814).

Emerson, Everett. *John Cotton*, Revised edition. Boston, 1990.

Evans, Margaret, ed. *Letters of Richard Radcliffe and John James of Queen's College, Oxford, 1755–1783*. Oxford, 1888.

Evanson, Philip. 'Jonathan Boucher: The Mind of an American Loyalist'. *Maryl.Hist.Mag.* 58 (1963).

Ewer, John. *Sermon Preached before the Incorporated Society for the Propagation of the Gospel in Foreign Parts, at Their Anniversary Meeting in the Parish Church of St. Mary-le-Bow, On Friday February 20, 1767*. New York, 1768.

Filmer, Robert. *Patriarcha and Other Political Works of Sir Robert Filmer.* Peter Laslett, ed. Oxford, 1949.

Fitzpatrick, John C., ed. *The Writings of George Washington.* vols. 9, 10. Washington, 1933.

Flick, Alexander C. *Loyalism in New York During the American Revolution.* New York, 1901, 1969 edition.

—— ed. *Minutes of the Albany Committee of Correspondence, 1775–1778; Minutes of the Schnectady Committee, 1775–1779.* II. Albany, 1925.

Foote, Henry Wilder. *Annals of King's Chapel, from the Puritan Age of New England to the Present Day.* 2 vols. Boston, 1882, 1896.

Ford, Worthington C., ed. 'John Wilkes and Boston'. *Mass.Hist.Soc.P.* 47 (1914).

Foster, Joseph. *Alumni Oxonienses 1500–1714.* 4 vols. Oxford, 1891–2; 1715–1886. 4 vols. London, 1887–8.

Foster, Stephen. *The Long Argument: English Puritanism and the Shaping of New England Culture, 1570–1700.* Chapel Hill, 1991.

Fowler, William M., Jr. *Samuel Adams: Radical Puritan.* New York, 1997.

Gardiner, Samuel R. *History of England from the Accession of James I to the Outbreak of the Civil War, 1603–1642.* London, 1886.

Gavin, Frank. 'The Rev. Thomas Bradbury Chandler in the Light of His (Unpublished) Diary, 1775–1785'. *C.Hist.* I (1932).

Gegenheimer, Frank. *William Smith: Educator and Churchman, 1727–1803.* Philadelphia, 1943.

Germann, William. 'The Crisis in the Early Life of General Peter Muhlenberg'. *P.M.H.B* 37 (1913).

Goldie, Mark. 'Danby, the Bishops and the Whigs', in Tim Harris, Paul Seaward, and Mark Goldie, eds. *The Politics of Religion in Restoration England.* Oxford, 1990.

Gordon, Ann D. *The College of Philadelphia, 1749–1779: Impact of an Institution.* New York, 1989.

Graham, John. *Some Remarks upon a late Pamphlet Entitled, A Letter from a Minister of the Church of England, to His dissenting Parishioners. Shewing How Far the Book is From Answering the Titles and How Remote the Matters of Fact Therein Mentioned, Are From the Truth; Together with a Brief indication of the Presbyterians From Those Reproaches Therein Cast upon Them.* [Boston], 1733.

—— *Some Remarks upon a Second Letter from the Church of England Minister, to His Dissenting Parishioners* (Boston, 1736).

Greaves, R. W. 'The Working of the Alliance, A Comment on Warburton', in G. V. Bennett and John D. Walsh, eds.*Essays in Modern English Church History in Memory of Norman Sykes.* Oxford, 1966.

Greene, Jack P., ed. 'William Knox's Explanation for the Revolution'. *W.M.Q.* Third Series 30 (1973).

Griffith, David. *Passive Obedience Considered: in a Sermon Preached at Williamsburgh, December 31st, 1775.* Williamsburgh, [1776].

Guenther, Karen. 'A Faithful Soldier of Christ': The Career of the Reverend Dr. Alexander Murray Missionary to Berks County, Pa., 1762–1778'. *H.M.P.E.C.* 55 (1986).

Gwatkin, Thomas, *A Letter to the Clergy of New York and New Jersey, occasioned by an Address to the Episcopalians of Virginia.* Williamsburg, 1772.

Hall, Michael Garibaldi. *Edward Randolph and the American Colonies, 1676–1703.* Chapel Hill, 1960.

Hambrick-Stowe, Charles E. *The Practice of Piety: Puritan Devotional Disciplines in Seventeenth-Century New England.* Chapel Hill, 1982.

Harris, George. *The Life of Lord Chancellor Hardwicke.* 3 vols. London, 1847.

Hawks, Francis L. and Perry, William Stevens. *Historical Notes and Documents.* Claremont, 1874.

—— *Collections of the Protestant Episcopal Historical Society for the Year 1851.* New York, 1851.

Headley, Joel T. *Chaplains and Clergy of the Revolution.* New York, 1864.

Heylyn, Peter. *Cyprian us Anglicus or, the History of the Life and Death of the Most Reverend and Renowned Prelate William by Divine Providence, Lord Archbishop of Canterbury.* London, 1671.

Hickes, George. *Two Treatises: one of The Christian Priesthood; the other of the Dignity of the Episcopal Order, Written ... to Obviate the Erroneous Opinions ... and False Assertions in a Late Book Entituled The Rights of the Christian Church [by M.Tindal].* London, 1707.

Hill. Christopher. *Puritanism and Revolution.* London, 1962.

—— *Society and Puritanism in Pre-Revolutionary England.* New York, 1964.

Hills, George Morgan. *History of the Church in Burlington, New Jersey.* Trenton, 1876.

Hiner, Ray Jr. 'Samuel Henley and Thomas Gwatkin: Partners in Protest'. *H.M.P.E.C.* 37 (1968).

Historic Manuscript Commission. *The Manuscripts of the Earl of Dartmouth, Historic Manuscript Commission Report. Fourteenth Report.* II. London, 1895.

Hobart, Noah Hobart. *A Serious Address to the Members of the Episcopal Separation in New-England. Occasioned by Mr. Wetmore's Vindication of the Professors of the Church of England in Connecticut.* Boston, 1743.

—— *Ministers of the Gospel Considered as Fellow Labourers; A Sermon Delivered at the Ordination of the Reverend Noah Welles at Stamford, Dec. 31, 1746.* Boston, 1747.

Hocker, Edward W. *The Fighting Parson of the American Revolution; a Biography of General Peter Muhlenberg, Lutheran Clergyman, Military Chieftan, and Political Leader.* Philadelphia, 1936.

Holmes, Abiel. *The Life of Ezra Stiles.* Boston, 1798.

Holmes, Thomas J. *Increase Mather. A Bibliography of his Works.* 2 vols. Cleveland, 1931.

Hooker, Richard. *Of the Laws of Ecclesiastical Polity. Books VI, VII, VIII.* P. G. Stanwood, ed. Cambridge, 1981.

Hopkins, Samuel. *An Enquiry Concerning the Promises of the Gospel.* Boston, 1765.

Humphrey, David C. *From King's College to Columbia, 1746–1800.* New York, 1976.

Hurd, Richard, ed. *The Works of William Warburton.* II. London, 1788–94.

Hurt, John. *The Love of Our Country. A Sermon preached before the Virginia troops in New Jersey.* Philadelphia, 1777.

Hutchinson, William T., ed. *The Papers of James Madison.* II. Chicago, 1962.

Hutton, Ronald. *The Restoration: A Political and Religious History of England and Wales, 1658–1667.* Oxford, 1985.

—— *Charles the Second, King of England, Scotland, and Ireland.* Oxford, 1991.

[Inglis, Charles]. *By an American. The True Interest of America Impartially Stated, in Certain Strictures on a Pamphlet Entitled Common Sense.* Philadelphia, 1776.

—— *Letters of Papinian: in Which the Conduct, present State and Prospects, of the American Congress, are Examined.* New York, 1779; London, 1779.

—— *The Duty of Honoring the King, Explained and Recommended: in a Sermon Preached in St. George's and St. Paul's Chapels, New York, on Sunday, January 30, 1780, Being the Anniversary of King Charles I.* New York, 1780.

Isaac, Rhys. *The Transformation of Virginia, 1740–1790.* Chapel Hill, 1982.

Jefferson, Thomas. *A Summary of the Rights of British Americans. Set Forth in Some Resolutions Intended for the Inspection of the Present Delegates of the People of Virginia Now in Convention.* Williamsburgh, 1774.

Johnson, Samuel. *A Letter from A Minister of the Church of England to His Dissenting Parishioners. Containing a Brief Answer to the Most Material Objections Against the Establish'd Church That Are to be Found in De Laune's Plea, The Answer to the Bishop of Derry, The Plain Reasons for Separating, &c. and Together with Plain Reasons for Conformity to the Church of England.* New York, 1733.

—— *A Second Letter from a Minister of the Church of England to His Dissenting Parishioners, In Answer to Some Remarks made on the Former, by one J. G.* Boston, 1734.

—— *A Third Letter from a Minister of the Church of England to the Dissenters, Containing Some Observations on Mr. J. G'.s Remarks on the Second.* Boston, 1737.

Jones, Thomas F. *A Pair of Lawn Sleeves: A Biography of William Smith, 1727–1803.* Philadelphia, 1972.

Journal of the Commissioners for Trade and Plantations, April 1704–May 1782. 14 vols. London, 1920–38.

Katz, Stanley Nider. *Newcastle's New York: Anglo American Politics, 1732–1753* Cambridge, 1968.

Keeble, N. H. *Richard Baxter: Puritan Man of Letters.* Oxford, 1982.

Keith, George. *The Doctrine of the Holy Apostles & Prophets the Foundation of the Church of Christ, As it was Delivered in Sermon at Her Majesties Chappel, at Boston in New-England, the 14th of June 1702.* Boston, 1702.

—— *A Reply to Mr. Increase Mather's Printed Remarks on a Sermon Preached by G. K. at Her Majesty's Chappel in Boston, the 14th of June, 1702, In Vindication of the Six Good Rules in Divinity There Delivered. Which He hath Attempted (though Very Feebly and Unsuccessfully) to Refute.* New York, 1703.

—— *A Journal of Travels from New Hampshire to Caratuck, on the Continent of North America.* London, 1706.

Kirby, Ethyn Williams. *George Keith (1638–1716).* New York, 1942.

Klein, Milton, ed. *The Independent Reflector or Weekly Essays on Sundry Important Subjects More Particularly adapted to the Province of New York.* Cambridge, 1963.

—— *The American Whig. William Livingston of New York.* New York, 1990.

Klingberg, Frank J. *Anglican Humanitarianism in Colonial New York.* Philadelphia, 1940.

—— *Carolina Chronicle: The Papers of Commissary Gideon Johnston, 1707–1716.* Berkeley, 1946.

Knollenberg, Bernhard. *Origin of the American Revolution: 1759–1766.* New York, 1960.

—— 'Thomas Hollis and Jonathan Mayhew: their Correspondence, 1759–1766'. *Mass.Hist.Soc.P.* 69 (1956).

Knox, R. Buick. *James Ussher, Archbishop of Armagh.* Cardiff, 1967.

Knox, William. *The Claims of the Colonies to an Exemption from Internal Taxes Imposed by Authority of Parliament, Examined: In a Letter from a Gentleman in London, to his Friend in America.* London, 1765.

Labaree, Leonard Woods. *Royal Government in America: A Study of the British Colonial System before 1783.* New Haven, 1930.

—— *Royal Instructions to Colonial Governors, 1671–1776.* 2 vols. New York, 1935.

—— *Conservatism in Early American History.* New York, 1948.

Lake, Peter. *Moderate Puritans and the Elizabethan Church.* Cambridge, 1982.

—— *Anglicans and Puritans? Presbyterianism and English Conformist Thought from Whitgift to Hooker.* London, 1988.

Langford, Paul. *The First Rockingham Administration, 1765–1766.* Oxford, 1973.

Laslett, Peter. 'Sir Robert Filmer: The Man versus the Whig Myth'. *W.M.Q.* Third Series 5 (1948).

Launitz-Schurer, Leopold, Jr. 'A Loyalist Clergyman's Response to the Imperial Crisis in the American Colonies: A Note on Samuel Seabury's Letters of a Westchester Farmer'. *H.M.P.E.C.* 44 (1975).

Leaming, Jeremiah. *A Defence of the Episcopal Government of the Church: Containing Remarks On two late, noted Sermons on Presbyterian Ordination.* New York, 1766.

Leslie, Charles. *Case of the Regale and of the Pontificate, Stated in a Conference Concerning the Independency of the Church upon any Power on Earth in the Exercise of Her Purely Spiritual Power and Authority.* 1700.

—— *The Religion of Jesus Christ the Only True Religion, or a Short and Easie Method with the Deists, Wherein the Certainty of the Christian Religion is Demonstrated by Infallible Proof from Four Rules, Which are Incompatible to any Imposture That Ever Yet Has Been, or That Can Possibly Be. In a Letter to a Friend.* Boston, 1719.

Leventhal, Herbert, and Mooney, James E. 'A Bibliography of Loyalist Source Material in the United States'. *P.A.A.S.* 85 (1975); 90 (1980).

Livingston, William. *A Letter to the Right Reverend Father in God, John, Lord Bishop of Landaff; Occasioned by Some Passages in his Lordship's Sermon on the 20th of February, 1767, in Which the American Colonies are Loaded with Great and Undeserved Reproach.* New York, 1768.

Lohrenz, Otto. 'The Right Reverend William Harrison of Revolutionary Virginia, First "Lord Archbishop of America"'. *H.M.P.E.C.* (1984).

—— 'The Reverend Thomas Feilde, Loyalist Acting Rector of St. Andrews: An Identification'. *Staten Island Historian*, new ser., 2 (1984).

—— 'The Discord of Political and Personal Loyalties: The Experiences of the Reverend William Andrews of Revolutionary Virginia'. *Southern Studies* 24 (1985).

—— 'The Reverend William Davis of Colonial Virginia: Was He Immoral or Conscientious'? *Northern Neck of Virginia Historical Magazine* 36 (1986).

—— 'The Reverend John Hamilton Rowland of Revolutionary America and Early Shelburne'. *Nova Scotia Historical Review* 7 (1987).

—— 'Clergyman and Gentleman: Archibald Campbell of Westmoreland County, 1741–1774'. *Northern Neck of Virginia Historical Magazine* 39 (1989).

—— 'Parson and Patrons: The Clerical Career of Thomas Johnston of Maryland and Virginia, 1750–1790'. *A.Epis.Hist.* 58 (1989).

—— 'The Reverend Ichabod Camp: First American to Preach on the Ohio and Mississippi Rivers'. *The Filson Club History Quarterly* 65 (1991).

—— 'An Analysis of the Life and Career of the Reverend David Currie, Lancaster County, Virginia, 1743–1791'. *A.Epis.Hist.* 61 (1992).

—— 'The Reverend Alexander White of Colonial Virginia: His Career and Status'. *Fides et Historia* 24 (1992).

—— 'The Reverend Thomas Davis: President of the Sons of Liberty, Norfolk, Virginia, 1766'. *The Valley Forge Journal* 6 (1992).

—— 'Forgotten Clerical Loyalist: Alexander Cruden of Revolutionary Virginia'. *The Loyalist Gazette* 32 (1994).

—— 'A Mental Casualty of the American Revolution: The Reverend James Herdman of Virginia'. *The Loyalist Gazette* 33 (1995).

—— 'Parson and Local Man of Affairs: George Gurley of Southampton County, Virginia'. *The Southside Virginian* 12 (1994), 13 (1995).

—— 'The Reverend Thomas Smith of Revolutionary Virginia: A Case Study in Social Rank'. *Journal of Religious Studies* 19 (1995).

—— 'The Reverend John Wingate: An Economic Casualty of Revolutionary Virginia'. *Journal of American Culture* 18 (1995).

—— 'William McKay, Rector of North Farnham Parish in Richmond County, 1744–1775'. *Northern Neck of Virginia Historical Magazine* 46 (1996).

—— 'The Revolutionary Adventures of a Loyalist Anglican Minister: William Duncan of Isle of Wight County, Virginia'. *The Loyalist Gazette* 34 (1996).

—— 'Unobtrusive Rector of Hamilton Parish: James Craig of Eighteenth-Century Virginia'. *Fides et Historia* 28 (1996).

—— 'The Advantage of Rank and Status; Thomas Price, a Loyalist Parson of Revolutionary Virginia'. *The Historian* 60 (1998).

—— 'The Reverend John Brunskill of Revolutionary Amelia County, Virginia: A Revisionist Biographical Sketch'. *Southern Studies*, new ser., 5 (1994).

—— 'Anglican Parson, Alleged Sodomite, and Loyalist Perjurer: John Milner of Colonial and Revolutionary New York and Virginia'. *The Social Science Journal* 36 (1999).

—— 'The Life, Career, and Political Loyalties of the Reverend Thomas Hall of Revolutionary Virginia and Leghorn, Italy'. *Fides et Historia* 31 (1999).

—— 'Ardent Military Chaplain: Fitzhugh McKay of Revolutionary Virginia'. *Daughters of the American Revolution Magazine* 133 (1999).

—— 'Parson and Bigamist: Thomas Wilkinson of Colonial and Revolutionary Virginia'. *Southern Studies*, new ser., 7 (1996).

—— 'Clergyman and Committeeman: Thomas Lundie of St. Andrew's Parish, Brunswick County, Virginia'. *The Kentucky Review* 15 (2000).

—— 'The Troubled Clerical Career of Andrew Morton of Colonial New Jersey, North Carolina, and Virginia'. *Lamar Journal of the Humanities* 25 (2000).

—— 'A Neglected Scottish Clergyman: Arthur Hamilton of Revolutionary Virginia and Maryland'. *Scottish Tradition* 25 (2000).

—— 'Clergyman, Teacher, and Indicted Loyalist: John Bruce of Norfolk and Princess Anne Counties, Virginia'. *The Loyalist Gazette* 41 (2003).

—— 'Parson and Vagrant: The Life and Career of Lewis Gwilliam of Revolutionary Pittsylvania County, Virginia'. *Lamar Journal of the Humanities* 27 (2002).

—— 'The Reverend Abner Waugh: The "Best Dancer of the Minuet in the State of Virginia"'. *The Kentucky Review* 15 (2003): 28–40.

—— 'The Reverend William Coutts of Revolutionary Prince George and Henrico Counties, Virginia: Was He a Tory or a Whig'? *The Early America Review* 5 (2004, online).

—— 'Jacob Townshend: An Enigmatic Loyalist of Revolutionary Hampshire'. *The Appalachian Quarterly* (2004).

—— 'Thomas Jefferson's Unlucky Loyalist Friend: The Reverend James Ogilvie'. *The Loyalist Gazette* 42 (2004).

—— 'Thomas Davis, Jr.: Officiating Clergyman at the Funeral and Burial of President George Washington'. *A.Epis.Hist.* 73 (2004).

—— 'The Economic and Social Effects of the American Revolution on the Reverend William Vere of Virginia's Eastern Shore', *Southern Studies*, new ser. 11 (2004).

—— 'Highly Respected Anglican Clergymen: John Cameron of Virginia, 1770–1815', *A.Epis.Hist.* 74 (2005).

—— 'Parson, Naturalist, and Loyalist: Thomas Fielde of England and Revolutionary Virginia and New York', *Southern Studies*, new ser., 12 (2005).

Lovejoy, Davis S. *The Glorious Revolution in America*. New York, 1972.

Loveland, Clara O. *The Critical Years. The Reconstitution of the Anglican Church in the United States of America: 1780–1789*. Greenwich, 1956.

Lustig, Maay Lou. *Robert Hunter, 1666–1734: Augustan Statesman*. Syracuse, 1983.

Lydekker, John Wolfe. *The Life and Letters of Charles Inglis. His Ministry in America and Consecration as First Colonial Bishop, from 1759 to 1787*. London, 1936.

Mackesy, Piers. *The War for America, 1775–1783*. Lincoln, NE, 1993.

MacLean, Horace V. 'The Reverend Ranna Cossit'. *Journal of the Canadian Church Historical Society* 5 (1963).

Maier, Pauline. *From Resistance to Revolution: Colonial Radicals and the Development of American Opposition to Britain, 1765–1776*. New York, 1974.

—— 'The Pope at Harvard: The Dudleian Lectures, Anti-Catholicism, and the Politics of Protestantism', *Mass.Hist.Soc.P.* XCVII (1985).

Mampoteng, Charles. 'The New England Clergy in the American Revolution'. *H.M.P.E.C.* 9 (1940).

Manning, James. *A Sketch of the Life and Writings of the Rev. Micaiah Towgood*. Exeter, 1792.

Manross, William Wilson. *A History of the American Episcopal Church*. Third edition revised. New York, 1959.

Maseres, Frances, *Occasional Essays on Various Subjects, Chiefly Political and Historical: Extracted Partly from The Publick Newspapers*. London, 1809.

Mather Cotton. *The Serviceable Man. A Discourse Made Unto the General Court of the Massachusetts Colony, New England, At the Anniversary Election*. Boston, 1690.

—— [Mather, Cotton]. *Diary of Cotton Mather. Mass.Hist.Soc.Coll.* Seventh series. 7. Boston, 1911.

Mather, Increase. *A Brief Discourse Concerning the Unlawfullness of the Common Prayer Worship. And of Laying the Hand on and Kissing the Booke in Swearing*. [Cambridge, 1686].

—— *A Narrative of the Miseries of New-England, by Reason of an Arbitrary Government Erected there, under Sir Edmund Andros* (Boston, 1688).

—— *A Testimony Against Several Prophane and Superstitious Customs Now Practiced by some in New-England, The Evil Whereof is Evinced from the Holy Scriptures, and from the Writings both of Ancient and Modern Divines*. London, 1687; Boston, 1688.

—— *Some Remarks on a Late Sermon, Preached at Boston in New England, by George Keith M. A. Shewing That his Pretended Good Rules in Divinity, Are Not Built on the Foundation of the Apostles & Prophets*. Boston, 1702.

—— *Some Remarks, on a Pretended Answer, to a Discourse Concerning the Common-Prayer Worship. With an Exhortation to the Churches in New-England, to Hold Fast the Profession of Their Faith without Wavering*. Boston, 1713.

Mathews, Alice Elaine. *Society in Revolutionary North Carolina*. Raleigh, 1976.

Mayhew, Jonathan. *A Discourse on Rev. XV 3d, 4th. Occasioned by the Earthquakes in November 1755*. Boston, 1755.

—— *A Defense of the Observation on the Charter and Conduct of the Society for the Propagation of the Gospel in Foreign Parts Against an Anonymous Pamphlet Falsely Intitled A Candid Examination of Dr. Mayhew's Observations, &c., and also Against the Letter to a Friend Annexed Thereto, said to Contain a Short Vindication of Said Society. By One of its Members*. Boston, 1763.

—— *Observations on the Charter and Conduct of the Society for the Propagation of the Gospel in Foreign Parts; Designed to Shew Their Non-Conformity to Each Other. WithRemarks on the Mistakes of East Apthorp, M. A., Missionary at Cambridge, in Quoting and Representing the Sense of the Said Charter, &c. As also Various Incidental Reflections Relative to the Church of England, and the State of Religion in North-America, Particularly in New England*. Boston, 1763.

—— *Remarks on an Anonymous Tract, Entitled An Answer to Dr. Mayhew's Observations on the Charter and Conduct of the Society for the Propagation of the Gospel in Foreign Parts. Being a Second Defense of the said Observations*. Boston, 1764, London, 1765.

Meade, William. *Old Churches, Ministers and Families of Virginia*. 2 vols. Philadelphia, 1857.

Middlekauff, Robert. *The Mathers. Three Generations of Puritan Intellectuals, 1596–1728*. New York, 1971.

Miller, John. New York *Considered and Improved, 1695*. New York, 1970 edition.

Miller, Perry. *The New England Mind from Colony to Province*. Cambridge, 1953.

Miller, Rodney K. Miller. 'The Political Ideology of the Anglican Clergy'. *H.M.P.E.C.* 45 (1976).

Mills, Frederick V. Sr. 'The Internal Anglican Controversy Over an American Episcopate, 1763—1775', *H.M.P.E.C.* 44 (1975).

—— *Bishops by Ballot: An Eighteenth-Century Ecclesiastical Revolution*. New York, 1978.

Mills, W. Jay, ed. *Glimpses of Colonial Society and the Life at Princeton College, 1766–1773, by One of the Class of 1763*. Philadelphia, 1903.

Morgan. Edmund S. *The Gentle Puritan, A Life of Ezra Stiles, 1727–1795*. New Haven, 1962.

—— *Inventing the People. The Rise of Popular Sovereignty in England and America*. New York, 1988.

Morgan. Edmund S. and Helen M. Morgan. *The Stamp Act Crisis: Prologue to Revolution*. Chapel Hill, 1953.

Morgan, Robert. 'Ranna Cossit', in Phyllis Blakely and John N. Grant, eds. *Eleven Exiles, Accounts of Loyalists of the American Revolution*. Toronto, 1982.

Morrill, J. S. 'The Church in England, 1642-9', in John Morrill, ed. *Reactions to the English Civil War, 1642–1649*. London, 1982.

—— 'The Attack on the Church of England in the Long Parliament, 1640–1642', in Dereck Beales and Geoffrey Best, eds. *History, Society and the Churches: Essays in Honor of Owen Chadwick*. Cambridge, 1985.

Morse, Jedidiah, *Annals of the American Revolution: or a Record of the Causes and Events which Produced and Terminated in the Establishment and Independence of the American Republic*. Hartford, 1824, 1968 edition.

Muhlenberg, John Peter Gabriel. 'Orderly Book of General John Peter Gabriel Muhlenberg, March 26, - December 20, 1777'. *P.M.H.B.* 33 (1909).

Muhlenberg, Henry Augustus. *The Life of Major General Peter Muhlenberg of the Revolutionary Army*. Philadelphia, 1849.

Murdock, Kenneth B. *Increase Mather. The Foremost American Puritan*. Cambridge, 1925.

—— *Literature and Theology in Colonial New England*. Cambridge, 1939.

Neill, Edward Duffield. 'Rev. Jacob Duché, the First Chaplain of Congress'. *P.M.H.B.* 2 (1878).

Nelson, John K. *A Blessed Company: Parishes, Parsons and Parishioners in Anglican Virginia, 1690–1776*. Chapel Hill, 2001.

Nelson, William. *The Controversy over the Proposition for An American Episcopate, 1767–1774. A Bibliography of the Subject*. Paterson, NJ, 1909.

Nelson, William H. *The American Tory*. New York, 1961.

Nobakken, Elizabeth I., ed. *The Centinal: Warnings of a Revolution*. Newark, DE, 1980.

O'Callaghan, E. B., ed. *Documents Relative to the Colonial History of the State of New York*. Vol. VIII. Albany, 1857.

Oliver, Andrew and James Bishop Peabody, eds. *The Records of Trinity Church, Boston, 1728–1830*. Boston, 1980.

Paine, Thomas. *Common Sense; Addressed to the Inhabitants of America*. Third edition. London, 1776.

Palmer, Gregory. *Biographical Sketches of Loyalists of the American Revolution*. Westport, 1984.

Parker, Mattie Erma Edwards. ed. *North Carolina Charters and Constitutions, 1578–1698*. Raleigh, 1963.

Patterson, W. B. *King James VI and I and the Reunion of Christendom*. Cambridge, 1997.

Pearson, A.F. Scott. *Thomas Cartwright and Elizabethan Puritanism, 1535–1603*. Gloucester, 1966 edition.

Perry, William S., ed. *Journals of General Conventions of the Protestant Episcopal Church in the United States, 1785–1835*. I. Claremont, 1874.

—— *The History of the American Episcopal Church 1587–1883*. 2 vols. Boston, 1885.

—— *Historical Collections Relating to the American Colonial Church*. 5 vols. Hartford, 1871–8.

—— *The Alleged 'Toryism' of the Clergy of the United States at the Breaking out of the War of the Revolution*. N.p., 1895.

Phillimore, Robert. *The Ecclesiastical Law of the Church of England London*. 1873.

Pilcher, George W. 'Virginia Newspapers and the Dispute Over the Proposed Colonial Episcopate, 1771–1772'. *The Historian*. XXIII (1960).

—— 'The Pamphlet War on the Proposed Virginia Anglican Episcopate, 1767–1775'. *H.M.P.E.C.* 30 (1961).

Porteus, Beilby. *The Works of Thomas Secker, LL. D., Late Lord Archbishop of Canterbury, to which is prefixed a Review of His Grace's Life and Character*. 6 vols. London, 1811.

Potter, John. *A Discourse on Church Government, Wherein the Rights of the Church and the Supremacy of Christian Princes Are Vindicated and Adjusted.* London, 1707.

Powell, William S. *North Carolina through Four Centuries.* Chapel Hill, 1989.

Proceedings and Acts of the General Assembly of Maryland. Baltimore, 1894–1904.

Prynne, William. *Sixteen Quaeres Proposed to our Lord Prelates.* Amsterdam, 1637.

Prynne, William and Bastwick, John. *A New Discovery of the Prelates Tyranny, in Their Late Prosecutions of Mr. W. Pryn.* No place, 1641.

Ranlet, Philip. *The New York Loyalists.* Knoxville, 1986.

Reeves, Thomas C. 'John Checkley and the Emergence of the Episcopal Church in New England'. *H.M.P.E.C.* 34 (1965).

Rhoden, Nancy L. *Revolutionary Anglicanism: The Colonial Church of England Clergy during the American Revolution* (Basingstoke, 1999).

Rightmyer, Nelson Waite. *Maryland's Established Church.* Baltimore, 1956.

—— 'The Holy Orders of Peter Muhlenberg'. *H.M.P.E.C.* 30 (1961).

Rivers, Isabel. *Reason, Grace, and Sentiment: A Study of the Language of Religion and Ethics in England, 1660–1780.* Cambridge, 1991.

Robbins, Caroline. 'The Strenuous Whig, Thomas Hollis of Lincoln's Inn'. *W.M.Q.* Third Series VII (1950).

—— *The Eighteenth-Century Commonwealthman.* Cambridge, 1959.

Roche, John F. *The Colonial Colleges in the War for American Independence.* Millwood, NY, 1986.

Royster, Charles. *A Revolutionary People at War: The Continental Army and American Character.* Chapel Hill, 1979.

Rudé, George. *Wilkes and Liberty: A Social Study of 1763 to 1774.* Oxford, 1962.

Sabine, Lorenzo. *Biographical Sketches of Loyalists of the American Revolution.* 2 vols. Boston, 1864.

Sainsbury, John. *Dissaffected Patriots: London Supporter of Revolutionary America, 1769–1782.* Montreal, 1987.

Sayre, John. *From the New-York Journal, Mr.Holt.* Philadelphia, 1776?

Schlesinger, Arthur M. *Prelude to Independence: The Newspaper War on Britain, 1764–1776.* New York, 1957.

Schneider, Herbert and Carol, eds. *Samuel Johnson President of King's College: His Career and Writings.* 4 vols. New York, 1929.

Seabury, Samuel. *A Modest Reply to a Letter from a Gentleman to his Friend in Dutchess County. Lately published by an Anonymous Writer.* New York, 1759.

—— [Seabury, Samuel], *Free Thoughts on the Proceedings of the Continental Congress, Held at Philadelphia Sept. 5, 1774, Wherein Their Errors are Exhibited, Their Reasoning Confuted and the Fatal Tendency of Their Non-Importation, Non-Exportation, and Non-Consumption Measures, are Laid Open to the Plainest Understanding; and the Only Means Pointed Out for Preserving and Securing our Present Happy Constitution in A Letter to the Farmers, and other Inhabitants of North America in General, and to Those of the Province of New York in Particular.* New York, 1774.

—— [Seabury, Samuel]. *By A. W. Farmer. The Congress Canvassed: or, an Examination into the Conduct of the Delegates at Their Grand Convention Held in Philadelphia, September 1, 1774. Addressed to the Merchants of New York.* New York, 1774; London, 1775.

——[Seabury, Samuel]. *A View of the Controversy Between Great Britain and Her Colonies: Including a Mode of Determining Their Present Disputes, Finally and*

Effectually; and of Preventing All Future Contentions. In a Letter to the Author a Full Vindication of the Measures of the Congress, from the Calumnies of Their Enemies. New York, 1774; London, 1775.

—— [Seabury, Samuel]. *An Alarm to the Legislature of the Province of New York, Occasioned By Present Political Disturbances, in North America, Addressed to the Honourable Representatives in General Assembly Convened.* New York, 1775; London, 1775.

—— *St. Peter's Exhortation to Fear God and Honor the King, Explained and Inculcated: In a Discourse Addressed to His Majesty's Provincial Troops, in Camp at King's Bridge, On Sunday the 28th September 1777.* New York, 1777.

Secker, Thomas. *An Answer to Dr. Mayhew's Observations on the Charter and Conduct of the Society for the Propagation of the Gospel in Foreign Parts.* London, 1764; Boston, 1764.

—— *Letter to the Right Honourable Horatio Walpole, Esq.; Written January 9, 1750/1, by the Right Reverend Thomas Secker ... Concerning Bishops in America.* London, 1769.

Seibert, Frederick Seaton. *Freedom of the Press in England, 1476–1776.* Urbana, IL, 1952.

Shaw, Peter. *American Patriots and the Rituals of Revolution.* Cambridge, 1981.

Shipton, Clifford K. *Sibley's Harvard Graduates, Biographical Sketches of those who attended Harvard College.* Vols. 4–17. Cambridge, 1933–1975.

Sibley, John Langdon. *Biographical Sketches of Graduates of Harvard University, in Cambridge, Massachusetts.* 3 vols. Cambridge, 1873–85.

Silliman, Charles A. *The Episcopal Church in Delaware, 1785–1954.* Wilmington, 1982.

Silverman, Kenneth. *Selected Letters of Cotton Mather.* Baton Rouge, 1971.

—— *The Life and Times of Cotton Mather.* New York, 1984.

Slafter, Edmund F. *John Checkley, or the Evolution of Religious Tolerance in Massachusetts Bay, 1719–1774.* 2 vols. Boston, 1897.

Smith, Horace W. *Life and Correspondence of William Smith.* I. Philadelphia, 1880.

Smith, Page. *John Adams.* I. New York, 1962.

[William Smith], *Plain Truth; Addressed to the Inhabitants of America, Containing Remarks on a Late Pamphlet, Entitled Common Sense. By Candidus.* Philadelphia, 1776; London, 1776; Dublin, 1776.

—— *A Sermon on the Present Situation of American Affairs, Preached in Christ Church, June 23, 1775. At the request of the Officers of the Third Battalion of the City of Philadelphia, and District of Southwark.* Philadelphia, 1775; Wilmington, 1775; London, 1775; Bristol, 1775; Belfast, 1775; Dublin, 1775.

—— *An Oration in Memory of General Montgomery, and of the Officers and Soldiers, who fell with him, December 31, 1775, Before Quebec: Drawn up and delivered February 19, 1776, at the desire of the Honorable Continental Congress.* 2nd ed. London, 1776.

Sosin, Jack M. 'The Proposal in the Pre-Revolutionary Decade for Establishing Bishops in the Colonies'. *J.Eccl.H.* 13 (1962).

—— *Agents and Merchants: British Colonial Policy and the Origins of the American Revolution, 1763–1775.* Lincoln, NE, 1965.

Sprague, William B. *Annals of the American Pulpit; or Commemorative Notices of Distinguished American Clergymen of Various Denominations, from the Early Settlement of the Country to the Close of the Year Eighteen Hundred and Fifty-Five.* V. New York, 1859.

Spurr, John. *The Restoration of the Church of England, 1646–1689.* New Haven, 1991.

Steiner, Bruce E. *Samuel Seabury, 1729–1796: A Study in the High Church Tradition.* Athens, 1971.

—— *Connecticut Anglicans in the Revolutionary Era: A Study in Communal Tensions.* Hartford, 1978.

Stevens, B. F. *Facsimile of Manuscripts in European Archives Relating to America, 1773–1783.* Vol. 24, Nos. 2045, 2067, 2075. London, 1895.

Stiles, Ezra Stiles. *A Discourse on the Christian Union; the Substance of Which was Delivered before the Reverend Convention of the Congregational Clergy in the Colony of Rhode Island, Assembled at Bristol, April 23, 1760.* Boston, 1761.

Stowe, Walter H. ed. 'The Clergy of the Episcopal Church in 1785'. *H.M.P.E.C.* 20 (1951).

—— 'Autobiography of Bishop William White'. *H.M.P.E.C.* 22 (1953).

Sweet, William W. 'The Role of the Anglicans in the American Revolution'. *H.L.Q.* XI (1947).

—— *Religion in Colonial America.* New York, 1943.

Sydnor, William. 'Doctor Griffith of Virginia: Emergence of a Church Leader, March 1779–June 3, 1786'. *H.M.P.E.C.* 45 (1976).

—— 'Doctor Griffith of Virginia: The Breaking of a Church Leader, September 1786–August 3, 1789'. *H.M.P.E.C.* 45 (1976).

—— David Griffith – Chaplain, Surgeon, Patriot'. *H.M.P.E.C.* 44 (1975).

Sykes, Norman. *Edmund Gibson: Bishop of London, 1669–1748. A Study in Politics and Religion in the Eighteenth Century.* Oxford, 1926.

—— *Church and State in England in the XVIIIth Century.* Cambridge, 1934.

—— *From Sheldon to Secker: aspects of English Church History 1660–1768.* Cambridge, 1959.

Tatum, Edward H., Jr., ed. *The American Journal of Ambrose Serle, Secretary to Lord Howe, 1776–1778.* San Marino, 1940.

Taylor, Robert J. *The Papers of John Adams.* I. Cambridge, 1977.

Taylor, Stephen. 'William Warburton and the Alliance of Church and State'. *J.Eccl.Hist.* 43 (1992).

—— 'Whigs, Bishops and America: The Politics of Church Reform in Mid-Eighteenth-Century England'. *The Historical Journal* 36 (1993).

Thomas, Peter D. G. *British Politics and the Stamp Act Crisis: The first phase of the American Revolution, 1763–1767.* Oxford, 1975.

—— *John Wilkes: A Friend to Liberty.* Oxford, 1996.

Tiedmann, Joseph S., Presbyterianism and the American Revolution in the Middle Colonies, *C.Hist.,* 74 (2005).

Towgood, Michaiah. *The Dissenting Gentleman's Answer to the Reverend Mr. White's Three Letters; in Which Separation from the Establishment is Fully Justified; the Charge of Schism is Refuted and Retorted; and the Church of England and the Church of Jesus Christ are ... Compared, and Found to be Constitutions of a Quite Different Nature.* New York, Boston, 1748.

Trevor-Roper, Hugh R. *Archbishop Laud, 1573–1645.* Second edition. Hamden, CN, 1962.

Trott, Nicholas, *The Laws of the British Plantations in America, Relating to the Church and Clergy, Religion and Learning.* London, 1721.

Trinterud, Leonard J. *The Forming of an American Tradition.* Philadelphia, 1949.

Tucker, Josiah. *Four Tracts together with Two Sermons on Political and Commercial Subjects.* Gloucester, 1774.

Turner, Charles H. B. *Some Records of Sussex County Delaware*. Philadelphia, 1909.

Tuttle, Julius Herbert. 'The Libraries of the Mathers'. *P.A.A.S.* 20 (1911).

Tyacke, Nicholas. 'Puritanism, Arminianism and Counter-Revolution', in Conrad Russell, ed., *The Origins of the English Civil War*. London, 1973.

Tyler, Moses Coit. *The Literary History of the American Revolution, 1763–1783*. 2 vols. New York, 1897.

Updike, Wilkins. *A History of the Episcopal Church in Narragansett, Rhode Island, Including a History of Other Episcopal Churches in the State*. Second edition. Daniel Goodwin, ed. Boston, 1907.

Van Tyne, Claude Halstead. *The Loyalists in the American Revolution*. New York, 1902.

——— *The Causes of the War of Independence*. Boston, 1922.

Villers, David H. '"King Mob" and the Rule of Law: Revolutionary Justice and the Suppression of Localism in Connecticut, 1774–1783', in Robert M. Calhoon, M. Timothy M. Barnes, and George A. Rawlyk, eds. *Loyalists and Community in North America*. Westport, 1994.

Vivian, Jean H. 'The Reverend Isaac Campbell: An Anti-Lockean Whig'. *H.M.P.E.C.* 39 (1970).

Voorst, Carol van. *The Anglican Clergy in Maryland, 1692–1776*. New York, 1989.

Wade, Mason. 'Odyssey of a Loyalist Rector'. *Vermont History* 48 (1980).

Wallace, David Duncan. *South Carolina, A Short History, 1520–1948*. Columbia, SC, 1951.

Warburton, William. *Alliance of Church and State*. London, 1736.

Warden, G. B. *Boston, 1689–1776*. Boston, 1970.

Weaver, Glenn. 'Anglican-Congregational Tensions in Pre-Revolutionary Connecticut'. *H.M.P.E.C.* 26 (1957).

Weeks, Joshua. 'Journal of Rev. Joshua Weeks, Loyalist Rector of St. Michael's Church, Marblehead, 1778–1779'. *Essex Institute of Salem, Historical Collections*. LII (1916).

Weis, Frederick Lewis. *The Colonial Churches and the Colonial Clergy of the Middle and Southern Colonies, 1607–1776*. Lancaster, 1938.

Welles, Noah. *The Real Advantages Which Ministers and People May Enjoy Especially in the Colonies by Conforming to the Church of England; Faithfully Considered, and Impartially Represented in a Letter to a Young Gentleman*. [New Haven], 1762.

——— *The Divine Right of Presbyterian Ordination asserted, and the Ministerial Authority Claimed and Exercised in the Established Churches of New England, Vindicated and Proved: In a Discourse Delivered at Stanford [i.e., Stamford], Lord's Day, April 10, 1763*. New York, 1763.

Wertenbaker, Thomas J. *The Golden Age of Colonial Culture*. New York, 1949.

Weston, Edward. *The Englishman Directed in the Choice of his Religion, Reprinted for the Use of English Americans, with a Prefatory Address Vindicating the King's Supremacy and Authority of Parliament, in Matters of Religion, and Thereby Demolishing All the Pleas of Dissenters for Separation, according to the Concessions of the Dissenting Gentleman's Answer to the Rev. Mr. White's Letters. Pages 3, and 53. Being Also a Justification of the Church of England Against the Misrepresentation of that Answer*. Boston, 1748.

Wetmore, James. *Eleutherius Enervatus or An Answer to a Pamphlet, Intituled, the Divine Right of Presbyterian Ordination, &c. Argued. Done by Way of Dialogue between Eusebius and Eletherius, Together with Two Letters upon this Subject, some Time agoe Sent to the Supposed Author of That Pamphlet*. New York, 1733.

—— *A Vindication of the Professors of the Church of England in Connecticut Against the Invectives Contained in a Sermon Preached at Stanford by Mr. Noah Hobart, Dec. 31, 1746, in a Letter to a Friend*. Boston, 1747.

White, Gavin. 'The Consecration of Bishop Seabury'. *The Scottish Historical Review* 63 (1984).

Whitehill, Walter Muir. *Boston: A Topographical History*. Cambridge, 1963.

Whiteman, Anne. 'The Re-Establishment of the Church of England, 1660–1663'. *Transactions of the Royal Historical Society*. Fifth Series. 5 (1955).

—— 'The Restoration of the Church of England', in Geoffrey F. Nuttal and Owen Chadwick, eds. *From Uniformity to Unity, 1662–1962*. London, 1962.

—— *The Compton Census of 1676: A Critical Edition*, Oxford, 1986.

Whitmore, William Henry, ed. *The Andros Tracts. The Prince Society*. II Boston, 1870.

Wickwire, Franklin B. *British Subministers and Colonial America*. Princeton, 1966.

Wigglesworth, Edward. *Sober Remarks on a Book Lately Reprinted at Boston, Entituled, A Modest Proof of the Order & Government Settled by Christ and His Apostles in the Church. In a Letter to a Friend*. Boston, 1724.

Wilderson, Paul W. *Governor John Wentworth & the American Revolution: The English Connection*. Hanover, 1994.

Willcox, William B., ed. *The Papers of Benjamin Franklin*. Vol. 21, New Haven, 1978.

Williams, John. *A Brief Discourse Concerning the Lawfulness of Worshipping God by the Common Prayer. Being in Answer To a Book. Entituled, A Brief Discourse Concerning the Unlawfulness of the Common-Prayer Worship. Lately Printed in New-England, Let all Things Be Done Decently, and in Order, I. Cor. 14. 40*. London, 1693.

Williamson, Audrey. *Wilkes: 'A Friend of Liberty'*. London, 1974.

Wilson, Bird. *Memoir of the Life of the Right Reverend William White*. Philadelphia, 1839.

Wood, Gordon S. *The Creation of the American Republic, 1776–1787*. New York, 1969.

—— *The Radicalism of the American Revolution*. New York, 1992.

Woolston, Thomas. *A Discourse on the Miracles of Our Saviour, in View of the Present Controversy Between Infidels and Apostates*. London, 1727.

Woolverton, John Frederick. *Colonial Anglicanism in North America*. Detroit, 1984.

Young, B. W. *Religion and the Enlightenment in Eighteenth-Century England: Theological Debate from Locke to Burke*. Oxford, 1998.

Ziff, Larzer. *The Career of John Cotton: Puritanism and the American Experience*. Princeton, 1962.

—— ed. *John Cotton and the Churches of New England*. Cambridge, 1968.

Zimmer, Anne Young and Kelly, Alfred H. 'Jonathan Boucher: Constitutional Conservative'. *J.A.Hist*. 58 (1972).

Zimmer, Anne Y. *Jonathan Boucher, Loyalist in Exile*. Detroit, 1978.

Zobel, Hiller B. *The Boston Massacre*. New York, 1970.

Database

Bell, James B. 'The Colonial American Clergy of the Church of England Database'. www.JamesBBell.com.

Index

Act of Uniformity, 1662, 53, 56
Adams, John, xi, xiv, 3, 4, 90,
   91–106, 127, 211, 212, 215, 216
Adams, Samuel, xi, xiii, xiv, 16, 90,
   91–106, 138, 212, 215, 216
Addison, Eleanor, 131, 148
Alison, Francis, 109, 110
Almon, John, 100, 102
American Philosophical Society, 181
American Prelate, Anglican Bishop,
   Church of England Bishop,
   Colonial Bishop, *see* Episcopacy
American Revolution, *see*
   Revolutionary War
Ames, Nathaniel, 137
Anabaptists, 18, 114
Andrews, Samuel, 138
Andros, Edmund Sir, 6, 7, 13, 15, 78,
   213
Anglicans, 4, 5, 9, 213
Anglicisation, 6, 27
Apthorp, Charles, 69
Apthorp, East, 69, 70, 72, 74, 75, 102,
   211
Archbishop of Canterbury, xii, xvi, 27,
   74, 75, 191, 193
Archbishop of York, 27
Arnold, Jonathan, 40
Auchmuty, Samuel, 117, 149
Avery, Ephraim, 203

Babcock, Luke, 135, 138, 203
Bailey, Jacob, 125, 127–30, 133
Bailyn, Bernard, 16, 43
Baldwin, Alice M., 217
Baltimore, Lord, Charles Calvert, 17
Banner, James M. Jr., xviii
Baptists, 22, 27, 114, 167, 207, 208,
   213
Barron, Steve, xvii
Barton, Thomas, 76, 133, 134, 135,
   197
Barwick, John, 52

Bass, Edward, 135, 185
Bastwick, John, 48
Batwell, Daniel, 204
Baxter, Richard, 51, 55
Beach, Abraham, 117
Beach, John, 39, 200
Becket, William, 31
Berkeley, George, 34
Bernard, Francis, Governor, 72
Bernard, Nicholas, 51
Bishop of London, xii, xv, xvi, 24–5,
   27, 30, 31, 191, 193, 213
Bissett, George, 201
Blackburne, Francis, Archdeacon of
   Cleveland, 69, 100–103, 120
Blair, James, 57, 114
Blair, John, 22–23
Blount, Nathaniel, 208
Boehme, Anthony W., 15
Book of Common Order, 47
Book of Common Prayer, xiii, 4, 5, 7,
   8, 9, 10, 11, 12, 28, 42, 46, 48, 49,
   50, 51, 52, 53, 54, 55, 94, 102,
   186, 198, 201, 206, 207, 217, 219
Boston, 4, 33, 34; Christ Church, 35,
   214; Freeholders, 103, 104;
   Harbour, 103
Boston Gazette, The, 33, 92, 93, 95, 96,
   100, 216
Boston Massacre, 92, 103, 119, 188, 217
Boston Newsletter, 33
Boston Port Act, 135
Boston Tea Party, 92, 119, 188, 217
Boucher, Jonathan, x, 130–31, 133,
   140–49, 170, 175, 190, 219
Bowie, John, 138, 139
Bradshaw, Paul F., 44, 48
Bray, Thomas, 21, 27; Maryland
   Visitation, 1700, 18
Bridenbaugh, Carl, xiv, 33
British Army Chaplains, 134, 203
Browne, Arthur, 39, 75
Browne, Daniel, 26, 35

Browne, Isaac, 203
Bryan, George, 109
Bunker Hill, 140, 168, 188
Burke, Edmund, 189
Burnet, Gilbert, Bishop of Salisbury, 35, 56
Burton, Henry, 48
Bute, John Stuart, Lord, 189
Butler, Joseph, Bishop of Durham, 63
Byles, Mather Jr., 218

Calvin, John, 44
Calvinism, 47, 58, 73
Calvinists, 79, 213
Campbell, Isaac, 177–78
Camm, John, 115, 116
Campbell, Archibald, ninth earl of Argyll, 11
Caner, Henry, 60, 76, 85, 199, 200, 211, 218
Carlisle Peace Commission, 192
Cartwright, Thomas, 46
Cary, Thomas, 23
Centinel The, 109–110
Chandler, Thomas Bradbury, 82, 87–90, 91, 93–4, 95, 102, 108, 109, 110, 115, 117, 118, 120, 149, 156, 157, 158, 165–69, 170, 181, 186, 187, 190, 203, 214
Chaplains to
Continental Army, 175–77
Provincial Legislatures, 130, 143
Royal military forces, 138
Charlton, Richard, 117
Chauncy, Charles, xii, 33, 56, 70–1, 91, 96, 107, 120, 139, 168, 187, 214
Checkley, John, xi, xiii, 33–41, 42, 214
Circular Letter, 91
Civil War, Puritan Revolution in England, 49, 50, 196
Civil War, United States, 199
Clark, J. C. D., x, xvii, 96, 146, 213
Clark, William, 136–37
Clergymen, birthplaces, birth years, colleges attended, 241–45
Coercive Acts, 1774, xiv, 123, 124, 156, 157, 188

College of New Jersey (now Princeton University), 112
Colman, Benjamin, 34
Committees of Correspondence, Maine, 128, 129; Massachusetts, 92; Pennsylvania, 183
Committees of Public Safety, 123, 124, 125, 129, 131, 132, 135, 138, 139, 144, 148, 155, 159, 164, 170, 173, 183, 195, 205, 216, 219, 220
Comprehension Bill, 1680, 55
Compton, Henry, Bishop of London, 6, 7, 19, 21, 27, 30, 31, 33, 66, 81, 98, 190, 213
Concessions and Agreement, 22
Confession of Faith, 8
Congregational Church, 25, 64, 73, 108, 211, 214, 219
Congress of ministers, 66, 79, 190
Leaders, 4, 34, 36, 60, 80, 104, 107, 189, 195
Ministers, xii, 29
Ministry and ordination, xiii, 34, 35
New Lights, 58
Old Lights, 58
Congregationalism, 59
Congregationalists, xiv, 14, 38, 49, 158, 212, 213
Continental Association, 123, 135, 138, 139, 157, 159, 195
Continental Congress, First, xiv, 92, 106, 123, 124, 127, 128, 135, 138, 139, 140, 150, 154, 156, 157, 158, 159, 160, 162, 163, 164, 166, 167, 168, 176, 177, 179, 183, 184, 186, 195, 196, 198, 201, 204, 206; Second, 92, 144–45, 150
Conventions of clergymen, Anglican, 82, 83, 87, 113, 114, 120, 200, 213
Cooke, Samuel, 203
Cooper, Myles, 82, 117, 148, 158, 190, 203
Cornbury, Edward Hyde, Lord, 20
Cornwallis, Frederick, Archbishop of Canterbury, 84, 102
Cossitt, Ranna, 135
Cotton, John, 5, 42

Council of Trade and Plantations, Committee of Trade and Plantations, Board of Trade and Plantations, xii, 3, 5, 19, 27, 67, 204, 218, 221
Cranmer, Thomas, Archbishop of Canterbury, 44, 45
Cromwell, Oliver, 6, 49, 50, 51, 52, 137
Cromwell, Richard, 52
Cross, Alfred Lyon, xiv,
Crown, xiv, 25, 30, 31, 67, 120, 171, 221
Currency Act, 1764, 82
Cushing, Charles, 129
Cutler, Timothy, xiv, 38, 156, 214; at Yale, 26, 35

Daniel, Robert, Governor, 23
Dartmouth, Legge, William, Lord, xi, 149, 153, 189, 190, 193, 194, 212
Davenport, Addington, 70
Declaration of Independence, xii, xiv, xvi, 124, 135, 151, 152, 183, 184, 188, 198, 213, 218, 220, 221
Declaration of Rights, 207
Delaune, Thomas, 158
Delaware, University of, 110
Dibblee, Ebenezer, 200
Dickinson, John, 109
Dickinson, Jonathan, 37, 38, 66, 203, 214
Dissenters, xv, 3, 12, 19, 20, 22, 23, 24, 25, 27, 28, 40, 62, 67, 68, 72, 87, 89, 90, 98, 103, 118, 134, 150, 152, 211, 216
Dobbs, Arthur, Governor, 25
Doddridge, Philip, 65
Dodwell, Henry, 30
Doty, John, 138, 203
Drummond, Robert Hay, Archbishop of York, 61, 90, 216
Duché, Jacob, 146, 147, 179–80, 183
Dudley, Joseph, 10, 27, 28
Dummer, William, Lt. Governor of Massachusetts, 38
Dutch Reformed Church, 18, 58, 214
Dyer, Mary, 108

Ecclesiastical Courts, 215
Eddis, William, 142
Eden, Robert, Governor, 143
Edes, Benjamin, 92
Edict of Nantes, 11
Edmiston, William, 135
Edwards, Jonathan, 58
Eliot, Andrew, 184
English Church, Church of England, Anglican Church, as a cause of the American Revolution, 211–21
Episcopacy, bishop, prelate, x, xi, xiii, xiv, xv, xvi, 3, 4, 8, 9, 10, 15, 19, 29, 30, 31, 32, 34, 36, 38–9, 40–1, 43, 44, 45, 46, 48, 49, 50, 51, 52, 53, 54, 55, 56, 57, 59, 60–1, 62, 63, 64, 65, 66, 68, 70, 71, 74, 76, 77, 78, 79, 80, 81, 85, 86, 87–90, 91, 94, 98, 99, 100, 104, 107, 109, 110, 112, 115, 116, 118, 119, 120, 143, 144, 150, 154, 163, 165, 169, 184, 187, 190, 191, 192, 193, 198, 205, 211, 213, 214, 215, 216
Episcopal Church in Scotland, 57, 110, 149, 164
Episcopalians, 212
Evelyn, John, 5
Ewer, John, Bishop of Landaff, 149–50

Fanning, Edmund, 164
Fayerweather, Samuel, 201
Filmer, Robert, 145–46
Fitzroy, August Henry, Duke of Grafton, 210
Fletcher, Benjamin, 18–19
Foxcroft, Thomas, 70
Franklin, Benjamin, 150, 181
Frazer, James, 136
Freeman, James, 219
French and Indian War, 150, 181, 189
French Protestants, 26
Fundamental Constitutions, 22

Galloway, Joseph, 157, 192
Garden, Alexander, Jr., 208
Gauden, John, Bishop of Exeter, 51, 52
German Protestants, 26
Germaine, George Sackville, First Viscount Sackville, 189

German Reformed Church, 206
Gerry, Elbridge, 216, 217
Gibson, Edmund, Bishop of London, 38, 40, 61, 62, 65, 66, 177
Gordon, Patrick, 20
Gordon, William, 23
Governors, royal commissions and instructions, 218, 221
Graham, James, 3
Graham, John, 39
Graves, John, 201
Grenville, George, 215, 216
Griffith, David, 174–75, 186
Gwatkin, Thomas, 115, 117, 118, 119

Half-Way Covenant, 7
Hamilton, Alexander, 158, 161
Hancock, John, 91, 92, 97
Harrison, Henry, 183
Harvard College, 5, 8, 10, 13, 35, 58, 69, 73, 91, 92, 115, 125, 136, 156, 202, 216, 219; Dudleian Lecture, 70, 87
Henley, Samuel, 115, 116, 117, 119
Henry, Patrick, lawyer, 219
Henry, Patrick, minister, 205
Herring, Thomas, Archbishop of Canterbury, 63, 67
High Churchman, xiii, 34
Hill, Wills, Lord Hillsborough, 84, 189, 210
Hind Richard, 152
Hoadly, Benjamin, 34, 68
Hobart, Noah, 58–66, 80, 214
Hollis, Thomas, 68–9, 72, 74, 75, 100–101, 102
Hooker, Richard, 39
Hopkins, Samuel, 86
Horrocks, James, 115, 116, 117
Howe, William, General, 182, 199
Huguenot, 108
Hunter, Robert, Governor, 20, 31, 213
Hurt, John, 175–77, 186
Hutchinson, Anne, 108
Hutchinson, Thomas, Chief Justice, Massachusetts, 140
Hyde, Edward, 51, 52, 53

Independents, 18, 29, 32, 40, 49, 50, 52
Inglis, Charles, 117, 131–33, 134, 149–55, 158, 163, 170, 190, 192, 193, 194, 203
Intolerable Acts, 103, 106, 119, 217
Isaac, Rhys, 119

Jackson, Clare, 57
Jacobite, xiii, 34, 65
James, John, 142, 143
Jefferson, Thomas, 119, 219
Johnson, Samuel, 26, 35, 36, 39, 40, 65, 87, 109, 115, 165, 216
Johnston, Gideon, 31

Keith, George, 27, 28–29
Kempe, John, Attorney General, New York, 192
Kennett, White, 34
King and Royal Family, prayers, 128, 131, 135, 152, 184, 196, 197, 200, 201, 205, 207
King Charles I, 47, 49, 50, 154
King Charles II, 5, 22, 51, 52, 54
King George II, 81
King George III, 81, 124, 128, 201, 217
King Henry VIII, 42
King James I, 47
King James II, 57, 58
King Philip's War, 7
King William III, 12, 15, 18, 57
King's Chapel, Boston, 34, 76, 200, 214, 218, 219
King's College (now Columbia University), 87, 108, 113, 115, 138, 148, 157, 158, 165, 202, 203, 220
Kneeland, Ebenezer, 138
Knollenberg, Bernhard, xiv
Knox, John, 47
Knox, William, xi, 187–94

Laud, William, Archbishop of Canterbury, 42, 47, 48, 53, 56, 78
Laudians, 51
Leaming, Jeremiah, 133, 137–38
Leland, John Jr., 205
Leonard, Daniel, 140

Leslie, Charles, 34, 35, 38
Lexington and Concord,
    Massachusetts, xiv, 3, 128, 136,
    140, 168, 188, 195, 200
Livingston, William, 108
*London Chronicle or Universal Evening
    Post*, 100
London, Samuel, 151
Loyalists, xiv, 123, 126, 136, 137,
    138, 139, 140, 144, 154, 162, 163,
    170, 185, 190, 195–210, 217, 218,
    219, 222–40
Lutherans, 27, 206; German, 108,
    171, 172, 207; Swedish, 108,
    172

MacPherson, John, 112
Madison, James, clergyman, 173
Maier, Pauline, 96, 123, 195
Manross, William W., 20
Markham, William, Archbishop of
    York, 193
Marprelate Tracts, 46
Marshall, Thomas, Colonel, 174
Maryland, Church Act, 17, 18,
    Provincial Convention of
    clergymen, 120
Massachusetts Bay Colony, xiii, 6, 14
Massachusetts, General Court, 92
Mather, Cotton, xii, xiii, 7, 8, 9,
    13–17, 34, 38, 59, 70, 78, 80, 107,
    139, 214
Mather, Increase, xii, xiii, 4–13, 14,
    15, 17, 28–29, 42, 68, 80, 94, 107,
    108, 139, 214, 216, 218
Mather, Richard, 5, 11, 42
Mauduit, Israel, 74
Mauduit, Jasper, agent for
    Massachusetts Colony, 72
Mayhew, Jonathan, xii, 43, 67–80, 84,
    85–7, 90, 92, 107, 125, 138, 168,
    187, 211, 214
Methodist, 114
Miller, Ebenezer, 72
Miller, John C., xiv, 18, 19
Mills, Frederick V. Sr., xvi
Mooney, James E., xvii
Morley, George, 52

Moravians, 24, 208
Morgan, Edmund S., 78
Morris, Lewis, 20, 27, 28,
Morris, Robert, 183
Morse, Jedidiah, 3, 211
Muhlenberg, Henry Melchior, 171
Muhlenberg, John Peter Gabriel, 171,
    172, 174, 186
Munro, Henry, 203
Myles, Samuel, xiv, 15, 28, 38, 214

Navigation Acts, 6
Nelson, John K., 26, 119
New England Courant, 33
New Jersey, College of (now Princeton
    University), 37, 203
New York, Ministry Act, 1693, 18, 19,
    20; New York City, 4
Newark Academy, 110
Newcastle, Duke of, 63, 64, 190
Nichols, James, 136, 137, 200
Nicholls, Samuel, 65
Nicholson, Francis, Governor, 27, 114
Niles, Hezekiah, 211
Niles National Register, 211
Nonconformists, 21, 35, 36
Non-Importation Association, 91–2,
    135–36, 157, 159
North, Frederick, Lord, 193
North Carolina, Church established,
    24; State Constitution, 25; Vestry
    Acts of 1701, 22; 1704, 22; 1715,
    24; 1741, 24; 1754, 25; 1758, 25;
    1760, 25; 1762, 25; 1765, 25;
    1768, 25; 1774, 25
Nova Scotia, 154, 201, 218

Oakes, Urian, 8
Oaths
    Of Allegiance, 129, 135, 154, 155,
        183, 199, 204, 206, 221
    At ordination, 128, 133, 200
Odell, Jonathan, 203
Ogilvie, John, 117
Osbaldeston, Richard, Bishop of
    Carlisle, 110
Osborne, Thomas, earl of Danby, 6
Otis, James, 97

Paine, Thomas, *Common Sense*, 140, 150–51
Palfrey, William, 97, 100
Panton, George, 203
Parker, Samuel, 184–85, 186
Parkhurst, John, 148
Parliament, xi, xiv, xvi, 3, 18, 30, 31, 42, 48, 49, 50, 51, 53, 65, 72, 90, 93, 103, 109, 112, 120, 126, 139, 141, 143, 144, 147, 157, 161, 163, 167, 168, 171, 215, 216, 221
Passive obedience and non-resistance, 146, 175, 178, 198
Paterson, William, 112
Patriots, xiv, 133, 135, 137, 150, 153, 162, 168, 170–86, 195–210, 218, 222–40
Pelham, Henry, 62
Pennsylvania Assembly, 180
Peters, Richard, 202
Peters, Samuel Andrews, 125, 185
Petty, William, second earl of Shelburne, 61
Philadelphia Academy, 108, 171, 181
Philadelphia, College of (now University of Pennsylvania), 108, 179, 180, 183, 202, 220
Political Register The, 97, 100, 106
Political sentiments of the clergymen, 195–210, 222–40
Porter, John, 23
Potter, John, Archbishop of Canterbury, 61
Pownall, Thomas, Governor, 168
Poyer, Thomas, 20
Presbyterian, 48, 49, 55, 57, 71, 153
Presbyterian Church, xiv, 17, 18, 22, 26, 27, 32, 50, 58, 59, 79, 107, 108, 109, 114, 158, 163, 167, 206, 207, 208, 213, 214; New Sides, 58; Old Sides, 58; Corporation for the Relief of Poor and Distressed Presbyterian Ministers, 110
Presbyterian ordination, 36–7, 38
Presbyterians, 38, 52, 54, 58, 64, 158
Presbyterianism, 50, 76
Preston, John, 203
Price, Richard, 184

Protestant Episcopal Church in the U.S.A., 186, 199, 219
Provincial Conventions, Maine, 126, 128; Maryland, 144, 206, 207, Massachusetts, 92; New York, 138; North Carolina, 209
Provoost, Samuel, 183, 185, 186
Prynne, William, 48, 53
Puritan, xiii, 7, 8, 10, 15, 36, 45, 49, 51, 71, 93, 94, 95, 139, 167, 213, 220
Puritanism, 47, 51
Puritans, 9, 13, 46, 47, 48, 49, 53, 54, 59, 60, 80, 207

Quakers, 17, 18, 21, 22, 23, 26, 28, 32, 34, 39, 76, 100, 108, 150, 167, 181, 196, 204, 206, 207, 208, 214
Quartering Act, 1765, 82, 217
Quebec Act, 1774, xiv, 104, 106, 140, 157, 217
Queen Anne, 31, 81, 213
Queen Elizabeth I, 45
Queen Mary, 12, 45

Radcliff, Robert, 7, 15
Ramsay, David, xiv
Randolph, Edward, Customs Commissioner, xiii, 6, 10, 21, 94
Reading, Philip, 197
Revere, Paul, 106, 107
Revolutionary War, x, xi, xiv, xv, xvi, xvii, 4, 21, 29, 42, 134, 135, 174, 178, 187, 188, 198, 199, 200, 202, 204, 208, 211, 212, 215, 216, 217, 218, 219, 220, 221
Rittenhouse, David, 134
Rivington, James, 153
Robinson, John, Bishop of London, 66
Rockingham, Charles Watson-Wentworth, Marquis of, 61
Roman Catholics, 12, 17, 18, 21, 42, 87, 94, 104, 106, 206
Royal American Magazine, 106
Royster, Charles, 176
Rush, Benjamin, 180, 182, 183, 196

Saltonstall, Gurdon, 26
Sancroft, William, Archbishop of
    Canterbury, 94
Savoy Conference, 8
Sayre, John, 113, 135
Scotland, 47, 56; Parliament, 57
Scots-Irish, 26–7
Scott, James, first Duke of
    Monmouth, 11
Scott, John, 133
Seabury, Samuel Jr., 82, 96, 117, 149,
    156–65, 170, 186, 187, 190, 192,
    203
Secker, Thomas, Archbishop of
    Canterbury, xiv, 61, 63, 67, 68,
    81, 83, 84–5, 90, 92, 98–100, 102,
    106, 108, 190, 211, 214, 215, 218;
    Bishop of Oxford, 40
Serle, Ambrose, 149, 153, 163, 192,
    193, 212, 213
Sharpe, Kevin, xvii
Sheldon, Gilbert, Archbishop of
    Canterbury, 6
Sherlock, Thomas, Bishop of London,
    61, 62, 63, 64, 65, 66, 67, 98,
    102, 103, 190
Sherlock, William, 62
Sirmans, M. Eugene, 21
Smith, William, 109, 110, 171, 179,
    180–83, 186, 187
Society for the Propagation of
    Christian Knowledge among the
    Indians of North America, 68
Society for the Propagation of the
    Gospel in Foreign Parts, S.P.G., x,
    xi, xii, xv, xvi, 15, 17–32, 43,
    63, 64, 65, 66, 67, 68, 69, 70, 72,
    73, 75, 76, 77, 80, 84, 85, 87, 90,
    92, 93, 96, 102, 103, 123, 125,
    127, 134, 136, 149, 152, 156, 162,
    164, 171, 190, 191, 198, 200, 204,
    208, 210, 213, 214, 215, 216;
    Anniversary Sermon, 40, 41, 67,
    81, 149–50, 193
Solemn League and Covenant, 50, 196
Sons of Liberty, 91, 96, 97, 100, 103,
    125, 136, 166, 168
South Carolina, 21, Church Act, 1706,
    21; Common House of Assembly,
    21; Proprietors, 22

Sparrow, Anthony, 51
Spurr, John, 51
Stamp Act, 1765, x, xiii, 16, 78, 82,
    89, 90, 91, 92, 93, 95, 109, 111,
    140, 143, 165, 181, 187, 188,
    194, 215, 216, 217
State of the clergymen, 1775 and
    1783, 195–210
Stiles, Ezra, 76–8, 79, 108, 110, 169
Stoddard, Solomon, 7, 14
Subscriptions for the Relief of the
    Clergy of the Church of England
    in North America, 210
Suffolk Resolves, 123, 125, 156, 157,
    160, 167, 190
Suffragan Bishop, 30, 31, 61, 98
Sugar Act, 1764, 78, 81–2, 91

Talbot, John, 28, 29–30, 31, 63
Taylor, Stephen, xvi, xvii
Tea Act, 1773, xiv, 103, 167
Tenison, Thomas, Archbishop of
    Canterbury, 30
Tennent, Gilbert, 58
Tennent, William, 58
Terrick, Richard, Bishop of London,
    83, 110
Thirty-nine Articles, 46, 55, 72, 112
Thompson, James, 174
Thorne, Sydenham, 135
Thruston, Charles Mynn, 173, 174
Tillotson, John, Archbishop of
    Canterbury, 35, 55, 56
Todd, Christopher, 205
Toleration Act, 5, 14
Towgood, Micaiah, 71, 72, 74, 120
Townsend, Epinetus, 203
Townshend Acts, 90, 91, 109, 217
Townshend, Charles, Lord, 62,
    63, 210
Trinity Church, Boston, 218;
    New York City, 149, 158, 219
Tryon, William, Governor, 136, 207
Tucker, Joseph, Dean of Gloucester
    Cathedral, 110–12
Tufts, Cotton, 92
Tyler, Moses Coit, 140

Unitarian Church, 219
United Brethren, 24

Urquhart, William, 20
Ussher, James, Archbishop of Armagh, 48, 51, 54, 63

Vardill, John, 202
Viets, Roger, 136, 137
Virginia, church established, 26; Company of London, 114, 204, 218; Convention, 1775, 175; General Assembly, 114, 118; House of Burgesses, 118, 119, 172, 219; House of Delegates, 173; Militia, 205; Fund for the Relief of Widows and Orphans of Clergy, 115

Walker, Henderson, 23
Walpole, Horace, 190
Walpole, Horatio, 65
Walpole, Robert Sir, 62, 63, 98–9, 102
Walsh, John, xvii
Walter, William, 218
Warden, G. B., 16, 33
Washington, George, 131, 142, 148, 179–80, 219
Weeks, John Wingate, 133, 135
Weiser, John Conrad, 171
Welles, Noah, 59
Wentwroth, Thomas, 47
Westminster Assembly, 50

Wetmore, James, 38–9, 60
White, William, 171, 179, 183–84, 186, 219
Whitefield, George, 58, 70
Whitgift, John, Archbishop of Canterbury, 46
Wigglesworth, Edward, 36, 66, 70, 214
Wilkes, John, xiv, 90, 91–106, 139, 216
William and Mary, College of, 115, 173, 206, 220
Williams, Elisha, 34
Williams, John, Bishop of Chichester, 12
Willie, William, Acting Commissary, 119
Winslow, Edward, 133
Wiswall, John, 125–27, 133
Wood, Gordon S., 16
Wrangel, Carl Magnus von, 171
Wythe, George, 173

Yale College, 34, 115, 125, 138, 156, 164, 169, 202; Apostates, Commencement 1722, 25–6, 35, 59, 60, 82, 156
Yorke, Philip, first earl of Hardwicke, 63, 64

Zimmer, Anne Y., 141–42